Vampires, Zombies, and Monster Men

Vampires, Zombies, and Monster Men
by Daniel Farson

Aldus Books · Jupiter Books

Series Coordinator: John Mason
Design Director: Günter Radtke
Picture Editor: Peter Cook
Editors: Mary Senechal
Eleanor Van Zandt
Copy Editor: Mitzi Bales
Research: Frances Vargo
General Consultant: Beppie Harrison

SBN 490 00334 6
© 1975 Aldus Books Limited London
First published in the United Kingdom
in 1975 by Aldus Books Limited
17 Conway Street, London W1P 6BS
Distributed by Jupiter Books
167 Hermitage Road, London N4 1LZ
Printed and bound in Italy by
Amilcare Pizzi S.p.A.
Cinisello Balsamo (Milano)

Frontispiece: a female vampire attacks her prey.
Above: a hideous German version of the wild man.

EDITORIAL CONSULTANTS:

**COLIN WILSON
DR. CHRISTOPHER EVANS**

Of all monsters, we fear the man-monsters most: terrible figures preying on their fellows, whether drinking their blood or sapping their vitality and reason until the victims move like mindless zombies. Man can erect protection against many of the dangers of the natural world, but where does protection lie against the vampire, rising from his grave to fatten on the living, or the werewolf, ravaging people like a wild beast? Even the delicate fairy of nursery story tales can lash out malignantly. All the folk traditions have gruesome tales to tell in whispers over a dying fire, but what reality do the tales have in the bright light of day? From what corner of his own subconscious has man drawn their images? The world is often a dark place—and in the darkness lurks a predatory human shape.

1

The Legend of the Vampire

Above: the common vampire bat, small and hideous, feeds like the vampire of legend on blood, mainly drawn from living cattle.

One night in January 1973 John Pye, a young British police officer, was called to investigate a death. Within an hour what had seemed like a routine mission turned into one of the strangest cases any policeman can have encountered. Police Constable Pye found the dead man's room plunged in darkness. The man had apparently been so terrified of electricity that there were no light bulbs in his room. But gradually the beam from the policeman's flashlight revealed an extraordinary scene. P.C. Pye was looking at a fortress prepared against an attack by vampires. Salt was scattered around the room and sprinkled over the blankets. A bag

A creature that takes as its nourishment the lifeblood of others has held a particular horror and fascination for people all over the world and throughout history. Some believe in real vampires; practically everyone shivers at the evil doings of Dracula, whether in literature or on the screen. Bela Lugosi, shown here attacking the actress Helen Chandler in the 1931 movie *Dracula*, grew so fond of the role that he arranged to be buried in his black Dracula cloak lined with scarlet—the color of blood.

"The vampires did get him in the end"

Below: *Vampire*, a painting by the modern Norwegian artist Edvard Munch. This view of woman as a devourer of man has deep sexual undertones, as do many elements of the legends about vampires.

of salt rested by the dead man's face, and another was laid between his legs. The man had mixed salt with his urine in various containers. Outside on the window ledge he had placed an inverted bowl that covered a mixture of human excreta and garlic.

The dead man was Demetrious Myiciura, a Polish immigrant who had left his country for Britain 25 years earlier. He had worked as a potter in Stoke-on-Trent in the heart of England's pottery district. That is where he met his bizarre death. It would certainly be hard to imagine a place more remote from the traditionally vampire-haunted forests of Transylvania in Romania. Stoke-on-Trent is an industrial town, set in a landscape mutilated by factory chimneys and slag heaps. Opposite the station is a large old-fashioned hotel in front of which is a statue of the town's most famous citizen—Josiah Wedgwood, who made pottery a major industry. There is the usual imposing town hall. Otherwise the streets of little houses are uniformly black and narrow. It is all the more surprising, therefore, to come across the line of large old-fashioned dwellings where Myiciura had made his home. The houses look gloomy and somehow eerie. They are called, simply, "The Villas," and it was at number 3 that Myiciura met his death.

The body was duly removed for examination. At the inquest the pathologist reported that Myiciura had choked to death on a pickled onion. The coroner thought this unusual, but commented that it was not unknown for people "to bolt their food and die." Meanwhile the young policeman could not forget what he had seen. He had gone to the Public Library and read the *Natural History of the Vampire* by Anthony Masters. His suspicions were confirmed: salt and garlic are traditional vampire repellants, and the mixture on Myiciura's window ledge was intended to attract the vampires who would then be poisoned by the garlic. When told of this, the coroner ordered a reexamination of the alleged pickled onion. It was found to be a clove of garlic. As a final desperate measure to ward off the vampires, this wretched man had slept with a clove of garlic in his mouth, and the garlic had choked him to death. So in a roundabout way, the vampires did get him in the end.

What, then, are these vampires that literally scared Myiciura to death? Vampires are corpses, neither dead nor alive, that rise from the grave at night and suck the blood of the living. They gradually drain the blood of their victims, who must then become vampires in turn. The legendary home of the vampire is in Eastern Europe, notably Romania. It was there, in the province of Transylvania, that British author Bram Stoker set his famous story of Dracula. His Count Dracula, with arched nostrils, blood-red lips, and long sharp teeth, has come to typify our image of a vampire. But like the legendary vampires, Dracula could readily change into an animal such as a wolf or a bat. A vampire might even become a vapor to filter around the window frames in search of his or her chosen victim. When their gruesome feast of blood is over, the vampires crawl back into their coffin, where they can easily be recognized by the excellent state of preservation of their body. No matter how long vampires have been buried, it is said, they look as if they were still alive. Garlic, salt, or a crucifix may drive them off, but the only way to destroy

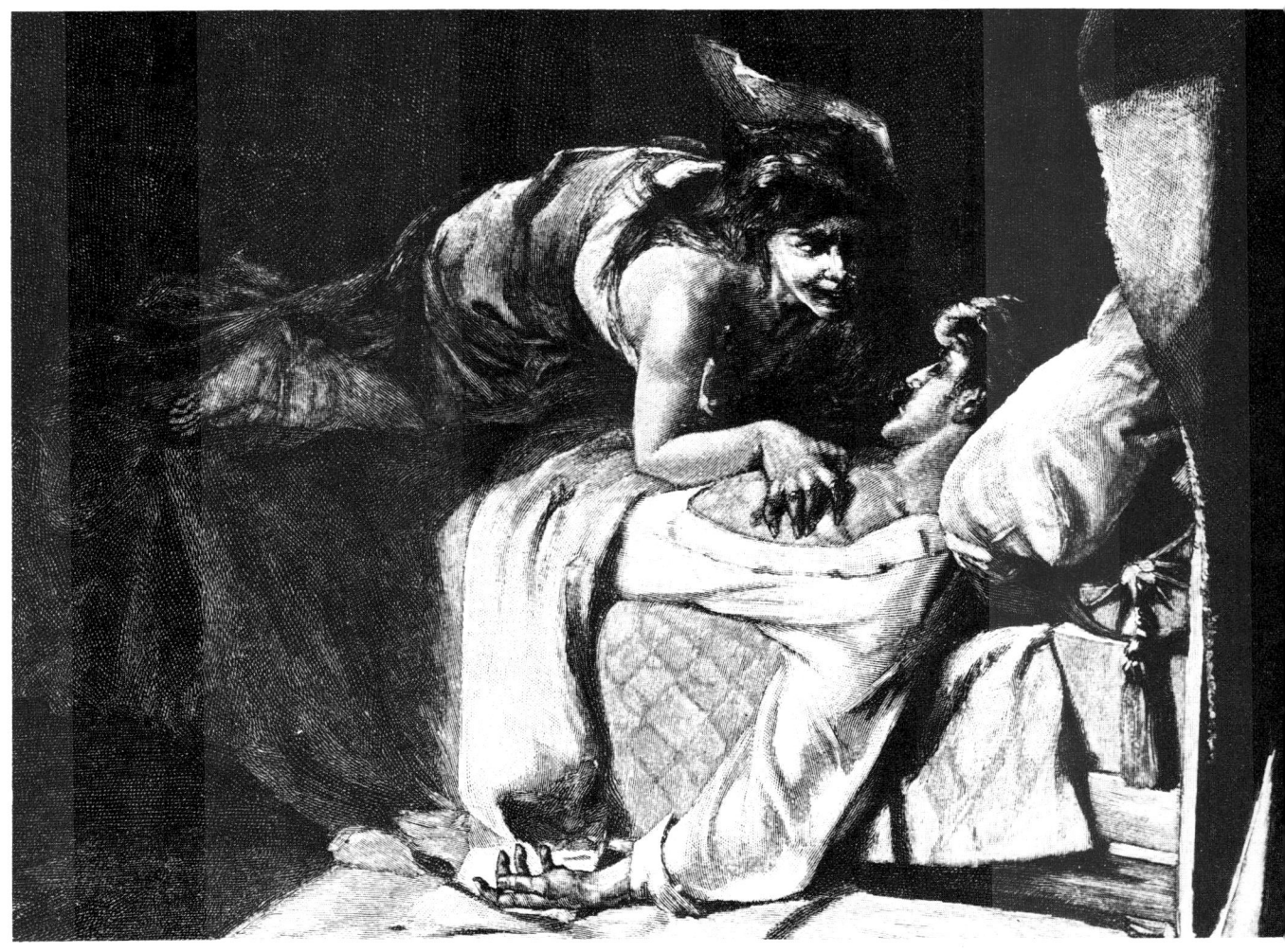

Above: a 19th-century engraving of a female vampire, preparing to sink teeth and nails into her victim. The strong sexual aspect of vampirism is obvious here, as the predatory female hovers over the defenseless man in bed.

them is to plunge a stake through their heart—at which time they give a horrible death shriek. They may need to be beheaded and burned as well.

A primitive superstition? Perhaps. Nevertheless, Myiciura believed it. He was convinced that vampires exist—and not just in the faraway forests of Transylvania. Demitrious Myiciura believed that he was being threatened by vampires in a British city in the 1970s.

"This man genuinely believed," remarked the coroner afterward. He denied that Myiciura was mad, although "obsessed perhaps." The Pole, who was born in 1904, had lost everything in World War II. His farm had been taken over by the Germans, and his wife and family had been killed. He arrived in England after the war with nothing.

"I've been a lawyer for a long time," said the coroner, "dealing with courtroom cases of all kinds. I've seen all sorts of depravity, all sorts of nonsense, but I can visualize what was behind this man. A lot of evil had happened to him. All right, he thought, I'll cling to evil, and he happened to believe in vampires. I am convinced, even after this inquest, that this man genuinely was afraid of vampires and was not trying to kill himself."

Even in New York, surely a most unlikely hunting ground for

Tourists seeking Count Dracula: down the Transylvanian roads roll Dracula bus tours with eager tourists looking for thrills in the mist, black crosses on the hills, and gloomy ruined castles brooding over the dark valleys.

Left: a tourist soaks up the atmosphere on his Dracula vacation.

Left: a British package tour bus exploring the Dracula country. Bran Castle, a well-preserved fortress associated with ancient Romanian nobility, looms behind. Could it have been Dracula's home?

Below: a souvenir doll of Vlad Tepes, which means Vlad the Impaler. This medieval Romanian ruler was cruel and barbaric, earning his nickname from his bloodthirsty habit of impaling his enemies on spikes. He also called himself Dracula. But Romanian tourist officials today object to attempts to link Vlad with the vampire Dracula because Vlad upheld Christianity.

Left: two Romanian women with Dracula plum brandy bottled for the souvenir-thirsty tourists.

vampires, there have recently been two strange cases reported by writer Jeffrey Blyth. A girl calling herself Lillith told two psychic researchers that she met a young man in a cemetery who tried to kiss her. It is not clear what she was doing in the cemetery in the first place, but instead of consenting to the kiss she plunged her teeth into the man's neck with such a surge of strength that she drew blood. "I never considered myself a Dracula," she said, "but rather a very evil person who liked the taste of blood." The second vampire was a young man named Carl Johnson who crept into his sister's bedroom while she slept, gently pricked her leg, and sucked her blood. This gave him a thirst, he said, and he could feel himself gaining in strength as he drained his victim.

Such cases indicate that far from being a legend of the past, vampirism exists today, if only in people's minds. Indeed, there has been an amazing revival of interest in vampires on both sides of the Atlantic. There is a Dracula Society in London and another in California. Modern British writers have studied the vampire, and professors in the United States and Canada have published learned books and papers on the subject. Countless movies are still made about Dracula and vampires—and so are studies of the movies. In Britain, a national poll revealed that the actor Denholm Elliot was the most "dreamt of" person in the country after he had portrayed Count Dracula on television. It has also been discovered recently that mental patients tend to identify themselves with Count Dracula as much as with Napoleon.

The latest to climb on the bandwagon are the travel agencies. Pan American blazed the trail when they offered a "Package Tour

Above: a meeting of the Dracula Society in London at which the club was presented with the gift of the cloak worn in films by Christopher Lee as Dracula. Below: British children can have a gory blood-red treat if they choose "Count Dracula's Deadly Secret" ice cream-on-a-stick.

Above: an abandoned churchyard, often the home of vampires, so heavy with melancholy that one can almost imagine the uneasy dead moving through the silent tombstones. It was painted by the 19th-century German artist Caspar David Friedrich, much of whose work was heavy with gloom.

with a Toothy Grin" in 1972, and the first British Airways "Dracula Tour" set out for Romania in 1974. Now the Romanians themselves have awakened to the extraordinary tourist potential that lies on their own Transylvanian doorstep. They are planning to cash in on this horror counterpart of Disneyland by selling Count Dracula on the souvenir stalls and by opening The Castle Dracula Hotel in 1977. The hotel will be in the Borgo Pass made famous in the Stoker story of Dracula, and taped wolves will howl at prearranged spots as the tourists drive to their destination through the mists at nightfall.

For the most part this modern preoccupation with vampires is little more than a harmless fantasy. But there are elements, such as the recent desecration of graveyards in Britain, that are disturbing. The graveyard activity reached an unpleasant climax with the so-called vampire hunters of Highgate Cemetery in London. Highgate Cemetery was once a place of splendor. It was designed by the best 19th-century British architects and landscape gardeners, and has graceful avenues of trees for the bereaved families to stroll through. It has deteriorated, however, and is so thickly overgrown that the atmosphere is sinister even on a bright sunlit morning. Reports of black magic are all too believable, and the work of vandals is only too evident.

The case of the vampire hunters was brought to public notice in 1974 with the trial of 28-year-old David Farrant, the self-styled High Priest and President of the Occult Society. Publicity was limited because the details of the case seemed too bizarre for the ordinary newspaper reader. However, the headline writers created some interest with lines like "Capers among the Catacombs" and "Casanova witch a failure as a lover." The jury was told of naked girls dancing on desecrated graves. This prompted the judge to comment with dry legal wit that they must have found it extremely chilly in October.

Here is what happened. One hundred vampire hunters had converged on Highgate Cemetery after reports of a seven-foot vampire seen hovering over the graves. The startled jury learned that iron stakes had been driven through mutilated corpses after the tombs had been smashed in. (The bodies were later returned to their graves by the cemetery staff as discreetly as possible in order to spare the feelings of relatives.) An architect who had parked his car just outside the cemetery gates returned to find a headless body propped against the steering wheel. Photographs of a naked girl on a grave were found in Farrant's home, and when a police inspector called on one of the witnesses he found that "he had salt around the windows of the room, salt around

Above: David Farrant, who called himself High Priest of the Occult Society, was jailed in 1974 after a sensational trial for vampire-hunting ceremonies he conducted in Highgate Cemetery, London. Below: the author, great-nephew of Bram Stoker who wrote *Dracula*, pictured in Highgate Cemetery.

the doorway, and a large wooden cross under his pillow." It was also revealed that voodoo dolls with pins through their chests had been sent to possible witnesses against Farrant.

Farrant was charged with damaging a memorial to the dead, entering catacombs in consecrated ground, and interfering with and offering indignity to the remains of a body "to the great scandal and disgrace of religion, decency, and morality." Admitting that he had frequented the cemetery, he denied all the charges and conducted his own defense. Referring to "this horrible interference," the judge sentenced him to jail for almost five years.

It is tempting, and probably correct, to dismiss such cases as a form of unhealthy aberration. Yet not far from Highgate Cemetery lives a man who takes reports of vampirism seriously. The Reverend Christopher Neil-Smith is a leading British exorcist and writer on exorcism. He can cite several examples of people who have come to him for help in connection with vampirism. "The one that particularly strikes me is that of a woman who showed me the marks on her wrists which appeared at night, where blood had definitely been taken. And there was no apparent reason why this should have occurred. They were marks almost like those of an animal. Something like scratching." He denies that this might have been done by the woman herself. She came to him when she felt her blood was being sucked away, and after he performed an exorcism the marks disappeared.

Another person who came from South America "had a similar phenomenon, as if an animal had sucked away his blood and attacked him at night." Again, the Reverend Neil-Smith could find no obvious explanation. There was a third case of a man who, after his brother had died, had the strange feeling that his lifeblood was being slowly sucked away from him. "There seems to be evidence this was so," says Neil-Smith. "He was a perfectly normal person before, but after the brother's death he felt his life was being sucked away from him as if the spirit of his brother was feeding on him. When the exorcism was performed he felt a release and new life, as if new blood ran in his veins." Neil-Smith rules out the possibility of a simple psychological explanation for this, such as a feeling of guilt by the survivor toward his brother. "There was no disharmony between them. In fact he wasn't clear for some time that it [the vampire] *was* his brother."

The clergyman describes a vampire as "half animal, half human," and firmly refutes the suggestion that such things are "all in the mind." "I think that's a very naive interpretation," he says. "All the evidence points to the contrary." Concluding that there is such a thing as vampirism, he identifies this strange belief as a persistent form of devil worship.

Many people will say that Neil-Smith is easily taken in. Most will dismiss reports of vampirism in the modern world as so much nonsense. And yet, as Hamlet tells Horatio in Shakespeare's play, "There are more things in heaven and earth, Than are dreamt of in your philosophy." But do these undreamed of things include vampires? On the face of it, how can anyone believe that corpses can rise from their coffins at night to suck the

Opposite: *Kiss of the Vampire*, done by the Polish-born painter Boleslas Biegas in 1916. His huge winged vampire looks nothing like the familiar Count Dracula, but is in keeping with the earlier folk beliefs that vampires could take many various forms. Biegas frequently painted vampires of fantastic appearances in themes that were openly sexual in nature.

Below: Reverend Christopher Neil-Smith, a High Anglican priest who does a great deal of exorcism. Although Reverend Neil-Smith has permission to practice from the Bishop of London, the Church of England tends to view his highly emotional exorcisms with dubious reserve. During the process of exorcism, both the minister and the person being exorcised shake violently as the vicar's prayer fades into a fervent mutter. He claims over 3000 successful exorcisms, but is quick to add that not all cases of disturbed behavior can be explained by demonic possession, and that in many cases a patient can be cured only by orthodox psychiatry.

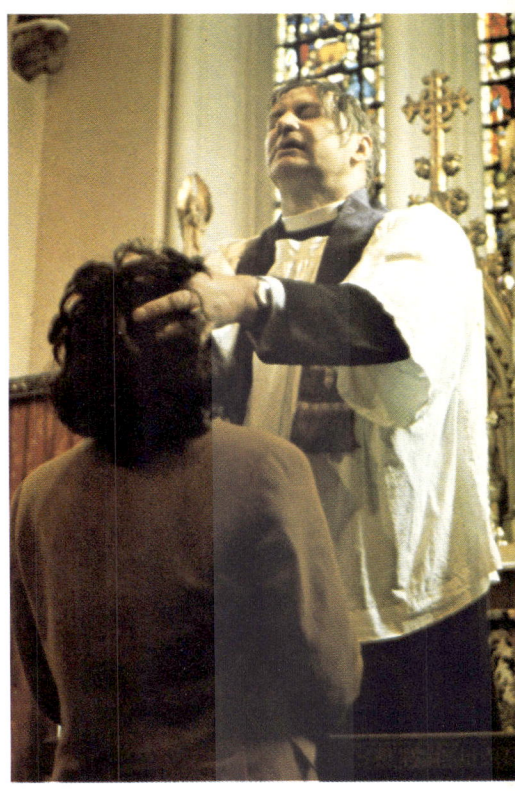

Blood has had a place in religious rites since antiquity, in the East as in the West. Sometimes it was to be offered up to the gods from a sacrificial animal or human, and sometimes it was to be drunk by the participants in the holy ceremony.

Left: even the gentle Buddhists found a place for fierce masks as defense against enemies. This Tibetan one is a receptacle, probably for blood or holy water, in the shape of a guardian figure.

Below: an aspect of the Hindu goddess Kali symbolizing the dark side of woman—death, war, disease, and blood sacrifice. The small figures at the side are other aspects of Kali, which are regenerated with her own blood. Kali is still worshiped widely in Bengal. The name of the huge city Calcutta is an anglicized form of Kalighata, a temple built in honor of the dread goddess.

blood of the living, make new vampires of their victims, and return to the grave before daybreak? Skeptical minds find this incredible. Some even say it is the silliest superstition of all.

Yet people have believed in vampires all over the world since the earliest recorded times. Legends reach back many centuries before Christ to ancient Assyria and Babylonia—and always vampirism includes the drinking of blood, the life-giving fluid.

Aztecs poured blood into the mouths of their idols. In India, rajahs drank blood from severed heads. In China, the family would guard a corpse the night before burial lest a dog or cat jump over the body and transform it into a vampire. This belief is echoed in a book called *Antidote Against Atheism* written in the 17th century by Dr. Henry Moore. He tells the story of Johannes Cuntius of Silesia in central Europe, whose dead body was scratched by a black cat before the funeral. Sure enough, Cuntius was later reported to have reappeared, and to have drunk blood. When his body was duly dug up again, it was said to be in the typical well-preserved vampire condition.

The ancient Greeks, and the Romans after them, believed in a type of female vampire called a *lamia* who seduced men in order to suck their blood. Later the Greeks had another word for the vampire: *vrukalakos*, a creature who was able to revive the dead and whose victims would then feast on the living. Anyone—male or female—with red hair, a birthmark, or even blue eyes was suspected of being a vampire. Blue eyes are rare in Greece. But those born on Christmas Day, a seventh son, a person with a hare lip, or anyone in the slightest bit unusual were also suspect, so many people would easily fit the description of vampires.

Vampires were so rife on the Greek island of Santorini, now called Thera, that Greeks would say "send a vampire to Santorini" just as we talk of "taking coals to Newcastle." In 1717 a distinguished French botanist, Joseph de Tournefort, stated that throughout "the whole Archipelago there is no Orthodox Greek who does not firmly believe that the devil is able to reenergize and revitalize dead bodies."

Closer to home and as recently as 1874, a man in Rhode Island dug up his daughter and burned her heart because he believed she was draining the lifeblood from the rest of his family.

The true home of the vampire, however, lies in Eastern Europe, and the vampire legend as we know it today grew up in Romania and Hungary around the start of the 16th century. The word itself comes from a Slavonic term, and did not exist in English until the 1730s. At that time, reports of vampires were numerous in Eastern Europe. These accounts were picked up by travelers whose writings about them spread the vampire story all over Europe. Fiction then made the vampire famous. In the 19th century best-selling horror writers seized on the vampire tale. Even great poets like Byron, Goethe, and Baudelaire tried their hand with the vampire theme. It was British author Bram Stoker, however, who finally took the many jumbled strands of the vampire legend and wove them into the classic *Dracula*, published in 1897. His mixture of fact and fiction has dominated our conception of a vampire ever since.

Stoker never went to Transylvania which is now a province of Romania, and where his story opens. But his research into museum records and guidebooks on the area was extremely thorough, and *Dracula* contains a great deal of authentic Slavonic folklore. The choice of Transylvania as Dracula's homeland was an apt one. The swirling mists, the peasants in colorful national costume, and the wooden crucifixes beside the Borgo Pass that Stoker described in his book are all still there. In this part of Europe, vampirism was a part of life—and death. As the Reverend Montague Summers, a leading historian of vampirism, wrote, ". . . in Romania we find gathered together around the Vampire almost all the beliefs and superstitions that prevail throughout the whole of Eastern Europe."

We tend to think of the vampire as pale, gaunt, and emaciated. This is misleading, for after a feast of blood the creature would be replete, red-lipped, and rosy-hued. In some ways this image of the vampire as something sleek with blood is even more horrifying. But, deathlike or robust, do such beings exist? Many early authorities were tempted to think so, including the French monk Dom Augustin Calmet. He was the author of one of the earliest learned studies of vampires, published in 1746. Calmet strived to maintain an open mind, but he wrote: "We are told that dead

Above: a Pakistani boy in what is now Bangladesh dances in ecstacy as he is possessed by spirits, and drinks the blood of a goat. Eventually his state of high excitement gives way to a deep trance, from which he wakes restored to his normal self.

Vikram and the Vampire

Long ago in India there lived a soldier-king whose name was Vikram. He was proud and brave and cunning. Clever as he was, he was once tricked by a sorcerer into promising to do anything the evil magician ordered. He was set the task of getting a vampire out of a certain tree and bringing it back to the sorcerer. Vikram found the vampire hanging head down in the tree.

Vikram cut the creature down, but it scrambled back up again. This happened seven times until at last the vampire, sighing that "even the gods cannot resist a thoroughly obstinate man," allowed itself to be taken. However, the vampire struck a strange bargain with Vikram: it would tell some stories and ask some questions about them. If Vikram could keep silence and never answer, the creature would reward him. But if he made any response at all, the vampire would return to the tree.

Ten tales the vampire told, and ten times Vikram could not keep from making a response. Each time the vampire returned to the tree, but each time Vikram recaptured it. The eleventh time Vikram managed to hold his tongue. The vampire's reward was to tell him of a plot against his life. Forewarned, Vikram escaped unscathed.

men . . . return from their tombs, are heard to speak, walk about, injure both men and animals whose blood they drain . . . making them sick and finally causing their death. Nor can the men deliver themselves unless they dig the corpses up and drive a sharp stake through these bodies, cut off their heads, tear out the hearts, or else burn the bodies to ashes. It seems impossible not to subscribe to the prevailing belief that these apparitions do actually come forth from their graves."

Other eminent writers had no doubts about the existence of vampires. Jean-Jacques Rousseau, the famous French philosopher of the 18th century, declared, "If ever there was in the world a warranted and proven history, it is that of vampires. Nothing is lacking: official reports, testimonials of persons of standing, of surgeons, of clergymen, of judges; the judicial evidence is all-embracing."

In our own time Colin Wilson, author of *The Occult* (1971), agrees. He says: "There *must* have been a reason that these vampire stories suddenly caught the imagination of Europe. Obviously *something* happened and it seems unlikely that it was pure imagination." He, too, refers to the documentation: "Examples of vampirism are so well authenticated that it would be absurd to try to maintain a strictly rationalist position."

There is a surprising weight of evidence in support of the vampire legend, much of it collected and endorsed by army surgeons. In the Yugoslavian village of Meduegna near Belgrade, for example, a group of doctors investigated an epidemic of vampirism. On January 7, 1732 Johannes Flickinger, Isaac Seidel, Johann Baumgartner, and a lieutenant colonel and sublieutenant from the capital of Belgrade signed the medical report. They testified to an examination of 14 corpses. Only two—a mother and baby—were found to be in a normal state of decomposition. All the others were "unmistakably in the vampire condition."

There were so many such reports of vampirism in the mid-18th century that it was said by one surgeon to have "spread like a pestilence through Slavia and Walachia . . . causing numerous deaths and disturbing all the land with fear of the mysterious visitors against which no one felt himself secure."

A classic case history of the time concerned a Hungarian soldier who was billeted on a farm near the Austro-Hungarian frontier. He was eating with the farmer and his family one evening when they were joined by an old man. The soldier noticed that the family seemed extremely frightened of the man, who simply touched the farmer on the shoulder and then left. Next morning the soldier learned that the farmer was dead. Apparently the old man was the host's father, and had been dead for 10 years. When he visited and touched his son, he both announced and caused that son's death.

The soldier told the story to other men in his regiment, and the old man was soon labeled a vampire. For although he had not taken blood from his son, his coming showed him to be a member of the living dead, and he had certainly brought about his son's death. The affair was beginning to spread alarm among the soldiers, so it was investigated by the infantry commander, some other officers, and a surgeon. The farmer's family was questioned

Above: Malay vampire demons. The one on the left sucks the blood of women in childbirth. The other attacks children and drinks their blood because, in life, her infant was stillborn.
Left: this figure with vampire-like fangs frightens off evil spirits. It is from the Nicobar Islands off the coast of India.

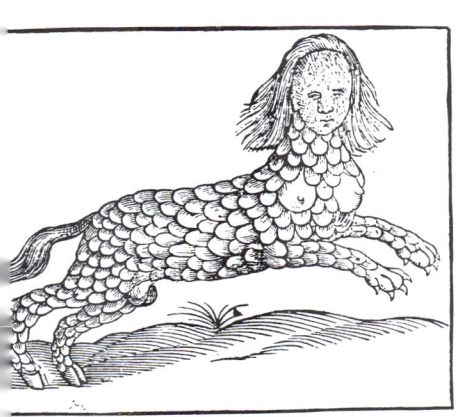

Left: the ancient Greeks believed that Lamia was an evil spirit with vampire habits. One of her forms was as a serpent with the face and breasts of a woman.
Right: in adapting another old belief about Lamia, the poet Keats made her able to change herself into a beautiful young woman. This illustration for Keats' poem shows the charming Lamia who had won the heart of his hero Lycius. The poem ends in tragedy when Lamia changes back into a serpent.

under oath, testimony was taken from villagers, and eventually the old man's grave was opened. His body looked like that of a man who had died recently—not 10 years earlier—and "his blood was like that of a living man." The commander of the regiment ordered that the vampire's head be cut off, and the body was laid to rest again.

During their inquiry the officers were told of another vampire who returned at 10-year intervals to suck the blood of members of his family. It is a notable feature of vampire stories that the vampire's relatives or lovers are usually the first to suffer attack. One case in a remote village in Yugoslavia concerned a particularly pernicious vampire who killed three of his nieces and a brother within a fortnight. He was interrupted just as he was

Right: a Romanian woman lighting candles in devotion. The natural religious piety and simultaneous superstition of the peasantry created a fertile ground for the legend of the vampire to flourish.

Below: the brooding turrets and battlements of Bran Castle seem to come straight from *Dracula*, but Stoker put his Dracula's home in Burgo Pass where no castle exists. Bran Castle, however, today attracts tourists interested in the vampire legends.

Above: Bram Stoker, the author of *Dracula*. He took the threads of the vampire legend and bound them together into the terrifying novel of the vampire count of Transylvania. Stoker claimed that his inspiration came from a nightmare he suffered after having too much crab for supper. The book was an instant success when it was published in 1897, and his Count Dracula has moved malignantly through films, plays, and other books ever since then.

starting to suck the blood of his fifth victim—another beautiful young niece—and he escaped.

A deputation, whose members' credentials seem impeccable, was sent from Belgrade to investigate. The party consisted of civil and military officials and a public prosecutor. They went to the vampire's grave as dusk fell, accompanied by the villagers. The man had been buried three years before, but when the investigators opened his grave they found his body intact with hair, fingernails, teeth, and eyes all in good condition. His heart was still beating, unbelievable as that seems. When the investigators thrust an iron stake through the corpse's heart a white fluid mixed with blood burst out. They then cut off the head with an ax. Only when the body was finally reburied in quicklime did the young niece who would have been the vampire's fifth victim begin to recover.

Usually in such cases a terrible smell was reported around the corpse, but that is hardly surprising. One body was described graphically as "puffed and bloated like some great leech about to burst," and when the customary stake was plunged into the breast of another, "a quantity of fresh scarlet blood issued, and from the nose and mouth as well; more issued from that part of his body which decency forbids me to name." There was another poignant case when tears sprang from the vampire's eyes as he gave his last scream of anguish.

One of the chief reasons for people's acute fear of vampires is their alleged power to infect victims with their own insatiable lust for blood. According to some traditions, only people who die from loss of blood after repeated vampire attacks will become vampires themselves. Other vampire tales maintain that one or two attacks are enough, and that any victim of a vampire will come back as a new vampire after his or her natural death. The vampire is said to hypnotize its victims while it feeds so that the person remembers nothing of the gruesome experience, but simply complains of disturbed sleep and a strange lack of energy. Thus the vampire can safely return night after night to the same victim if it wishes until that victim grows progressively more anemic and dies. Sometimes there are tell-tale puncture wounds on the victims' neck. In that case, if they believe in vampires, they may well suspect their plight.

An example of how one vampire creates another was reported to the Imperial Council of War in Vienna in the 1730s. It involved a Hungarian soldier, Arnold Paole. He had been killed when a cart fell on top of him, but he was said to have returned from the dead 30 days later and claimed four victims who eventually died "in the manner traditionally ascribed to vampires"—presumably from the typical weakness attributed to loss of blood. Friends remembered Paole saying that he had been attacked by a vampire himself during military service on the Turko-Serbian border. But he thought he had cured himself of any possible infection by the traditional remedy of eating earth from the vampire's grave, and rubbing himself with its blood. This had obviously failed, however, for when Paole's body was exhumed, it "showed all the marks of an arch vampire. His body was flushed; his hair, nails, and beard had grown, and his veins were full of liquid blood which splashed all over the winding sheet." The local Governor

Above: the burial of a suicide. It was the custom to bury anyone who had taken his own life under a cross at the intersection of two roads. Only then could the living be sure that the tormented soul would not rise to vampirize the community he had left behind. Below: staking a corpse in its coffin was one of the much-used methods of disposing of a vampire. Other methods included burial face down, decapitation, or placing garlic in the corpse's mouth.

ordered the inevitable stake to be thrust through the heart, and the vampire uttered the familiar shriek. Then the body was burned. The same procedure was also applied to the four recent victims in case they became active.

All these precautions apparently proved futile. Five years later there was a further outbreak of vampirism in the same area, and 17 people died. One woman claimed that her son, who had died nine weeks earlier, had attempted to strangle her while she slept; she died three days afterward. The governor demanded another inquiry, and it was learned that Arnold Paole had attacked animals as well as humans during his reappearance as a vampire. Parts of the flesh of these animals had been eaten and, in due course, had caused the new epidemic. This time all the new in-

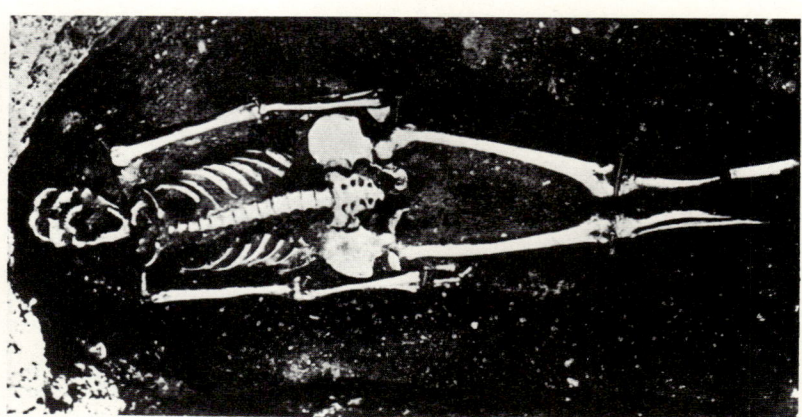

Above: this skeleton of a person buried about 400 years ago had been fastened to the coffin with rivets at the joints of the body. The burial took place in England in the days when people believed both that witches lived among them, and that the dead could rise. This body was probably that of someone said to be a witch, and so nailed down when buried to keep its unquiet spirit from haunting everyone.

fected vampires were exhumed, staked, decapitated, and burned. For good measure their ashes were thrown into the river. This seemed to be effective at last, and the terror was over.

Local bishops frequently sought the advice of the Pope on the vampire problem, but they received little help. The Church maintained, with some justification, that such phenomena were delusions. However, at one point the Vatican issued the cautious advice that suspect bodies should be exhumed and burned. Dom Calmet is one of the few authorities who quelled his occasional doubts and managed to remain objective. He showed a rare compassion for the vampires, especially if they were really innocent victims of superstition: "They were killed by decapitation, perforation, or burning, and this has been a great wrong; for the allegation that they returned to haunt and destroy the living has never been sufficiently proved to authorize such inhumanity, or to permit innocent beings to be dishonored... as a result of wild and unproved accusations. For the stories told of these apparitions, and all the distress caused by these supposed vampires, are totally without solid proof." Ever open-minded, however, he eventually came to the conclusion that, "This is a mysterious and difficult matter and I leave bolder and more proficient minds to resolve it."

Dom Calmet rightly uses the word "mysterious," and this element of mystery may be one simple reason for the lasting fascination of the vampire legend.

There are other vampire stories, however, which are far from entertaining and which stem from genuine fear. It was part of the vampire legend that people who were outcasts of society in life would remain outcasts after death, and might return as vampires. This compares to the Western European folklore that an evil-doer—or the victim of evil—is often fated to return after death as a ghost. The Church may have found it useful not to discourage this belief that served as a warning to the guilty. In Eastern Europe around 1645, it was stated that people who had led a "wicked and debauched life" or had been "excommunicated by their bishop" were likely to be condemned to the fate of the vampire, forever searching for the peace that was denied to them. The same threat applied to all suicides; those buried without the proper religious sacraments; perjurers; people who died under any kind of curse; and, in Hungary, to the stillborn illegitimate children of parents who were also illegitimate. In other words, anyone who had defied the social conventions of the times might become a vampire after death.

A vampire's grave is reputed to stink, and the creature's breath is said to smell foul from its diet of blood. The appearance of a vampire is also often heralded by an appalling odor. Interestingly, an abominable smell is also a frequent element of possession by the devil even today, and features prominently in the popular book and film *The Exorcist*. A vampire story that demonstrates this aspect well was recounted by Dr. Henry Moore in 1653, and concerns a Silesian. The story goes as follows: "One evening when this theologer was sitting with his wife and children about him, exercising himself in music, according to his usual manner, a most grievous stink arose suddenly, which by degrees spread itself to every corner of the room. Hereupon he commended him-

The Vampire of Croglin Grange

Croglin Grange was an English manor house that overlooked the nearby church in the hollow. It was rented by two brothers and their sister. One night as the sister lay in bed she became uneasily aware of something moving across the lawn toward the house. Mute with horror, she saw a hideous brown figure with flaming eyes approach. It scratched at her window with bony fingers, and one pane fell out. It reached in, unlocked the window, and before she could scream, sank its teeth into her throat.

Her brothers were wakened by the commotion, but by the time they reached her room the creature had vanished and the girl lay unconscious and bleeding. One brother tried to follow the attacker, but lost it.

The girl recovered and bravely insisted on returning to the house. Nearly a year later, she again woke to see the creature scratching at the window. Her brothers, who since the first attack slept armed, came running. They found the creature in flight. One brother fired and hit it, but it escaped into the churchyard. When the two men entered the churchyard vault, they discovered all the coffins broken open except one. In that coffin was the vampire—and it had a bullet wound in its leg.

Below: Stoker was not the first to make sensational fiction out of the ancient theme of vampires. Nearly 50 years earlier Varney the Vampyre appeared as a pulp serial with an inexhaustible flow of drama in 220 episodes.

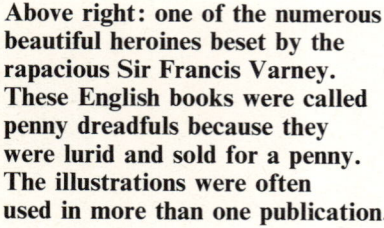

Above right: one of the numerous beautiful heroines beset by the rapacious Sir Francis Varney. These English books were called penny dreadfuls because they were lurid and sold for a penny. The illustrations were often used in more than one publication.

self and his family to God by prayer. The smell nevertheless increased, and became above all measure pestilently noisome, insomuch that he was forced to go up to his chamber. He and his wife had not been in bed a quarter of an hour, but they find the same stink in the bedchamber; of which, while they are complaining one to another, out steps the specter from the wall, and creeping to his bedside, breathes upon him an exceedingly cold breath, of so intolerable stinking and malignant a scent, as is beyond all imagination and expression."

This smell sounds like a symbol of impending plague, and was frequently interpreted as such. As early as 1196 the historian William of Newburgh told of a "lecherous husband" who returned from the grave to terrify people in his home town. He said: "For the air became foul and tainted as this fetid and corrupting body wandered abroad, so that a terrible plague broke out and there was hardly a house which did not mourn its dead, and presently the town, which but a little before had been thickly populated, seemed to be well nigh deserted, for those who had survived the pestilence and these hideous attacks hastily removed themselves to other districts lest they should also perish."

Two young men, plainly braver than the rest, traced the living corpse to its grave and cut its head off with a spade so that the red blood gushed out. The body was then burned. This destruction

Left: soldiers burst into a room at the home of Sir Francis Varney and discover a body staked in the coffin by a riotous mob. The great hammer with which the stake had been pounded down lies on the floor, carelessly discarded.

Above: the vampire at his awful pleasure, near the end of the lengthy opus. At last, and rather abruptly (the publisher must have ordered the series ended without much notice), Varney "tired and disgusted with a life of horror," flings himself into a volcano.

of the corpse in the fashion of a vampire succeeded. "No sooner had that infernal monster been thus destroyed," the story goes on, "than the plague, which had so sorely ravaged the people, entirely ceased, just as if the polluted air was cleansed by the fire which burned up the hellish brute who had infected the whole atmosphere."

It is interesting to see how the infernal monster is used as a scapegoat for the plague, with the added condemnation that he was a lecherous husband, as if his behavior when he was alive was responsible for the whole calamity. It is true that epidemics of vampirism and plague did tend to go together: in 1729 it was said that any plague where, "within a few hours five or six persons fell ill in the village," would automatically be linked to vampirism. But it is not a case of the vampires causing the plague. On the contrary, periods of plague created the perfect atmosphere for a belief in vampires.

There are, therefore, several perfectly reasonable explanations for the proliferation of the vampire legend; but nevertheless the doubts remain. As the curtain fell on the first stage production of *Dracula*, the producer Hamilton Deane came out in front of the curtain to warn the audience to take care as they went home. "Remember," he cried in sepulchral tones, "There are such things!" Well, are there?

Why Believe in Vampires?

"Bring out your dead!" That cry was horrifyingly familiar to the people who lived in times of plague. Carts piled high with corpses would trundle by night after night, bound for the burial pit. A red cross marked the doors of the stricken, and the sick were often abandoned even by their own family for fear of contagion. Streets became blocked with decomposing bodies as the living left the towns to the dead and dying. It is easy to understand how terrified people must have been by this devastating disease that flared up periodically in Europe from ancient times right down to the 18th century. Never knowing where it might strike or when it might end

One explanation for the persistent belief in vampires through the ages is that of premature burial, which was long common. It can be seen how vampire stories arose when a disarranged or bloody corpse—created by a grim death struggle within coffin or vault—had been dug up for some reason. Premature burial has also been a popular theme for horror stories. Right: the heroine of a macabre tale by Edgar Allan Poe in which she is buried alive. Her twin brother senses that she still lives, but dares not investigate. When she escapes and enters his room, they both fall dead.
Below: a 19th-century engraving titled "The Dead Body Moves."

"The priests believed that the dancers were possessed by the devil"

Below: St. Vitus, a Christian martyr of the 4th century associated with the cure of disease. His name was given to the wild dance that swept Europe in the Middle Ages after centuries of intermittent plague. This was because many of the seemingly possessed dancers went to chapels of St. Vitus throughout Germany, where the mania started, to pray for a cure. Later the name St. Vitus Dance was applied to the disorder which, like the medieval dance, is marked by uncontrolled jerking movements of the body.

must have made the plague more alarming even than warfare. Such an epidemic would leave an area depressed mentally as well as physically, creating the ideal climate for panic.

The worst plague of all was the Black Death which swept through Europe in the 14th century. It claimed millions of victims—a quarter of Europe's population. When the Black Death finally began to subside, a strange delusion took possession of whole communities in the region that is now Germany. It was known as the Dance of St. Vitus, and the nervous disorder that is marked by jerky involuntary movements is still known by that name today. The dancers seemed to lose their senses, performing wild leaps, screaming, and foaming at the mouth. Regardless of the dismayed crowds that watched them, they danced together for hours in this strange state of delirium until they fell from sheer fatigue. They saw nothing and heard nothing except for some who were haunted by religious visions. In spite of this, the priests believed that the dancers were possessed by the devil, and tried to pacify them by exorcism.

The dancing spread to Belgium and northern France. At one time streets in the town of Metz, France were choked by over a thousand dancers. The only solution was to encourage the dancing, which was sometimes done with the aid of hired musicians. Then the dancers would reach the final stage of exhaustion more quickly, and collapse on the ground apparently lifeless. Slowly, however, they began to recover.

This frenzied dancing seems to have been a form of collective hysteria—a result of the nervous strain left by the Black Death. In the same kind of hysteria, rumors of vampirism would be especially likely to spread in times of pestilence, and would grow in the retelling. Another explanation for stories of vampires is even more convincing: the high frequency in those days of premature burial or of accidental burial alive. This was all the more probable in times of plague when people were terrified of infection, and disposed of bodies as hastily as possible.

Strangely enough it has always been difficult to ascertain exactly when death occurs. Far from being rare, premature burial happened frequently in the past, and similar accidents can still happen today. As recently as 1974 doctors in a British hospital were dissecting a body for a kidney transplant when they realized to their horror that the corpse was breathing. This is not an isolated case. Recently in a southern state of America, an unmarried mother-to-be became so agitated at the sight of a policeman knocking on her door that she collapsed, and was certified as dead. A week after her burial, her mother arrived and insisted on seeing the body for herself. When the grave was opened it was discovered that the baby had been born, and that the mother's fingers had been worn down in the effort to scratch her way out of the coffin.

If we can make such mistakes today with all our medical knowledge, imagine how easy errors must have been in the days when such states as catalepsy (a trancelike condition which might last for several weeks), epilepsy, or apparent death from suffocation or poison were not properly recognized.

Above: the artist Pieter Breughel painted the life he saw around him in 16th-century Flanders—which included one of the mass dancing crazes of the times. As shown in this drawing, dancers were sometimes encouraged by others to reach final exhaustion and so to start their recovery.

Left: an engraving by a 17th-century artist of the frenzied dance that took place in a churchyard on Christmas Eve a few hundred years before, and started one of the mad dance epidemics of the Middle Ages. At one point the priest's son tried to pull his sister away—but her arm came out in his hand! The dancers were excommunicated by their priest and ordered to dance for a year without a rest.

31

Right: this 19-century painting is not of a vampire about to leave his grave, but of a victim of premature burial during one of the the European plagues. Belgian painter Antoine Wiertz called his work *Buried Alive*. It depicts the horror of a person who, buried as dead in undue haste, awakens to claw his way desperately out of his coffin—only to find himself sealed in the bone-littered fastness of his vault forever.

Right: an engraving from 1604 showing ghosts rising. They are the souls of victims of the Black Death who had been buried alive in 1347. The Black Death was one of the most severe of the plagues, carried across Europe by rats. It laid waste cities and wiped out the entire population of hundreds of towns and villages.

A state resembling death may even be induced deliberately, as by the fakirs of India.

Even those who were simply in a drunken stupor might have awakened to find themselves interred forever in the darkness. It is hard to imagine a more appalling fate: first the gradual realization of what had happened, then the panicky and hopeless attempts to get out, and finally the slow suffocation. If the grave of someone prematurely buried was broken into by body snatchers seeking a body for dissection or by robbers hoping to find a valuable ring on one of the fingers, it would be discovered that the body had twisted into a different position in the cramped space. The searchers would probably find also that the shroud was torn and bloody, that there was blood on the fingers and nails from the wretched person's efforts to claw a way out, and that the mouth was bloody from being bitten in the final agony. How easily these signs could be attributed to vampirism.

Buried Alive!

Of all the horrors possible, one of the most terrible must be to be buried alive. Yet there are many true tales of unfortunates who revived from deathlike states to find themselves irrevocably locked away in their own coffins, there to struggle in anguish until real death at length released them. Edgar Allen Poe used this theme in one of his macabre tales. In it a woman falls ill with a mysterious disease and dies. For three days after, the corpse lay waiting for the funeral. On the fourth day after death it was sealed away in the family vault, with all appropriate ceremony and care.

Three years later the husband himself opened the vault for another family member who had died. To his horror, a shrouded skeleton fell into his arms. It was the remains of his wife. Poe tells us that less than two days after her burial she had awakened from seeming death and, struggling within her coffin had thrown it from the ledge to the floor of the vault. This fall had cracked it open. The frantic woman had apparently seized a piece of the broken coffin to bang against the door of the vault in a vain appeal for help. There she had died, her shroud entangled in the ironwork. Thus she remained, and thus she rotted, erect.

Dr. Herbert Mayo, Professor of Anatomy at King's College, London, realized this truth in 1851 and wrote: "That the bodies, which were found in the so called Vampyr state, instead of being in a new or mystical condition, were simply alive in the common way, or had been so for some time subsequent to their interment; that, in short, they were the bodies of persons who had been buried alive, and whose life, where it yet lingered, was finally extinguished through the ignorance and barbarity of those who disinterred them." In other words, some alleged vampires might still have been alive when the stake was plunged through their heart. Dr. Mayo quoted the case of a man who was believed to have become a vampire, and who was exhumed. "When they opened his grave," Mayo says, " . . . his face was found with a color, and his features made natural sorts of movements, as if the dead man smiled. He even opened his mouth as if he would inhale fresh air. They held the crucifix before him, and called in a loud voice, 'See, this is Jesus Christ who redeemed your soul from hell, and died for you.' After the sound had acted on his organs of hearing, and he had connected perhaps some ideas with it, tears began to flow from the dead man's eyes. Finally, when after a short prayer for his poor soul, they proceeded to hack off his head, the corpse uttered a screech and turned and rolled just as if it had been alive . . . "

In Moravia in the 18th century a postmaster was thought to have died from epilepsy. When some years later it became necessary to transfer various graves, his body was disinterred and it was discovered that he had been buried alive. The doctor who had signed the death certificate lost his reason over it.

In 1665 a terrible outbreak of plague decimated the population of England, claiming nearly 150,000 victims. One symptom of the disease was an acute drowsiness that brought an overwhelming desire for sleep. Since bodies were hurried out of the houses at night, it is hardly surprising that those deeply asleep might be taken for dead—especially as they were buried hastily in communal pits without the proper formalities of a funeral. A hundred or more years later, premature burial was still so common that it gave rise to this limerick:

"There was a young man of Nunhead
Who awoke in his coffin of lead,
'It's cosy enough,' he remarked in a huff,
'But I wasn't aware I was dead.'"

Even at the beginning of this century premature burial occurred so often in the United States that there was said to be a case of it every week. In one instance a young woman from Indianapolis was to be buried two weeks after her seeming death, which several doctors had attested to on the death certificate. Her young brother clung to her body as it was removed for burial, and in the confusion a bandage around the woman's jaw fell loose. It was then noticed that her lips were quivering. "What do you want?" the boy cried. "Water," whispered the woman, who subsequently recovered and lived to an old age.

The director of an American school for orphans was declared dead on two occasions. She was only saved the second

Left: imagine the shock of on-lookers when a dead woman sits up in her coffin, as this engraving shows. This happened in 1728 when Margaret Dickson, hung for the murder of a child, later revived. The law protected her from being tried for the same crime again, and she lived in good health for another 30 years.

Left: this 18th-century Swiss engraving tells a grim tale of the premature burial of a pregnant woman. Her baby was born after burial—and both died in what must have been an agony.

Below: catalepsy—a state like a coma in which even breathing may stop—can occur from hypnotism, as shown here, or from hysteria. Edgar Allan Poe was fascinated by the danger of burial alive while in the cataleptic state, and used variations on the theme in his spine-chilling stories.

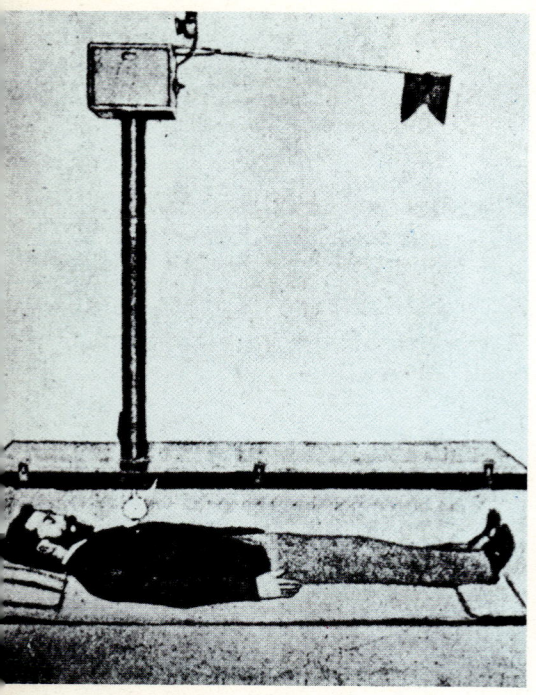

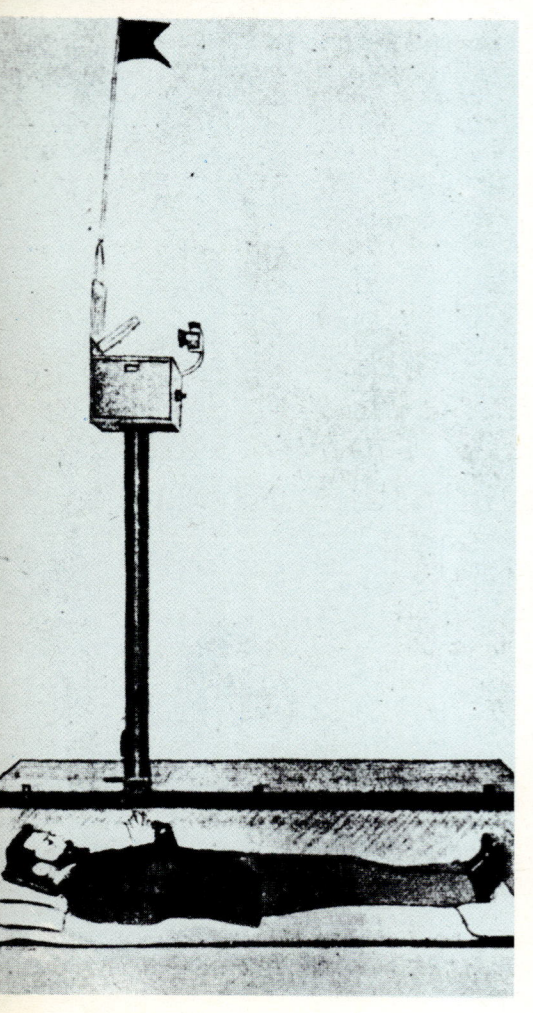

Left: an extraordinary device invented by a Russian, Count Karnicki, in 1901 to avoid the possibility of premature burial. Basically it consists of a tube and a sealed box. The tube is inserted into the coffin as soon as it is lowered into the grave. The box will still remain visible. Inside the coffin is a glass ball, resting on the chest of the body. If the corpse makes any movement at all, the glass ball releases a spring, and the lid of the box flies open, thus providing both light and air to the coffin below. Simultaneously a flag rises about four feet above the ground, and a bell rings. The gadget at the front of the box is an electric lamp, which will provide the unfortunate soul buried alive with some light after sunset while he awaits his rescue.

time when the undertaker happened to pierce her body with a pin and saw a drop of fresh blood ooze from the wound. Washington Irving Bishop, a stage thought reader in America who frequently entered a state of trance, was once considered dead until a cut made at the autopsy revealed he was alive. A similar case concerned a powerful Churchman of Spain whose heart was brought to view, and was seen to beat while he was being embalmed. At that moment he regained consciousness, and "even then had the sufficient strength to grasp with his hand the scalpel of the anatomist" before he finally died.

In creating his arch-vampire Dracula, Bram Stoker may well have drawn on stories he had heard as a child of a great cholera epidemic that, like the plague, created an atmosphere of panic and increased the likelihood of premature burial. This epidemic affected the whole of Europe. In 1832 it reached County Sligo in the West of Ireland, where Stoker's mother Charlotte, then a young girl, was living with her family. Her house was besieged by desperate looters among the last survivors in the village, and the story was told that when she saw a hand reaching through the skylight, she took an axe and cut it off. She told Stoker about Sergeant Callan, a giant of a man whose body was too big to fit in his coffin. To make it fit the undertaker took a hammer to break his legs. At the first blow of the hammer the supposed cholera victim sprang back to life, and he was seen around for many years afterward.

Premature burial, therefore, is one logical explanation for bodies that have moved and twisted in their graves. Another is that a dead body shrinks naturally, and as the corpse shrinks, the hair and nails appear to grow longer. There are also medical explanations for such apparent phenomena as the scream that the body is supposed to utter as the stake is plunged through the heart. Finally, the soil in which a body is buried can explain why it remains so well preserved. For example, on the Greek island of Santorini, where vampires were said to be so abundant, the volcanic nature of the soil would help keep the bodies intact longer.

These explanations do not account for the reports of vampires who have left their graves and are seen outside them at night. Yet even here there is a straightforward answer suggested by Dennis Wheatley, a best-selling writer on the occult. In times of extreme poverty, beggars would take shelter in graveyards, and make family vaults or mausoleums their macabre homes. Driven by hunger, they would have to leave these tombs by night to forage for food in the neighborhood. If such figures were glimpsed in the moonlight it is understandable that they might be thought of as vampires. An empty grave can be explained simply as the work of a body snatcher who had stolen the corpse to sell for medical dissection.

All these logical explanations fail to account for the persistence of the vampire legend, however. It goes deeper. Indeed, much of the fascination for vampires lies in the subconscious.

On one level there is the basic desire for reunion with dead loved ones. "It is believed," wrote British psychologist Professor Ernest Jones in *On the Nightmare,* "that they [the dead] feel an overpowering impulse to return to the loved ones whom they had left. The deepest source of this projection is doubtless to be found in the wish that those who have departed should not forget us, a wish that ultimately springs from childhood memories of being left alone by the loved parent." He concludes, "The belief that the dead can visit their loved ones, especially by night, is met with over the whole world." It is certainly the case that the majority of reports show alleged vampires returning to their loved ones and families.

What about the traditional symbolism of blood as the vital essence of life? To the vampire the sucking of blood is a form of transfusion, and this life restorer is a remedy that goes back through history. Early Australian tribes used to treat their sick by opening the veins of male friends, collecting the blood in a bowl, and feeding it to the invalid in its raw state.

Bloodsucking may also be an image for the way in which certain people seem to feed on the energy of others, draining them of vitality. Most of us have come across someone whom we might call a parasite, a sponger, or a leech. Vampire would be an equally suitable description. An encounter with such a person can leave us feeling absolutely exhausted. It has been noticed in hospitals that some people can even have this effect on machines, causing them to drop in electric current.

The draining of another's energy is particularly likely to happen in a marriage, family, or other close emotional relationship—traditionally the vampire's favorite feeding ground. There are also real cases of a strong personality exerting an unnatural influence over a weaker one. One example of this is how Ian Brady controlled Myra Hindley in their wholesale torture and killing of children in the British Moors Murders. Another is the power of Charles Manson over the group called his family. In this connection we might recall the vampire's reputed power to hypnotize a victim while draining its strength.

Above all there is a powerful sexual element in vampirism, which is undoubtedly one of the main reasons for its continuing fascination. This aspect of the vampire theme was played down in the 19th century when, although cruelty and violence were acceptable topics for publication, sex was heavily censored. However, some Eastern European vampire tales state quite frankly that bloodsucking was not the only activity the vampire had in mind when he or she chose a victim. It is certainly part

Was My Father a Vampire?

Do vampires still walk in Romania? In 1974 a gypsy woman told of her father's death when she was a girl. According to custom, she said, the body lay in the house awaiting the ceremonial final dressing by the family. After this ceremony it would be carried to the grave uncovered, so that everyone could see that the man was truly dead.

When the family lifted her father's legs to put them in his burial clothes, the limbs were not stiff. Neither were his arms nor the rest of his body. Rigor mortis had not set in. The family stared horrified at him and at each other, and the fearful whispering began.

The story spread among the villagers—people who remembered, or thought they remembered, the vampires that used to roam in the darkness of night. One unmistakable sign of a vampire is an undecomposed body, kept lifelike by the regular feasting on the blood of the living. Fear licked through the village, and the inhabitants soon came to the house armed with a wooden stake.

The family—bewildered, uncertain, and grief-stricken—fell back. The men tore off the corpse's covering sheet and, in the traditional manner, thrust the stake through the dead man's heart. The vampire—if such it was—was vanquished.

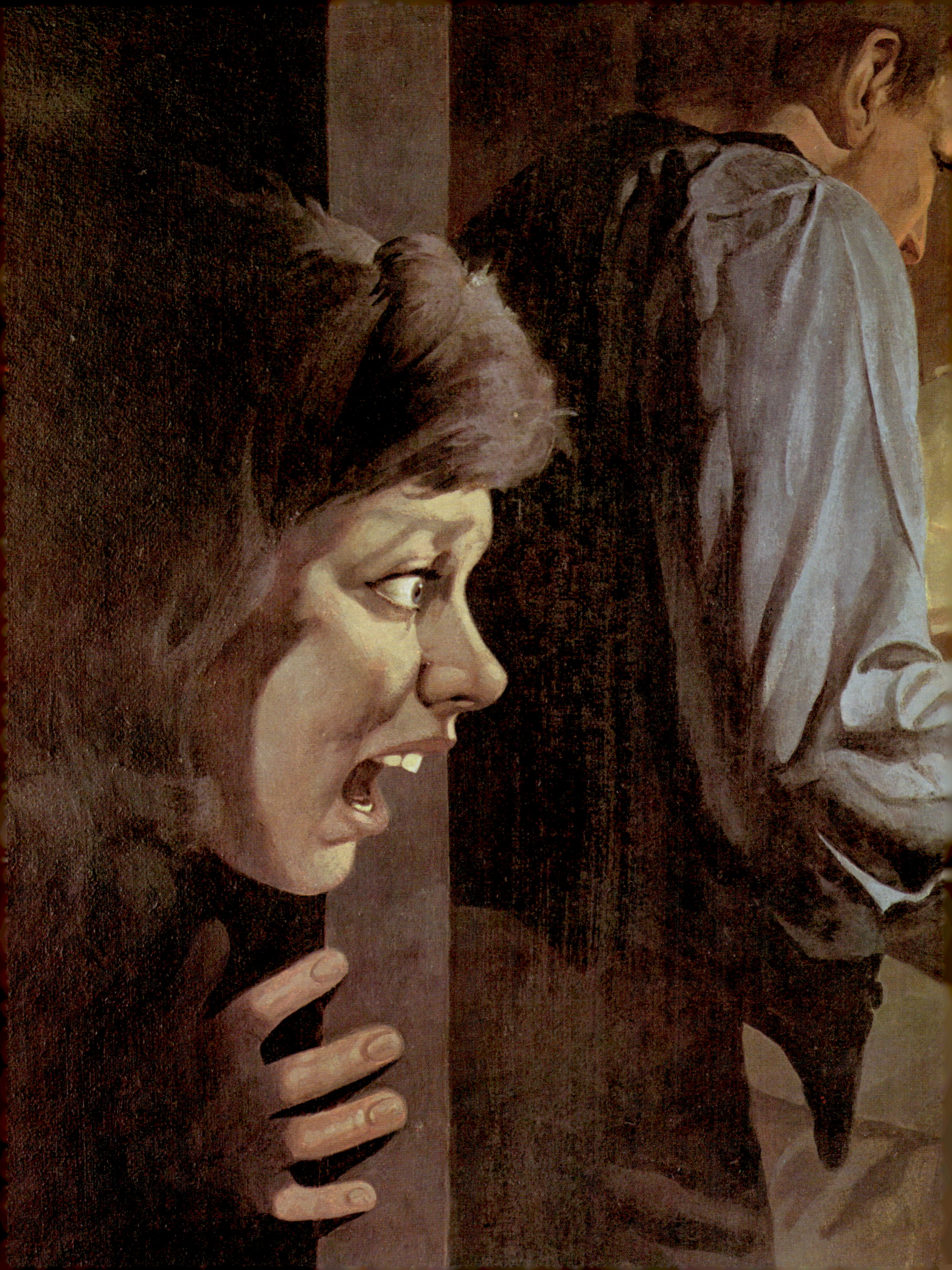

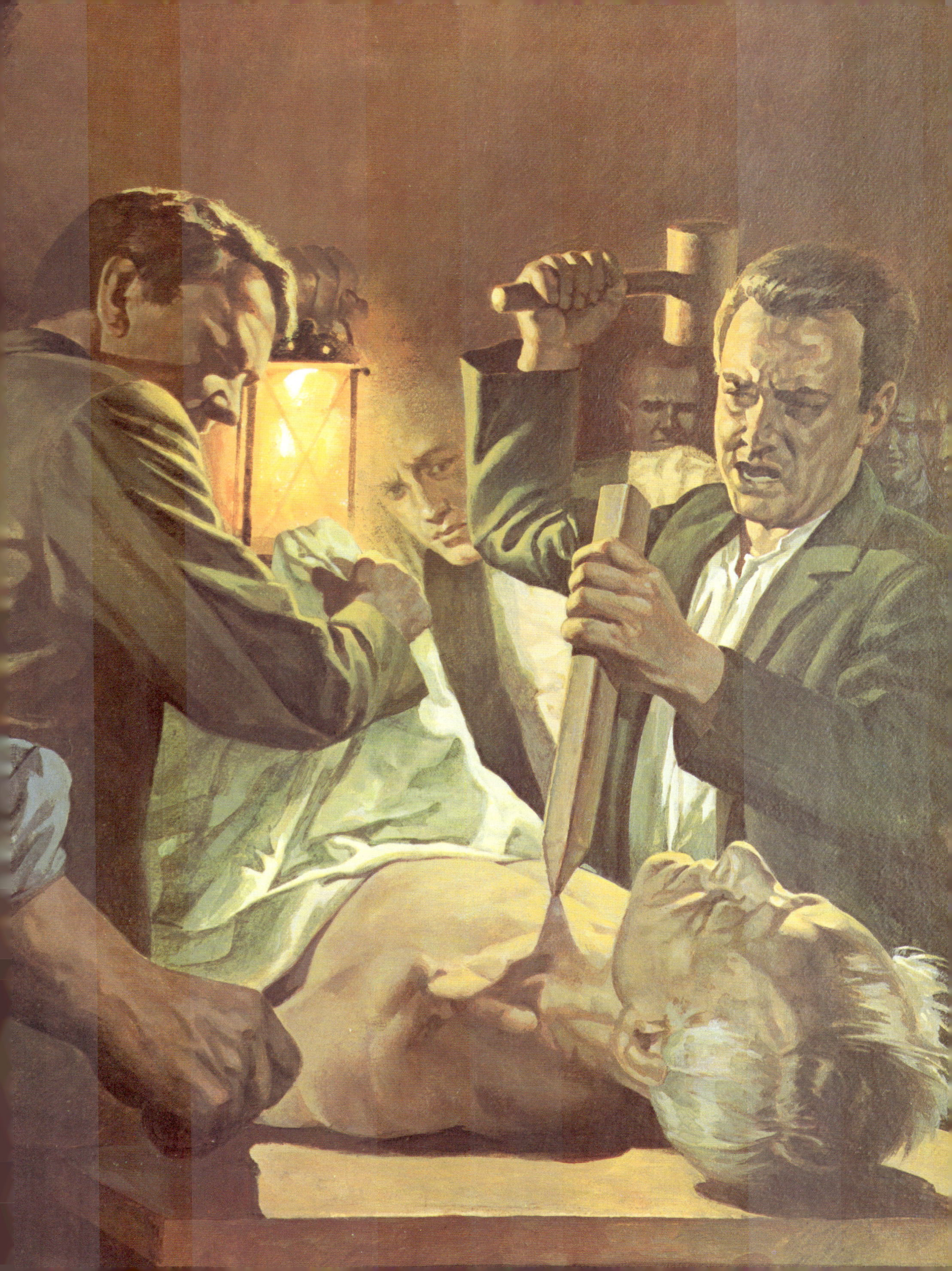

Opposite: one of the many erotic vampires painted by Boleslas Biegas in the period around World War I. Called *Vampire in the Form of an Explosion*, it is explicitly sexual in its depiction of female vampire and male prey.

Below: a post-card on sale in Vienna around 1900. It offers sexual titillation as a male vampire towers above his naked female victim, whose lifeblood is draining away from her body.

of the legend that male vampires prefer beautiful young girls, while female vampires practice their hypnotic charms on handsome young men.

The vampire's biting kiss on the victim's throat in order to suck out blood has an erotic and sadistic content that has not escaped the attention of psychologists. Ernest Jones says that "The act of sucking has a sexual significance from earliest infancy which is maintained throughout life in the form of kissing." A bite, according to Freud, is a part sadistic, part erotic kiss. Blood is also deeply linked with sexuality. "It has long been recognized by medico psychologists," wrote Montague Summers in his history of vampirism, "that there exists a definite connection between the fascination of blood and sexual excitement." Modern psychologists also note that blood and bloodletting are frequently associated with the erotic fantasies of their patients.

Freud believed that "morbid dread always signifies repressed sexual wishes." British writer Maurice Richardson, a contemporary expert on vampirism, agrees. The vampire embodies repressed sexual desires and sexual guilt that date from infancy, he maintains. Though we may not like to admit it, sex is a major part of the vampire's appeal. Writing about Bram Stoker's *Dracula* Richardson declares: "From a Freudian standpoint, and from no other does the story really make any sense; it is seen as a kind of incestuous, necrophiliac, oral-anal-sadistic all-in wrestling match. And this is what gives the story its force. The vampire Count, centuries old, is a father figure of huge potency."

Christopher Lee, the movie actor who has become famous for his portrayal of Dracula, describes the vampire Count as a "superman." "He offers the illusion of immortality, the subconscious wish we all have for limitless power, a man of tremendous brain and physical strength with a strange dark heroism. He is either a reincarnation or he has never died," says Lee. It is interesting to note that of the two greatest horror novels ever written one, *Frankenstein*, deals with the creation of life, and the other, *Dracula*, with the perpetuation of life.

Lee continues: "He [Dracula] is a superman image with an erotic appeal for women who find him totally alluring. In many ways he is everything people would like to be, the antihero, the heroic villain, and, like the much maligned Rasputin, part-saint and part-sinner. Men find him irresistible because they cannot stop him and, to women, he represents the complete abandonment to the power of a man."

Christopher Lee's best-known predecessor in the role of Count Dracula was the Hungarian actor Bela Lugosi. His version of Dracula, directed by Tod Browning in 1931, was an early horror film and is the oldest talkie still playing commercially. After the movie, Lugosi received piles of fan mail from women admirers. The appeal of the vampire had already infected Hollywood long before, however, with the creation in 1913 of the *vamp*. This word, still used today especially in advertising copy, was coined deliberately to launch the first movie star created by publicity. This was Theda Bara, whose name is an anagram of "Arab Death." She was shown to the

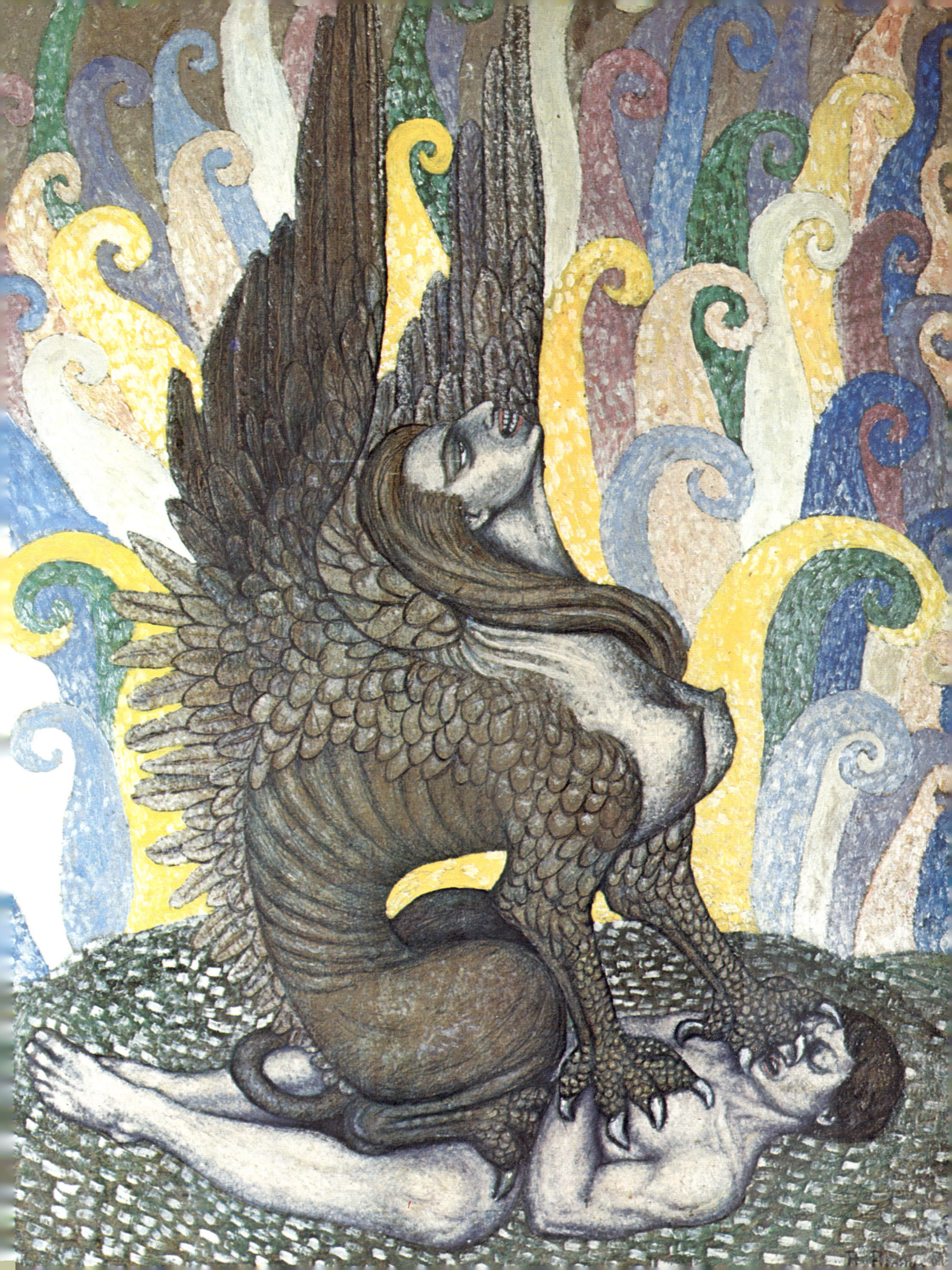

Below: a poster for the movie *Dracula*, made in 1931. The star was Bela Lugosi, a Hungarian cavalry officer who had drifted to Hollywood. His ominous good looks and broken accent made his portrayal of the Count famous.

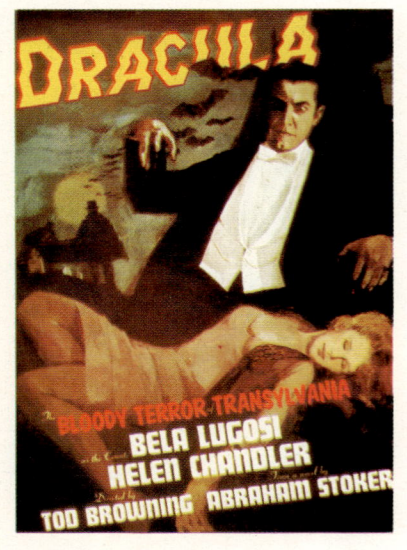

Below: a still from the movie. Lugosi as Dracula is about to sink his fangs into a vulnerable female throat. The film built a powerful atmosphere of horror—mainly by telling Stoker's story relatively straight—and was an enormous influence on later work.

public in *A Fool There Was* in which she had the celebrated line "Kiss me, my fool," and she was photographed in seductive poses—once crouching over a male skeleton. In *The Kiss of the Vampire* in 1916, the vamp reveled in the destruction of men. It was said of her: "She just wanted to ruin her victims and then laugh at them. She was bad!"

The erotic female vampire is just as much a part of the classic vampire legend as her male counterpart. She is described as voluptuous and wanton, irresistible, heartlessly cruel. Like the male vampire she has full red lips—supposedly the result of sucking blood, but also traditionally regarded in folk belief as a sign of excessive sensuality. Even the pure must succumb to her macabre charms. By day, however, all vampires are powerless. Some legends continued the erotic theme in their instructions for detecting a vampire's grave while the creature was asleep. A virgin boy or girl was supposed to ride naked over the graveyard on the back of a coal black virgin stallion that had never stumbled. The horse would shy when it came upon a vampire's tomb, it was said.

We now see that there are psychological reasons for the appeal of the vampire as well as logical explanations for vampire beliefs. But the big question remains unanswered: are there really such things as vampires—not the living person who drains us of vitality, nor the occasional individual who develops a mania for blood, but the bloodsucking cousin of the ghost, the so-called living dead? As an expert on vampires, Montague Summers came to this conclusion: "Consciously or unconsciously it is realized that the vampire tradition contains far more truth than the ordinary individual cares to appreciate and acknowledge."

A century ago people would not have believed that we would be able to sit in our homes, watch a square box, and through it see a man land on the moon. There may well be another, spiritual world around us of which we are still unaware.

When someone dies, a close friend or relative frequently gets an instinctive feeling that the death has happened, even hundreds of miles away. Sometimes the death is dreamt of. Occasionally, the dying person is seen by another at the very moment of death. In a similar way the sighting of vampires could be a time lapse, a version of the experience known as *déjà vu* in which one feels one has been in a strange place before. Some people believe that the sighting of flying saucers is a look into the future when such transport will be common. Conversely, alleged glimpses of the Loch Ness Monster may be a look back into the prehistoric past when monster creatures abounded.

Such a case of time out of joint would help to explain the Irish legend of a funeral cortege which, having just buried their local priest in the neighboring hills, noticed a clerical figure coming toward them. As he passed, they were shocked to recognize the man they had just laid to rest. Hurrying to his home they found his mother in a state of extreme agitation because her dead son had appeared at the house an hour before. Had this happened in Eastern Europe, the priest might well have been dubbed a vampire, particularly if there were any other unusual or mysterious circumstances in the way he died.

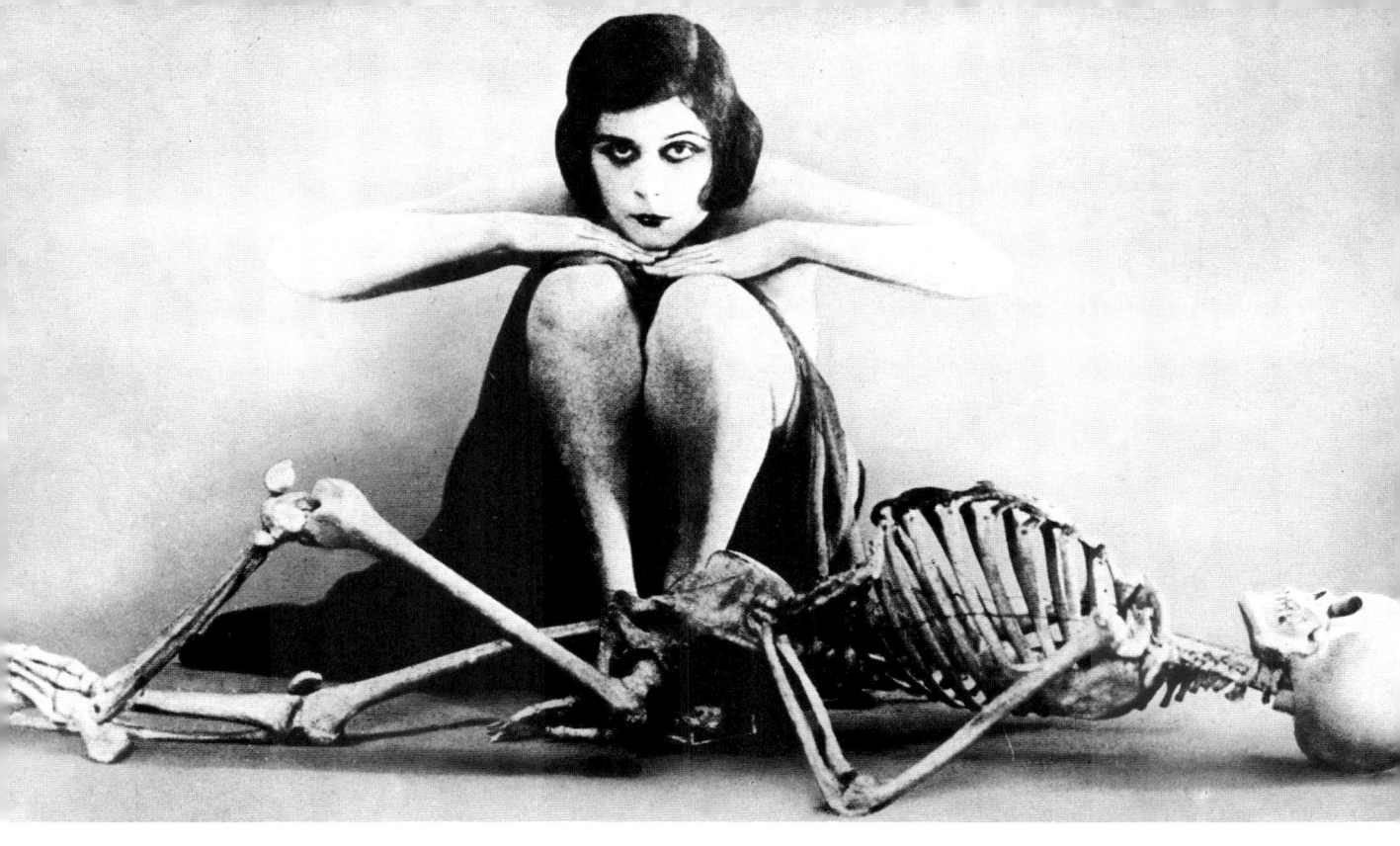

A more complex theory concerning the existence of vampires was put forward by the late Dion Fortune, a leading modern occultist. Like many occultists she believed in the *astral body*—the spiritual second body that can separate itself from the physical body and take on a life of its own. She maintained that by a trick of occultism, it is possible to prevent disintegration of the astral body after the death of the physical body. She referred to a case she had encountered involving some dead Hungarian soldiers who were reported to have become vampires, and to have made vampires of their victims. She suggested that these soldiers "maintained themselves in the etheric double [astral body] by vampirizing the wounded. Now vampirism is contagious; the person who is vampirized, being depleted of vitality, is a psychic vacuum, himself absorbing from anyone he comes across in order to refill his depleted sources of vitality. He soon learns by experience the tricks of a vampire without realizing their significance, and before he knows where he is, he is a full-blown vampire himself."

After death separation of the astral body from the physical body is permanent. But occultists believe that the astral body can also escape from the physical body during a person's life, and that it may take on some other form—that of a bird or animal, for example. Could this provide further grounds for a belief in the existence of vampires? Dion Fortune firmly believed in the ability of powerful feelings to create thought forms that possess a separate existence. Highly charged negative feelings might therefore cause the astral body to assume the form of an evil monster or ghost—possibly a vampire.

Discussing Dion Fortune's theory in *The Occult*, Colin

Above: Theda Bara, the first screen vamp, was also one of the first Hollywood actresses to be made into a star by a publicity campaign. She was not a bloodsucking vampire like Dracula, but ate up her male victims in a figurative way. In this publicity photograph she crouches over a male skeleton with a smoldering and chilling look of conquest.

Left: Christopher Lee as the screen Dracula comes into the bedroom to claim his human prey.

Below: in this scene from the 1960 movie *Brides of Dracula*, Peter Cushing looks sadly into the coffin of the vampire's victim. He played van Helsig, the arch enemy of Count Dracula.

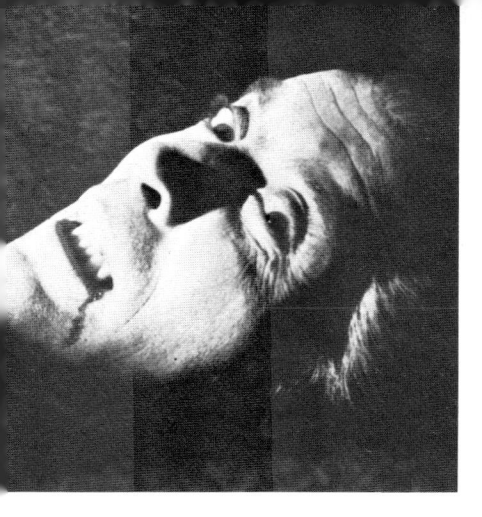

Above: Count Dracula, played by Christopher Lee, lies replete, blood on his fangs and chin. The terrible Count can only sleep in the coffin that contains earth from the grave in which he was originally buried. Traditionally, if a vampire's coffin was burned, the vampire dissolved into dust.

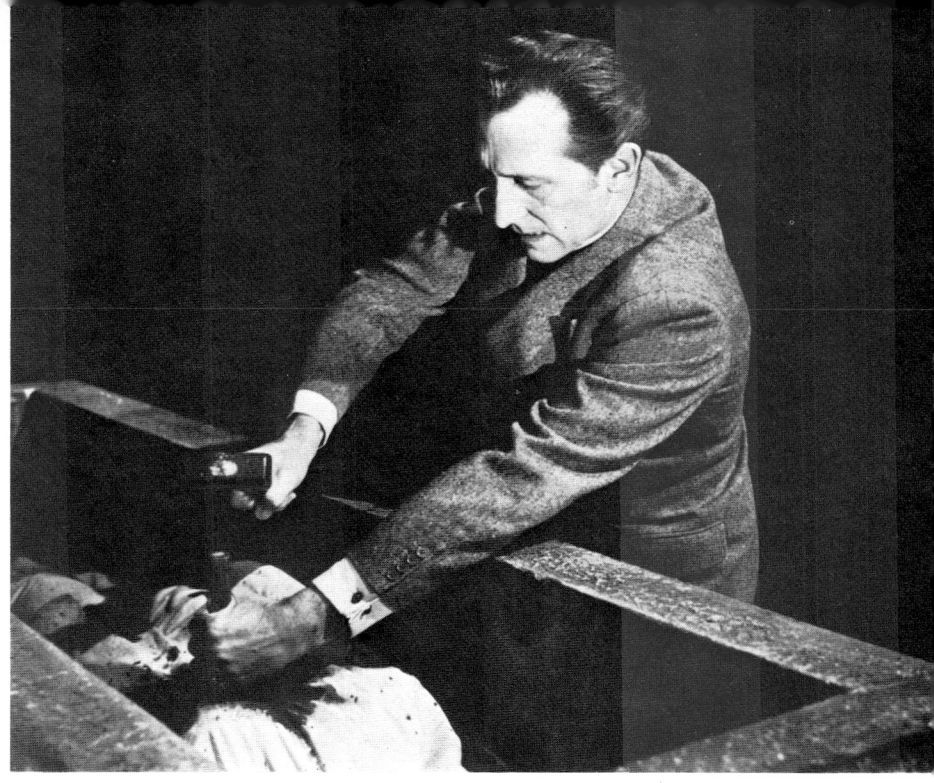

Above: from the start of the British series of Dracula films in 1958, Peter Cushing played the vampire fighter van Helsig. Here in the first of the movies, *Horror of Dracula*, he kills a vampire one common way by driving a stake through its heart.

Wilson agrees that "strange forces can erupt from the subconscious and take on apparently material shape." He quotes the story of a young Romanian peasant girl Eleonore Zugun. Eleonore showed a psychical investigator "devil's bites" on her hands and arms. As he sat with her she cried out, and marks of teeth appeared on the back of her hand, developing into bruises. A few minutes later she was bitten on the forearm, and the investigator could see deep teeth marks. Was this a ghost, asks Wilson, or Eleonore's own subconscious mind out of control? Perhaps it wasn't even Eleonore's mind, he suggests. "It might have been *somebody else's* mind."

"The subconscious mind is not simply a kind of deep seat repository of sunken memories and atavistic desires," says Wilson, "but of forces that can, under certain circumstances, manifest themselves in the physical world with a force that goes beyond anything the conscious mind could command." He feels that this might explain the mystery of vampires, and indeed of all so-called occult phenomena.

Can a mental image be projected as a physical reality? Can the subconscious mind create monsters or ghosts that attack and destroy? Can the astral body of a dead person attach itself to a living person, feeding off him as a vampire in order to maintain life?

Many people would say that the only vampires we might possibly encounter are living people whose private fantasy life and peculiar aberration is that of the bloodsucking vampire. If this side of a person becomes dominant, he might even believe himself to be a vampire. If his fantasy assumes the shape of a wolf, he may act like a wolf. But the nagging question remains: is there ever a moment when that person actually *becomes* a vampire or a wolf, through some external influence we do not yet understand?

3

Man Into Beast

In the year 1598, in a remote patch of forest in Western France, an archer and a group of armed countrymen came across the naked body of a boy. The corpse had been horribly mutilated and torn. The limbs, still warm and palpitating, were drenched with blood. As the Frenchmen approached the body, they caught sight of what appeared to be two wolves running off between the trees. The men gave chase, but to their amazement, they found they had caught, not a wolf, but what proved to be a man—tall, gaunt, clothed in rags, and with matted, verminous hair and beard. To their horror they noticed that his hands were still stained with fresh

Surrounded by a threatening and harsh world, humans often longed to acquire the power and ferocity of wild beasts—especially the savage wolf in Europe. Could anyone really change into an animal? In folk belief through the ages the answer was "yes"—and people went in fear of the werewolf.

Above: a werewolf attacking a victim, from a 16th-century German treatise on kinds of witchcraft.

Right: hidden by the darkness of a forest at midnight, men—and women— hunched over a fire and recited words of an ancient ritual in the hopes that they would find themselves magically transformed into the wolf they wished to be.

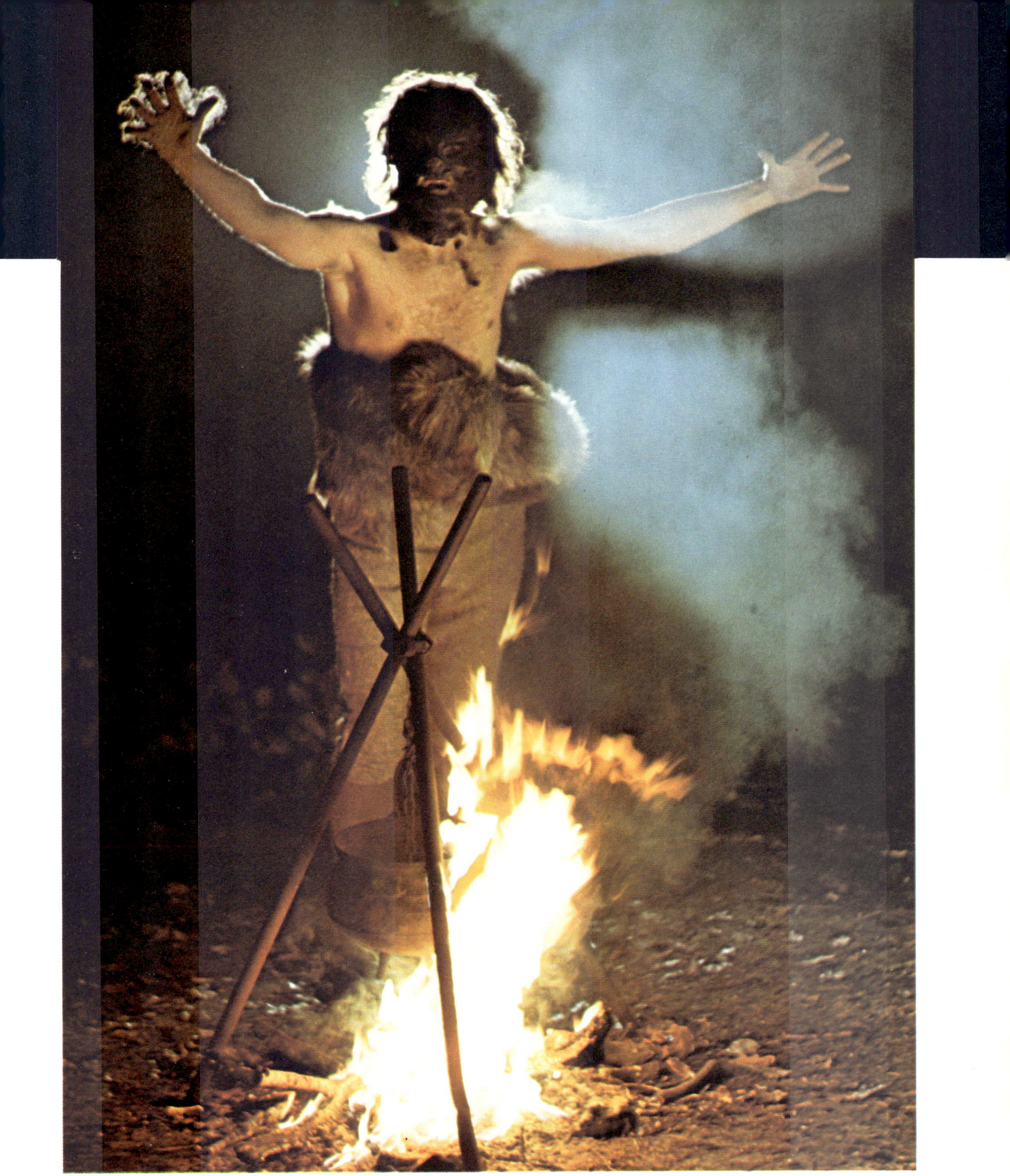

"The werewolf and the vampire have much in common..."

Below: a werewolf devouring a young victim. Though werewolves are closely allied to witches and witchcraft—the metamorphosis is generally seen as a ritual of black magic—werewolf legends, like those of vampires, have a strong and obvious sexual element.

blood, and his claw-like nails clotted with human flesh. The man, it turned out, was a wandering beggar named Jacques Roulet, and he was brought to trial at the town of Angers in August, 1598. And if the discovery of Roulet was a shock to the people of Angers, the trial proceedings were shattering.

Roulet confessed to the court: "I was a wolf."

"Do your hands and feet become paws?"

"Yes, they do."

"Does your head become like that of a wolf?"

"I do not know how my head was at the time; I used my teeth."

In reaching their verdict the court had to decide whether Roulet was a werewolf, as he claimed, or a lycanthrope, which is related but different. A werewolf or werwolf is a living person who has the power to change into a wolf. The word comes from Old English *wer*, meaning man, and wolf. A *lycanthrope* is someone suffering from a mental illness that makes him believe he is transformed into a wolf. This word comes from the Greek for wolfman. In either case, Roulet could have faced execution. But the court showed a compassion rare for its time. Judging Roulet to be mentally sick—and therefore a lycanthrope—they sentenced him to a madhouse for only two years.

A true werewolf was generally believed to undergo an almost complete transformation into a wolf, unlike the werewolf of Hollywood movies who remains basically human in appearance. Much controversy arose in the past over people who were said to disguise the fact that they were wolves by wearing their fur on the inside. It was claimed that such people looked ordinary enough, but that their skin was inside out. When they were torn apart—as hundreds of innocent people were at various times in past centuries—the hair, or wolf fur, could be seen on the other side of the skin.

The werewolf and the vampire have much in common. In fact it was often assumed that a werewolf would become a vampire after death unless special precautions, such as exorcism, were taken. Anyone who ate the flesh of a sheep killed by a wolf was liable to become a werewolf. A person who ate a wolf's brains or drank water from his footprints was certain to become one. In some places, eating certain large and sweet smelling flowers or drinking from a stream where a wolfpack had drunk was a sure way to turn into a wolf.

Anybody with small pointed ears, prominent teeth, strong curved fingernails, bushy eyebrows that met over the nose, a third finger as long as the second on each hand, or even a lot of hair—especially on the hands and feet—was immediately suspect. However, if you are tempted to take a closer look at your friends next time you see them, remember that the eyes of a werewolf always remain human.

Like the belief in vampires, these beliefs stemmed from peoples' ignorant fear of anyone who was different. In some traditions it was easy to become a werewolf by accident. In others, you had to be especially evil to merit such a fate. Some tales suggest that a bestial person would return after death as a wolf. Ghostly werewolves, however, are extremely rare in folklore, which is where the werewolf differs most from the vampire. The vampire is akin to the ghost. The werewolf is very much a living person, and more akin to the witch in that he or she may actively seek to become a werewolf. This can be done by entering into a pact with a demon known as the Wolf Spirit or with the Devil himself.

Surprising though it may seem, many people actually wanted to become werewolves and, in addition to the magical methods already mentioned, went through elaborate rituals in the hope of doing so. The right moment for such a change was at midnight by the light of a full moon. The would-be werewolf drew a magic circle and built a fire over which he placed a cauldron containing a potion of herbs and drugs. Then he smeared his body with an ointment made from the fat of a newly killed cat, mixed with ingredients like aniseed and opium. Around his waist he bound a belt made of wolf's skin. Kneeling inside the circle as the magic potion simmered, he chanted an incantation that went something like this:

"Hail, hail, hail, Great Wolf Spirit, hail!
A boon I ask thee, mighty shade. Within this circle I have made,
Make me a werewolf strong and bold,
The terror alike of young and old.
Grant me a figure tall and spare;
The speed of the elk, the claws of the bear;

Above: the title page picture from Sabine Baring-Gould's *The Book of Were-wolves*, published in 1864. It was the first serious look at the whole werewolf myth. Baring-Gould, an expert on many aspects of medieval folklore, was a clergyman who wrote novels and hymns, among them the well-known *Onward Christian Soldiers*.

A reconstruction of the ritual designed to turn human into wolf.

Left: the would-be werewolf, having drawn his magic circles on the ground and built his fire, puts the specified herbs and drugs into a boiling cauldron.

Right: making his invocation to the "devilish hosts," he strips naked to the waist and smears his body with an ointment made from the fat of a newly dead cat, mixed with more drugs and herbs.

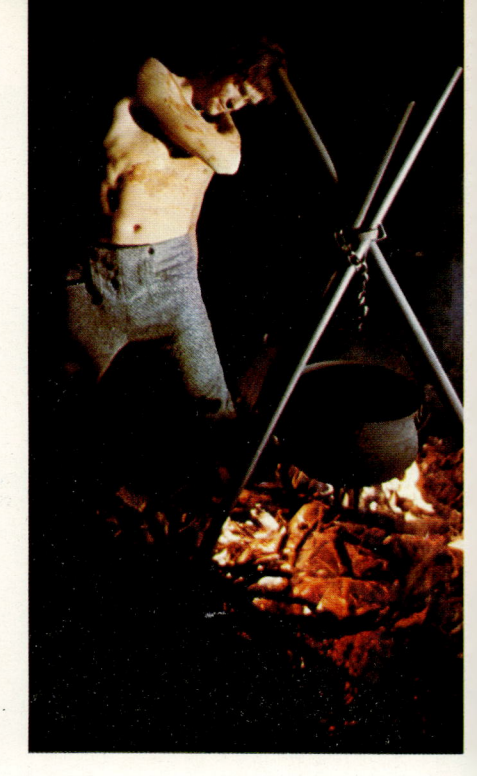

The poison of snakes, the wit of the fox;
The stealth of the wolf, the strength of the ox;
The jaws of the tiger, the teeth of the shark;
The eyes of a cat that sees in the dark."

Such a powerful plea might sound irresistible. To the skeptical mind, however, it is significant that the simmering potion included large amounts of poppy seed, and the salve contained opium. This suggests that the initiate may have been in a drugged condition. The incantation concluded with the cry:

"Make me a werewolf! make me a man eater!
Make me a werewolf! make me a woman eater!
Make me a werewolf! Make me a child eater!
I pine for blood! human blood!
Give it to me! Give it to me tonight!
Great Wolf Spirit! give it to me, and
Heart, body, and soul, I am yours."

If the ritual had been correctly carried out, the aspirant would then begin to change into a wolf. Tall and phantomlike, his figure would glow in the darkness until it assumed the "form of a tall thin monstrosity, half human and half animal, gray and nude, with very long legs and arms, and the feet and claws of a wolf." Once fully transformed, he would indulge in the werewolf's traditional nighttime activities of hunting, killing, and eating. The commonest reason for wishing to become a wolf was said to be a desire for revenge.

The man or woman who has achieved the power of metamorphosis will change into a wolf at sunset every night until death, reassuming human shape at dawn. Some folk tales say that the werewolf must roll in the dirt or the morning dew in order to change back into a human; others that the transformation occurs automatically at daybreak. A werewolf that is wounded or killed immediately becomes human again. Usually the creature

Above: putting on the belt made out of a wolf's skin (in some versions of the ritual an entire wolf skin was required), he waits for a demon to give him the power of transformation into a wolf. Right: the magical metamorphosis into the terrible werewolf begins.

Right: once someone has acquired the power of metamorphosis, it is believed that he or she will automatically change into a wolf at sunset every night until death.

Right: *The Witches Kitchen* by Francisco de Goya shows warlocks changing themselves into wolflike creatures. It is one of six paintings on witchcraft done by this Spanish master in 1798, and indicates Goya's strong interest in exploring the realities of the subconscious mind.

Above: a werewolf savaging a baby as depicted by the 16th-century German painter Lucas Cranach. In this case the man hasn't changed into a wolf physically, but has merely taken on the beast's predatory behavior.

can be caught or destroyed like an ordinary wolf, but the most effective way of killing a werewolf is to shoot it with a silver bullet. The corpse must then be burned rather than buried.

To most people all this sounds like a welter of primitive superstition, and it is significant that reports of werewolves decreased as cities spread into the countryside. Such tales have always been commonest in remote regions where the wolf was the foremost beast of prey. Today, when the wolf has all but disappeared from the United States and many European countries, it may be hard for us to imagine the terror this animal inspired in our ancestors. In northern countries especially, the wolf was a deadly enemy, hated and feared for its ferocious attacks on flocks and people alike. But the wolf also seemed eerie, moving mainly by night, ghostly gray and silent, almost invisible except for the slanting eyes that glowed red by firelight and yellow-green by moonlight.

Add to this its spine-chilling howl—said to be an omen of death—and it is not surprising that the wolf came to be regarded as an evil, almost supernatural monster. Wherever there were wolves there were also reports of werewolves, whom people feared with a panic verging on hysteria.

Nevertheless there are eminent authorities on werewolves who do not regard the idea of a human turning into a wolf as superstitious fantasy, and who take reports of werewolves seriously. Sabine Baring Gould, author in 1865 of the *Book of Were-wolves, Being an Account of a Terrible Superstition*, maintained that because the legend was so persistent "everywhere and in all ages, it must rest upon foundation of fact." He claimed that "Half the world believes, or believed in werewolves."

Writing in this century, Elliott O'Donnell agrees, and declares that there is no conclusive evidence that the people who claimed to be werewolves were shams. It was a characteristic of trials for lycanthropy that the accused seemed eager to confess. He suggests that many of the accused had been victimized and confessed under torture, which is doubtless true. But even if they were shams, O'Donnell thought this "would in nowise preclude the existence of the werewolf." He becomes less convincing, however, when he asserts that werewolves were created by "malevolent forces, the originators of all evil."

As with vampirism, reports of werewolves have been documented all over the world since ancient times. As early as the 5th century B.C. Herodotus, who is known as the "father of history," wrote: "Each Neurian changes himself once a year into the form of a wolf and he continues in that form for several days, after which he resumes his former shape." In the 2nd century A.D. a Roman doctor observed that "lycanthropia is a species of melancholy which can be cured at the time of the attack by opening a vein and abstracting blood."

Petronius, the 1st-century Roman satirist, tells a werewolf story with a universal theme. It concerns a servant who accompanied a soldier on a night's journey out of town, and was aghast to see him strip off his clothes by the roadside and change into a wolf. With a howl the creature leaped into the woods and disappeared from view. When the servant reached his destination, he was told that a wolf had just broken into the farm, and had savaged the cattle before being driven away by a man who had thrust a pike into the animal's neck. Hurrying home at daybreak, the servant came to the place where the soldier's clothes had been, but he found only a pool of blood. Back home, the soldier lay wounded with a doctor dressing his neck.

This epitomizes a constant theme of the werewolf legend: the wolf is wounded in a fight and a human being is later discovered suffering from the same wound. A story from the Middle Ages tells of a Russian noblewoman who doubted that anyone could change into an animal. One of her servants volunteered to prove her wrong. He changed into a wolf and raced across the fields, chased by his mistresses' dogs which cornered him and damaged one of his eyes. When the servant returned to his mistress in human form he was blind in one eye.

Another famous case took place in the Auvergne region of central France in 1558. A hunter out in the forest met a neigh-

"I am becoming a wolf..."

An American Indian and his three children lived alone in the forest away from their tribe. When he lay dying, he made his older boy and girl promise they would look after their younger brother.

Soon, however, the older brother began to long for the company of the tribe. He told his sister, who agreed that she was lonely as well. "But remember our father's words," she said. "Shall we forget the little one?" In spite of her reminder, the boy left. Weary of her duty, the girl also left her little brother, and set off for her former home.

She found her older brother married and happy, and soon decided to stay in the village with him. Her little brother waited in vain for her to come back. He grew hungry and cold. He crept out only at night to eat what the wolves had left behind. Soon, having no other friends, he sought out their company, and they were good to him.

One day the older brother was out in his canoe, fishing on the great lake. He heard the voice of a child singing, "My brother, my brother! I am becoming a wolf!" He leaped out on the shore, running after his brother and calling to him. But the younger boy, already half a wolf, fled after his new brothers, the wolves, into the depths of the forest.

boring nobleman who asked him to bring him back some game if the hunt was successful. The hunter was later attacked by a savage wolf, but was able to drive it away after slashing off one of its paws. He put the paw in his pouch as a memento, and set off for home. On the way he stopped at the nobleman's chateau and told him of his adventure. Reaching in his pouch for the wolf's paw, he was amazed to find a delicate female hand in its place. The nobleman was even more astonished as he recognized the gold ring on one of the fingers. Dashing upstairs he found his wife bandaging the bleeding stump of her wrist. She confessed to being a werewolf, and was burned at the stake.

Just as the vampire has its traditional home in Eastern Europe, the forests of France seem to have been the natural home of the werewolf. Reports of werewolves, called *loups-garoux* in French, reached epidemic proportions in the 16th century. As many as 30,000 cases were listed between 1520 and 1630.

Below: an engraving of the capture and hanging of a werewolf by the townsfolk of Eschenbach, Germany in 1685. The werewolf, which had ravaged the children of the town, tried to leap over a well to get the cockerel that had been placed on the other side as bait. It missed its mark, fell into the well, and was easily taken.

One of the most famous werewolves in history is a stooping, bushy-browed hermit called Gilles Garnier. On September 13, 1573, authorities in the French town of Dôle gave permission for a werewolf hunt after several local children had been found killed and partially eaten. The permission read: "And since he has attacked and done injury in the country to some horsemen, who kept him off only with great difficulty and danger to their persons, the said court, desiring to prevent any greater danger, has permitted and does permit, those who are dwelling in the said places, notwithstanding all edicts concerning the chase, to assemble with pikes, halberds, and sticks, to chase and pursue the said werewolf in every place where they many find or seize him; to tie and to kill, without incurring any pains or penalties." Clearly the peasants were convinced that a werewolf was to blame before they had even started the hunt. It is extraordinary that in all such reports there is never any suggestion that the victims might have been seized by a real wolf.

Two months later a group of villagers heard the screams of a child and the baying of a wolf. Hurrying to the spot—expecting to find a werewolf—they discovered a small girl, badly mauled, and thought they recognized Garnier in the wolf that raced away. When a 10-year-old boy disappeared six days later, they raided the hut of "the hermit of St. Bonnet," as Garnier was known, and arrested both him and his wife.

Garnier made two immediate confessions. One concerned a 12-year-old boy killed in a pear orchard the previous August. Garnier had been about to eat the boy's flesh when he was interrupted by some men. They testified that Garnier was in the form of a man, not a wolf. On October 6, in a vineyard near Dôle, Garnier had attacked a 10-year-old girl, this time in the guise of a wolf. He killed her with her teeth and claws, stripped her, and ate her, enjoying the meal so much that he brought some of the flesh back for his wife's supper. On the evidence of this confession Garnier was burned alive on January 18, 1574.

Thirty years later the similarly named Jean Grenier, a handsome 14-year-old shepherd boy, confessed to a series of crimes in the Bordeaux area of southwest France. For what his confession is worth, he admitted to having eaten more than 50 children. Sometimes, he said, he lay in wait in the woodlands until dusk fell and his transformation into a wolf took place. Then he watched for victims from a thicket beside a favorite pool. Once he surprised two girls, bathing naked; one escaped, but he devoured the other. When he was provoked by extreme hunger, he said, he hurled himself fearlessly into a crowd until he was driven off.

Grenier confessed with suspicious eagerness, reciting his crimes with such relish that he even caused laughter in the crowded courtroom when he talked of pursuing an old woman only to find her flesh "as tough as leather." He also complained about a child in this way: "When I lifted it out of its crib, and when I got ready for my first bite, it shrieked so loud it almost deafened me." There had been killings in the area, and three girls testified against Grenier, so his detailed confession was believed. However, Grenier accused other people of being werewolves too, and the judge found the evidence so appalling that he sent Grenier

Below: this engraving of 1765 shows the dreaded Wild Beast of Gévaudan at some of its nefarious doings. It terrorized several districts in France with attacks that took the lives of more than 100 people. It was said that the Wild Beast could deal paralyzing blows with its long tail, and that it ran with supernatural speed.

Below: another engraving of the Beast of Gévaudan. Local peasants were convinced it was a warlock in a wild beast's shape. It was finally killed by a royal archer.

The Phantom Werewolf

The story is told that in the 1880s a professor was taking a vacation by a small lake in Wales. One day he discovered what looked like a particularly large dog's skull, and brought it back to the house. That evening his wife was alone when she heard a snuffling and scratching at the kitchen door. Going in to make sure the door was locked, she saw at the window the head of a huge creature, half human, half animal. The jaws and teeth were those of a wolf, but the eyes were human and intelligent. She ran to the door and bolted it. Then, terrified, she heard the creature moving around the house, rattling the latches. At that moment she heard her husband returning with a guest. She just managed to unlock the door for them before she fainted dead away.

When she revived she told them the story, and they waited up that night to see if the monster would return. It did. There glaring through the window was a wolf with a man's eyes. They snatched a gun and ran toward it, but the shape darted away. It went down to the lake and vanished without a ripple into the depths.

The next day the professor took the skull and threw it into the deepest part of the lake. They never saw the werewolf again.

to a higher court for further investigation of the strange case.

The houses of the people named by Grenier were searched, and although nothing was found, Grenier's father and a neighbor were arrested. Monsieur Grenier impressed the higher court judge with testimony that his son was a well-known idiot who boasted that he had slept with every woman in the village. Nevertheless, Grenier continued to confess with such conviction that his father and the neighbor were reexamined. Under torture they admitted that they had sought young girls "to play with, but not to eat."

Grenier was sentenced to be burned, but the case had caused such a stir that it was eventually reviewed by the high court of justice in Bordeaux. Judge de Lancre recorded this testimony by the youth: "When I was 10 or 11 years old, my neighbor del Thillaire introduced me, in the depths of the forest, to the Maître de la Fôret [Lord of the Forest], a black man, who signed me with his nail, and then gave me and del Thillaire a salve and a wolf skin. From that time I have run about the country as a wolf." Grenier maintained that he went hunting for children at the command of this Lord of the Forest, changing his shape with the help of the salve and the wolf skin after hiding his clothes in the thicket.

Like the beggar Roulet before him, this self-confessed werewolf was treated with a rare degree of understanding. The high court called in two doctors who decided that the boy was suffering from "the malady called lycanthropy, which deceives men's eyes into imagining such things," although they added that the illness was the result of possession by an evil spirit. Judge de Lancre gave an intelligent summing up, which must apply to many similar contemporary cases of alleged werewolves: "The court takes into account the young age and the imbecility of this boy, who is so stupid and idiotic that children of seven and eight years old normally show more intelligence, who has been ill fed in every respect and who is so dwarfed that he is not as tall as a 10 year old... Here is a young lad abandoned and driven out by his father, who has a cruel stepmother instead of a real mother, who wanders over the fields, without a counselor and without anyone to take an interest in him, begging his bread, who has never had any religious training, whose real nature was corrupted by evil promptings, need, and despair, and whom the devil made his prey."

The boy's life was spared, and he was sent to a monastery which the judge visited several years later. He found that Grenier's mind was completely blank, unable to comprehend the simplest things, yet the young man still maintained he was a werewolf and that he would eat more children if he could. Also, he wanted "to look at wolves." Grenier died in 1610 as a "good Christian," but it is not altogether surprising that anyone in the region with the name of Garnier or Grenier was regarded with suspicion for a long time afterward.

The case of a whole family of werewolves was recorded in western France in 1598. Two sisters, their brother, and his son were known as the Werewolves of St. Claude. One of the girls, Peronette, was plainly suffering from lycanthropic hysteria, and ran about on all fours. She attacked two children who were

Above: illustrations from a 16th-century pamphlet *The Life and Death of Peter Stubb*, the German werewolf. Stubb, under torture, claimed that he had a magic belt that changed him into a wolf. He was found guilty although his accusers were unable to find any trace of the belt, and sentenced to death by horrible tortures.

picking fruit in an orchard, and when the four-year-old boy tried to defend his sister, she seized a knife and gashed him in the throat. Before he died he testified that this wolf had human hands instead of paws, and the enraged peasants tore Peronette to pieces before she could be brought to trial. Her sister was then accused of also being a lycanthrope who had the additional evil gift of producing hail. She was said to sleep with the devil who came to her in the shape of a goat. Their brother Pierre confessed that he turned himself into a wolf, and that the three would chase people or animals around the country "according to the guidance of their appetite" until they were exhausted. His son testified that he covered himself with a magic salve to turn into a wolf, and that he had gone hunting with his two aunts and had killed some goats.

The judge visited the wretched family in jail. "I have seen those I have named go on all fours in a room just as they did when they were in the fields," he said, "but they said it was impossible for them to turn themselves into wolves, since they had no more ointment, and they had lost the power of doing so, by being imprisoned. I have further noted that they were all scratched on the face and hands and legs; and that Pierre Gandillon was so much disfigured in this way that he bore hardly any resemblance to a man, and struck with horror those who looked at him." This last sentence is revealing. If Pierre had been disfigured since birth, he may well have desired the company and guise of animals. The verdict was not merciful this time, however, for the entire family was burned to death.

The most notorious German werewolf was Peter Stubb or Stump, who was tried in Cologne in 1589. An historian has written of his trial: "It is interesting to note the ease with which

LE LOUP-GAROU.

Jean-Claude vivait en paix : mais il avait des poules et croyait aux sorciers.	Il va donc un beau jour trouver le père Grenouille, qui passait pour un de ces derniers, et lui conte :	Qu'il a vu de ses propres yeux, un animal étrange emportant deux de ses poules.
C'est un *loup-garou*, lui répond le père Grenouille : moyennant un écu je vous en débarrasserai.	Jean-Claude, rentré chez lui, dort sur ses deux oreilles.	Dès son lever, il va visiter son poulailler : il lui manque encore deux poules !
Il confie son aventure à un de ses voisins.	Qui lui conseille de mettre un piége à loup devant son poulailler : ce qu'ils font aussitôt.	Puis ils entrent tous deux chez Jean-Claude.
Et se mettent à jouer aux cartes pour passer le temps.	Ils entendent bientôt des cris vers le poulailler.	Et trouvent dans le piége à loup, le père Grenouille en Loup-Garou.

Propriété de l'Éditeur. (Déposé.)

Fabrique de PELLERIN, Imprimeur-Libraire, à EPINAL

otherwise intelligent persons rationalized the impossible and made negative evidence into positive proof." This is another poignant case of a man destroyed by his own confessions—forced from him under torture—and who was prejudged before his trial began. Stubb claimed he had a magic belt that transformed him into "a greedy devouring wolf, strong and mighty, with eyes great and large, which in the night sparkled like brands of fire, a mouth great and wide, with most sharp and cruel teeth, a huge body, and mighty paws."

The accusers searched the valley where Stubb said he had left this belt, but found nothing. However, this did not prevent the magistrates from believing Stubb's confession. On the contrary, they declared "it may be supposed that the belt has gone to the devil from whence it came." Their revenge was terrible. Stubb was condemned to have "his body laid on a wheel, and with red hot burning pincers in ten several places to have the flesh pulled from the bones; after that, his legs and arms to be broken with a wooden axe or hatchet; afterward to have his head struck off from his body; then to have his carcase burned to ashes."

In surprising contrast to these horrifying real-life stories there are reports of protective werewolves, which sound about as unlikely as "benign vampires." In Portugal there was said to be a type of werewolf that never attacked anyone and fled if approached, whimpering pitifully—a cowardly werewolf if ever there was one. Sometimes a person who had become a werewolf by accident would welcome the wound that transformed him back into permanent human shape again. A case recorded in Britain in 1214 tells of a carpenter who fought off a wolf, severing its paw. The animal instantly turned into a man who, though crippled, expressed his gratitude.

France is the favorite locale for protective werewolves as well as savage ones. One French tale concerns an abbot who drank too much at a country fair and was so overcome with the wine and sun on his journey home that he fell off his horse. He hit his head on a stone and bled so profusely that the scent attracted a pack of wildcats that lived in the forest. As the wildcats moved in, a werewolf bounded to the abbot's rescue—and even escorted the tipsy, bleeding monk back to his monastery. There the wolf was welcomed and its wounds were treated. At dawn, however, it resumed human shape—that of a stern Church dignitary who reprimanded the abbot most severely for his conduct, and stripped him of his privileges. A moralistic, if protective, werewolf.

Left: a French cartoon strip of 1860 by Epinal with a humorous twist on the usually grim werewolf theme. In the top panel, the peasant Jean-Claude confides to Father Grenouille, reputedly a magician, that he has seen a strange animal carrying off his chickens. In the second strip, Father Grenouille takes some money to get rid of what he said was a werewolf, and Jean-Claude sleeps in contentment that all will be well. But he finds two more chickens gone. In the next panel, he tells all to a neighbor who helps him set a wolf trap. In the bottom strip the two friends await the arrival of the wolf. They hear cries from the chicken house—and there, securely caught in the trap they set, is Father Grenouille dressed up in a wolf's suit.

The Lady is a Wolf

By the admission of William Seabrook who tells the story, it was perfectly true that Nastatia Filipovna was not ordinary. A Russian aristocrat who had fled the revolution, she seemed slightly larger than life. She was tall and powerful with challenging tawny eyes. She had a fearful temper, but also charm when she chose to use it. She didn't like reality—it bored her—but although she fell into a self-induced trance easily, she didn't like that world either.

Then she decided to try the *I Ching*, the ancient Chinese method of opening the mind to future possibilities. For Nastatia Filipovna it seemed to open a door. "But it's opening into the outdoors!" she murmured. "Everything is white—everywhere snow. I am lying in the snow... I am lying naked in my fur coat... and I am warm."

She moved restlessly and muttered: "I'm running lightly like the wind... how good the snow smells!" She began to make unhuman sounds, like a wolf baying. Alarmed, her friends tried to rouse her. Her face changed. Her tawny eyes wide open, the wolf-woman sprang straight for a friend's throat. She fell short. Her companions snared her in blankets and held ammonia under her nose. She came out of it.

But Nastatia Filipovna remembered. And she liked it.

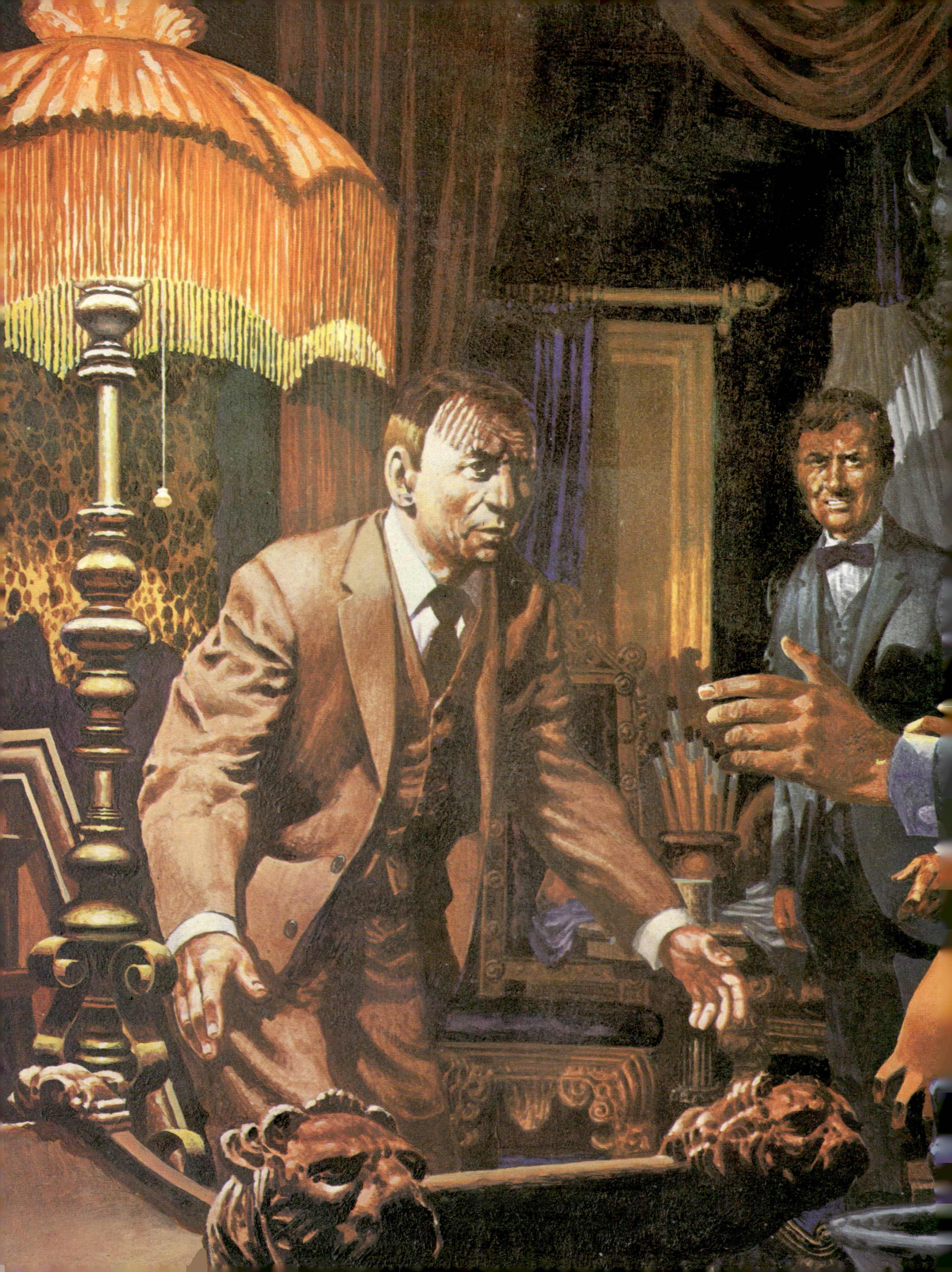

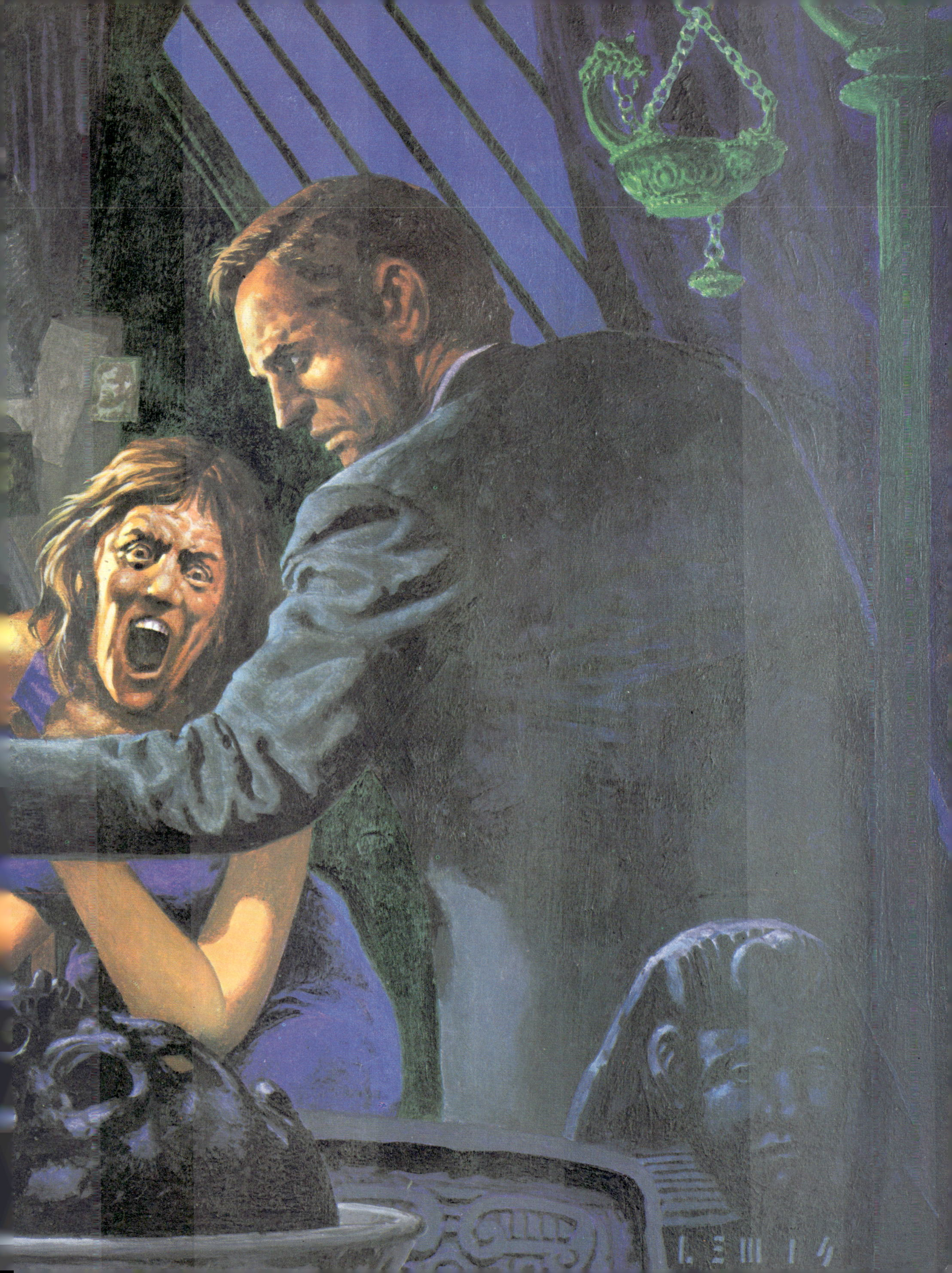
LEWIS

Below: a 16th-century engraving of the ancient Greek Lycaeon, a probable forerunner of the werewolf. According to myth, Lycaeon sought to please the god Zeus by sacrificing a child and offering its flesh to that mighty power. As a punishment for this action, Zeus changed Lycaeon into a wolf.

Another story concerns the captain of a schooner employed in attacks on the Huguenots—French Protestants—fighting against Catholic persecution in the 16th and 17th centuries. After one such raid the captain's ship foundered in the wide waters of the Rhone estuary, and he would have drowned if someone had not come to his rescue and dragged him ashore. Reaching out his hand in thanks, the captain was dismayed to find himself grasping a huge hairy paw. Convinced that this must be the devil, who had saved him as a reward for his atrocities against the Huguenots, the captain fell on his knees and asked for the forgiveness of God. The wolf waited grimly, then lifted the sailor up and took him to a house on the outskirts of a village. Once inside, the captain saw the werewolf's face clearly in the light of a lantern, and fell headlong to the floor in an effort to escape. Again, the wolf lifted him gently, and then gave him food before leaving him in a locked room. The captain ran to the window, but it was barred. Then he noticed the horribly mutilated body of a woman lying in a corner of the room, and he feared that the same fate was intended for him. But the next morning the werewolf returned in human shape. He was a Huguenot minister, and he revealed that the woman was his wife, cruelly murdered by the captain's crew when they ransacked the village the day before. He himself had been forced aboard the captain's ship in order to be tortured and drowned.

"Well," said the minister, "I am a werewolf; I was bewitched some years ago by the woman Grenier [again that name] who lives in the forest at the back of our village. As soon as it was dark I metamorphosed; then the ship ran ashore, and everyone leaped overboard. I saw you drowning. I saved you . . . you who had been instrumental in murdering my wife and ruining my home! Why? I do not know! Had I preferred for you a less pleasant death than drowning, I could have taken you ashore and killed you. Yet, I did not, because it is not in my nature to destroy anything." Needless to say, the captain was so moved by this act of mercy that he became a devoted friend of the Huguenots until the day of his death.

It is a romantic tale, and this may be one reason for the appeal of the werewolf legend. There may even be a fragment of fact behind the tales of protective werewolves. Modern studies indicate that the wolf is not necessarily the voracious monster it is traditionally made out to be. Rescues of a human being by an animal are not unknown, and there may have been isolated cases in the past in which a wolf was responsible for saving a man's life. Nevertheless, it is the image of the wolf as a cruel and ferocious beast that prevails. Kindly werewolves are rare, and the werewolves of legend are almost always bent on the vicious killing and devouring of their victims.

The concept of a man or woman turning into a wolf is no more outrageous than that of a corpse emerging from the coffin at night to drink human blood. Yet it is somehow even harder to believe in werewolves than in vampires. This may be partly because the werewolf fits so neatly into folklore. The monstrous wolfman made the ideal character for a good horror tale to tell around the fire in remote regions, where there was little to talk about apart from the wild animals of the forest and perhaps the even wilder characters in the village. Werewolves were alleged to be especially partial to small boys and girls, so they would serve as a natural threat for the peasants to their children. "Don't go out in the woods tonight or the werewolf will gobble you up," they might say, just as London Cockneys warned their children not to roam the streets of the East End after the murders of 1888 "or Jack the Ripper will get you."

But the belief in werewolves has deeper roots. The metamorphosis of men into animals is part of primeval legend, a power attributed to the gods and heroes of mythology. The Scandinavian god Odin turned into an eagle; Jupiter, the Roman god, became a bull; Actaeon was changed into a stag by the Greek goddess Artemis. There are counterparts of the werewolf in almost all parts of the world, varying according to climate: were-tigers in India; were-leopards, were-hyenas, and even were-crocodiles in Africa; and were-bears in Russia, which also had its fair share of werewolves. In his book on werewolves, Elliott O'Donnell quotes eyewitness accounts of an Indian youth who changed into a tiger, and of two Javanese children who turned into jaguars. Significantly, were-animals are always creatures that inspire fear; you never hear of a were-tortoise.

The *berserkers*—ancient Norse warriors who fought with murderous frenzy—exploited the fearsome reputation of wild animals by wearing bearskins in battle. These gangs of Nordic fighters would work themselves into a state of diabolical madness as they hurled themselves into the attack, howling like animals and foaming at the mouth. Our word

Above: an illustration from a book about Marco Polo's adventures in the Far East, showing the people of the Andaman Islands in the Indian Ocean as having dog heads. The 13th-century Venetian traveler was only repeating tales he had heard in India, but he found his European audience ready to believe such stories as fact. Below: a were-jaguar is South America's equivalent of werewolf.

Above: marauding raids of fur-clad barbarians, like this one painted by a 19th-century artist, helped bring on the period known as the Dark Ages. It is thought that one group of plunderers from Scandinavia, who dressed in full bearskins, may have given rise to werewolf stories. For what poor villager, fleeing in fear before a wild horde of bestial attackers, could tell the difference between men wearing fur skins and wolves?

berserk, meaning violently enraged, comes from the *bear sark*—bearskin—the berserkers wore. Just as the word lives on, so the memory of these barbaric warriors may have contributed to the werewolf legend. To the peaceful villagers whose community was attacked one day by fur-clad berserkers and another by a pack of howling wolves, there can have seemed little enough difference between the two. Both might have seemed like men dressed as animals—or like men completely transformed into raging beasts.

Others trace the werewolf legend back further still to the time when prehistoric man began to don animal disguise for the hunt, and to invoke the spirit of a powerful animal in the hope of inheriting that animal's strength. In his book *Man Into Wolf* Dr. Robert Eisler, a British writer with a profound knowledge of ancient history and legend, develops a fascinating theory of the origins of the werewolf idea. Eisler's explanation starts with the idea that man was once a peaceful vegetarian, but was driven to seek new food by changing conditions—such as the arrival of an Ice Age. He was forced to eat meat, to cover himself with animal skins, to hunt, and to imitate the behavior of ferocious wild animals in his struggle to survive. Gradually man himself acquired the same blood lust, probably even turning to cannibalism in times of extreme food shortage. This traumatic upheaval left its scars that lingered on in man's unconscious, says Eisler, giving rise among other things to the werewolf legend.

There are also more straightforward explanations. Furs were

worn in winter as a protection against cold, and a fur-clad figure might easily be mistaken for an animal. Werewolves might have been children who had been lost or abandoned in the forest, raised by a pack of wolves, and therefore practicing all the skills of the wild animal. But Eisler's theory is still the most attractive. Writing about the concept of *metempsychosis*— the passing of a soul from one body to another after death— Baring Gould refers to "the yearnings and gropings of the soul after the source whence its own consciousness was derived, counting its dreams and hallucinations as gleams of memory, recording acts which had taken place in a former state of existence."

To some extent this echo exists in us all. The counterpart of the female vamp is the male wolf—a man who pushes his attentions on women—and he is still with us today, complete with wolf whistle. The werewolf is a monster of the unconscious, "the beast within" that may still emerge in our dream life. American psychoanalyst Dr. Nandor Fodor has recorded a number of dreams reported by patients in which the werewolf theme figures prominently, complete with all the brutal details of transformation, savage attack, and killing.

At its fiercest extreme, however, this primeval instinct is seen most clearly in the secret societies of the Leopard Men in West Africa, who continue to disguise themselves as leopards up to the present day. Although it is most unlikely that man can change into wolf, it is certain that man frequently imitates the wildest of animals, even to assuming their skins.

Above: a man with a medical condition in which quantities of hair grow on the body. The existence of an unfortunate like this before the disorder was understood could go far to explain werewolf tales. Below: movie make-up to produce the same effect. Michael Landon in *I Was a Teenage Werewolf*.

4

The Walking Dead

"The eyes were the worst. It was not my imagination. They were in truth like the eyes of a dead man, not blind, but staring, unfocused, unseeing. The whole face, for that matter, was bad enough. It was vacant, as if there was nothing behind it. It seemed not only expressionless, but incapable of expression. I had seen so much previously in Haiti that was outside ordinary normal experience that for the flash of a second I had a sickening, almost panicky lapse in which I thought, or rather felt, 'Great God, maybe this stuff is really true...'"

This was how William Seabrook described his encounter with one of the most horrifying

The power and mystery of voodoo has fascinated many visitors to the lovely island of Haiti. Some of them have tried to understand the place the secret rituals have in the lives of ordinary people, and some of them have come close enough to sense the overwhelming impact of the gods and goddesses who claim their worshipers in a wild and ecstatic possession.

Above: Maman Célie, the proud old priestess and sorceress who presided over William Seabrook's initiation into voodoo ritual.

Right: a man representing a zombie, face whitened and clad in a shroud, being led by a rope during a street procession.

67

"A body without soul or mind, raised from the dead through sorcery"

creatures ever to step from the realms of the supernatural. For Seabrook was face-to-face with a zombie—a walking corpse. And in that moment he was prepared to believe all he had heard about zombies since he first arrived on the island of Haiti.

The zombie's fate is even worse than that of the vampire or the werewolf. The vampire returns to his loved ones. He may be recognized and lain to rest. The werewolf may be wounded and regain human form. But the zombie is a mindless automaton, doomed to live out a twilight existence of brutish toil. A zombie can move, eat, hear, even speak, but he has no memory of his past or knowledge of his present condition. He may pass by his own home or gaze into the eyes of his loved ones without a glimmer of recognition.

Neither ghost nor person, the zombie is said to be trapped, possibly forever, in that "misty zone that divides life from death." For while the vampire is the living dead, the zombie is merely the walking dead—a body without soul or mind raised from the grave and given a semblance of life through sorcery. He is the creature of the sorcerer, who uses him as a slave or hires him out—usually to work on the land.

Haiti is the home of the zombie, and the island abounds with stories of people who have died, been buried and reappeared as a walking corpse sometimes years later. One of the most famous cases, first recorded by American writer Zora Hurston in 1938, is still recounted in Haiti today. It concerns Marie, a lovely young society girl who died in 1909. Five years after her death, Marie was seen by some former school friends at the window of a house in Haiti's capital Port-au-Prince. The owner of the house refused to allow anyone to investigate, and Marie's father was reluctant to push the matter. Later, however, the house was searched, but by then the owner had disappeared and there was no trace of the girl. Meanwhile the news had spread all over Port-au-Prince, and to satisfy public opinion Marie's grave was opened. Inside was a skeleton too long for the coffin. Neatly folded alongside the skeleton were the clothes in which Marie had been buried.

People say that Marie had been dug up and used as a zombie until the sorcerer who had held her captive died, and his widow turned her over to a Catholic priest. After her schoolmates had seen her, it was said that her family smuggled her out of Haiti, dressed as a nun, and sent her to a convent in France. There she was later visited by her brother.

It is a sad aspect of most zombie stories, however, that no one generally comes to zombies' aid. Family and friends may never learn of the zombie's plight, or if they do, they are much too frightened to intervene. One mother told Zora Hurston about her son who had died and been buried. After the funeral friends stayed overnight with the grieving woman and her daughter. During the night the boy's sister awoke to the sound of chanting and of blows in the street outside. Then she clearly heard her brother's voice. Her screams awoke the rest of the house, and everyone looked out of the windows. Outside a grim procession was wending its way along the street, and in its midst was the boy they had buried that very day. As he stumbled sightlessly by, they all heard his anguished cry. "But such is the

Below: the American writer W. H. Seabrook. Impressed by voodoo magic, he concluded that it only existed in the mind and emotions.

terror inspired by these ghouls," wrote Zora Hurston, "that no one, not even the mother or sister, dared to go out and attempt a rescue." The procession shuffled out of sight. The boy's sister subsequently went insane.

Why are the Haitians so terrified of zombies? What might happen to relatives who try to free their dead loved one? Do zombies even exist? To answer all these questions we need to look at Haiti's past, and in particular at the beliefs and practices of Haiti's voodoo religion.

Voodoo is a unique combination of African, Roman Catholic, and even some American Indian beliefs plus traditional occult practices from Europe. Its deepest roots are in Africa, and voodoo began with the arrival in Haiti of large numbers of African slaves. This terrible traffic in human life, started when Haiti belonged to Spain in the 16th century, gathered momentum in the late 17th century when the island passed into French hands. Haiti was France's wealthiest colony—and depended on slave labor to stay that way. European traders on the west coast of Africa, already supplying millions of slaves to the plantations of the New World, were only too ready to meet France's growing demands. On the rare occasions when the French authorities needed to justify this trade, they did so on the grounds that slavery was the best means of converting the heathen African to Christianity. Many slaves did become members of the Catholic Church, but they adapted the doctrines of Christianity to their own temperaments and needs, and blended Christian rites with their own religious rituals—a

Above: a modern Haitian's painting of a voodoo ritual. In the actual performance, the drummers will gradually intensify their throbbing rhythm until the dancers reach a climactic state of ecstasy.

Above: a woman kneeling in the doorway of a church in Haiti. Haiti is a Catholic country, but for most people—some who know Haiti well claim it is for all—voodoo has compelling force in everyday life. It has been said, only half in joke, that Haiti is "90% Catholic, 100% Voodooist."

combination that was to persevere down the centuries. Even today many Haitians practice both voodoo and Catholicism, despite the disapproval of the Church.

Slaves were brought to Haiti from every part of Western Africa, but the majority came from areas dominated by the Yoruba-speaking peoples. These groups had a strong belief in possession by the gods. Torn from their homeland and their families, transported under appalling conditions to a strange land, the slaves nevertheless carried with them their traditions, their belief in magic and witchcraft, and the memory of the gods and ancestors they had worshiped in the forests of Africa. In Haiti these were to form the basis of voodoo. The new religion became a solace and a rallying force for a suffering and uprooted people, and it was swiftly banned by the French authorities. Driven underground, voodoo grew stronger and more sinister.

Slavery was big business. The thousands who died during or after their journey were continually replaced. By the 1750s, 30,000 slaves were being landed in Haiti every year. As one generation of slaves succeeded another, a terrible yearning set in, and nostalgia for the past fed the flames of rebellion. The first attempt for independence in Haiti took place in 1757. Macandal was the leader of this rebellion of fanatical fugitives, but he was captured by the French and burned to death. Several revolts followed, forcing the proclamation of Haitian independence in 1804. With the retreat of the French colonists who were the upholders of the Christian faith, the voodoo religion became firmly established.

Voodoo is a formalized religion with its own gods and forms of worship. But it also has its sinister side—the voodoo of black magic, sorcery, and superstition, of monsters, murder, and raising the dead. Blood is an essential part of some ceremonies, usually involving the sacrifice of such animals as pigs, hens, and cockerels.

Voodoo ceremonies take place in *tonnelles*. These may be either simple rough huts with mud floors or an elaborate building, but they always contain a covered area for ritual dance. It is during the dance that worshipers undergo the central experience of voodoo worship—possession by the gods. The dancing, chanting, and throbbing of drums are said to generate an atmosphere in which god and worshiper may become one, and at the height of the dance the worshipers enter a state of trance—a sort of collective dilirium—which ends in collapse.

A dancer may be possessed by any one of a huge number of gods and spirits, many of whom are still known by their African names. During possession the dancer is believed to *become* the god or spirit, adopting not only the god's personality but his or her physical appearance, gestures, and behavior. Thus a dancer possessed by the ancient spirit Papa Legba—guardian of the gateway to the other world and god of crossroads, whose symbol is a crutch—becomes apparently old and lame. Others, recognizing the spirit, run forward with sticks and crutches to help him. A sea god will row with invisible oars. A flirtatious female god will make a possessed man or woman assume mincing, flaunting gestures. A traditional goddess from Dahomey called

Right: a voodoo priestess, a *mambo*, possessed by the Ocean god Agwe, rocks on a chair to symbolize the motion of a boat. In the background is a wall painting of Aida Ouedo, Virgin Mary. Among the voodoo gods she is the wife of the serpent god Dambella. Another wall painting shows St. George who symbolizes the voodoo god Langueson. The curious blend of pagan African religion and folk Catholicism that forms voodoo leads to the juxtaposition of deities that strikes outsiders as incongruous.

Below: a grisly exhibit of two shrunken mummified figures known as Clahuchu and his Bride, photographed in Haiti. The exhibitor claimed they were discovered in 1740, the last of the lost tribe of Ju-Ju or Devil Men. He also said that the skin, horns, and hooves have been x-rayed and found to be human.

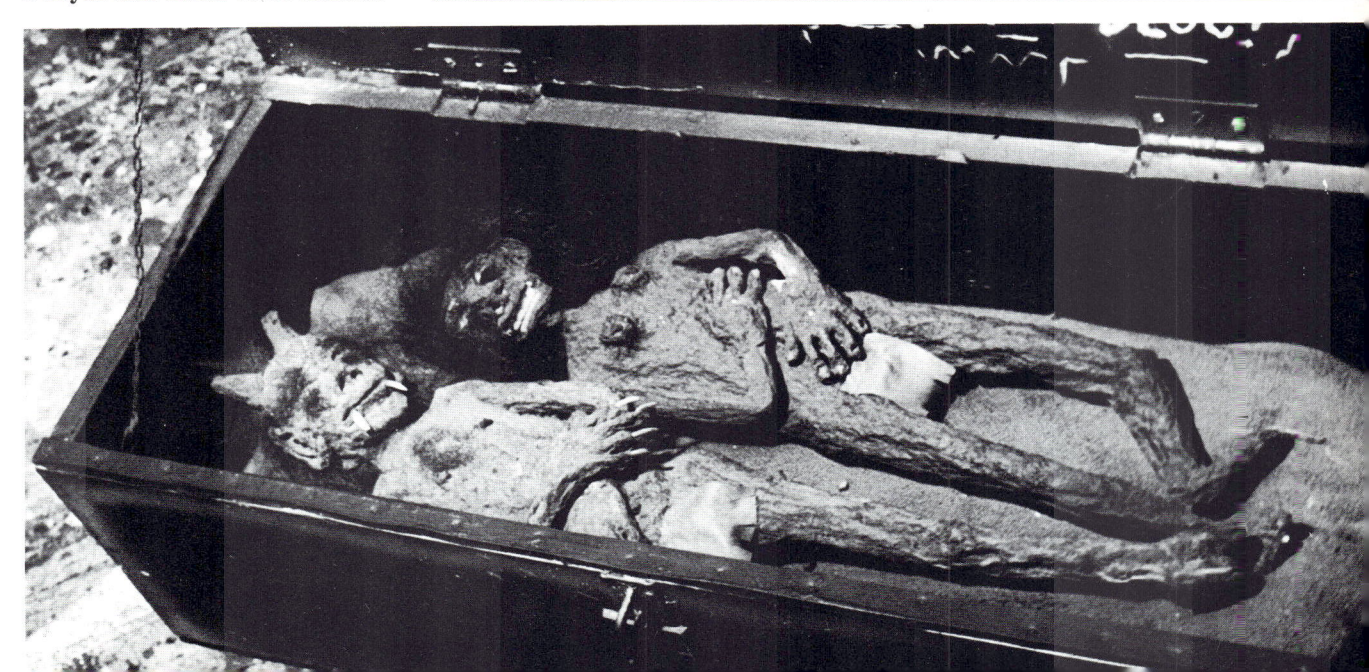

Agassa—a royal union of panther and woman—continues to exert her power in Haiti, causing possessed dancers to stiffen their fingers into claws. Evil spirits might throw a dancer into convulsions. Possession can last for several hours and be so absolute that the possessed walk on burning coals or hold their hands in boiling water without flinching, just as the members of some African tribes used to cut off their own fingers in a state of trance.

A British visitor to Haiti, Patrick Leigh Fermor, gives this interpretation of how possession—or the supposed incarnation of the gods in their worshipers—takes place. In his book *The Traveller's Tree*, written in 1950, he notes, "Every Haitian . . . from his earliest childhood, is spiritually geared for the event of incarnation; and he knows that the moment of miracle occurs in the dark *tonnelle* where the air is afloat with mysteries, and where the drums are already violently reacting on his nerves and brain . . . and so, when he has been brought by the drums, the dance, and the divine presence to a state of hysteria and physical collapse, a dormant self-hypnosis, finding no opposition, leaps to the surface of his brain and takes control."

Certainly it has been established by electrical recordings of the human brain that it is particularly sensitive to rhythmic stimulation. The *hungan*, or voodoo priest, may therefore increase suggestibility by altering the pitch and pace of the ceremonial rhythms. Hungans are also known to use magical powders and herbs as aids to possession, and it is said that even a substance as ordinary as pepper may be enough to bring on possession in the feverish atmosphere of a voodoo ceremony.

Whatever the trigger that induces possession, voodoo worshipers believe that the god cannot take over their body unless their soul is first displaced. The soul is believed to consist of two spirits: the *gros-bon-ange* (big good angel) and the *ti-bon-ange* (little good angel). The ti-bon-ange is what we might call a person's conscience. The gros-bon-ange is his essential soul—everything that makes him what he is.

Without the gros-bon-ange, the ti-bon-ange and the body lose contact. It is the gros-bon-ange that is displaced during possession, so that a person is no longer himself but the god who has taken over his body. Normally possession ends spontaneously, and the worshiper's gros-bon-ange is automatically restored to him. But sometimes the return to oneself will only happen with

Above: a young participant in a voodoo-like ceremony in Dahomey, Africa, identified as the home of most of the slaves brought to Haiti. It has been figured that 10,000 slaves were sold annually from one city alone. The word "voodoo" in Dahomey means a god, a spirit, or a sacred object.

Left: slave traders loading black Africans for shipment abroad as slaves. Some apologists for the slave trade have presented the theory that slave cargoes were made up of the less capable people. In fact, most slaves were prisoners of war—which might merely have meant that a more powerful king had conquered their ruler—or were considered guilty of a crime, whether a matter of common wrongdoing, sorcery or disrespect to the king.

Above: tribal chiefs in their ceremonial costumes, their faces whitened with ashes, await the beginning of the temple ceremonies. As in Haiti, spirit possession is characteristic of the traditional religion of southern Dahomey, the place of origin of most Haitian slaves. Left: a Dahoman man in trance balances on a rooftop, chanting and waving his ceremonial wand.

the hungan's help. Great care is also taken after a person's death to provide his disembodied soul with an alternative dwelling place. The soul, which first spends some time at the bottom of a river, is recalled by the hungan during a special ceremony, and placed in a sacred jar—a substitute for the physical body. It then becomes an ancestral spirit who will advise and protect his family.

This idea of the soul lies at the heart of many voodoo superstitions, including the belief in zombies. For a soul that has been displaced for the ceremony of possession may fall into evil hands. Having one's soulless body possessed by a god is devoutly to be wished, but it also opens up the possibility of a body being taken over by the evil machinations of the sorcerer.

The voodoo sorcerer, or *bokor*, is a terrifying character who communes with the dead and practices all the darkest arts on behalf of himself and his clients. Sometimes hungan and sorcerer are one and the same person, for it is said that a priest must be well acquainted with the techniques of sorcery if he is to combat them successfully. A hungan might fight a curse with white magic one day, and cast a spell with black magic the next. Hungans can invoke good spirits, or evil ones like the *Zandor* who turn people into snakes or vampire bats. Voodooists maintain, however, that the true hungan will have nothing to do with sorcery, and there certainly are bokor who are not voodoo priests. The bokor inspire criminal societies, worship the devil, and gather in cemeteries to practice the sinister cult of the dead.

Such sorcerers make powders out of cemetery earth and dead men's bones to "send the dead" against an enemy. Spreading the powder outside the victim's door or across some path he often takes is enough to paralyze or kill him, unless another hungan works some counter-magic in time. Another dreaded custom is the dressing of a corpse in the clothes of an intended victim and concealing it in some secret place to rot away while the living person goes mad searching for it. As students of Haitian belief have pointed out, if the victim knows what is happening and believes in the force of the magic, it can easily have fatal results.

Haitians tell spine-chilling tales of corpses being dragged from the grave to serve the cruel will of the sorcerer. In his book *The Magic Island*, written in 1936, William Seabrook records this story of a young wife, Camille, and her husband Matthieu Toussel. On their first wedding anniversary Toussel took his wife to a feast soon after midnight. He insisted that Camille wear her bridal dress and she, being afraid of him, obeyed. As the couple entered a candlelit room laid for a banquet, Camille saw that there were four other guests, all in evening clothes. But none of them turned to greet her. Toussel excused their behavior, promising that after dinner all four men would drink and dance with her. His voice was odd and strained. Camille could see the fingers of one guest clutched, motionless, around a tilted, spilling wineglass. Seizing a candle she looked into his face—and realized she was sharing a banquet with four propped-up corpses.

The panic-stricken girl ran for her life, but she never recovered from her nightmare experience. Friends who returned to the scene later the same day found everything laid out exactly as she had described—but no trace of the silent guests nor of Toussel, who is said to have fled the island.

Legend or fact? The machinations of a sorcerer husband or the imaginings of an unbalanced wife? The Haitians who told Seabrook this story believed it was true. They knew other stories like it. Haitian children are raised on tales of black magic, bogies, and sorcerers' spells. Their mothers warn them never to play with their shadows, and tell them that the bokor or the *tonton macoute*—traveling voodoo magician—will get them if they don't behave—a threat that could have proved only too true under Haiti's dictator Dr. Francois Duvalier, whose strong private army was dubbed the *tontons macoute*.

It is this atmosphere of fear and superstition that has bred

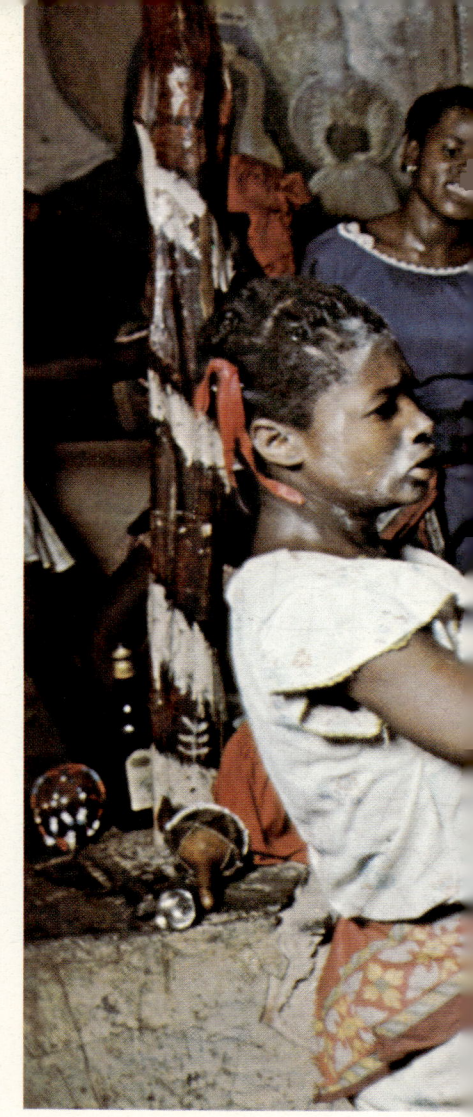

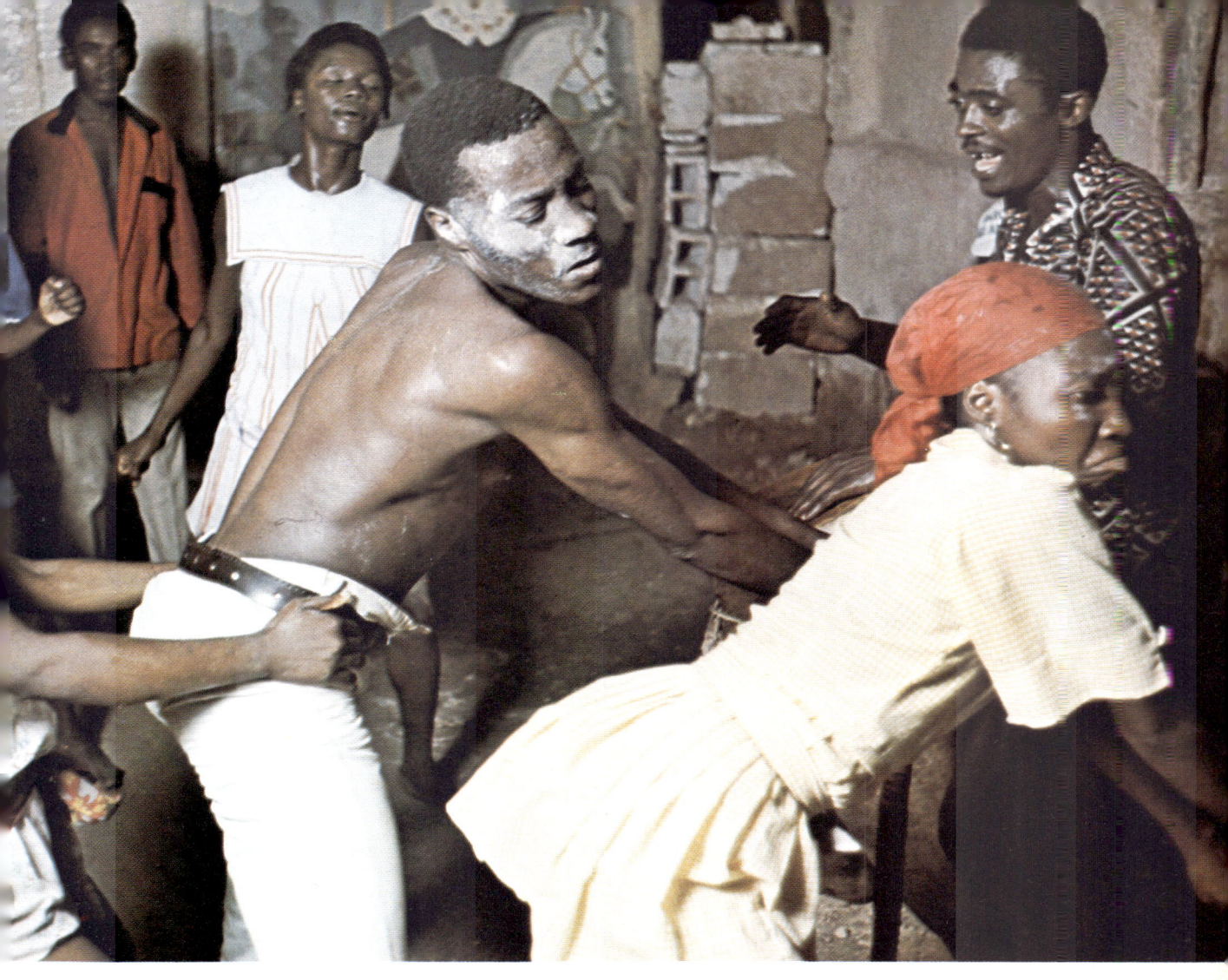

Above: voodoo dancers in Haiti, possessed by Papa Guédé and his associates, the gods of death. This is shown by the whitened faces.
Left: a girl possessed by Petro Simbi with the sword that is the mark of that particular god's control over one of his devotees.
Right: a woman in trance. The drawing in powdered cornmeal in the ground under her arms shows the marks of the serpent god Damballa.
Below: dancers moaning and writhing together, taken over by gods.

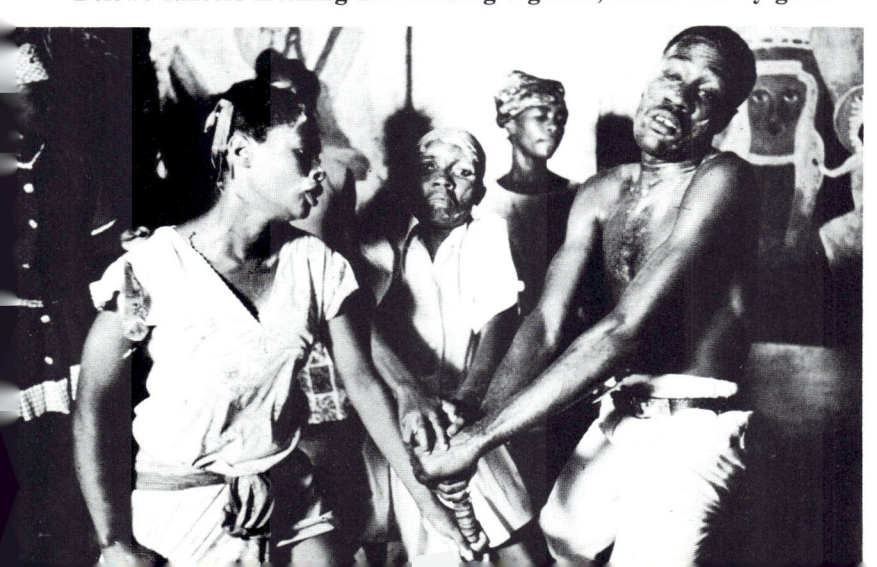

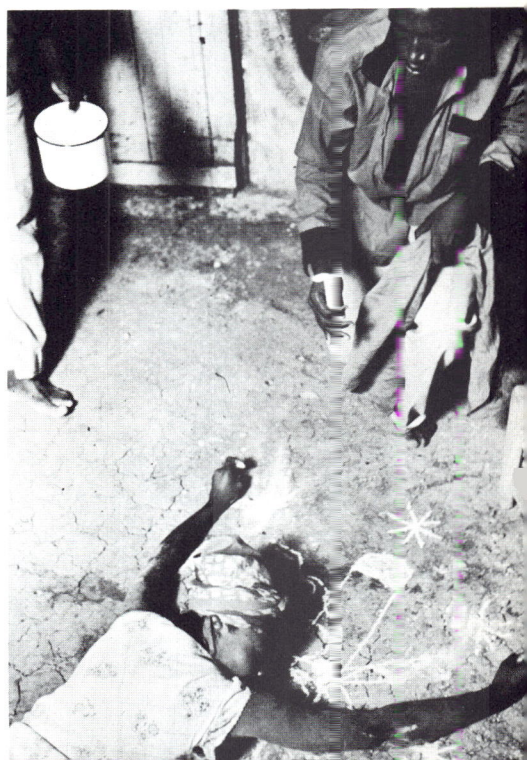

Right: a voodoo drum during a ceremony in Haiti. The drum is not just a musical instrument, but is also a sacred object. It is endowed with the mysterious power of a vaguely defined life-force. **Below:** an uninitiated woman in an advanced state of possession by the serpent god Damballa. In general, those inexperienced with possession by the gods react the most wildly, and the believers associated with the temple hover over them to make sure that they will not actually hurt themselves.

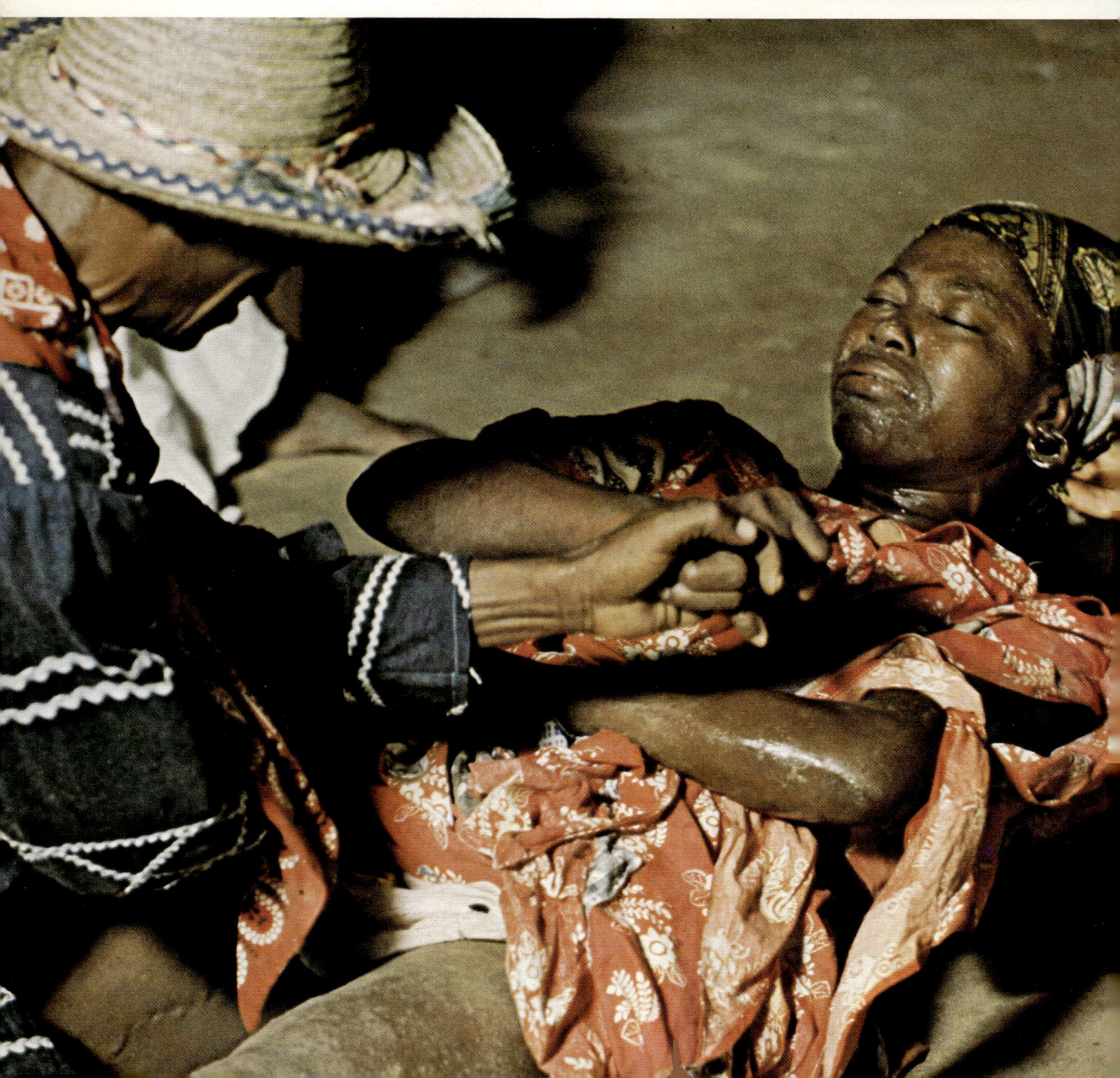

belief in the zombie. From cemetery cults and disinterred bodies it is but a short step to the idea of a corpse brought back to half-life by black magic—and some would say this was Toussel's intention for his dinner guests. Of all the supernatural horrors that sorcery may reserve for the unwary, becoming a zombie is the most dreaded fate of all, and a threat that even the most sophisticated may find hard to shrug off. Alfred Metraux, author of *Voodoo in Haiti*, made a study of zombies in the late 1950s. He says, "At Port-au-Prince there are few, even among the educated, who do not give some credence to these macabre stories."

One of the macabre stories that Metraux recorded concerns a young girl who rejected the advances of a powerful hungan. He stalked off, muttering threats about her future. Sure enough, the girl grew ill and died. For some reason, she was buried in a coffin too short for her, and her neck had to be bent to fit her in. While this was going on, a candle near the coffin was overturned, burning the girl's foot. Years later, people claimed to have seen the girl, apparently alive and clearly recognizable by her stoop and the burn on her foot. It was said that the jealous hungan had made her into a zombie, and kept her as a servant in his house until so much attention was drawn to the case that he was obliged to set her free.

This hungan was motivated by revenge—a common reason for the creation of zombies. Other times, zombies are made simply to provide cheap and uncomplaining labor when any suitable corpse will do. More rarely, they are the carefully chosen victims of a pact with the forces of evil, who demand payment in human souls for services rendered. For while Christians talk of selling one's soul to the devil, a voodoo follower sells the souls of others. In return for power, wealth, or some other favor, he must pledge the souls of those nearest and dearest to him. Each year the horrible sacrifice must be repeated until there are no more relatives or beloved friends left to give, and the person must then give himself. He too surrenders his soul. Then his body, like theirs, becomes a zombie.

Such pacts are made with the help of the bokor, and only he can create zombies. After dark he saddles a horse and rides, backward, to the victim's house. Placing his lips against a slit in the door he sucks out the person's soul, and traps it in a corked bottle. Shortly afterward the victim falls ill and dies. At midnight on the day of burial, the bokor goes with his assistants to the grave, opens it, and calls the victim's name. Because the bokor holds his soul, the dead person has to lift his head in answer. As he does so, the bokor passes the bottle containing the soul under the corpse's nose for a single brief instant. The dead person is then reanimated. Dragging him from the tomb, the bokor chains his wrists and beats him about the head to revive him further. Then he carefully closes the tomb, so no one will notice it has been disturbed.

Led by the bokor and his associates, the victim is first taken past his own house. This is said to insure that he will never again recognize his home and try to return there. He is then taken to the bokor's house or a voodoo temple, and given a secret drug. Some say this is an extract of poisonous plants

Voodoo Dancers

It begins like any other party—except that the guests are gathering in the mountains or plains of Haiti, and it is warm enough that they wear the least possible amount of clothing, finery though it is. At first people gather around the edge of the dance space to eat and drink. Then the drums begin.

The man leaps out into the center. He is the *mait' la danse*. He moves easily with the rhythm, prancing like a magnificent horse, then standing still and moving with slow suggestive undulations. The crowd watches, rapt. Then the mistress of the dance is beckoned into the center, and the two dance with a single rhythm, moving closer until they are almost touching—but not quite. They retreat and approach again. Gradually, as the drums pound relentlessly, the rattles add their own excitement, and the shrill singing begins. There are songs of doggerel that mock friends and comment bitingly on the relationship of men and women, sad songs, happy songs, silly songs. Other dancers move onto the floor. It becomes crowded, hot, and exciting. The steady four-four beat gets more hypnotic and insistent. The endless, effortless swaying of hips and buttocks seems to depersonalize the dancers, producing a cosmic perpetual motion.

like datura (jimson weed) or belladonna (deadly nightshade), which were sometimes used by the slaves of colonial days to kill their masters. Others maintain that the potion is made of drops that fall from a corpse's nose.

There are other methods of ensnaring a person's soul. A jar containing herbs and magical objects may be placed beneath a dying man's pillow to draw off the soul, or the soul of an insect or small animal may be substituted for the human soul. In neither case does the victim realize what is happening. It is even possible to take the soul from a person already dead. Whatever the method used, the soul plays the same part in the ritual at the tomb, and after the giving of the magic drug, all is complete. The victim has become a zombie—a hideous, mesmerized, walking corpse, ready to do the sorcerer's will.

Elaborate precautions are taken to prevent the sorcerer from raising the dead and creating a zombie. A family that can afford it may bury its dead beneath solid masonry. Others will make sure that the grave is dug in their own back yard or close to a busy road with plenty of passers-by. Since only a fresh or well-preserved corpse will serve the bokor's purpose, relatives may keep a continuous watch at the tomb until the body has decomposed. Sometimes the corpse is killed again, being shot through the head, injected with poison, or strangled. Occasionally it is buried with a dagger in its hand to defend itself. Often the body is placed face downward in the grave with its mouth full of earth, or its lips are sewn together so that it cannot speak to answer when the sorcerer calls its name.

Above: part of the private army of Haiti's former dictator Dr. Francis "Papa Doc" Duvalier. This elite bodyguard was called the Tontons Macoutes, the name for traveling voodoo sorcerers. They were greatly feared, in part for their brutality and in part for supposed supernatural power. Right: a Tonton Macoute guarding the Duvalier family tomb. Papa Doc's grave now has a permanent military guard against the believed threat that sorcerers may attempt to seize his remains.

Once people become zombies they can never escape from their deathly trance unless they taste salt (frequently a symbol of white magic). They then become aware of their fate and, knowing they are dead, will return to the grave forever.

In his book *The Invisibles*, British anthropologist Francis Huxley tells a story he heard from a Catholic priest of a zombie who wandered back to his own village in 1959. He was taken to the police station, but the police were too frightened to do anything and simply left him outside in the street. After several hours someone plucked up the courage to give the zombie a drink of salt water, and he then stammered his name. Later his aunt, who lived nearby, identified him. According to her, he had died and been buried four years before.

Below: the woman said to be Felicia Felix-Mentor, discovered wandering around naked 29 years after her death. The photograph was taken in a hospital yard by Zora Hurston, who published the story. Called a zombie, she had completely lost the faculty of speech, and huddled fearfully under a cloth whenever she was approached, seeming to expect abuse and violent treatment. She appeared to be incapable of forming any kind of coherent thought.

Above: a Haitian graveyard. The cross in the foreground is not Christian but voodoo, hung with the garment of the person who is buried beneath it so that the evil spirits will be attracted to the clothing and leave the body in peace. Most people can only cover their graves with small stones, but families who can afford it put a heavy stone slab on the grave to prevent a sorcerer from stealing away the newly buried body and making it a zombie.

A priest was called and, after he arrived, the zombie revealed the name of the sorcerer for whom he and a band of other zombies had been forced to labor. The police, thoroughly scared now, sent a message to the sorcerer offering him his zombie back. However, two days later the zombie was found, well and truly dead this time—presumably killed by the sorcerer because of his damaging revelations. The sorcerer was eventually arrested, but his wife and the other zombies were never traced.

There is a strong element of doubt in many zombie tales. Evidence is often missing or incomplete. Other stories are less easy to dismiss. Catholic priests and Protestant clergymen report having seen people die, conducted their burial service, shut the coffin lid, and watched the grave closed—only to see that person days or weeks later not dead but staring, inarticulate, and apparently insane.

Zora Hurston notes that such creatures were occasionally brought to a missionary by a bokor who had been converted—or by a sorcerer's widow who wished to be rid of them. She herself was one of the few visitors to Haiti to see, touch, and actually photograph a zombie. The zombie was Felicia Felix-Mentor, who had died of a sudden illness in 1907. In 1936 she was found wandering naked on the road near her brother's farm. Both her brother and her husband identified her as the woman they had buried 29 years before. She was in such a wretched condition that she was taken to the hospital, and it was there, a few weeks later, that Zora Hurston saw her. "The sight was dreadful," she wrote later. "That blank face with the dead eyes. The eyelids were white all around the eyes as if they had been burned with acid. There was nothing that you could say to her or get from her except by looking at her, and the sight of this wreckage was too much to endure for long."

So zombies or zombielike creatures do exist. But are they really walking corpses? Is it possible for a dead body to be given the semblance of life? Montague Summers, an authority on witchcraft and black magic, once wrote: "That necromancy can seemingly endow a dead body with life, speech, and action is not to be disputed, but the spell is invariably of short continuance and the operation, from the confession of sorcerers, is considered to be one of the most difficult and most dangerous in all witchcraft, a feat only to be accomplished by wizards who are foulest and deepest in infernal crime."

A spell of "short continuance" would hardly explain the reappearance after 29 years of Felicia Felix-Mentor. A far more likely explanation is that so-called zombies have never been dead at all. Some people have suggested that zombies are simply the doubles of persons who have died. If so, why do such doubles always have the characteristic zombie appearance and gait? Zombies are known for their expressionless and often downcast eyes, their blank faces, and shambling walk. They appear not to hear when spoken to, and their own speech, uttered in a nasal twang, is almost always incoherent. Often it consists only of grunts or guttural noises deep in the throat.

These are often the hallmarks of the mentally defective, and it seems probable that many alleged zombies are in fact morons concealed by their family and deliberately made out to be dead until they are seen again, perhaps many years later. Alfred Metraux was introduced to a zombie only to find a "wretched lunatic." On the next day this zombie was identified as a mentally deficient girl who had escaped from her home, where her parents normally kept her locked up.

Students of Haiti have pointed out that the harsh treatment meted out to zombies is no worse than the treatment of the mentally sick, who are commonly beaten to cow them into compliance. Once he had recovered from his initial shock at the sight of those "staring, unfocused, unseeing eyes," William Seabrook too concluded that the zombies he had seen were "nothing but poor ordinary demented human beings, idiots, forced to toil in the fields," rather than half-alive corpses.

Old Friends Meet

The exasperated man who stopped to fix a flat tire was a person of education and property. This did not prevent him from getting involved with a zombie, however. Here is how it happened. An old man standing near the disabled car said that a friend of the hard-pressed traveler would soon pass by to help. In the meantime, he offered the man some coffee at his house. The man accepted, and went with him. During their talk over coffee, the old man claimed to be a *bokor*, a voodoo sorcerer. His guest was politely skeptical. At this the sorcerer eyed him speculatively, and asked if he had known a certain Mr. Célestin who had died six months earlier. They had been dear friends, his guest replied. "Would you like to see him?" the bokor murmured. He cracked a whip six times and a door opened. Shambling, submissive, empty-eyed, Célestin entered—in life a man of the traveler's own class. Full of pity, the traveler instinctively moved to hand the zombie his cup. The sorcerer swiftly stopped him. Nothing is more dangerous, he explained, than to give a dead person something from hand to hand.

The zombie waited passively. The bokor explained that Célestin had been killed by another sorcerer's spell, and had been sold to him for $12.

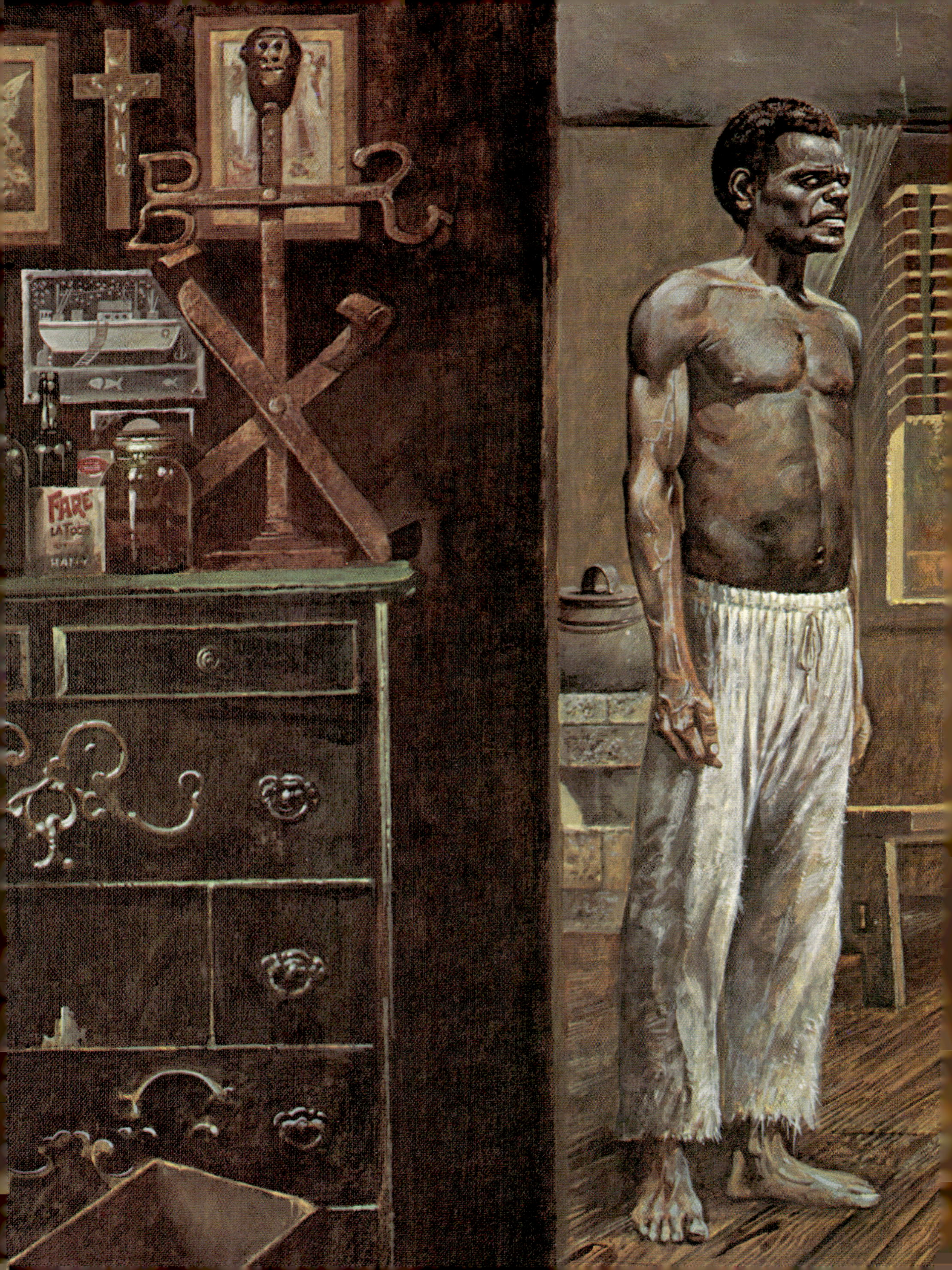
FARE

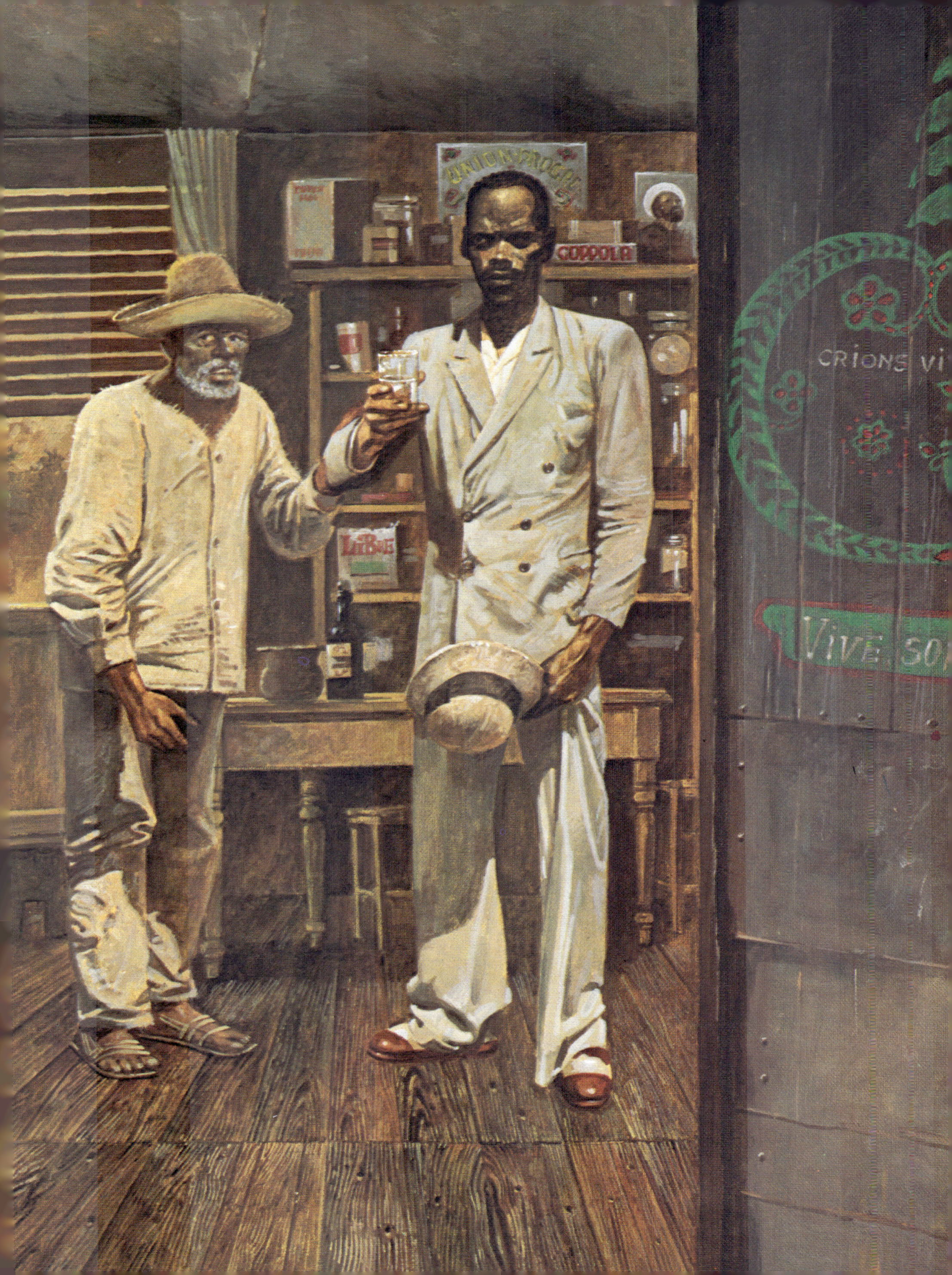
COPPOLA
CRIONS VI
VIVE SO

84

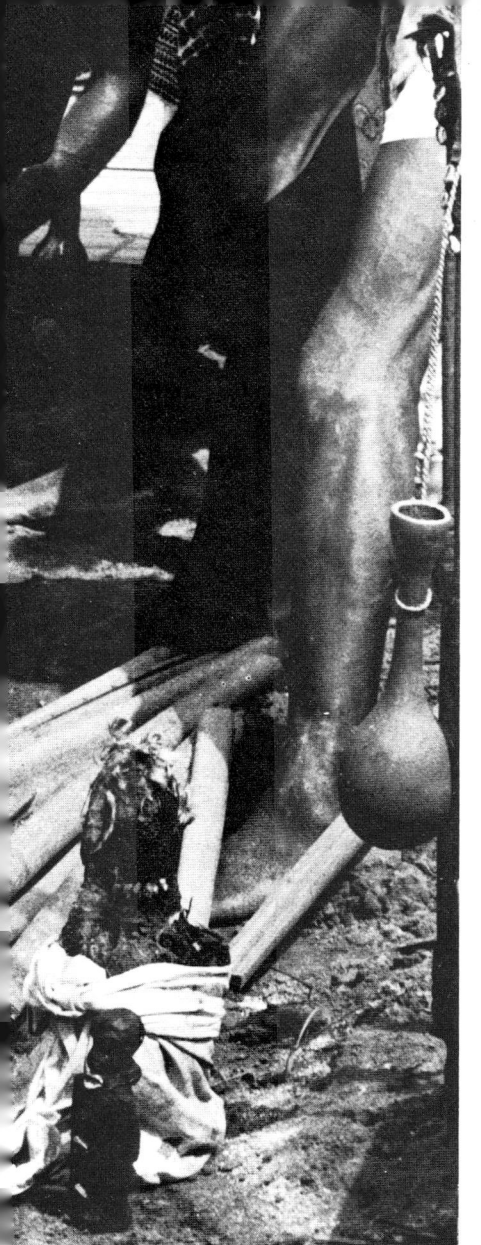

Above: an African religious rite in Dahomey in which a person is drugged into such a deep trance that his coma lasts for seven to nine days. During this time the person is wrapped in a sheet and buried. He is unearthed and recalled to life by the high priest.

Left: the zombie in Hollywood. In a 1943 movie called *I Walked with a Zombie*, Darby Jones played the tall walking corpse known as Carre Four. Here he is met by Francis Dee, who was the nurse to a planter's sleep-walking wife.

What, then, of the reliable witnesses who have testified to the burial of some so-called zombies? Were they lying? Not all zombies started out as morons. What about the person friends remember as a sane, intelligent individual, who suddenly reappears as a vacant, gibbering wreck of his former self? This has to be a different kind of case.

The answer comes from a surprising source—Article 246 of the old Haitian Criminal Code. "Also to be termed intention to kill," it states, "is the use of substances whereby a person is not killed but reduced to a state of lethargy, more or less prolonged, and this without regard to the manner in which the substances were used or what was their later result. If following the state of lethargy the person is buried, then the attempt will be termed murder."

From this it can be inferred that a zombie may really be a person buried and mourned by his family, and dragged from the grave by the bokor as the legend says. But he has been buried alive after being drugged into a deathlike trance from which he may never recover.

A prominent Haitian doctor interviewed by William Seabrook was convinced that at least some reported zombies were victims of this kind of treatment. Doctors with whom Zora Hurston discussed the case of Felicia Felix-Mentor agreed. "We discussed at length the theories of how zombies come to be," she writes. "It was concluded that it is not a case of awakening the dead, but a semblance of death induced by some drug—some secret probably brought from Africa and handed down from generation to generation . . . It is evident that it destroys that part of the brain which governs speech and will power. The victims can move and act but cannot formulate thought. The two doctors expressed their desire to gain this secret, but they realized the impossibility of doing so. These secret societies are secret. They will die before they will tell."

The idea, if not the making, of the zombie almost certainly originated in Africa, where legendary tales are still told of sorcerers who can raise the dead. The true zombie, however, is unique to Haiti. While cynics would say that so-called zombies must be lunatics or people temporarily in a state of trance, there are undoubtedly cases that can only be explained on a deeper and more sinister level. Today voodoo is often exploited as a tourist attraction, and spectacular displays of black magic may be mounted for the entertainment of foreigners and natives alike. Francis Huxley tells, for instance, of a magistrate who saw a hungan take a body from the grave and apparently reanimate it. Inside the grave the magistrate found a tube leading out to the air. The "corpse" was really the hungan's accomplice, and had been able to breathe in comfort while awaiting his resurrection.

Haitians know about hoaxes like this. Yet many of them still believe in zombies, and have a deep-rooted fear of joining their ranks. For while zombies may not be raised from the grave, they may well be people reduced by drugs to a state that is scarcely distinguishable from death. Who would say which fate is the worse? In either case, the zombie is truly one of the walking dead.

5

Who Believes in Fairies?

"An Epoch-making Event—Fairies Photographed." So ran the title of an article published in a leading British magazine in 1920. Alongside the article was the photograph of a young girl surrounded by a group of tiny, fairylike figures. Another photograph showed a second girl beckoning to a little gnomelike creature with wings. The girls were Frances Griffiths and Elsie Wright. They had photographed each other, and since neither had ever handled a camera before, clever trickery was unlikely. The writer of the article was Sir Arthur Conan Doyle, respected author of the famous Sherlock Holmes stories.

The fairy world is a place of small unpredictable creatures—the best are capricious and easy to offend and the worst are ugly and malignant toward mortals. Above: like witches, fairies can fly, but they use stems and twigs instead of broomsticks, or ride other little creatures as steeds. Right: Oberon, the King of the Fairies, painted in great splendor. Mother-of-pearl inlays on the oil paints give this picture a shimmering radiance. Although ordinary male fairies are most often reported to be wizened and hairy, the kings and knights are generally as beautiful as their fairy ladies, dressed in filmy and irridescent finery. Oberon was the consort of Queen Mab and the father of the changeling Robin Goodfellow, who in turn fostered mischievous sprites called Pucks.

87

"Sometimes hideous, often terrifying, and occasionally evil beings"

Below: 13-year-old Elsie Wright and a fairy friend in a picture taken by 10-year-old Frances Griffiths. Elsie had already snapped Frances with a group of fairies. That was in 1917 in the small English village of Cottingley. Three years later the two photographs were used with a magazine article and started a great wrangle over their genuineness. It has never been proven definitely that they were faked.

Within days the magazine with the picture and article on the Cottingley Fairies was sold out. News of the photographs spread around the world, and started a controversy that remains unresolved to this day. The girls seemed genuine—and so did the photographs. Even some skeptical investigators found themselves wondering whether there might be such a thing as fairies after all.

Do you believe in fairies? Most of us would probably answer emphatically "No." Of all supernatural phenomena the fairy seems about the most unlikely. The idea of fairies is so absurd that we even use the expression "fairy stories" to describe obvious lies. Yet the creator of Sherlock Holmes, that master of logic, felt sure enough to state publicly that he believed in fairies. And Conan Doyle was not alone. Air Chief Marshal Lord Dowding, a leader of the British Royal Air Force during World War II and a powerful personality if ever there was one, believed implicitly in fairies. This rational and rather stern man would occasionally show visitors a book of fairy photographs, and talk with as much conviction about fairies as about military tactics. Other responsible and apparently well-balanced people, including clergymen, professors, and doctors, have argued that such creatures exist—and some testify to having seen them. What they saw, however, were rarely dainty little creatures with gossamer wings, like those Frances Griffiths and Elsie Wright had photographed. They were sometimes hideous, often terrifying, and occasionally evil beings.

Belief in fairies was once universal, and the fairy was considered a formidable force to be reckoned with. Evans Wentz, author of *The Fairy Faith in Celtic Countries* and an authority on the subject, noted that, "There seems never to have been an uncivilized tribe, or a race or nation of civilized men who have not had some form of belief in an unseen world, peopled by unseen beings." Wentz maintains that, "fairies actually exist as invisible beings or intelligences." Examining the fairy world as "a fact of chemistry," Wentz came to the conclusion that Fairyland is a real place, existing "in an invisible world within which the visible world is immersed like an island in an unexplored ocean, and that it is peopled by more species of living beings than this world, because incomparably more vast and varied in its possibilities."

The inhabitants of Fairyland are certainly "vast and varied." Fairies come in all shapes and sizes. Although they are often tiny, they may be eight or more feet tall, and can sometimes change their shape at will. Fairies often adopt semihuman form, and love to meddle in human affairs. They may use their magical powers to capture or paralyze mortals, to steal crops or slay cattle with darts, to trip people up, or to bring bad luck. The appearance of some fairies may herald a human death. Other fairies are generous and helpful, bringing gifts or cleaning people's houses—but even they must be treated with care. There is no such thing as a wholly good fairy. Even the gentlest may become spiteful if provoked. Fairies are at best capricious, and at worst downright malevolent. Apart from the tiny fairy of romantic legend, their ranks include leprechauns, pixies, hobs, brownies, banshees, imps, goblins, bogeys, nature spirits, and many others. Their powers vary, but most are ill-disposed

Left: tiny elves feasting in the fuchsia, a watercolor by Richard Doyle, 19th-century artist.
Elves are prominent in northern European mythology, originally divided into light elves and dark elves. These were apparently the source of the fairy folk of Germanic folklore, who, like elves, were mischievous and malicious. **Below: one of the gnomes in England's special Gnome Garden. It is in the town of Polperro.** "Gnome" was a name invented by the medieval scholar-magician Paracelsus to describe the elementals of the earth. They were dwarfish spirits which live underground, guarding buried treasure. According to Paracelsus, they move through the earth as easily as we move through air.

toward people and are more likely to harm than help.

Stories of fairies are told the world over, but fairy belief is strongest in the British Isles. Even there, however, fairies vary from region to region. The most beautiful fairies come from Ireland—graceful, stately, little creatures known as the Dana o'Shee. They dwell in the realm of eternal beauty and remain forever young. The Dana o'Shee live like the knights and ladies of the Age of Chivalry with their own king, queen, and royal court. They wear rich jeweled dress and love sweet music, dancing, and hunting. Their favorite pastime is to ride out in procession, with their king and queen at their head, and this is when they are most likely to be seen by mortals.

Even the loveliest fairies are treacherous, however, and some

Above: fairies at a christening bestowing magical gifts on a chosen, usually royal, infant. The story probably derives from the Greek myth of the Fates who came to the cradle of Meleager. Below: Welsh fairies—in their darker aspect—trying to steal a baby from the arms of his mother, Jennet Francis. She was said to have hung on and kept her son, who became a famous preacher.

say they come from the realms of the dead. A person who is lured by their beauty or entranced by their music may be doomed. One story from Ireland tells of a man whose wife was held captive by the fairies. To rescue her he had to watch for the faries to ride past with her on Halloween, and throw a jug of fresh milk over her. But unbeknown to him the milk contained a few drops of water, and this broke the power of the spell. The wife fell from her horse, the fairies gathered around her—and the man never saw his wife again. Next morning the road was covered with the dead woman's blood. The fairies had taken their revenge.

The Irish also have a whole series of less sinister, if sometimes grotesque, "little folk." These are the mischievous commoners of Fairyland who love to play tricks on people, but may also be useful and industrious. Most famous of all is the leprechaun, who makes fairy shoes and looks after the huge pile of fairy gold that mortals long to discover. Some little folk lend humans a hand with domestic chores; others ask for human help in repairing their tiny furniture or agricultural tools, and offer gifts of good luck in return.

The pixies of Cornwall in Southwest England are also gift-givers, but they reserve their rewards for efficient homemakers, leaving silver coins for the keeper of a neat and tidy kitchen. Merry little people with red hair and snub noses, pixies are also full of pranks such as blowing out candles, kissing young girls, and rapping on walls. They delight in leading mortals astray, and Cornwall is full of tales about such a danger. People out walking at twilight may be suddenly overcome by a strange dizziness, and hear peels of discordant laughter all around them. Unless they turn their coats or their pockets inside out—a sure preventive against pixy magic—they are led a fine dance through hedges and ditches for hours on end. This is known as being "pixy-led." However, it is significant that pixies are also renowned for flying long distances to seek out well-stocked wine cellars, and being pixy-led, or pixilated, is still a common term for a merry form of drunkenness.

Brothers to the pixies are the brownies and hobs, who are forever helping out in the home or around the farm. They are known as tutelary or guardian faries, because they tend to remain attached to a particular family or place. Only if mistreated will they move elsewhere. Like most fairies, however, brownies react badly to any interference from the Church. A Scottish story tells of one brownie's devotion to a young woman. He helped her in love, organized her wedding, and brought the midwife when the girl was expecting her first child. Although the midwife was "scared of the brownies," he carried her safely on his back across the raging waters of a haunted pool. Hearing all this, the local minister insisted that such a good and faithful servant ought to be baptized. The minister hid in the stable where the brownie was about to begin work, then threw some holy water over him and started to say the words of baptism. Thereupon the brownie gave a scream of terror, disappeared, and was never seen again.

This story indicates the vague aura of evil and fear that hangs around even the friendliest fairies. A mishandled brownie may quickly become menacing. He is never so menacing, however, as another tutelary fairy of Ireland and Scotland, the banshee. A banshee's terrible wail is a warning of imminent death. "Banshee" comes from an Irish word meaning "fairy women," but a banshee is more like a female specter who haunts the members of a family or clan, weeping when one of them is about to die. In Scotland, she may be seen at a riverside washing the bloodstained clothes of the one who is to die. If a human can seize her, she must give the name of the condemned man or woman. The banshee is said to have one nostril, a large prominent front tooth, webbed feet, and eyes that are red from constant weeping. The wailing of several banshees together is believed to prophesy the death of a holy person.

The ugliest and most dangerous of all fairies are the goblins, imps, and bogey beasts. While some of these creatures are mere mischief-makers, most are truly evil. The imp seems to come straight from hell. He has been portrayed in 16th- and 17th-century paintings as a little devil with a round cap, pointed shoes, bushy tail, and naked feet in place of hands. In her book *The Personnel of Fairyland,* Katherine M. Briggs describes a particularly nasty specimen of imp known as the *Nuckelavee,* a spirit in flesh, who was found in the Scottish Lowlands. He lived in the sea. When he came on land he would ride a horse as terrible as himself, so that many thought horse and rider were one. His head was like a man's but ten times larger, his mouth was like a pig's, and he had no hair on his body, for the very good reason that he had no skin. The Nuckelavee's breath was

In one Irish fairy story Molly is stolen away by the fairies to be a baby nurse. Her unhappy husband John hears nothing of her for six weeks. Then a neighbor tells him a tale about her adventure as midwife to the fairy queen, when she saw Molly and found out how to save her: John must grab her and keep her in his clasp when the fairy band passes. Guided by the neighbor, John succeeds in saving his wife.

The Changeling Wife

We usually imagine fairies as tiny winsome creatures in the role of playmates for children —at least it is charming to think so. But Michael Cleary thought different. In 1894 in Ireland he roasted his wife to death because he believed she was a changeling substituted by the fairy folk. His wife's family helped in the torture because they also believed she had been cavorting with the fairies.

The wretched woman was held in the fire while she was challenged to prove her identity. "I am Bridget Boland, daughter of Patrick Boland in the name of God!" she shrieked; but her husband would not believe her. He continued his cruel treatment over a period of days, until his wife lay dead on the hearth. Her legs and abdomen, the lower part of her back, and her left hand were almost burned away.

When neighbors realized that no one had seen Bridget Cleary for several days, the rumors of strange happenings at the Cleary house grew stronger and reached the local law authorities. They arrested eight people, among them the husband of the dead woman, her father, an aunt, and three cousins. Her body was discovered in a shallow grave close to the house. Cleary apparently believed to the end that he had killed a witch, saying: "Did you not know that it was not my wife . . . she was two inches taller than my wife."

Michael Cleary was sentenced to 20 years' hard labor, and the others got various prison sentences. The dreadful affair was almost forgotten over the years. But Irish children, dancing in a ring in their street games, still sing:

"Are you a witch, are you a fairy,
Or are you the wife of Michael Cleary?"

said to destroy plants and sicken animals, so he was blamed for any crops that failed or animals that fell over the cliffs.

One old man who claimed to have encountered the Nuckelavee gave a horrifying account of a huge "man" with no legs, arms that reached to the ground, and a head that rolled so violently it threatened to tumble off. Worse of all was the creature's raw open flesh where its skin should have been, and its twisting yellow veins clotted with black blood.

Equally terrifying are the redcaps, a type of bogey beast from the Scottish border. They live wherever violence has been committed, murdering travelers and dying their red caps in their victim's blood. The Highland Baobhan Sith or glaistigs are fairy vampires, assuming the form of beautiful women but sucking the blood of men who dance with them. Water kelpies, in the shape of horses, take unwary riders into the deep water of a lake and devour them.

In contrast to the often malicious kinds of fairies are the nature spirits that inhabit streams and lakes, woods and mountains. Their task is to care for all growing things. Yet even these spirits can be awesome, especially the higher nature spirits that deal in basic forces and broad outlines such as storms, winds, and vast landscapes. Geoffrey Hodson, a clairvoyant who made careful notes of the many fairies he claimed to have observed, described a higher nature spirit—the guardian of a hillside—in his book *Fairies at Work and at Play*. "My first impression was of a huge, brilliant crimson, batlike thing, which fixed a pair of burning eyes upon me," he wrote. "The form was not concentrated into the true human shape, but was somehow spread out like a bat with a human face and eyes, and with wings outstretched over the mountainside . . . When first seen its aura must have covered several hundred feet of space, but in a later appearance, in which it again showed itself, the actual form was probably 10 to 12 feet high."

Fairies may thus vary in appearance all the way from angel creatures clad in white to shadowy, monstrous, and terrible shapes. Most fairies wear green, from the shimmering draperies of the most beautiful to the plain little suits of leprechauns and pixies. But some fairies wear many-colored clothes, and pixies occasionally go naked. Female fairies especially may be delicate and dainty, tiny enough to curl up inside a flower, but their menfolk are sometimes stunted and hideous. Brownies and hobs tend to be ugly unkempt creatures with huge nostrils but no noses, while the bogey beasts often change form at will, choosing the most unpleasant shape available.

Fairies have some characteristics in common, however, as stories about them show. They are particularly interested in fertility. They tend to smile benignly on lovers. They are often described as wanton and promiscuous in their own behavior. Nevertheless, relatively few fairy babies are born, and those that are tend to be weak and ailing. This gives rise to one of the nastiest habits of the fairies: stealing human babies from their cribs and leaving a changeling—an ugly, strange, or stupid child —in their place. The human parents who care for a changeling are rarely rewarded by the fairies, and custom says they should beat and ill-treat the child. Extreme cruelty to the changeling is

Above: although the fairies of folk tales come in a bewildering variety of sizes and can often change their shape at will, most people now have a mental picture of tiny delicate creatures. In this watercolor by Richard Doyle the dainty little fairy folk are shown teasing a butterfly, which is about their own size.

Below: another miniature fairy being carried off by a bee in an 1895 fairy story illustration.

Right: *Thumbelina*, the classic fairy story by Hans Christian Andersen, tells of a miniature lovely girl "not half so big as my thumb" who sleeps in a walnut shell under a rose leaf. She is taken by a fat yellow frog to be his wife but escapes, and at last finds refuge with a field mouse. He is kind to her but arranges another marriage—this time with a sleek black velvet mole. Thumbelina finds a swallow struck down by the cold before it could migrate south, and nurses it back to health. It then leaves, but just as poor Thumbelina is about to marry the mole, the swallow returns and, taking her on its back, flies "where oranges and lemons hung golden in the woods." There the fairy king takes her as his wife.

supposed to be the only means of getting ride of it and retrieving their own baby. If the human child is ever restored, however, it is usually only after many years.

Immortal though they may be, the fairies seem ever preoccupied with reinforcing their stock. They kidnap not only babies but also nursing mothers to nourish their own ailing offspring. They capture young girls as brides, and lead away strong or skilled young men to work for them. One of the most famous of all fairy stories, told in many versions, concerns a midwife called out one night by a strange looking elderly couple. The two take her to a cottage where a lovely young girl is in labor. When the child is born the old people give the midwife some ointment to rub on its eyes, but warn her to keep it well away from her own

Above: Thumbelina in her bed, discovered by the fat yellow frog.

93

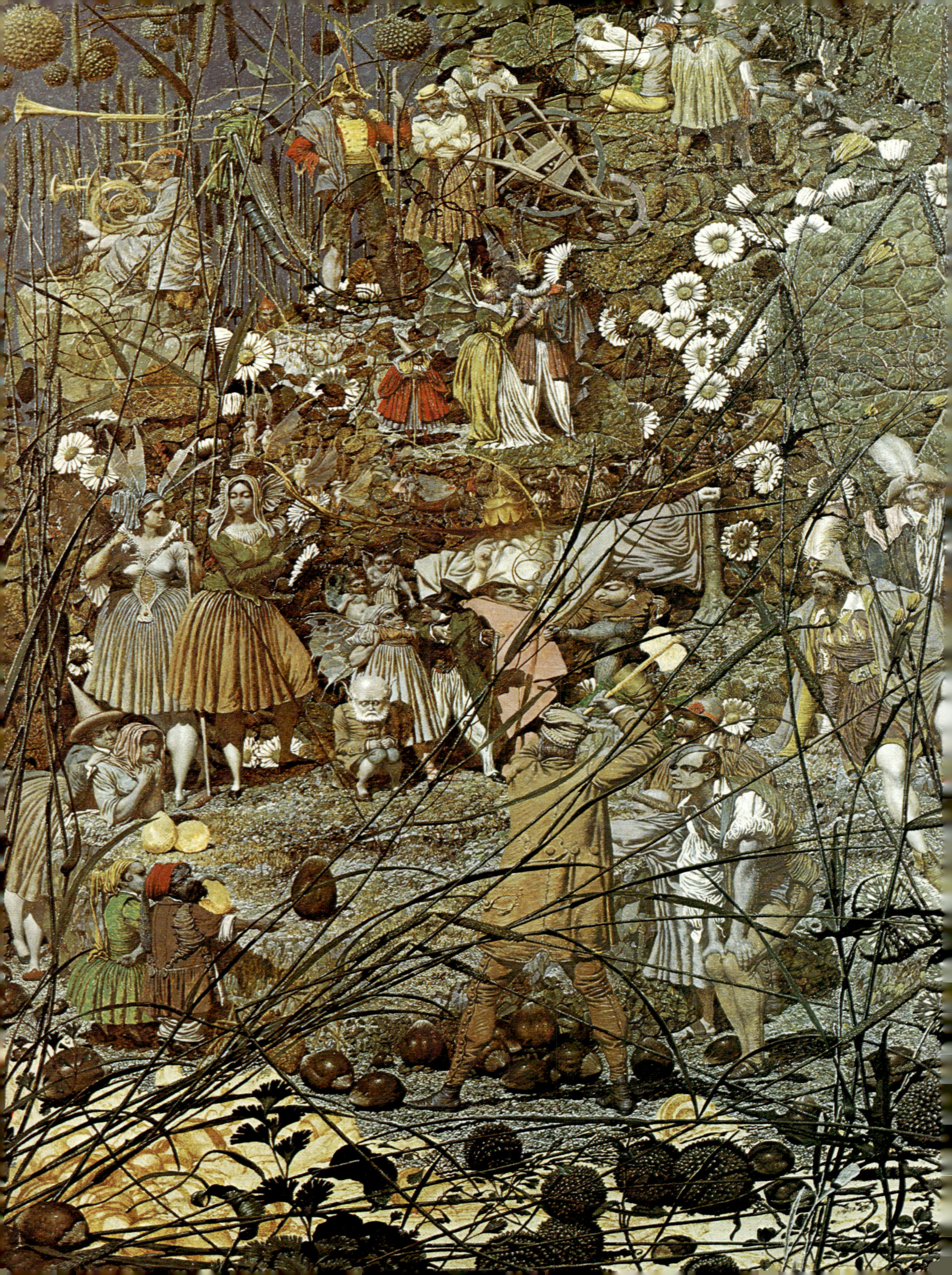

Left: an imaginative view of an intricate fairyland by Richard Dadd (1817-86), which he called *The Fairy Feller's Master-Stroke*. **In it all the figures are under a magic spell, which can only be broken by the cracking of a nut, and the Fairy Feller is attempting the task. It was painted by Dadd while he was an inmate of the Criminal Lunatic Asylum at the Bethlehem Hospital in London (the original Bedlam). He was confined there after an outburst of mania that led him to kill his father and attempt another murder. He never recovered sanity, but he continued to work and paint his hauntingly beautiful evocations of his troubled inner world.**

Below: a Pwca, or Puck, as seen by a Welsh peasant who sketched it with a bit of coal. Puck is a prankster who—when he appears as himself—is grotesquely elfish, quite unlike the delicate folk of Richard Dadd's fairyland.

eyes. Whether curious, careless, or anxious for the baby's welfare, the midwife disobeys the warning and touches her eyes with the ointment. Suddenly she sees a wild scene with the mortal mother in her bed surrounded by crowds of hideously ugly fairies, and the old couple the ugliest of all. The midwife hides her alarm and gets home safely. Some time later she sees the old fairy man and woman again, with other fairies who are stealing goods from a market stall. She challenges them, and they ask her which eye she can see them with. "Both," she replies—at which they blow on her eyes and she becomes completely blind.

Fairies typically dislike spies and eavesdroppers, often punishing them with blindness. Despite their own pilfering habits, they are hard on human thieves who covet fairy goods. They smile on those who have a free, open, and generous nature, sometimes disguising themselves to visit mortals and test them for these qualities. It is said that a family must leave a saucer of milk or a dish of beans on the window sill if they wish to bribe the fairies, and sometimes a pail of fresh water in the kitchen for them to bathe their babies. Those who neglect to do these things may be punished with painful cramps.

When pleased the fairies can be overwhelmingly generous, although they must be thanked profusely. An exception is the brownie or hob, and sometimes the pixy, who willingly works for humans without reward. There are many stories of people repaying fairies with the gift of a new suit, which delights them but usually results in their going away forever. Sometimes they fly off like witches, but they use a twig or a leaf instead of a broomstick.

Fairy history boasts of several leading personalities, such as the fairy Queen Mab. She is said to control our dreams, and is reputed to be only three-quarters of an inch high. A book published in England in 1588 and called *The Mad Pranks and Merry Jests of Robin Goodfellow* described this prototype of fairies as the son of a human girl and the fairy King Oberon. Some people have linked Goodfellow to the legend of Robin Hood, who dressed in the favorite green of the fairies. William Shakespeare used Robin Goodfellow and other leading fairy characters in his plays, and many other writers and poets have helped perpetuate fairy legends down the centuries.

Today we are all familiar with the fairies that figure in children's fiction, but what are we to make of case histories that are claimed as facts? Looking back we find that the earliest mention of fairies in England occurs around the 8th or 9th century. This concerns Anglo-Saxon charms against elf-shot—arrows believed to come from elves, and to cause disease in humans. Next comes the accounts of early chroniclers like Walter Map, who recorded the legend of King Herla and the Fairies in the late 12th century.

A chronicler of the early 13th century, Gervase of Tilbury, was the first to refer to very tiny fairies only half-an-inch high. They were known as portunes in England, but were apparently common in many parts of Europe. Another chronicler recorded the legend of Elidor, a little boy who used to visit the fairies in a subterranean fairyland devoid of sun, moon, or stars. The fairies were good and truthful, and Elidor moved among them freely until his doubting mother urged him to steal a golden ball from the son of the fairy king. On his way home with the ball, Elidor was tripped up by two fairies who took the ball and vanished. Elidor never found the fairy kingdom again.

The earliest records of changelings also date from medieval times. Most famous is the story of Malekin, a fairy claiming to be a human child stolen from her mother and given the gift of becoming invisible whenever she chose. Malekin would appear from time to time in the Suffolk area of eastern England, looking like a tiny child dressed in a white tunic. She would eat the food left out for her, and talk to the servants in broad Suffolk dialect. If she encountered a clergyman, however, she would converse with him in Latin.

Suffolk also became the home of the sad little Green Children, a brother and sister found at the entrance to a cave. Although they looked human, their skin was completely green and their speech unintelligible. Weeping and hungry, they nevertheless refused all food until offered beans, the fairies' favorite food, and for a long time they would eat nothing else. The green boy

Above: the first Cottingley Fairy photograph, taken by Elsie Wright, showed Frances Griffiths staring over a frolicking fairy band. The girls described the coloring of the fairies as shades of green, lavender, and mauve—darkest in their wings, and gradually fading into almost pure white in their bodies and floating draperies.

pined and died, but his sister gradually learned to eat mortal foods, and lost her greenness. She said the pair had come from a land of twilight, had lost their way in the caves, and had collapsed from the brightness and heat of the sun. The green girl married a local man and lived for many years, but was reputed to be "loose and wanton in her conduct."

The affair of the Green Children was said to have taken place in the mid-12th century, and is recorded by the chroniclers as fact. Down the centuries, there have been many more eyewitness accounts of fairies, especially in remote country areas.

By far the most remarkable documentation of fairies was the one in our own century, when Frances Griffiths and Elsie Wright photographed the Cottingley Fairies and Sir Arthur Conan Doyle wrote about them. For however incredible the story may seem, it has never been fully disproved. Let us look behind that 1920 title "An Epoch-making Event—Fairies Photographed."

In the summer of 1917 Frances Griffiths, a 10-year-old from South Africa, arrived to stay with her 13-year-old cousin Elsie Wright in the Yorkshire village of Cottingley. At the back of Elsie's house was a beautiful glen, a wild and secluded valley bordered by a stream. This soon became the girls' favorite spot, and it was there that they claimed to meet and play with the fairies. Not surprisingly, Elsie's parents did not take these stories seriously, but eventually, when Elsie begged him for the umpteenth time to let her prove she was telling the truth, Mr. Wright lent her his new camera. He slid one plate inside, set the camera, and showed Elsie how to operate it.

Within an hour the girls were back at their house, and later Arthur Wright developed the plate. There, unmistakably, was Frances Griffiths, her hand beneath her chin, and a troop of butterfly-winged fairies piping and prancing around her.

Amazed but unconvinced Mr. Wright again lent the girls the camera loaded with one plate. This time the photograph showed Elsie with a little winged gnome in tights, jerkin, and pointed cap about to jump onto her lap.

The Wright parents assumed that the girls must have used coutout figures. Elsie's father searched the glen for scraps of paper or cardboard cuttings, but found nothing. Nor was there any evidence to be found in the girls' bedroom. Still sure they were being deceived, but concerned at the girls' insistence on their story, the parents decided it was best to let the matter drop. The girls did not use the camera again, and the two photos were filed away on a shelf where they remained for three years.

In 1920 Mrs. Wright attended a local lecture. The speaker mentioned fairies, and Mrs. Wright told him about the photographs. As a result the two pictures were passed on to Edward L. Gardner, a leading member of the occult organization known as the Theosophical Society who had a particular interest in so-called spirit photography. Although unimpressed at first, Gardner had the negatives checked by Henry Snelling, a professional photographer and an expert in faked photography.

Snelling declared the two photographs to be genuine. "These two negatives are entirely genuine unfaked photographs of single exposure, open-air work, show movement in all the fairy

Above: a composite photograph by a British newspaper done to show how photographs like the pictures of the Cottingley Fairies could be created. The faked one shows Sir Arthur Conan Doyle, who wrote the article illustrated by the Cottingley Fairy photographs, with a tiny circle of frolicking fairy folk near his shoulder.

figures, and there is no trace whatever of studio work involving card or paper models, dark backgrounds, painted figures, etc. In my opinion, they are both straight untouched pictures."

It was then that Sir Arthur Conan Doyle added his considerable reputation to the case. He was planning an article on fairy lore for the Christmas issue of the *Strand Magazine*, and thought he might use the photographs to illustrate it. But first he needed additional proof of their authenticity. The negatives were tested by Kodak. They too declared that they could find no evidence of faking, although they did not rule out such a possibility.

Gardner then went to Cottingley and arranged for Elsie and Frances, now living in England, to try to take some more photographs. The girls, now aged 16 and 13, were each given a new camera and a set of secretly marked plates. Surprisingly, no independent witness went with them to the glen, perhaps because the fairies would only show themselves to sympathetic people and needed months to get used to strangers.

Although the weather was exceptionally bad over the next two weeks, the girls took three further photographs. Each revealed tiny fairy figures. The photographic company identified their marked plates, and after thorough analysis of the photographs, could detect no fraud. Gardner was convinced. He pointed out that the Wrights were not out for publicity, that they had insisted on concealment of their real names in Conan Doyle's article, and that they refused payment for the photographs. He also pointed out that faking would have taken considerable time, and would have required technical skills far beyond an amateur photographer.

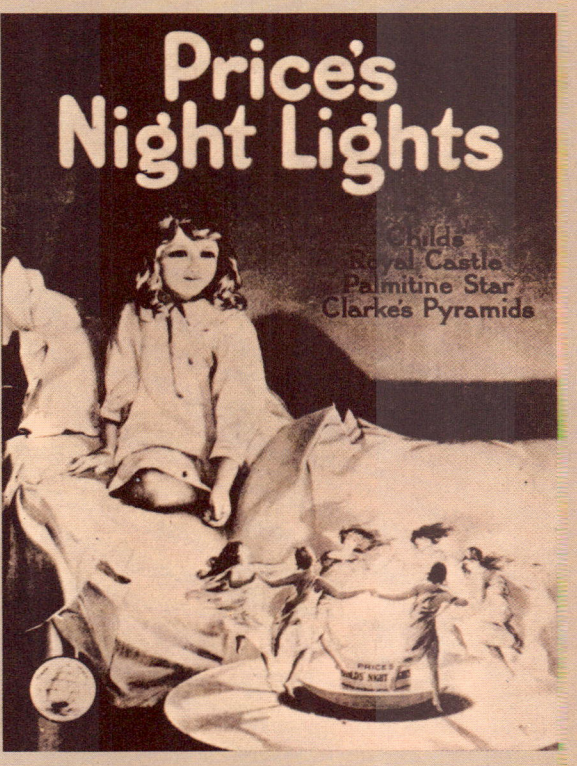

Relying on Gardner's report, Conan Doyle published his sensational story. He followed it up with another article in March 1921, and a book called *The Coming of the Fairies*. But he never visited Cottingley himself, nor spoke to the two girls. One man who did was the clairvoyant Geoffrey Hodson. After several weeks he too was convinced of the girls' honesty. He and Gardner concluded that both girls were clairvoyant, and that Frances was an exceptionally good medium whose ectoplasm was used by the fairies to materialize into the figures captured by the camera.

Seeing the photographs today a skeptic would not hesitate to say they were faked. The fairies are stereotyped little creatures, reflecting their conventional image to the tips of their gauze wings, and even wearing 1920 hairstyles. In the first and most famous photograph, Frances is staring straight ahead, apparently oblivious of the little figures frolicking in front of her. In the second, Elsie's hand looks abnormal—unusually large and apparently dislocated at the wrist. And although the girls continued to see the fairies, and claimed that the glen was swarming with all manner of fairy life, they never took more photographs.

Was there an element of self-deception on the part of the adults in the case? Critics point out that Gardner was deeply involved in the subject as an investigator of the paranormal; Hodson was a confirmed believer in fairies; Mrs. Wright was a Theosophist; and, for all his reputation as a logician, Conan Doyle had become a Spiritualist, turning to this belief in desperation at the death of a dearly loved son. Were they all perhaps a little too eager to believe in the Cottingley fairies?

The newspaper picture was done very simply by cutting out a fairy circle from a current advertisement and photographing it on a blank plate. The plate with the circle was superimposed on an ordinary picture of the celebrated author and presto! Sir Arthur was surrounded by dancing fairies.

Kludde, the Belgian Goblin

In the peaceful, pleasant countryside of Belgium, a goblin lurks they say. In the shadowy half-light of dawn or twilight, the goblin they call Kludde waits to pounce on innocents passing near his hiding places. Those who have heard the stories listen for the tell-tale sound—the clanking of the chain with which the evil goblin often beats his victims. For those who do not know about Kludde, the first thing they become aware of is the fearsome shape of a huge winged black dog, walking on his hind legs and approaching remorselessly. The faster you run, the faster he follows, slithering between the trees like a great snake. With a pounding heart you realize that it is impossible to escape him.

Kludde can use other shapes as well. He can appear as an enormous furry cat that purrs plaintively until the passer-by takes pity and then, letting out a blood-chilling yowl at the hand stretched out to pet him, he melts into the woods. Only then does the would-be befriender recognize the two small flames over Kludde's head.

Perhaps the goblin's strangest disguise is as a hideous bird, flapping over farms and wakeful farmers at night, cackling and crying out, "Kludde, kludde! Kludde, kludde!"

Gardner hotly denied this, pointing to a piece of evidence that emerged quite unexpectedly a year after Conan Doyle's article. A friend of Frances Griffiths in South Africa produced a copy of the first fairy photograph, which Frances had sent to her in a letter in 1917. Not only was this several years before the case was taken up publicly by Conan Doyle, but also Frances' letter dismisses the fairies in a single off-hand phrase amidst gossip about her dolls, her parents, and another photo of herself. This backs up Gardner's contention that, for Frances Griffiths, there was nothing extraordinary about seeing fairies and that, as Elsie Wright had told him, Frances had stared straight at the camera because she was far more interested in having her own photo taken than in fairies she could see any day. Gardner also defended the odd appearance of Elsie's hand, saying she did have exceptionally long hands and fingers. As for the ultra-typical looking fairies, Geoffrey Hodson maintained that fairies often choose to materialize in the forms that peasants or children have thought up for them, or in some image they particularly admire. "The surprise," he says, "would be if they were different."

According to Conan Doyle and Gardner, the girls did not manage to take any more photographs after 1920 because they had lost their childlike simplicity and innocence. In addition, although the girls continued to be good if limited clairvoyants, Frances' ectoplasm was no longer acceptable to the fairies, so they would not use it to take on photographable form. "The processes of puberty are often fatal to psychic power," wrote Conan Doyle. The rare combination of circumstances and people at Cottingley produced these photographs, said Gardner. Few attempts to photograph fairies have been successful since, and none have produced anything to match the results obtained by Elsie and Frances.

Cottingley today boasts a road with the name of "Fairy Dell," a reminder of a 20th-century sensation and an apparently inexplicable phenomenon. For in spite of the overwhelming publicity, which the Wrights could not in the end escape, no one ever convincingly disproved the fairy photographs. If the photographs were fraudulent, then the Wright family—or someone—apparently possessed a photographic genius that fooled every expert.

What if the photographs were genuine? Could there be such things as fairies after all? It is often said that modern city dwellers have lost the quality of clear-sightedness that would make them aware of such phenomena. Countryfolk and children are believed to be more psychic. Equally, countryfolk might be more gullible, and children more likely to fantasize, possibly in order to attract attention. In remote country areas people are raised on the old fairy legends, just as Haitian children are conditioned to the age-old superstitions of voodoo. Regional emphasis helps make the tales more meaningful. In Ireland, for instance, fairy stories stress such favorite Irish pastimes as dancing to the music of the pipers. In one tale, a villager who lived with the fairies for seven years reappeared without her toes because she had "danced them off." In many Celtic regions, anything unfamiliar might be given a fairy label: knolls were fairy mounds, or forts; a spiral of dust was a fairy wind; a sudden voracious appetite was explained as a fairy hunger; every rainbow had a fortune in fairy gold buried at the end of it.

It is reasonable to conclude that many eyewitness reports of fairies were simply mistaken identification. A procession sighted on top of a fairy mound might be made up of passing strangers or of small humans such as dwarfs and midgets. Sometimes a perfectly logical explanation is quickly found, as in the case of the mysterious white lady who appeared at night—and who proved to be a swan.

Nevertheless fairy beliefs persist, as D. A. MacManus, an expert on fairy lore, points out. He cites the 20th-century example of the legendary Fairy Black Dog, or *Poulaphuca*—a menacing variation of an Irish fairy that often assumes animal shape. The Fairy Black Dog is always jet black and stands shoulder high, with human eyes and great snarling teeth. One old man told MacManus that no one dared to cross a certain bridge alone after midnight for fear of the great black dog that haunted it. Checking up on this, MacManus found many local people who

Above: the treacherous water demon, the Kelpie, lurked by the lochs and rivers of old Scotland most often disguised as a horse. When a weary traveler would leap into its empty saddle, the Kelpie would rush into the water and devour its helpless victim. The next day, the victim's liver or entrails—all that then remained—would be washed ashore.

Above left: another view of fairies as attractive and gentle creatures. A water fairy, riding on the back of a friendly frog, seems to be talking with a fish. The whole scene is one of jollity and good fellowship amidst natural beauty.

Below: the Irish Sluagh, a host of evil spirits, flying together like a flock of birds. The souls of dead sinners, they try to take other souls along. Because they fly from the west, west windows were shut tight on a dying person lest his soul be intercepted before it could reach heaven.

Above: the dark elves of old Scandinavian mythology were a malignant and gloomy people, living in deep caves and quick to do evil in any way they could. They were capable of incredibly fine handiwork, however, and although they were recognized as demonic creatures, the gods on occasion asked them to make some objects. They made Thor's hammer, which would return to its owner when it was thrown. Below: the warm-hearted dwarf who rewarded the woodcutter's unloved youngest son for his genuine generosity with the gift of the golden goose. Because of the goose, the young man at last wins the princess as his wife.

Above: a 19th-century illustration of the French fairy tale *The Yellow Dwarf*, showing the beautiful arrogant princess, All-Fair, with the hideous little Yellow Dwarf who tricked her into agreeing to marry him. In the end, the Yellow Dwarf kills the King of the Gold Mines, whom All-Fair has come to love, to claim his bride. But All-Fair falls on the King's body and dies herself.

confirmed the story. One man said he had stopped to pump up his bicycle tire, and had seen a large black dog jump over the wall and stare at him. Having no doubt at all of its fairy nature, he uttered a rapid prayer and rode off as fast as his still flat tire would let him.

Such immediate acceptance of the black dog as a fairy shows how deep the superstition ran. MacManus himself dismisses the suggestion that the animal might simply have been a large wild black labrador, pointing out that such dogs were so common in the Irish countryside that people would have recognized the ordinary animal instantly.

He also denies any connection with the witchcraft tradition that a black dog is a witch's familiar. Yet this element of black magic may well help to explain the fear that the Black Dog and many other fairies arouse. In fact some people believe that certain fairies are artificial entities created by black magic.

Certainly European magicians of the 16th and 17th centuries had rites for conjuring up fairies or nature spirits. Geoffrey Hodson described one of these creatures, which were called *elementals*, as follows: "Entirely black in color, with a satanic cast of feature, it more nearly resembled the orthodox devil than anything I have ever seen... It was an elemental relic of ancient magic rites. In those distant days it was free, an evil demon, in form of a gigantic vampire. It was created and employed by a company of priests... to perform their evil designs."

In the Middle Ages, when almost everybody believed in fairies, the Church regarded them as fallen angels cast out by God, but continuing to challenge His power. Many 16th and 17th-century clergymen condemned fairies outright as "demons and devils from Hell." It was the Irish who found a more compassionate and comprehensive explanation for the many varieties of little people. Their theory, still current in Ireland today, is that the fairies are fallen angels all right, but were merely tricked by Satan, and were neither good enough to stay in Heaven nor bad enough to be consigned to Hell. God halted their fall so that the worst of them tumbled into caverns under the earth, becoming gnomes and goblins; others fell into waters and woods to become tiny fairies and nature sprites; and yet others landed near mortals' houses to labor forever as brownies and hobs.

Some say fairies occupy a place between humans and angels, calling them "spiritual animals." Others consider them strictly human, but carry the idea of them as inhabitants of a kind of limbo one step further. They say that fairies are the souls of dead people who were not good enough to be saved nor bad enough to be condemned, who died without the necessary religious rites, or whose life was prematurely cut short—an idea often cited as a reason why fairies are so attractive to Spiritualists. In other words, we are moving into the realm of ghosts.

Certainly it is the tradition in many Irish stories that some fairies belong to "the host of the dead." In other places too fairies are often specifically described as ghosts, particularly those of pagan peoples long dead. In her book *The Fairies in Tradition and Literature*, Katharine Briggs quotes a famous fairy story in which an unwilling visitor to fairyland says of her fairy captors: "They have little sense or feeling; what serves them in a way as such is merely the remembrance of whatever pleased them when they lived as mortals—maybe thousands of years ago"

Serious students of fairy belief have suggested that the fairies are in fact a folk memory of a prehistoric race of small people who once inhabited parts of France. Conquered and forced into hiding, they might well have dwelt in caves and hills, only venturing forth at night. Yet to their conquerors, unfamiliar with the local gods, traditions, and magical rites, these little people would continue to pose a powerful threat. Their situation would also make them expert thieves of just those items fairies are said to concentrate on: grain, milk, and other foodstuffs, cattle, and even brides. Possibly some would offer to work for the new settlers in return for food or clothing—hence the stories of helpful if odd-looking brownies and hobs.

Others trace the origins of fairy belief even further back—to

The Dwarf's Bribe

Like all members of the fairy family, dwarves are sometimes helpful. But they like to be bribed and hate to be thwarted. Here is the classic dwarf story.

Once a miller foolishly boasted that his daughter could spin gold from straw. The king took her away, locked her in with some straw, and ordered her to produce gold. A dwarf came to the poor girl's rescue. Taking her only possessions as bribes, he spun gold for two days running. On the third day the king promised the maiden marriage if she would spin gold once more. Having nothing left to give the dwarf, she promised her first-born child on the dwarf's insistence.

The maiden became queen and had a baby. The dwarf appeared and demanded his gift, but she was so persuasive that he made a new bargain: if she could tell him his name in three days, she could keep her child. After two days of guessing, no name was right. Then one of the royal messengers unexpectedly came across a funny little man singing: "Little does my lady dream/Rumpelstiltskin is my name."

Next day the happy queen told the dwarf his name. Rumpelstiltskin was so furious that he stamped his foot through the floor. But he kept his bargain—and the queen kept her baby.

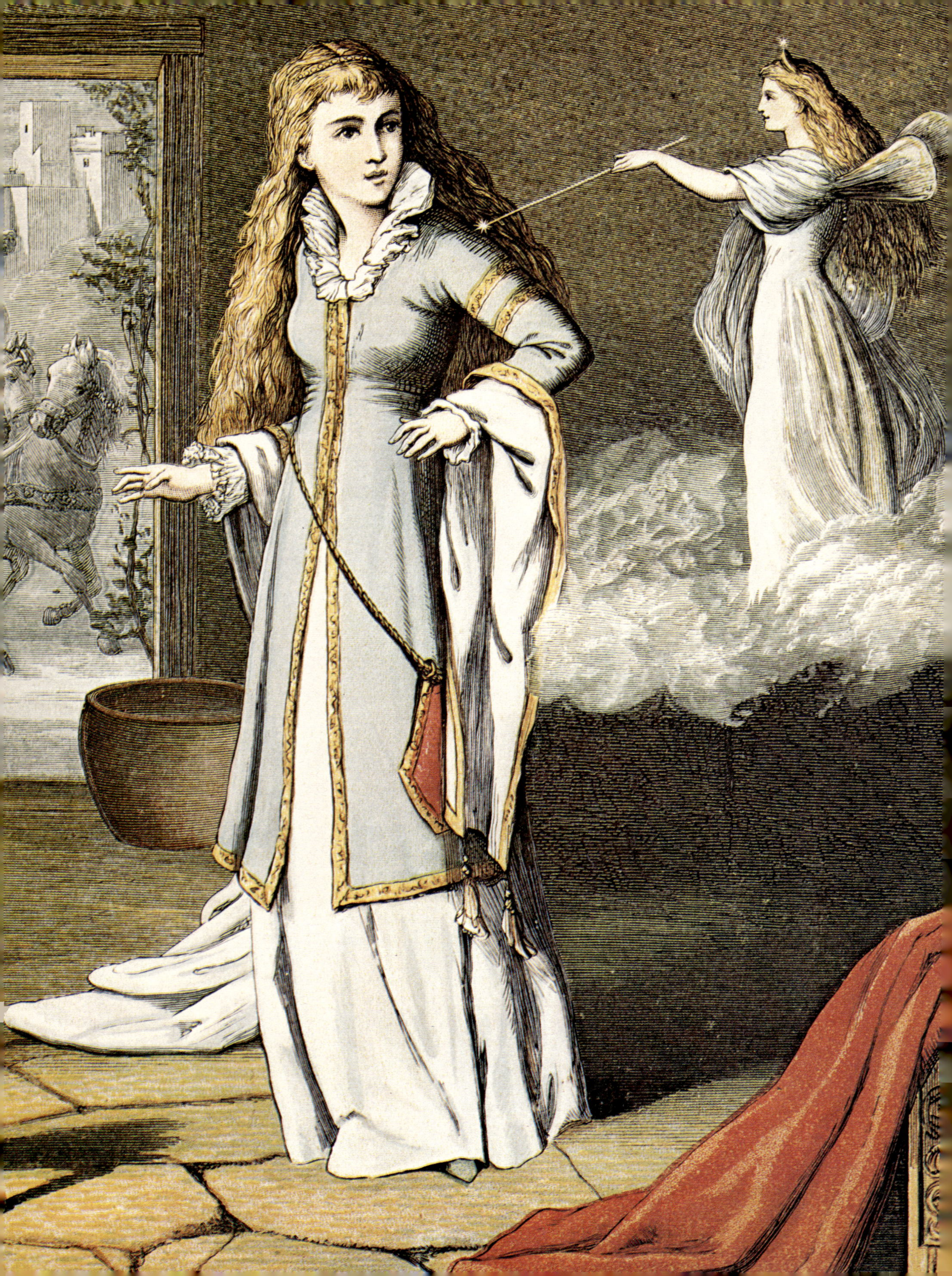

Left: Cinderella's open-handed fairy godmother is the kind of fairy most people think of as typical—tiny, beautiful, and eager to help the mortal under its protection with a wave of a magic wand. Although the fairy world has many clearly malicious as well as merely mischievous dwellers, the Cinderella story and its like takes the view that seems to have the widest appeal.

the gods and spirits worshiped in primitive times. The ancient spirits of streams and groves are almost certainly the direct ancestors of the nature spirit type of fairy. People buried beneath their own houses might become tutelary fairies, watching over their particular family. Katharine Briggs suggests that the typical minute stature of many fairies may arise from the primitive concept of the soul as a tiny creature that creeps from a person's mouth while he sleeps, and plays out his dreams.

The word fairy itself is believed to derive from the Latin *fata*—the Fates, or goddess guardians of man's destiny. They were believed to preside over the cribs of the newly born in the way that fairies did at Sleeping Beauty's christening. Nymphs and other lesser deities of mythology have evolved into fairies, and many interpret the beautiful Dana o'Shee as the lost gods of Ireland. The Irish poet W. B. Yeats, an influential writer on the fairy tradition, called fairies "the gods of the earth." He regarded them as immortal, and quoted with relish the old lady who told him that she did not believe in hell, "an invention got up by the priest," nor in ghosts, "who should not be allowed to go traipsing about the earth at their own free will," but she did believe in "faeries and little leprechauns, and water horses and fallen angels."

Many poets and mystic occult writers of every age and country have declared that behind the visible world are invisible chains and chains of conscious beings, who "are not of heaven but of the earth, who have no inherent form but change according to their whim, or the mind that sees them." According to Geoffrey Hodson, "the occultist sees no 'dead matter' anywhere —every stone thrills with life, every jewel has its attendant consciousness, however minute. The grass and trees are pulsing to the touch of tiny workers, whose magnetic bodies act as the matrix in which miracles of growth and color become possible."

Hodson and other modern believers in fairies, like Edward Gardner and Lord Dowding, regard almost all fairies as nature spirits whose specific function is to fertilize plants and insure that they grow and flourish. Hodson claims to have seen growing bulbs swarming with submicroscopic fairy creatures, each performing his appointed task. The more powerful nature spirits, he maintains, charge these humble workers with the necessary energy and, like managers, make sure they adhere to Nature's overall plan.

The more skeptical would say that fairies are merely an aspect of our own unconscious minds—symbols of repressed desires and fears. They would point to the universality of certain themes in fairy lore—the impotent human tied down with a thousand ropes of cobweb by a regiment of fairies, or the beautiful bride snatched up by the hairy and hideous fairy man.

Explanations for the strangely persistent belief in fairies are almost as varied as the fairies themselves. There is probably a grain of truth in all of them. But if 99 percent of reported fairy sightings can be explained, what about that other one percent? Can we believe, like Conan Doyle, that a whole new order of beings inhabit our planet, just the flicker of an eyelid away? Or has the ointment of civilization blinded us forever to the dreams and nightmares of Fairyland?

6

Wild Men of the Forest

However busy man has been in his work of imposing order on the natural world surrounding him, he has remained intrigued and half-admiring of life in the wild: of fierce, savage men and women not subject to the rules he has so carefully constructed for himself and his kind. The wild man and wild woman became an expression of this interest, and the mixed emotions behind it.

Right: this French miniature of the late 15th-century shows a wild family as fairly domesticated. By this period people tended to think of the wild man as more harmless than demonic.

Above: Tarzan of the apes, the wild man of the 20th century. He first appeared in a book by Edgar Rice Burroughs in 1914, and later gained great popularity as a hero of comic book and screen. Abandoned as a baby in Africa, Tarzan was brought up by apes.

"All of a sudden, a grown up wolf came out from one of the holes... This animal was followed by another one of the same size and kind. The second one was followed by a third, closely followed by two cubs one after the other....

"Close after the cubs came the ghost [in this case a hideous looking being of Indian folklore] hand, foot, and body like a human being; but the head was a big ball of something covering the shoulders and the upper portion of the bust, leaving only a sharp contour of the face visible, and it was human. Close at its heels there came another awful creature like the first, but smaller in size.

107

"Reared in the wild by wolves"

Their eyes were bright and piercing, unlike human eyes."

This excerpt is from the diary of Reverend J. A. L. Singh, a missionary in Bengal in the first part of this century. It describes the discovery of two feral children—little girls who had been reared in the wild by wolves. Very rare in real life, children reared by animals is a fairly common theme in mythology and popular literature.

In Rudyard Kipling's *Jungle Book*, the story of Mowgli gives this idea fanciful expression. As a toddler, Mowgli, a woodcutter's child, is nearly killed by a tiger, and is rescued by a family of wolves. Mother Wolf immediately becomes fiercely protective of the "man's cub," and manages to persuade the pack, which shows a high degree of social organization, to let

Left: Romulus and Remus, the legendary founders of Rome, being suckled by their foster-mother, a she-wolf. They had been taken from their mother (who had been reportedly seduced by Mars) by a jealous uncle and abandoned. Below: a boy found in the jungles of Sri Lanka in 1973, apparently having been adopted by a family of monkeys. When he was found he was about 10 years old. He could run swiftly on all fours, but could not speak or stand up.

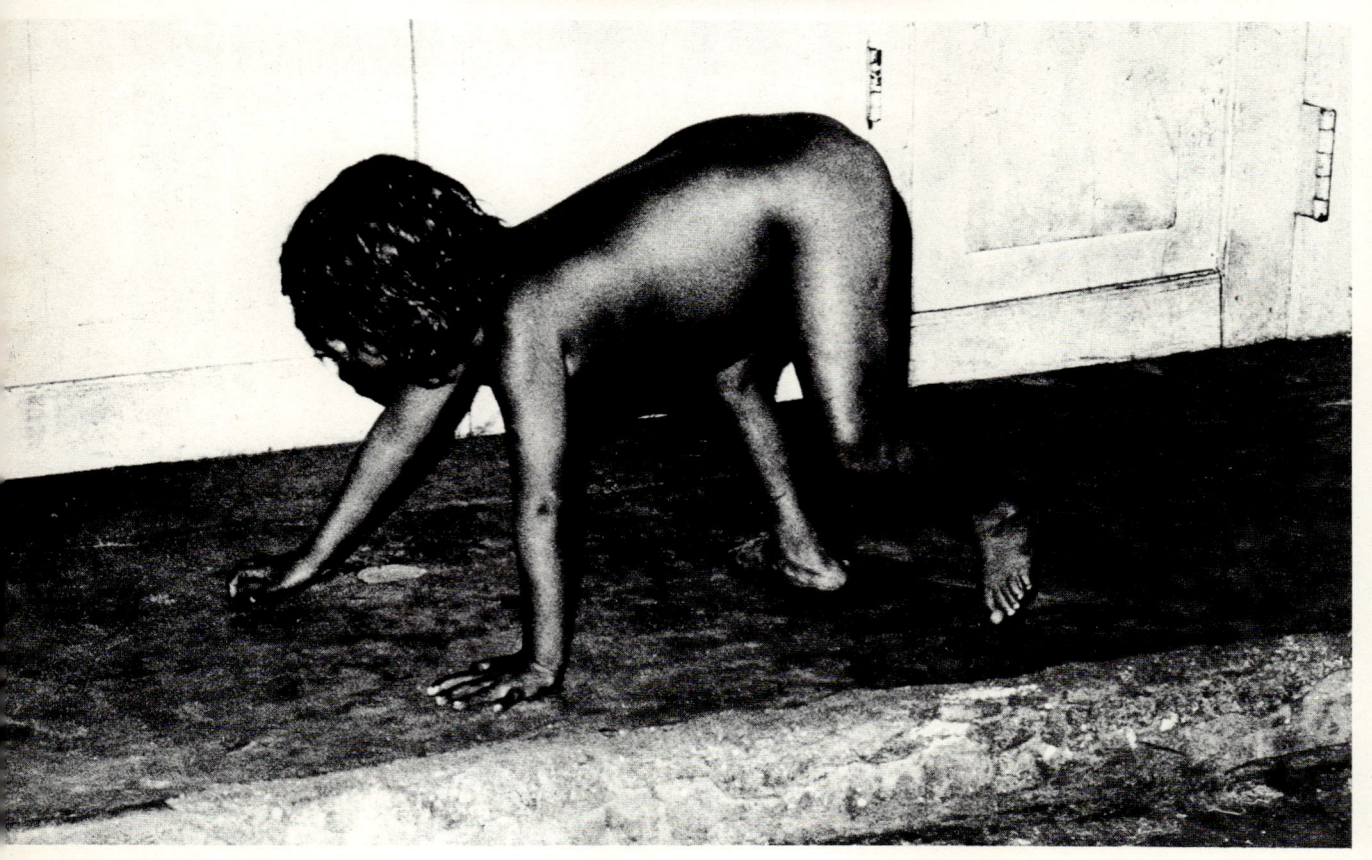

him stay. As he grows up, Mowgli learns the ways of the jungle and, like the animals, becomes acutely sensitive to "every rustle in the grass, every breath of the warm night air, every note of the owls above his head . . . ." He seems to enjoy a harmonious relationship with the pack, but secretly the young wolves sense and resent his superiority. Eventually he is forced to leave them and return to his human family—promising Father and Mother Wolf to return for a visit some day. "'Come soon,' said Mother Wolf, 'little naked son of mine; for listen, child of man, I loved thee more than ever I loved my cubs.'"

Our ambivalent attitude toward the wolf—part fear and part admiration—also emerges in the legend of Romulus and Remus, the twins who supposedly founded the city of Rome. Their mother, the princess Rhea Silvia, had been made a Vestal Virgin by order of her uncle, the usurper of her father's throne of Alba Longa. She claimed that the god Mars was the father of the children, but this distinguished supernatural parentage was of no immediate help to them. The king, fearing their claim to the throne, had them thrown into the Tiber River. They were rescued and suckled by a she-wolf, an animal sacred to Mars, and later cared for by a herdsman and his wife. When they grew up, the twins slew the usurper, restored their grandfather to the throne, and founded the city of Rome.

Although the legend claims that the city's name is derived from the names of the brothers, it is almost certain that the true story is the other way around: that Romulus and Remus were invented later in the history of Rome to provide an appropriately picturesque and mysterious origin for the great city. Stories of children brought up in the wild are fairly common in Greek legend, and the Romans, familiar with Greek literature, may have adapted this theme for their purpose. The role of Mars in the story—both as the alleged father of the twins and as the patron of wolves—is clearly an attempt to link Rome with the god of war.

However interesting their stories may be, Mowgli, Romulus, and Remus are, after all, definitely human beings, capable of adapting to human society when and if the necessity arises. Their wildness is artificially imposed. More intriguing is the idea of a creature who is man and yet not man, living in the wild, a perpetual threat to the community, possessed of man's baser, aggressive instincts and of a beast's strength—in short, a creature much like Neanderthal Man.

Today we know that before man in his present form appeared on the scene, more primitive forms inhabited various parts of the earth. In some areas two species may have coexisted for thousands of years, perhaps in a state of intermittent conflict until one of them died out. For example, although we have no proof of this, it may be that Neanderthal man, who inhabited central and southeastern Europe up until 32,000 to 35,000 years ago, was known to Cro-Magnon man, our ancestor who emerged about 28,000 to 32,000 years ago. If Neanderthal man was not already extinct, and if our ancestors knew him, it is possible that true stories of a man who wasn't quite man could have survived as a folk memory long after his type had disappeared. Similar overlappings of species, giving rise to similar

The Wolf Children

In 1920 in Bengal, India, the missionary Reverend J. A. L. Singh found two little girls who had been raised by a wolf pack. He discovered them originally because he had been asked to exorcise a "man ghost" that was frightening the local villagers. The ghost turned out to be the two girls, who emerged snarling from a cave with their wolf mother and two other cubs. The mother was killed by the nervous villagers, but the children were rescued by Reverend Singh and brought to an orphanage. He named them Kamala and Amala.

The two girls could run swiftly on all fours, but could not stand up. They ate only milk and raw meat, lapping and tearing like dogs. Their sense of smell was extremely well developed. They were never able to laugh, but when Amala died a year after capture, Kamala cried two tears.

Kamala survived nine years in human society, and learned to stand upright, eat cooked food, and speak a little. By the time she died she had a vocabulary of more than 30 words. She was thought to be about 16 when she died, but her mental age was about three. Although she had been nearly animal when she was found, her genetic adaptability proved itself: by her death, she was wholly human.

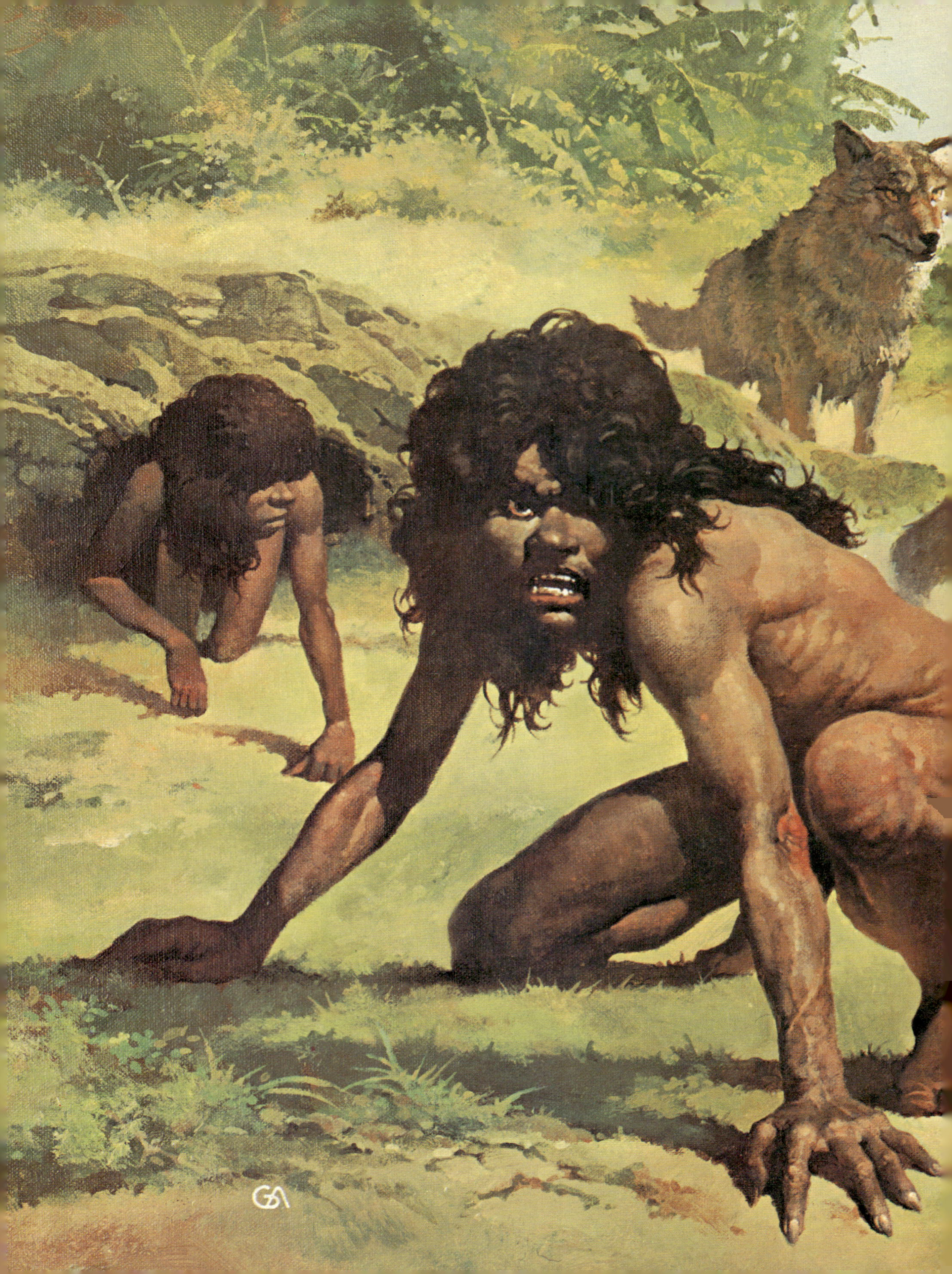

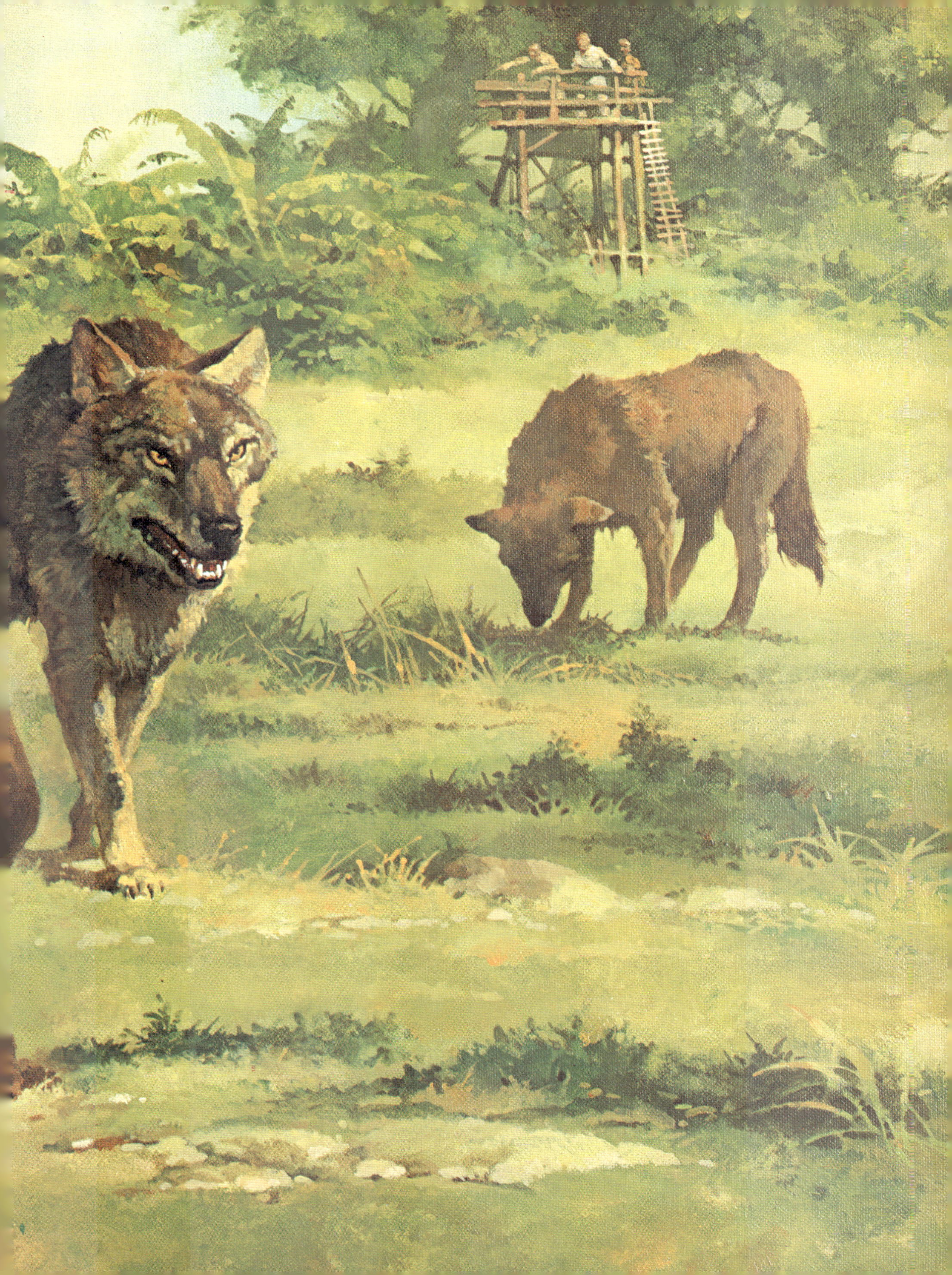

stories, may have occurred in other parts of the world. It may seem far-fetched to propose that a species that has not been seen for thousands of years could survive in people's minds as a threat today, but fears and superstitions have deep psychological roots and are more complex than usually thought.

Of course, it was not a *conscious* knowledge of evolution that kept the legend of the wild man alive. The people who believed it in the past, like most of those who believe it today, knew little or nothing about Neanderthal Man and his position in the theory of evolution. Medieval Europeans assumed that men had always looked as they did; stories and pictures of Adam and Eve proved it. If their belief in a wild man stemmed from a prehistoric source, the source itself had long since been forgotten. Perhaps the *unconscious* memory of prehistoric life and its dangers had somehow been transmitted from one generation to the next, in what the psychologist Carl Jung called the "collective unconscious." The readiness to believe in the wild man would then be lying hidden in everyone, requiring only certain conditions to keep the legend alive. These conditions are a body of mythology, scientific ignorance, and an occasional event that apparently backs up the myth.

Right: Mowgli, hero of Rudyard Kipling's *The Jungle Book*, returned to human society after being reared by a devoted wolf. Here he gets news of his former wild family from Gray Brother. **Below:** Tarzan in the wilds of Hollywood—Johnny Weissmuller with Maureen O'Sullivan as his wife Jane. Weissmuller had been an Olympic athlete and looked the part of the jungle hero he played more often than any other actor.

The best-known modern example of the wild man legend is the Abominable Snowman or Yeti of the Himalayas, whose existence is stubbornly believed both by local people and by foreign explorers of the region. No one ever manages to capture a Yeti or even to photograph one, although photographs exist of alleged Yeti footprints. But plenty of people claim to have seen one. Their descriptions vary widely, and go from five-foot-tall vegetarians to 15-foot meat eaters. The Yeti is often credited with prodigious strength, being able to rip up trees and throw boulders around like pebbles.

North America has its own version of the Yeti, called the Sasquatch in Canada and the Bigfoot in the United States. Long known to the American Indians, the Bigfoot is feared by the non-Indians as well. Every now and then even today an accident or a murder in remote mountainous parts of the continent are

If Tarzan had grown up in his proper home in England, he would have been the nobleman Lord Greystoke. In Burroughs' book he is in a sense still the noble, and becomes king of the apes and lord of the jungle.

attributed to this formidable creature. He is generally described as being about eight feet tall with huge feet, as the name suggests. The animal he most closely resembles is the ape—which, however, is not native to North America.

If with our present knowledge of natural history we can believe or half believe stories of semihuman creatures roaming the forests, it is not surprising that the people of the Middle Ages, who knew little about zoology, believed in the wild man. In fact, long after the Middle Ages, the Swedish botanist Linnaeus included the *Homo ferus*, wild man, in his *System of Nature* published in 1735. Linnaeus described this distinct human species as "four-footed, mute, and hairy," and cites several cases of feral children as evidence. A vivid description of the Alpine sub-species of the European wild man appears in Richard Bernheimer's book *Wild Men in the Middle Ages*:

"Huge and hairy and mute . . . he may be so large that his legs alone have the size of trees. His temper when aroused is terrible and his first impulse that of tearing trespassers to pieces. When moved to revenge, he may make lakes disappear and towns sink into the ground. He abducts women and devours human beings, preferring unbaptized children, and—according to a belief held in the Italian Tyrol and in the Grisons in Switzerland—makes a practice of exchanging his own worthless progeny for human offspring."

Belief in this formidable creature has all but disappeared in Europe except for certain small isolated communities in and around Switzerland. During the Middle Ages, however, the wild man myth in various forms flourished in most parts of the Continent and in the British Isles. His image, and those of his mate and offspring as well, appeared in tapestries, on pottery, and in engravings, woodcuts, and stone carvings. The main portal of the Church of San Gregorio in Valladolid, Spain, built in the late 15th century, is adorned with statues of hairy men instead of the expected figures of saints. At first glance this appears to be an astonishing glorification of a mythical beast by the Church. But in fact, the portal taken as a whole is a heraldic representation of King Ferdinand and Queen Isabella, whose coat of arms is carved above the doorway. In their period, the wild man was often represented as a protector or supporter of a family's coat of arms—and, therefore, of the family's honor. Like other creatures shown defending a heraldic shield, such as the lion, unicorn, and griffon, the wild man represented strength. He also represented fertility.

It is ironic that the wild man should eventually achieve respectability as the symbolic defender of monarch and faith, for throughout most of his history he had been regarded by the Church as at best an unfortunate spiritually blind creature condemned to a sort of limbo-on-earth, and at worst as a demon. He seems to have been left over from pagan beliefs in woodland gods and demons. The Greeks' woodland god Silenus was depicted as hairy and said to have superhuman strength. Roman writers including Virgil and Juvenal referred to a race of primitive man born from tree trunks. Somewhat more believably, the Roman historian Pliny states that in India there was a race of wild semihuman creatures with hairy bodies, yellow eyes, and

Left: a reconstruction of what a Neanderthal man probably looked like. Could he be the source of the wild man stories? This might be so if it is considered that the Neanderthals coexisted with our ancestors the Cro-Magnons for a time. The Neanderthals—a man not quite a man— might have lived on as a folk memory from this period of coexistence with the species that developed into man.

Below: a wild man of a medieval carnival from a 16th-century German manuscript. Winter carnivals were held in Nuremberg from 1449 until 1539, and were wild affairs. A police order of the 15th century complains about "wild men and other mummers" who are shouting, chasing people and "scuffling with them . . . and scratching them." Even when they were not assaulting the public, the uproar of the wild men must have been considerable—they entered at a dead run, shooting off concealed fireworks and clanging bells sewn to their costumes of fur and greenery.

Right: an illustration from one of the illuminated editions of *The Book of Marco Polo*. It depicts wild men of Asia in some grotesque forms. Polo heard about them on his extensive travels in China and India. (Bodleian Library, MS Bodley 264, fol. 260).

Below: a 17th-century engraving of a wild man discovered in Java.

canine teeth. He may have acquired this information from writings on the Indian campaign of Alexander the Great. It seems likely that the source of this wild man myth was some species of large monkey such as the eastern gibbon. Unable to speak in the human sense of the word, the apes nonetheless exhibit many human characteristics. It is not too difficult to understand how reports of large apes grew into wild men stories as they passed from one person to another.

The myth of the hairy wild man received a boost from the Bible itself, which contains a prophecy in Isaiah of forthcoming desolation in Palestine. It says, "the hairy ones will dance there." The Hebrew word *se'erim* is believed to have denoted a kind of hairy monster that lived in wild deserted areas. The translator, St. Jerome, was of the opinion that these "hairy ones" were possibly *incubi*—that, is, evil spirits who descend on sleeping women and ravish them—or satyrs, who have similar habits but attack women who are awake. In any case, the existence of the hairy wild man and his characterization as a lustful, immoral creature were fairly well established early in the Christian era.

The fact that no one ever actually saw one of these creatures naturally resulted in a variety of descriptions. Some wild men were depicted as giants that could joust with tree trunks and carry the carcass of a lion slung over the shoulder. Others are described as dwarf. Often they seem to be human size.

Nor were all wild men hairy. In England, particularly, the wild men were leafy, covered with moss and ivy. A humorous drawing of the 15th century shows two fighting wild men who are covered with a mixture of fur and scroll-like leaves. There is even a feathered species.

The wild man was a familiar part of many medieval festivals, and even today the wild man cavorts in the Carnival and

Twelfth Night festivities in some parts of Europe. The villagers of Oberstdorf in Germany perform a wild man dance in which they wear costumes of hay and lichen, and fierce looking masks carved of wood. Fur-clad wild men dance in Carnival celebrations in the Balkan countries and in Morocco. They are usually accompanied by other figures representing animals, including one wearing a female mask to represent the wild man's bride.

In some of the wild man dances and plays that are still performed we can discover how the people of the Middle Ages regarded this elusive but powerful being. One of the commonest plots of a wild man play—still enacted in the Balkans—involves a hunt for the wild man, his capture and killing, and often his resurrection. The story of the capture of the wild man seems to have been greatly popular during the Middle Ages. Normally the play would begin with the creature ranting and snorting around to the horrified delight of the audience. Eventually a group of villagers would catch up with him, and either kill him on the spot or lead him away in chains to face some court of justice. In some of these wild man plays, generally those performed in late spring or early summer, the wild man is brought to life again, apparently suggesting his importance as a symbol of fertility and the renewal of life. In Carnival performances he

Above: a sign hanging outside a modern London pub is a rendition of the leafy English wild man, Jack in the Green. He capered at spring festivals, and was often dunked in water to guarantee that enough rain would fall for crops.

Left: a German carnival mask. These masks, generally designed to present as fearsome an aspect as possible, were an integral part of the wild man costume. During the festivities of the French court in 1392, when Charles VI himself took part, someone took a torch to peer more closely at the masked dancers, and set them alight. Four died in flames. The king was saved only because his quick-witted aunt threw her cloak over him to smother the fire.

is usually left dead—possibly because in this context he represents the Carnival season itself, which ends with the arrival of Lent. In other words, the killing of the wild man represents the suppression of lust.

The wild man also figured in a riotous revel called a *charivari*, popular in France in the late Middle Ages. This was a kind of brawl combined with dance, performed on the occasion of the marriage of an unpopular person. Some of the participants in this malicious spectacle wore animal skins, while others cavorted in the nude. With their identities concealed under various bizarre masks, the dancers gave vent to their primitive instincts. Charivaris were occasionally performed at court, and on two occasions at least, the revelers included King Charles VI.

In other plays the wild man was the leader of the Wild Hunt, or Wild Horde. This group of demons, who with their hounds rode through the sky on dark nights, created a terrifying spectacle. The Wild Horde is one of the most widespread of European legends. The original leader of the Wild Horde is supposed to have been the Germanic god Wotan, but as the legend evolved, this role was sometimes taken by the wild man.

To complicate matters further, there was also a female version of the Wild Horde, led by a goddess such as Diana and including a vast company of female demons.

The identity of these female demons of the Wild Horde became confused with the wild woman—who is not merely the mate of the wild man, but a distinct being who occurs in regions where the male of the species is unknown. She varies considerably in size and appearance, and as in the case of the wild man, the Alpine version, called Faengge, is among the most formidable. Richard Bernheimer reports that she is "a colossal ogre of great strength and appalling ugliness. Bristly all over, she has a mouth forming a grimace that reaches from ear to ear. Her black, untended hair is interspersed with lichen, and according to a report from Switzerland, she has breasts so long that she can throw them over her shoulders [a characteristic shared by the female Yeti]. She is prone to eat human children."

Ugly as most wild women are reputed to be, they nevertheless have the power to bewitch men—first transforming themselves into beautiful young women if necessary. They also seem to have a love of combat, sometimes fighting the wild man for leadership of the Wild Horde.

Yet the tapestries and woodcarvings of the late Middle Ages often show the wild woman in a gentler mood, living companionably with the wild man in a pleasant woodland retreat. "Her appearance," says Bernheimer, "if exception be made of her shagginess, is distinctly human and even moderately attractive, and her behavior is usually that of a faithful housewife operating efficiently under the primitive conditions of a camping trip."

Such naive and charming representations of the wild man and his household show how people's attitude toward him had undergone a transformation—at least in more sophisticated circles. He was no longer the demonic creature feared by the peasantry, but a rather harmless, even ridiculous figure.

By the end of the Middle Ages, another attitude toward the

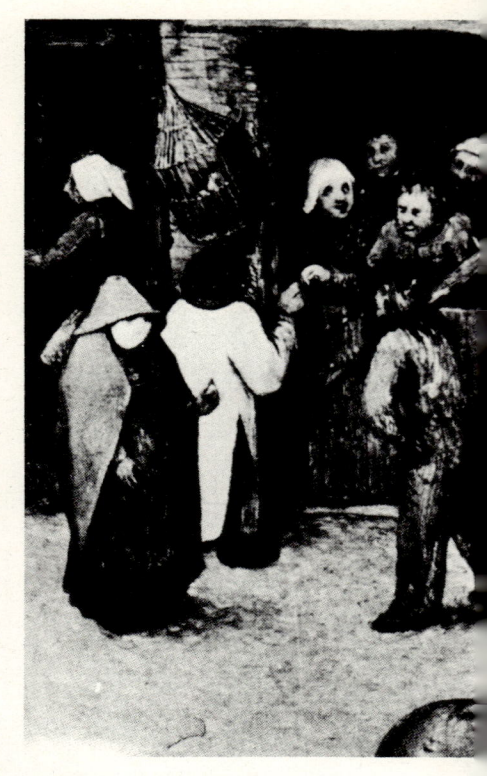

Above: the Play of the Death of The Wild Man, as recorded by Pieter Brueghel the Elder in the 16th century in Flanders. The emperor, identified by his crown and scepter, and a hunter armed with a crossbow, close in on the wild man. Meanwhile, a man with a white mask, disguised as a woman, lures the wild man by holding a ring out to him.

Right: the play is still performed in modern times, as shown in this scene in Bulgaria. Besides the frolicking of the wild men pictured here, the Bulgarians include the ceremony of pulling a plow—a clear reference to the traditional fertility role of the wild man.

wild man had emerged: that of admiration and envy. Among some writers, notably the German Hans Sachs, the wild man represented a healthy alternative to the artificiality and corruption, the strife and cruelty of society. Sachs' poem "The Lament of the Wild Man about the Unfaithful World" includes a detailed catalog of the vices of the world, followed by the wild man's extolling of the simple life he and his mate lead in the forest. "We feed on wild fruit and roots, drink the clear water of springs, and warm ourselves by the light of the sun. Our garment is mossy foliage and grass which serve also as our beds and bedspreads.... Company and pleasure we find in the wild animals of the woods, for since we do them no harm, they let us live in peace.... We exult in brotherly love and have never had any strife among us, for each does to the other as he would want him to do to himself."

This theme of the noble savage was not new. It had been popular in Greek and Roman writings, and it was to surface again in the latter 18th century. Apart from the question of its truth or falsity, this idea has probably never been widespread in any serious sense. Most people of Hans Sachs' day, or any other day, were much too involved in the world to give serious consideration to the advantages of living in the wild. It may be, however, that belief in the wild man satisfied some unconscious need to believe in such a possibility. Even the terrifying, bestial version of the wild man may have served a psychological purpose by exposing those aspects of human nature that society and religion tried to suppress.

Certainly the role of the wild man as our second self comes across strongly in stories of courtly love. Among the aristocracy, marriage and romantic love were kept separate. A lady might be married and yet also have a spiritual lover whose behavior toward her was marked by extreme respect, even worship. He performed brave actions to win her approval, offered her songs and poems, but never dared to approach her sexually.

Obviously maintaining such an artificial and idealized relationship would have been a strain on both parties. The interior struggle between courtly ideal and natural inclination found expression in innumerable stories and pictures of the knight subduing the wild man for the sake of the lady. Often the lady is abducted by the wild man and carried off to his cave. The knight appears on the scene just in time, and after a battle, slays the wild man.

A variation on the theme shows the lady herself subduing the creature. The wild man approaches the lady with his usual savagery, but is captured by her, tamed and civilized by the power of her love. This is clearly intended both as a tribute to the lady and as a plea from the suitor that she recognize his honorable intentions and grant him her love, thus making him a better man.

Often the aspiring lover pretended to go wild—that is,

Above: an etching by Albrecht Dürer in 1516 of the abduction of Prosepina, showing Pluto as a wild man. He carries off the struggling woman on a unicorn. Apart from virgins, the only conquerors of the unicorn—in 15th-century belief—were wild men, who overcame the fabled beasts by force rather than love.

Right: a French ivory casket used for jewels, dating from the 14th century, shows a knight in full armor rescuing a damsel from a wild man. In stories of courtly love—which among the medieval aristocracy was supposed to be spiritual only—the act of the knight in subduing the wild man was symbolic of his struggle to overcome lustfulness in order to keep his love for his lady pure.

Right: a coat of arms featuring the wild man. Some early coats of arms with wild men were a stereotyped reminder of pagan ceremonies with which a given place had been associated. Later the wild man became simply one of the host of heraldic beasts which like the unicorns, lions, griffons, and other savage beasts were guards on family shields.

temporarily insane—until the lady smiled on him. "The greater the warrior thus brought to grief," says Bernheimer, "the greater the implied prestige of the lady who had caused his fall. Indeed, some of the most renowned knights of romance, Yvain, Lancelot, and Tristan, fell victim to this strange occupational disease of knight-errantry."

This idea of pretended madness brings us to one of the factual bases for the myth of the wild man—namely, lunacy. The Book of Daniel tells us that King Nebuchadnezzar "was driven from men and did eat grass as oxen, and his body was wet with the dew of heaven, till his hairs were grown like eagles' feathers, and his nails like birds' claws." In the Middle Ages it was the custom to let some lunatics go free, and some of them went to live in the woods. It is easy to see how the fact of an irrational, perhaps violent outcast leading a crude existence in the forest could perpetuate the legend of the wild man.

The magician Merlin, best known to us as advisor to King Arthur, had another identity as a madman. A 12th-century epic, "Vita Merlini" by Geoffrey of Monmouth, describes how Merlin, first driven insane by the death of his brothers in battle, periodically reverts to madness and returns to the woods where he becomes a "sylvan man"—that is, a wild man.

To the Middle Ages, then, the wild man had many meanings. He could be an actual monster, an unfortunate lunatic, a demon, a symbol of physical love, an embodiment of the pure and simple life, or simply a decoration on a coat-of-arms. In one form or another he seemed to fill a need, for he flourished

121

Left: Nebuchadnezzar as a wild man, in a 15th-century manuscript illustration. Nebuchadnezzar, the Babylonian king written about in the Old Testament Book of Daniel, went through a period of madness. During that time he lived away from others, eating grass for food and letting his hair and nails grow wild. In the Middle Ages some mad persons were allowed to go free, and they usually drifted to the woods in order to live unmolested. However, they would be sure to be spotted at some time, and their probable wild behavior could easily lead to stories of the primeval wild man of the forest.

for several hundred years. And in parts of the world he continues to exist today—in people's minds, if not in reality.

Modern man is still fascinated by the wild man and wants to believe in him. In 1913 a man named Joe Knowles emerged from several months of wandering in the wilderness of Maine, claiming to have hunted and killed animals with his bare hands. This self-styled wild man was given an enthusiastic welcome by the citizens of Boston and other New England towns, who clearly were eager to believe in the possibility of living by one's wits alone in the wild. Later Knowles' claims were proved untrue, no doubt causing widespread disappointment.

A current example of the appeal of the wild man image is the hairy look favored by some young men. It is not merely a matter of wearing the hair long, which was fashionable and acceptable in society until the last century. It is a matter of leaving long hair uncombed and unwashed to suggest an intentional rejection of civilization, and an affinity with raw nature.

Similarly, in listening to some of the more extreme types of rock music popular in the last few years, and in observing modern dancing with its tacit rejection of form and its celebration of the primitive, we are tempted to think that the wild man has been absorbed into modern man's self-image. Our ancestors, engaged in building a society and formulating rules of conduct—which, of course, did not prevent their behaving with savagery in good causes sanctioned by Church and State—may have needed to express their own primitive tendencies in an imaginary wild man. Now that psychology has forced us to acknowledge the wild man that dwells within us, we are free to give him expression—at least in harmless symbolic ways such as unkempt hair and screaming pop stars. In time, the current wild man vogue will probably fade, just as the mythical forest-dwelling wild man of Europe has retreated into obscurity. But it is hard to imagine a day when the wild man in some form will have disappeared entirely from our imagination.

Above: this youth was found living like an animal in a wild part of France in the early 19th century. He was about 17 years of age. At first he was taken to be a hopeless idiot, but after five years of intensive study with a doctor who got interested in him, he learned to stand, speak a little, and do a number of simple tasks. Even so, he never became a normal human being: his range of emotion was limited, and his responses were often inappropriate. He died when he was 40 years old. **Right: a scene from the movie *L'Enfant Sauvage* made about the wild boy's life by François Truffaut in 1970.** Truffaut, who directed, also played the doctor.

123

7

Man as Monster

Running through the stories of vampires, werewolves, zombies, and all the other mysterious and sinister creatures that resemble living humans, is a mystery that is fascinating and terrible. This is the mystery of the human mind—an infinitely complex structure of fears, desires, repressions, aggressive tendencies, and ideals. We like to believe today that we approach the world with a scientific eye, and that our ideas follow the rules of logic. Most of us look back with horror at the superstitions that bound and limited the people of earlier times. In fact, some of the most vehement skeptics of the supernatural proclaim their skepticism with an almost

Standing with his brothers the vampires, the werewolves, and the other semihuman creatures of myth and legend is the most terrible monster of them all: man himself. Capable of great tenderness and humaneness, man has also shown himself capable of most shocking and iniquitous cruelties toward his fellows. Above: Peter Kürten, the soft-spoken, nicely dressed German craftsman who regularly combed the streets of Düsseldorf from February 1929 to May 1930 for victims. He savagely murdered women and children, and then—with relish—drank their blood. Right: a painting of the Devil. In Western religious belief the Devil is the supreme evil, symbol of the most dreadful wickedness in the world. Yet even he is most recognizable with a human face.

125

"In our myths we reveal ourselves"

fanatical fervor. They are seemingly terrified at the thought that there may after all be some truth in occult beliefs. Their repugnance is understandable, for when we look at the desperate lengths to which people's supernatural beliefs have driven them—the terrible witchcraft trials, for example—we may feel that it would be a good thing to ignore certain aspects of the supernatural in hopes that they might eventually shrivel up under the bright light of science.

To ignore the supernatural, however, would be to deprive ourselves of an important key to the mysterious workings of the human mind. In our myths we reveal ourselves.

Consider, for example, the fairly straightforward myth of the giant. There is nothing deeply profound about the fascination of giants. They simply represent our desire for superhuman power and strength and, less obviously, our awe of nature. In many cultures we find that the creation of the world is attributed to a giant, and it is easy to see how this explanation seemed plausible. The enormous size of many of the earth's natural features—oceans, mountains, canyons—would suggest, according to primitive logic, a gigantic creator. Similarly, the more violent moods of nature, such as thunderstorms and torrential rains, would naturally be interpreted as demonstrations of the god-giant's displeasure, or simply as reminders of his power. On a subtler level the forces of nature—or signs of the giant's activity—may symbolize the forces that man feels within himself and to some extent fears. The folklore of the British Isles is full of fanciful accounts of how hills, valleys, and other features of the landscape were formed by giants throwing around spadefuls of earth or flinging enormous rocks into the sea. In their poetry the Anglo-Saxons referred often to "the giants" who supposedly inhabited Britain before their own arrival. In this case, the myth seems to have rested not so much on natural phenomena as on

Right: stories of giants exist across the world. In Japan, the mythological hero Raiko, with his faithful lieutenants, slew a whole band of them. They were a particularly nasty breed that attacked women in the mountains and lived off human blood. Raiko vanquished them partly by bravery and partly by trickery: he and his men appeared at the giants' hidden mountain fortress dressed as monks, but fully armed under their robes, and offered them a magic inebriating drink. When the giants were wobbling genially around, the warriors threw off their disguise and beheaded them. The giant leader was so furious that he tried to hit the victorious Raiko with his severed head.

Left: an illustration from a 17th-century treatise on giants. The author believed that some huge bones found in a cave in Sicily in the 14th century were those of a giant said to live there by the Greeks. Most likely the bones remained from the prehistoric elephants now known to have inhabited Sicily.

Making of a Mountain

The Twins killed him. But there was a time, they say, when the Big Monster—half as tall as the tallest fir tree—prowled what is now Arizona. He looked like a huge ugly man, but he was a demon. He wore a suit of flint armor joined by threads made of the intestines of his victims. On his back he carried a huge basket in which he kept the humans he had seized to eat later. He was truly terrible. He ruled all the other monsters that killed humans, and he could not be killed by any weapon made by a mortal.

So the gods known as the Twins set out to destroy him. They came upon the Big Monster just as he swallowed a lake. Catching their reflection in the last drops, he shot his gigantic arrows at them. But they caught hold of the rainbow and used it to fend them off. Infuriated, the Big Monster started after them, and the Twins leaped over mountains and across deserts. The Big Monster drew closer with his immense strides. Just as his huge hands reached out to grab the Twins, there was a tremendous clap of thunder and a bolt of lightning which struck him on the head. With an earth-shaking shudder, he dropped where he stood.

The Twins cut off his head and tossed it eastward. There it now stands, known as Cabezon Peak.

Left: the giant discovers Hop o' My Thumb and his brothers in the fairy story by Perrault. This tale has the common theme of a normal —or tiny—human conquering or escaping the cruel giant by means of superior wits. In this story, the ogre decides to kill and eat the children on the spot, but his wife, of a more kindly disposition, urges him to wait until morning. During the night Hop o' My Thumb tricks the giant into killing his own daughters in their place.

Above: Jack the Giant Killer, having trapped the terrible giant in a pit, kills him with a pickaxe. This engraving comes from Routledge's Shilling Toy Book, published in 1872. The tale of brave Jack has been a popular one for over 200 years—Doctor Johnson admitted he had been reading Jack the Giant Killer, hoping that "so noble a narrative" might arouse in his own breast the soul of such enterprise.

the structures erected by the Romans during their 400-year domination of the island. To the Anglo-Saxons, the remains of Roman temples, fortifications, and aqueducts must have seemed beyond the ability of ordinary mortals. Hence, they assumed that the people who had constructed them were a race of giants.

It is interesting to note the widespread belief in such a race of giants. The book of Genesis alludes to such a people—the offspring of angels and earth women. In the Apocrypha there is a reference to a conflict between these giants and God. This myth eventually became transformed into the struggle between God and Satan and the banishment of Satan and his cohorts from Heaven, described in Milton's *Paradise Lost*.

In Norse mythology, the first living creature was a giant named Ymir. He begot both the human race as we know it and a race of frost giants. The Amerindians of northwestern United States and Canada have many legends of primeval giants with cannibalistic tendencies. Ancient Greek mythology gave us the huge Titans and the equally huge Gigantes, who had serpents for feet. British legend holds that the island was once inhabited by a race of giants who were vanquished by Brutus, the founder of the British race (no connection with the Roman Brutus). The two remaining giants of this breed, Gog and Magog, were brought to the newly established city of London, and made to serve as porters at the gate of the royal palace.

In this story we find another theme common to many myths about giants: that of the normal-sized being conquering the giant. Time and again we discover stories of the ferocious giant who terrorizes the community until a fearless and ingenious young man gets the better of him. The children's story of "Jack and the Beanstalk" is one familiar example of this theme. Somewhat more realistic is the bible story of David and Goliath.

The champion of the Philistines, Goliath is supposed to have measured "six cubits and a span" in height (about 10 feet). His coat of mail weighed 5000 shekels of brass (208 pounds), and his spear's head weighed 600 shekels. He challenged the Israelites to produce a man to fight with him as a way of deciding the outcome of the conflict between the two peoples—confident that through him the Philistines would surely win. As everyone knows, the boy David came forward and slew Goliath with one small stone from a slingshot.

An amusing variation on the theme of man as the outwitter of giants is a tale from the west of England. It seems that a Welsh giant bore a grudge against the mayor of Shrewsbury, and so decided one day to dam up the Severn River, flood that town, and drown its inhabitants. He set off with a great shovelful of earth and walked many miles. Somehow, he managed to bypass the town. Wandering around near Wellington, some 15 miles farther on, he met a cobbler who was returning from Shrewsbury. The cobbler carried a bag full of old shoes and boots to be mended. The giant called down to ask how far it was to Shrewsbury, adding that he intended to drown its citizens. The cobbler, not wishing to lose his good customers, assured the giant that he would never make it to Shrewsbury that day or even the next. "Why look at me! *I'm* just come from Shrewsbury, and I've had time to wear out all these old boots and shoes on the road since I started." So saying the cobbler showed the giant the bag filled with footwear. By now thoroughly fatigued, the giant decided to give up the project. He dropped the spadeful of earth on the ground beside him, and stomped home. The earth he dropped created the Wrekin, a prominent hill in the area.

This legend illustrates the tendency to defuse the giant myth by showing him as stupid—easily deterred by a spur-of-the-moment deception by a simple but quick-thinking craftsman.

Taken all together, the various giant legends seem to suggest that we created the giant partly in order to account for the natural world and partly to express our unconscious yearning to believe in and identify with larger-than-life humans. Having created this terrifying monster, we then had to create an accompanying myth in which we conquer the giant through our dexterity or our superior intellect.

In our complex relationship with animals, we reveal even more about our self-image, fears, and frustrations. An animal need not be fierce, strong, or poisonous to arouse strong feelings of antipathy. A common example is the domestic cat, a creature

Above: a little boy dances with a giant he has befriended in a story from a modern children's book. Unlike traditional giants, modern giants tend to be nice fellows. In this story, the giant unwittingly causes earthquakes and tornadoes by the tantrums he has because he can't whistle. The little boy teaches him how in return for a promise never to have another tantrum—and the storms stop. The adults are mystified, but the little boy knows what happened—and he isn't telling.

Right: Mau Mau terrorist leader Dedan Kimathi, who wore the leopard skin shown, was captured after a six-month manhunt through the jungles of Kenya. Kimathi was a clever and ruthless man who organized his men efficiently in the early stages of the Mau Mau movement to seize and take over European farms. But he was insecure and jealous, and his able subordinates were often exiled or summarily executed. As the Mau Mau movement began to fail, he and his remaining men retreated into the dense jungles where they fought a desperate, animal struggle for survival.

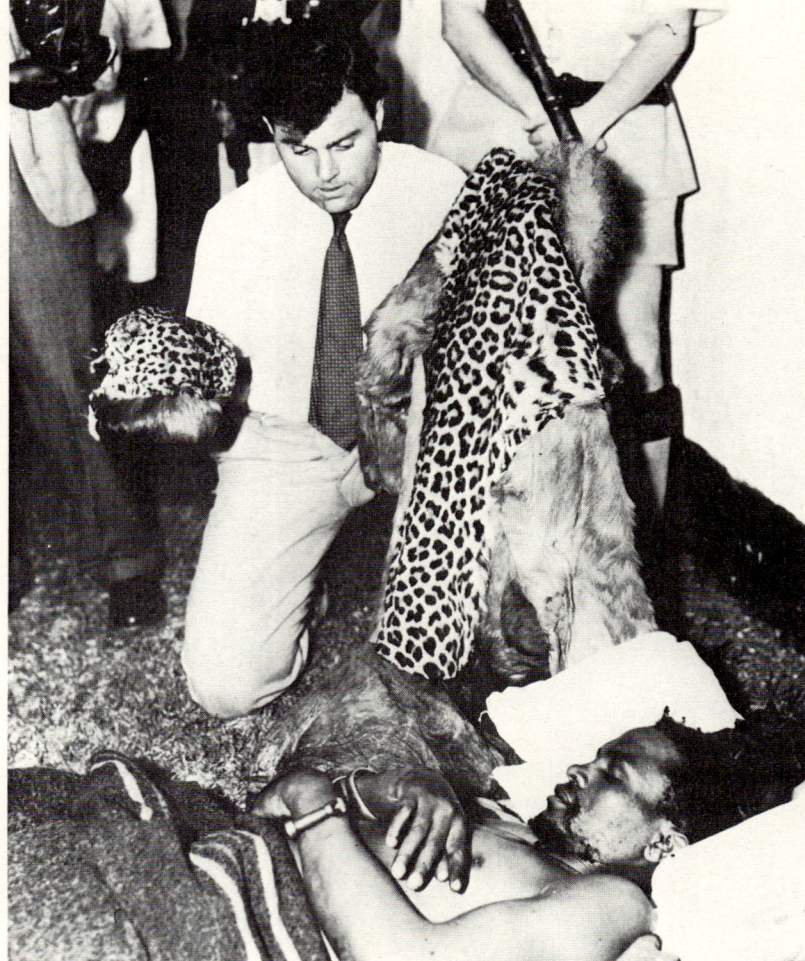

Above: clothing of a Leopard Man from the area once known as the Belgian Congo. In that area, the Leopard Society was apparently at its height during the 1930s, but dwindled away.

Above right: the terrible iron weapon forged like leopard claws.

harmless to man and generally considered beautiful, which nevertheless arouses irrational fear and loathing in some individuals.

Conversely, people often have strong feelings of identification with certain animals. In his book *The Naked Ape*, the zoologist Desmond Morris describes a study of children's preferences among animals. It revealed that the top 10 favorites were all mammals, and that all of them had one or more humanlike characteristic, such as flat faces, vertical posture as in the bear and the apes, and hair rather than feathers or scales. The lion appeared both in the 10 favorites list and in the 10 most disliked animals list. Morris suggests that the ambivalence of the response to the lion is due to its "attractive anthropomorphic characters" of expressive face and mane of hair on the one hand, and its violent predatory behavior—and great strength—on the other.

Some people identify with certain animals in an out-and-out way. Historically there is good reason for this. Primitive man throughout the world adopted animal disguise in order to hunt successfully. In Africa, a continent that must have seen some of the first and fiercest clashes between human and beast, animals assumed a special and lasting importance in African societies' approach to the supernatural. The hunter depended on the hunted, and man respected the strength of the animal to such an extent that he tried to form special bonds with it, and even to emulate it.

Some African tribes developed the concept of the "bush soul"—an animal with which a man identifies so completely that the two are one, inseparable and interchangeable. "The theory of an external soul deposited in an animal appears to be very prevalent in West Africa," wrote Sir James Frazer in *The Golden Bough*. "Every wizard is believed at initiation to unite his life with that of some particular wild animal." This bond was forged by means of a "blood brotherhood." By the ritual mingling of their blood, the sorcerer was believed to acquire the animal's strength and apparent invulnerability, while the animal became his familiar, ready to do his bidding and swift to kill those who offended his master. Frazer adds that such a blood relationship was never formed with a domestic animal, "but always a dangerous and wild beast, such as a leopard."

Identification with leopards produced a sinister result: societies of leopard men. Dressed in leopard skins and wielding three-pronged knives that simulate the claw marks of the leopard, these bands of killers terrorized the population of West Africa. Most of their victims were women. After killing the woman by slashing her jugular vein, the leopard man would cut off her breasts and eat them. This bloodthirsty cult has endured into the 20th century. In 1938, 400 local women were killed around Wamba in the Belgian Congo, now Zaire. One leopard man when caught took the police to 38 dead female bodies, all with their breasts cut off.

Africa also had its panther men who, like the leopard men and the werewolves of Europe, were believed to transform themselves into animals to kill and devour parts of their victims. During a visit to West Central Africa in the late 1920s, American author William B. Seabrook talked at length with an African clerk who had been caught wearing a panther skin with iron claws after murdering a girl on a jungle path. Tei, as the clerk was called, insisted that he really *became* a panther on such occasions, that the disguise was merely an aid to his transformation, and that being a panther was "nicer than being a man." As Seabrook pointed out, when Tei leaped howling from a tree in his panther garb, and tore the girl's throat with his claws, he must certainly have seemed like a real panther to her—as he did to those who witnessed the killing.

Another kind of power that we have desired throughout our history is the power to live forever. Among most people this has taken the form of religious beliefs in the immortaility of the soul, and perhaps a life in some other body after the death of the earthly body. In the myth of the vampire this desire appears in a

The Leopard Men

The sun was hot, but the green depths of the jungle were cool. The unseen inhabitants made their familiar squeaking and rustling animal noises as the girl walked along the path to her home. But suddenly there was a new sound—a wild cry. If the victim had had a chance to think before the cruel claws tore out her throat, she might have thought it was a leopard. She would have been wrong. The creature who killed her, and slashed off her breasts and ate them, was a man. His action was that of a beast.

He was one of the terrible leopard men, ritualistic killers who wear leopard skins and use steel claws. They belong to forbidden secret societies with roots in ancient pagan belief, and they claim they share the leopard's strength. They kill and mutilate, melt into the jungle, and emerge only to kill again. During much of their life they are ordinary men. But when they don their leopard-skin disguises, they become like the beasts they venerate, predators of the jungles. They keep everyone in fear.

The authorities try to stamp the cult out. Men are arrested and executed by the courts to stop the worst cases and serve as an example to the others. Still, in the jungles the leopards lurk. Some are animals. Some are men.

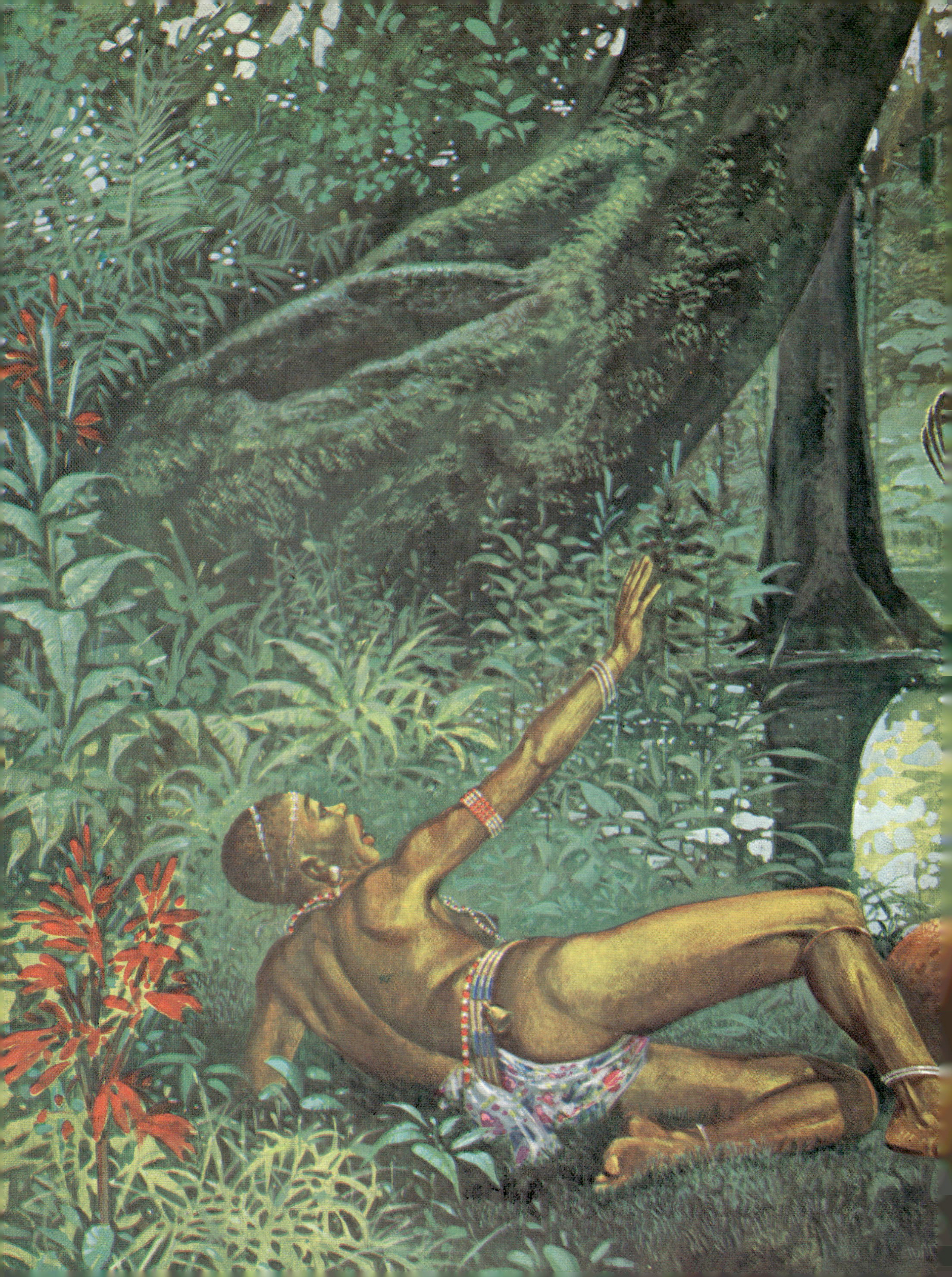

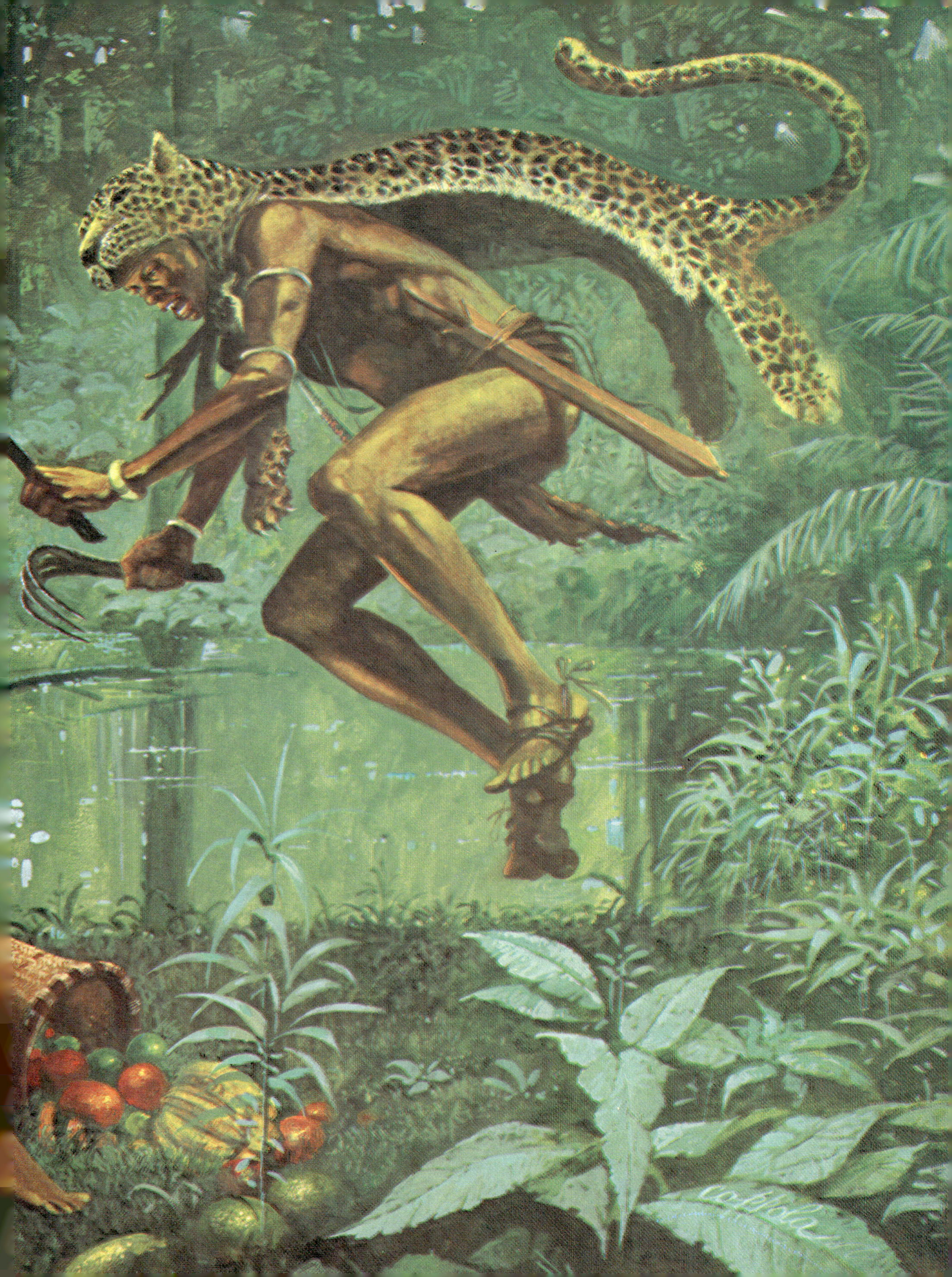

Left: Vlad Tepes—Vlad the Impaler—who ruled over Walachia, now part of modern Romania, as Vlad V in the 15th century. He signed his letters Vlad Dracula, which can be translated roughly as "son of the dragon, or devil." His father had been called "Dracul" because he used a dragon on his shield. Vlad Tepes' cruelties shocked even his own contemporaries, used to a fairly brutal level of warfare and punishment. His ingenuity in devising prolonged and agonizing deaths for those he considered his opponents was remarkable. He was a military genius, however, and his stand against the Islamic Turks convinced his own people that he was hero, in spite of all.

grotesque and perverted form. The vampire is able to preserve his own body by feeding on the blood of the living. Of course, the tellers of vampire tales profess abhorrence of such an idea, and those who really believe in vampires are genuinely terrified of them. Yet, to some people the idea has its attractions. The recently discovered fact that as many pyschotics identify with Count Dracula as identify with Napoleon suggests that this parasitical form of power is as alluring to some disturbed mentalities as military and politcal power is to others.

With some disturbed people the vampire fantasy is not a matter of imagining themselves to be Count Dracula, but of having a real pathological thirst for blood. For such people, as for the supernatural vampires who rise from their graves, the sucking of blood is a way of revitalizing themselves, if only symbolically or psychologically.

Blood has always had great significance for us apart from its obvious physical importance. Many people have identified blood with the soul—clearly an idea drawn from the fact that if a wounded person loses too much blood he will die. Some peoples ritually drink the blood of certain animals in the belief that by doing so they will acquire the qualities they admire in the animal. In early times, for example, Norwegian hunters drank the blood of the bear in order to acquire its great strength.

Many people suppose that the human vampire was named after the vampire bat, but in fact the naming was the other way around. The vampire bat, a native of Mexico and South America, was not discovered by scientists until the 19th century, long after the human vampire had become part of European mythology. The bat does not actually suck the blood of its victims—usually cattle or humans—but laps up the blood with its tongue after having pierced the skin with its teeth.

The vampire bat represents vampirism in a purely natural form. The bat simply requires a diet of blood in order to live. Of course, its behavior is dangerous because it can spread rabies. But the sinister and repulsive character of its attack is largely projected onto it by humans—partly as a reaction to the animal's ugly looks, which also make perfectly harmless bats cause a shudder, and partly because of associations with human vampirism.

Leaving aside extreme cases such as people who have a taste for blood and psychotics who are convinced they are Count Dracula, we are still confronted with the enormous popularity of vampire stories—and the popularity of the vampire himself—among perfectly sane people. The appeal of the stories can be explained on one level as the fun of being frightened. Any horror story, no matter how badly written, is almost guaranteed a certain amount of success. But the appeal of Dracula and his kind lies deeper. The desire for immortality, supported by the occasional discovery of a healthy looking corpse, may have created the vampire myth, but the continued appeal of the fictional vampire has more to do with sex than with immortality.

Any vampire story or film contains an obvious sexual element. Dracula's victim is usually a beautiful young woman; female vampires go for attractive men. The setting is usually the victim's bedroom. The attack itself is a perversion of the harmless love bite—or, from a different point of view, the love bite is a harmless version of the vampire's attack. In any case, the sexual connotations are clear. Moreover, they are clearly sadomasochistic—the vampire dominates, wounds, and eventually kills in an erotic situation. This seems to strike a responsive chord in many readers and film addicts. The prevalence of such sexual feelings can be inferred from the enormous amount of fan mail the actors who play Dracula receive from women.

It is also interesting to note the popularity of vampire stories in late 19th century England. In that repressed society the adventure, violence, and spookiness of the stories were played up, while the sexual element was played down. Even so, the sexual aspect was still very much present, and could be unconsciously enjoyed by respectable readers under the impression that they were just reading a good horror story.

By the end of the 19th century, some of the less socially acceptable aspects of the human character were beginning to be recognized—thanks largely to the pioneering work of Sigmund Freud. Today's educated adult takes for granted such concepts as infantile sexuality, and the conflicts within our conscious and unconscious minds. Clinical psychology has even shown us actual cases of multiple personality in which two or more distinct personalities inhabit the same body, coming out at different times. The true story of *The Three Faces of Eve* is such a case. Cases of more than one personality are apparently the result of conflicting elements within a person's psyche. The conflicts make the psyche split into separate personalities so that the contradictory drives can be expressed. Yet the complexity of human nature has been recognized by intelligent writers in every age. The most intriguing story of multiple personality, in fact, is a work of fiction written by Robert Louis Stevenson in the late 19th century.

The Strange Case of Dr. Jekyll and Mr. Hyde is, first of all, a superb horror story. As a horror story it lies roughly in the werewolf tradition inasmuch as the leading character had the power to transform himself into a dangerous and evil creature, altering his appearance and even his size in the process.

The physical differences between the respectable Dr. Jekyll and his fiendish other self Mr. Hyde have psychological significance. This is apart from the need of the writer to make them appear totally different to the other characters in the story. Hyde's smaller size and lightness of step seem to suggest the "easiness" of evil. At the same time there is the implication that Jekyll's stature and his heavier step indicate his morality. The hairy wild

Above: Vlad Tepes, cheerfully enjoying a meal, contemplates the final suffering of a forest of his victims impaled on stakes.

man theme appears in the descriptions of the hands, which says, "... the hand of Henry Jekyll ... was professional in shape and size; it was large, firm, white and comely. But the hand which I now saw, clearly enough in the yellow light of a mid-London morning, lying half-shut on the bedclothes, was lead, corded, knuckly, of a dusky pallor, and thickly shaded with a swart growth of hair." Some film versions of the story have shown Hyde with a hairy face as well, giving him a strong resemblance to the werewolf. But the author points out several times in the story that Hyde's face is not repulsive in any physical way. "'He's an extraordinary-looking man,' says one of the characters, 'and yet I really can name nothing out of the way.'" "He gave an impression of deformity without any namable malformation." It is the expression in Hyde's face, and particularly in his "displeasing smile" that makes other people react to him with revulsion. Jekyll comments on this when talking about his second

Right: self-styled law by the Ku Klux Klan on a hot summer night, with the bodies of the lynched men hanging limply over the heads of the satisfied mob.

Below: Goya in 1793 recognized the unreasoning wildness that simmers in any uncontrolled crowd of people. Here in a painting of a Spanish Ash Wednesday ritual called "Burial of the Sardine," a crowd heaves with barely contained wanton excitement.

Above: this gory Japanese print depicts a torture scene in which the torturer's unnatural calm makes her actions more horrible. It seems to prove that the worst monster of all is the human one.

personality. "... none could come near to me at first without a visible misgiving of the flesh. This, as I take it, was because all human beings, as we meet them, are commingled out of good and evil: and Edward Hyde, alone, in the ranks of mankind, was pure evil."

It is as a psychological thriller that the book achieves its greatness. Jekyll brings about his own destruction through his effort to separate the good and evil aspects of his own personality. He had wanted to do this to relieve the tension he experiences in trying to conquer his moral weaknesses and become the entirely serious upright gentleman he thinks he should be.

The fatal flaw in Jekyll's experiment is that he first tries the separation of good and evil when the baser aspects of his character are dominant. "At that time my virtue slumbered; my evil, kept awake by ambition, was alert and swift to seize the occasion; and the thing that was projected was Edward Hyde." When Hyde swallows the mixture Jekyll has concocted, he is transformed back into Jekyll—but it is the same old Jekyll with all his vexing inner conflicts. Because Hyde—the abstraction of Jekyll's unconscious and repressed aggressive tendencies—is "all of a piece," he is stronger than the uncertain Jekyll. Gradually Hyde destroys Jekyll.

Within six months of its publication in 1886 the book had sold 40,000 copies. It was the subject of dinner conversations and Sunday sermons. With its moral tone to offset the violence, it could hardly miss, but its popularity endures in our less moralistic age. It has been filmed several times, and no doubt someone will one day make a musical out of it.

In the years since *Dr. Jekyll and Mr. Hyde* was published, psychologists have approached the problem of our contradictory nature in a variety of ways, and have come up with a variety of explanations. For the average person, however, the problem remains something of a mystery—a mystery that continually shows new aspects of itself. There may be plausible sociological and psychological reasons why, for example, a Mafia killer or the commandant of a Nazi concentration camp can at the same time be an affectionate husband and father, but this seeming inconsistency still fascinates and appalls us.

The Bloodthirsty Countess

On the infamous roll of human monsters, the beautiful Countess Elisabeth Bathory of Transylvania holds a prominent position. In her blood-spattered castle torture chamber, the Countess—often in ecstatic transports of sexual pleasure—delighted in the slow torture and murder of 650 girls, sinking her teeth into their bodies and drinking their blood in the desperate effort to retain her youthful beauty. Her women accomplices scoured the countryside to find young virgins for her pleasure. It was the careless dumping of four bodies —drained of their blood—outside the castle that led the terrified local people to denounce the terrible Countess to the King.

She was truly extraordinary. Her immense cruelty seemed to be a separate part of her life. While her letters express conventional religious sentiments, she apparently never applied any sense of right or wrong to her blood rituals.

In 1611 her accomplices were brought to trial, found guilty, and cruelly executed. The Countess herself, protected by powerful relatives, was not tried. She was imprisoned in a small room whose windows and doors were walled up. There, after three years of icy blackness, the Vampire Lady died.

Many people who believe themselves incapable of inflicting pain on another person are content, and even eager, to see pain inflicted. The public executions that entertained our ancestors have largely disappeared, but the mangled bodies from a plane crash will attract hordes of horror seekers from miles around. The publishers of the American tabloid *The National Enquirer* know what they are doing by publicizing the most nauseating atrocities in huge type on the front page. The newspaper sells. When readers gasp and cry, "How awful!" do they really mean what they say? Or is there something in the story that secretly appeals to them? It is interesting to note that the trailers for films containing violence often consist mainly of the violent scenes. The brutality is assumed to be the most attractive aspect of the film—and this assumption is more than likely made on the basis of market research. A would-be suicide, hesitating on the ledge of a tall building, will attract a large crowd of the curious, and often there are a few who urge him on with "Jump! Jump!"

Of course, the mob as a monster is almost taken for granted. Riots do not surprise us anymore, and in any case we can account for them by explanations of pent-up resentment, racial hatred, fear—motivations that may not be excused, but may at least be understood.

Understanding fails us, however, when we approach stories of real human monsters—people for whom the infliction of pain on others is actually a source of pleasure. One such person was Vlad Tepes, ruler of Walachia (now part of Romania) from 1431 to 1477. He was partly famed for his courage in battle. When Vlad won a great victory over the non-Christian Turks, the bells of Christendom rang out in celebration as far away as the Island of Rhodes.

Vlad was known as Dracula, meaning devil or dragon. This was the name used by Bram Stoker for the bloodthirsty Count of his famous novel, but Vlad himself was not a vampire. Compared to the real Dracula's crimes, the bloodsucking habit of his fictional namesake seems like playfulness. It was Vlad's pleasure to impale his enemies on wooden stakes. "Tepes" means "the impaler." On one occasion, the triumphant Vlad impaled 20,000 of his enemies. The slightest provocation would serve as an excuse. After one victory Vlad and some guests sat down to dine, surrounded by his slowly dying victims. When one guest dared to comment on the screams and the stench, he was immediately impaled on a particularly tall stake so that he would be above the smells to which he had so unwisely objected.

In Gilles de Rais or Retz, a Marshal of France who lived at the same time as Vlad, we find a more complex character. Not only a brave soldier who fought alongside Joan of Arc, de Rais was also a cultured and apparently pious man. In 1440, however, he was brought to trial and accused of the murder of some 140 children. Moreover, it was charged that the murders were done with the utmost cruelty, and accompanied by sexual perversions. A contemporary account states: "The most monstrously depraved imagination never could have conceived what the trial reveals." Among other things he was charged with having sat on the bowels of a dying boy while drinking his blood. He apparently had an obsession with blood, and ordered his servant to stab the

Above: Gilles de Laval, Baron de Rais. A wealthy and powerful man, he was brave and courageous, cultured and pious in his public life. In his lurid private life, he had 140 children—selected for their beauty— murdered in the course of his monstrous sexual perversity.

Above right: the death of Gilles de Rais by strangling and burning.

Below: the Marquis de Sade, who also found sexual pleasure in inflicting pain on the object of his desire. His novels fully describe his vicious fantasies in which monstrous cruelties occur.

children in the jugular vein so that their blood would shoot over him. After being tortured himself, de Rais confessed publicly to all the charges, and begged forgiveness of the parents of his victims. He was burnt after first being strangled to death—an act of mercy granted to him for not recanting his confession.

Nearer to our own time is the case of Fritz Haarman, the Hanover Vampire. He was given this name because he killed so many of his victims with one fatal bite in the throat. He then cut them up and either ate the flesh himself or sold it as sausage meat. This was just after World War I when meat was scarce and butchers were none too fussy. Haarman was brought to trial in 1924 for the murder of 50 boys.

John George Haigh, the English acid-bath murderer hung in 1949, is reputed to have been a vampire. He himself claimed that he drank the blood of his victims, although this claim may have been an attempt to escape hanging by being certified insane. Basil Copper, one biographer of Haigh, says: "There is no doubt in my mind that John George Haigh was a vampire in the classical tradition, possibly the only true monster in this field in the 20th century."

Still alive in prison are two of the most infamous murderers of

Above: the headline that first appeared after Haigh's arrest.

Above: John George Haigh, the successful English confidence man who claimed he had murdered nine people mainly to drink their blood, but whose bank account grew in size after each killing. He disposed of the dead bodies in enormous water barrels filled with sulfuric acid. Although he pleaded insanity as his defense, he was convicted and hung.

Left: the 12-year-old Haigh as a choirboy in Wakefield Cathedral.

Right: Peter Kürten acted so normally that when he was arrested as "the Düsseldorf Monster" his neighbors were sure there had been a mistake. He confessed calmly to some 60 acts of arson, theft, rape, and savage murder. His first murder was the drowning of two playmates when he was only a child himself.

modern times, Ian Brady and Myra Hindley. Called the "Moors Murderers," this couple tortured and killed a number of children and recorded their screams on tape for future listening pleasure.

These horrifying examples of sadism bring us to the man who gave us the very word for such acts: the Marquis de Sade. De Sade never performed mass torture on the scale practiced by Vlad the Impaler, but this was due to lack of opportunity rather than squeamishness. De Sade's belief was that sexual pleasure not only can be achieved, but in fact is best achieved, through inflicting pain. He developed this theme at wearisome length and in excruciating detail in novels such as *Justine* and *120 Days of Sodom*.

During the period of his life when he was not in prison for his actions, he enacted his fantasies with various victims, some unwilling, but some surprisingly willing. His last years were spent in the asylum of Charenton where he was accompanied by the young actress Marie-Constance Quesnet.

A philosophy of a kind underlies de Sade's hideous practices. In an article for *Horizon* magazine entitled "Our Bedfellow, the Marquis de Sade," writer Anthony Burgess summarizes this philosophy. According to de Sade, he says, there is no God, but there is a goddess who is Nature. "We are wholly subject to her, being part of her, and we must fulfill in our own actions her most terrible and monstrous impulses. Nature is creative... but she is also destructive, reveling in earthquakes, in storms, floods, volcanic eruptions. But this destructive urge is in the service of creating new forms of life. A huge melting pot is always on the boil, and her old creations are thrown into it, to reemerge transmogrified. The devices of cruelty that man develops are a manifestation of quite impersonal, or rather prepersonal energy. Personal guilt is irrelevant, since the first law of life is to accept the world as it is."

Burgess points out that de Sade's image of man is, unfortunately, well supported by actual events. "In the depraved France of the prerevolutionary era, in the ghastly actions of the Terror, Sade could see ample evidence that man's appetites for pleasure were most satisfyingly fulfilled through the exercise of power and cruelty. His own private orgies, the extravagant fantasies of his books—what were these but reduced reflections of the conduct of the great world outside the château?"

De Sade's contemporary Jean Jacques Rousseau believed that man's depravity was due to the corrupting influence of society, and that he would be virtuous if he lived in a "state of nature." Returning explorers who brought tales of primitive tribes that not only fought each other like Europeans, but that also practiced cannibalism, shot a hole in this comforting theory of the noble savage. Savagery, it seems, is a kind of endemic disease that breaks out in various forms wherever humans live—in the forests of wild New Guinea as well as in the laboratories of academic New Haven.

We have explored the unpleasant truth that man is *potentially* a monster. As if this were not cause enough for despair, writer Oscar Kiss Maerth has recently advanced a theory that man is *essentially* a monster.

In his book *The Beginning Was The End*, he says that the

A Modern Vampire

Kuno Hofmann was a deaf-mute German laborer, a cripple who had spent nine years in mental hospitals. (He escaped 12 times.) According to the public prosecutors, he was perfectly sane and fully accountable for his actions. But his actions were extraordinary by any normal standards.

Between 1971 and 1972, the police have records of at least 35 occasions when Hofmann forced entry into graveyards and mortuaries near his home in Nürnberg. He made copies of the keys to the local cemetery where he stole among the tombstones, heading unerringly for the fresh graves. He chose his victims from death notices in the newspapers, and methodically made his way to a new corpse, stabbing into it with razor blades or a knife. Sometimes he cut the head off; sometimes he tore the heart out. Always he drank the blood. From his prison cell, Hofmann explained matter-of-factly that he did it to make himself "good-looking and strong.

In May 1972 Hofmann decided on a new approach. He found two young lovers in a car, shot them dead, and drank the blood from their wounds. It made him happy, he told police, adding that the young and pretty girl had been much better than the women in the graveyards.

141

evolution of man was due to cannibalism. He bases his argument partly on evidence that cannibalism was once practiced by humans in all parts of the world. According to Maerth's theory, this practice began among man's ape forebears who mainly ate the brain, as do the few head hunters still found today in some areas. The brain of humans was first prized by our forebears because it increased sexual activity, says Maerth. Only much later was it discovered that eating brain increased intelligence, and that this increased intelligence was permanent and hereditary. Various other biological changes, notably our loss of body hair, are attributed by the author to the chemical imbalance resulting from the eating of the pituitary gland of our own kind thousands of years ago.

Without going further into the details of this unusual theory, we may consider its fundamental meaning. It says that man did not evolve naturally, as modern science teaches, either accidentally or as part of a divine plan. He is a freak of his own making. All of his actions—not only his cruelty to his own kind and his ruthless exploitation of the natural world, but even his great intellectual and artistic achievements—are the actions of a monster.

Whatever arguments a scientist or a theologian might use to refute this theory, we are still left with the nagging thought that there is something monstrous about our species. There is more evil in the world than our minds can cope with. Most people probably try to ignore it as much as possible and concentrate on the mundane problems of living. Others devote themselves to humanitarian pursuits, and many of them succeed in curing some of the symptoms of the disease of savagery, if not the disease itself.

It may be that the supernatural monsters in which many of us believe are another way of coping with this all-pervasive evil. Subconsciously we may want to give our fears a form that is different from the real horrors we read of in the papers or, in earlier times, saw performed in the market square, and is in some sense more manageable. A vampire, terrifying though he may be, can be dealt with in a variety of approved ways. The zombie and the werewolf, as well as the diminutive malicious fairy and the blustering giant, express those evil tendencies we fear in ourselves and in others. By giving them a name and a shape, however grotesque, we get the illusion of having some degree of control over them.

The pathetic man in Stoke-on-Trent who died from choking on a clove of garlic intended to ward off vampires may really have been afraid of something else. Demitrious Myiciura had seen his native Poland overrun by the Germans in World War II. His farm was appropriated by the invaders, and his family was killed. Many people have survived similar experiences with their mental balance relatively undisturbed, but in Myiciura's case, the senseless violence of the war may have been more than he could stand. An individual is virtually helpless against such a juggernaut of evil. Who knows where it may strike again? No evasive action, no preventive measures are possible. But Myiciura did know how to deter vampires. They were an evil against which he could protect himself. So he believed in that evil.

Above: Brazilians eating human flesh. Although cannibalism was once practiced in Europe, as in all parts of the world, it was never accepted as part of the social order in contrast to other areas. Anthropologists usually give three reasons for the start of cannibalism: as the basis of a religious ceremony; as part of a magic ritual; and as an experiment in diet at some period when no other kind of meat was available and the grain diet had palled.

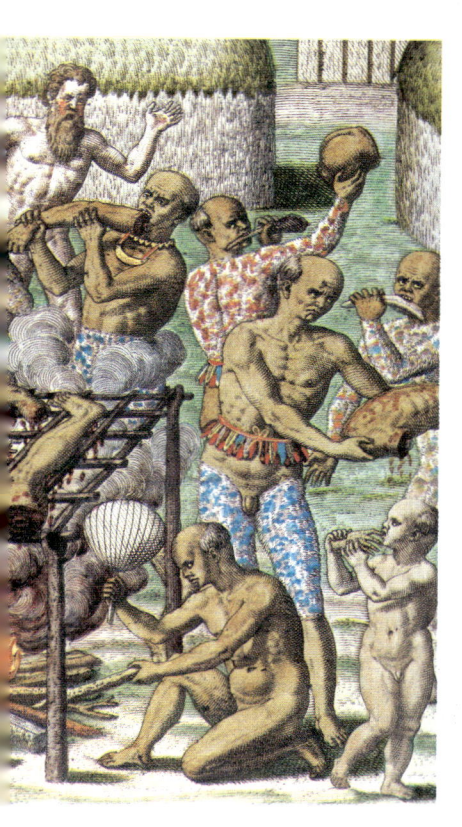

Right: *Satan Devouring His Son*, a depiction of cannibalism by Francisco de Goya. Western minds generally view cannibalism as the ultimate in bestiality. Yet it continues to fascinate people just as many monstrous aspects of human behavior fascinates them. It seems that our bewitchment with the monster is a bewitchment with our own darker selves— and our subconscious.

Picture Credits

Key to picture positions: (T) top (C) center (B) bottom; and in combinations, e.g. (TR) top right (BL) bottom left

2	Le Musée Adam Mickiewicz: La Société Historique et Littéraire, Paris/Photo J.-L. Charmet
4	Staatsbibliothek, Berlin
6	*Radio Times* Hulton Picture Library
7	National Film Archive
8	Munch-Museet, Oslo Kommunes Kunstsamlinger
9	Photo J.-L. Charmet, Paris
10(L)	Photos Allan Ballard/Camera Press Ltd.
10(BR)	Photo Mike Busselle © Aldus Books, courtesy Bruce Wightman and The Dracula Society
11(T)	Photo Mike Busselle © Aldus Books
11(B)	Courtesy Daniel Farson
12	Verwaltung der Staatlichen Schlösser und Gärten, Berlin
13(TR)	Press Association Ltd.
13(B)	B.B.C. copyright photo
14	Le Musée Adam Mickiewicz: La Société Historique et Littéraire, Paris/Photo J.-L. Charmet
15	Photo Alan Meak © Marshall Cavendish Ltd.
16(T)	Abbey Museum, Barnet/Michael Holford Library photo
16(B)	The MacQuitty International Collection
17	Roger Wood, London
18	Aldus Archives
19(TL)	Michael Holford Library photo
19(TR)	Aldus Archives
19(B)	Mary Evans Picture Library
20(L)	Mary Evans Picture Library
20(R), 21	Colin Maher
22(T)	Mary Evans Picture Library
22(BL)	The Bettmann Archive
22(BR)	Camera Press Ltd.
23-25	Gianetto Coppola © Aldus Books
26-27	Aldus Archives
28-29	Mary Evans Picture Library
30	Aldus Archives
31(T)	The Bettmann Archive
31(B)	Bibliothèque Nationale, Paris
32(B)	Aldus Archives
33	Musée Wiertz/Musées Royaux des Beaux-Arts, Bruxelles
34	Aldus Archives
35(T)(BR)	Mary Evans Picture Library
35(BL)	Photo J.-L. Charmet, Paris
36	Snark International
37-39	Bruno Elittori © Aldus Books
40	Photo J.-L. Charmet, Paris
41	Le Musée Adam Mickiewicz: La Société Historique et Littéraire, Paris/Photo J.-L. Charmet
42(T)	Snark International
42(B)	*Radio Times* Hulton Picture Library
43	National Film Archive
44-45	Snark International
46	Aldus Archives
47	Photo Mike Busselle
48	© Aldus Books The Mansell Collection
49	Aldus Archives
50-51	Photos Mike Busselle © Aldus Books
52(L)	Aldus Archives
52(R)	Photo Mas, Barcelona
53-54	Aldus Archives
55(T)	Mary Evans Picture Library
56-57	Aldus Archives
58	Photo J.-L. Charmet, Paris
59-61	Brian Lewis © Aldus Books
62	Photo J.-L. Charmet, Paris
63(T)	Aldus Archives
63(B)	Reproduced by permission of the Trustees of the British Museum
64	*Radio Times* Hulton Picture Library
65(TR)	Mary Evans Picture Library
65(B)	Ronald Grant
66	William Seabrook, *The Magic Island*, George G. Harrap & Co. Ltd., London, 1929
67	Romano Cagnoni, London
68	*Radio Times* Hulton Picture Library
69	Kurt Bachmann
70	Courtesy Daniel Farson
71(T)	Romano Cagnoni, London
71(B)	Bill Hamilton/Camera Press Ltd.
72(T), 73	Jean Luc Magneron/Sygma
74-75	Romano Cagnoni, London
76(T)	J. Cooke/Photo Researchers Inc.
76(B)	Romano Cagnoni, London
77	Aldus Archives
78	Guido Mangold/Camera Press Ltd.
79(R)	Hasse Persson/Camera Press Ltd.
80(L)	Kryn Taconis/Magnum
80(R)	From *Tell My Horse* by Zora Neale Hurston. © 1938 by Zora Neale Hurston. © renewed 1966 by Joel Hurston and John C. Hurston. Reproduced by permission of J. B. Lippincott Company
81-83	Gianetto Coppola © Aldus Books
84(T)	Jean Luc Magneron/Sygma
84(B)	National Film Archive
86	Picturepoint, London
87	Sotheby's, Belgravia/Photo Philippe Garner
88	Brotherton Collection, University of Leeds
89	Picturepoint, London
90-92	Aldus Archives
93(R)	Derek Witty/George Rainbird Ltd.
94	The Tate Gallery, London/Picturepoint, London
95	Aldus Archives
96	Brotherton Collection, University of Leeds
98-99	From the collection of Peter Haining
100(L)	Aldus Archives
100-101(TC)	The Mansell Collection
101(R), 102(L)	Aldus Archives
102(R)	Derek Witty/George Rainbird Ltd.
103	Photo Derek Witty/George Rainbird Ltd. With permission of Methuen Children's Books Ltd. publishers of *Household Tales by the Brothers Grimm*, illustrated by Mervyn Peake
104	Derek Witty/George Rainbird Ltd.
106	Edgar Rice Burroughs, Inc.
107	Bibliothèque Ecole Beaux-Arts, Paris/Giraudon
108(T)	Victoria & Albert Museum, London/Photo David Swann © Aldus Books
108(B)	Syndication International Ltd., London
109-111	Gino d'Achille © Aldus Books
112(L)	*Radio Times* Hulton Picture Library
112(R)	Rudyard Kipling, *The Jungle Book*, by permission of Macmillan London Ltd.; Doubleday & Company Inc., New York
113	Edgar Rice Burroughs, Inc.
115(L)	Zdenek Burian, Prague/Dilia
115(R)	Stadtbibliothek, Nürnberg
116(T)	Bodleian Library, Oxford
116(B)	Photo J.-L. Charmet, Paris
117(T)	Photo Mike Busselle © Aldus Books
117(B)	T. Schneiders/ZEFA
118	Kunsthistorische Museum, Wien
119(B)	K. Scholz/ZEFA
120(T)	Aldus Archives
120(B)	The Metropolitan Museum of Art, New York, Gift of J. Pierpont Morgan, 1917
121(T)	British Library Board
122(T)	Bayerische Staatsbibliothek, München
122(B)	Mary Evans Picture Library
123	Bilderdienst Süddeutscher Verlag
124	Ullstein Bilderdienst, Berlin
125	Photo J.-L. Charmet, Paris
126	Victoria & Albert Museum, London/Michael Holford Library photo
127(TL)	Ullstein Bilderdienst, Berlin
127(TR)	Aldus Archives
128(L)	The Mansell Collection
128(R)	Derek Witty/George Rainbird Ltd.
129	Illustration © 1972 by Philippe Fix, from *The Book of Giant Stories* by David L. Harrison. With permission of McGraw-Hill Book Co. and Jonathan Cape Limited, London, 1974
130(T)	Camera Press Ltd.
130(B)	Royal Museum of Central Africa, Tervuren, Belgium
131-133	Gianetto Coppola © Aldus Books
134(T)	Kunsthistorische Museum, Wien/Photo Meyer K.G.
134(B)	Aldus Archives
136	Ac. S. Fernando/Giraudon
137(T)	Black American News Service, Detroit
137(B), 138	Photos J.-L. Charmet, Paris
139(TL)(B)	The Mansell Collection
139(TR)	Snark International
140(BL)	Syndication International Ltd., London
140(BR)	Bilderdienst Süddeutscher Verlag
141	Press Association Ltd.
142	J. E. Bulloz
143(R)	Museo del Prado, Madrid/Giraudon

Monsters and Mythic Beasts

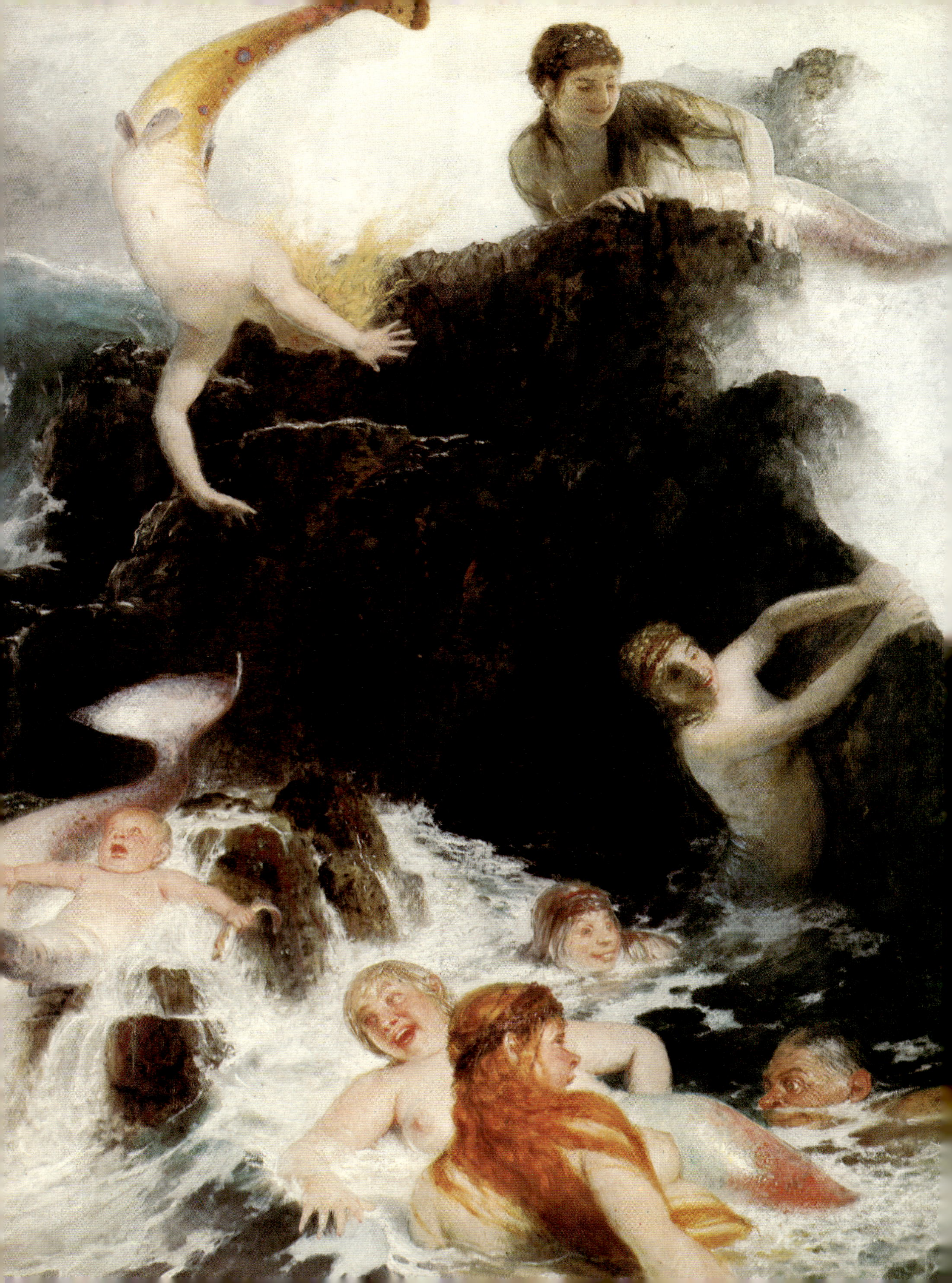

Monsters and Mythic Beasts
by Angus Hall

Aldus Books · Jupiter Books

Series Coordinator: John Mason
Design Director: Günter Radtke
Picture Editor: Peter Cook
Editor: Sally Burningham
Copy Editor: Mitzi Bales
Research: Marian Pullen
General Consultant: Beppie Harrison

SBN 490 00335 4

© 1975 Aldus Books Limited. London

First published in the United Kingdom
in 1975 by Aldus Books Limited
17 Conway Street. London W1P 6BS

Distributed by Jupiter Books
167 Hermitage Road. London N4 1LZ

Printed and bound in Italy by
Amilcare Pizzi S.p.A.
Cinisello Balsamo (Milano)

**Frontispiece: mermaids and mermen at play in the sea.
Above: the Greek hero Jason encounters a sea monster.**

EDITORIAL CONSULTANTS:

COLIN WILSON
DR. CHRISTOPHER EVANS

When we are children the world seems infinitely wide and filled with endless wonders. As we grow older we like to believe that science has taken command of our environment, that the living creatures are classified and the trackless wastes mapped. However, there is much of our earth that is barely known, and from such mysterious places come persistent stories of fantastic beasts—some of which have been told since man was man. A few, like the dragon, the mermaid and the unicorn, seem clearly fictional. But what about huge sea serpents, giant Bigfeet or Yeti, monsters of the lakes? Have a few prehistoric creatures survived in unexplored pockets of inaccessible places to this very day? The evidence is both abundant and curiously mixed. Will we ever have all the answers? Do we want to?

1

Dragons in Myth and Mind

The dragon is probably the most widely known of all monsters and mythic beasts. For centuries, all over the world, it has played a role in art, in myth, and in religion. St. George and the dragon is only one of many legends about this symbolic creature. One version of the St. George myth has it that the people of the North African city of Silene, in what is now Libya, had lived for a long time in fear of an evil dragon outside their gates. At first they had placated it each day with several sheep, but soon it was demanding both a man and a sheep. Then, not content with this, it wanted more delectable flesh and insisted on the sacrifice of young

The dragon is a fine and fabulous beast, flicking his reptilian tail far and wide across the world, at home on the banners of a medieval army riding gallantly into battle or in the splendors of the sumptuous Chinese courts. Above: a fake dragon probably dating from the 16th century when such fakes often appeared in Europe. This one more than likely started life as a harmless little tree lizard found in Java and known as a "flying dragon." Being only about four inches long, it was said to be a "dragon baby." The wings would be parts of bats' wings cunningly sewn into place. Right: the romantic view of St. George rescuing the beautiful princess from the dragon was a popular subject of paintings in the Middle Ages. This one was by a 15th-century Flemish artist.

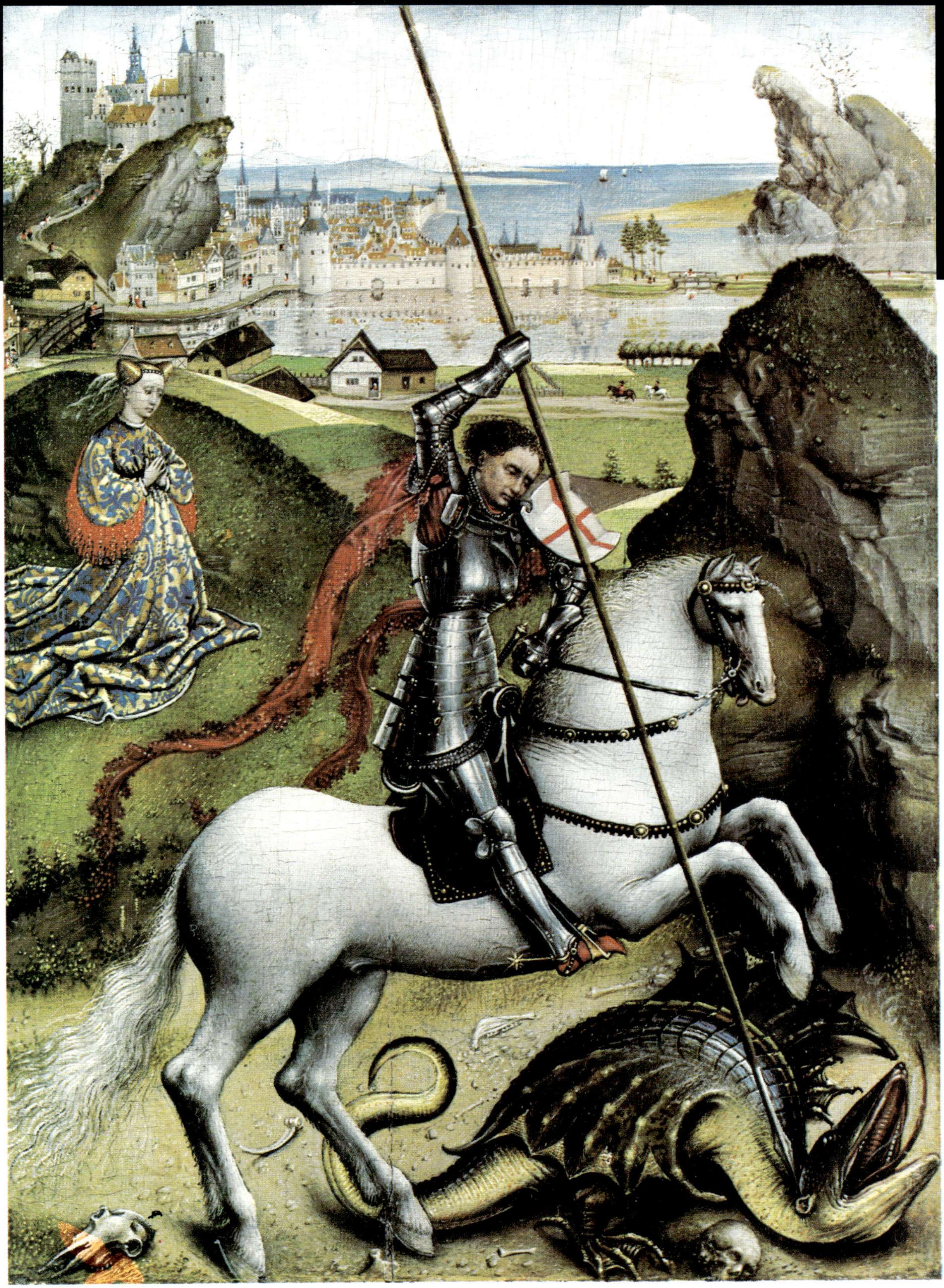

"Universal symbolic significance"

Below: a chapel altar painting by Albrecht Dürer in 1505 shows St. George with the dragon he slew. In this legend, St. George's killing of the dragon is symbolic of Christianity's superiority to Paganism and victory over evil.

virgins. The king decided that the young girls of the city should draw lots each day to determine who would be the next victim. One day to his horror the lot fell to his daughter, the beautiful Princess Sabra. In vain the king pleaded with his subjects for her life. They were adamant. He must abide by the rule that he himself had made.

Sick at heart, the king saw his beloved daughter led off to the spot where the dragon was eagerly waiting. But at that moment a strange knight appeared on horseback. It was George of Lydda, on his way to see the Roman Emperor Diocletian and plead for the lives of Christian slaves. Making the sign of the cross with his sword, he spurred his horse against the dragon. They fought until the beast fell wounded to the ground. George told the princess to fasten her belt around the dragon's neck and lead it into Silene. The people honored George as a hero, and when he told them he had been made powerful by the Christian God, they accepted Christianity. George then took his sword and cut off the dragon's head. By an odd coincidence the town of Silene is near the place that Perseus, a hero of Greek mythology, is said to have rescued the beautiful Andromeda from a terrifying sea dragon.

The fight between St. George and the dragon is usually interpreted as an allegory showing the triumph of Christianity over the powers of darkness. But legends and traditions found in many different places show that this struggle had an earlier and more universal symbolic significance. In countries as far apart as

China and England we find that the dragon, from early times, represented the principle of fertility. He was born each spring from an egg underneath the water and, like Nature at that season, he grew and flourished. Each year as Nature waned the old dragon had to be killed to make way for the new dragon that would be born the following spring. When in the Western Christian tradition the dragon became synonymous with evil, the killing came to symbolize not merely the end of the year, but also the victory of God over the Devil. The slaying of the dragon for this reason has been associated with many Christian saints besides St. George, and with secular figures as well.

Modern psychology takes still another view of the dragon myth. The struggle with the dragon has been interpreted as symbolizing our own internal struggle between deep-seated lusts and unconscious drives on the one hand, and the demands of conscience on the other. The fertility legend is likewise given a new slant. The dragon is seen as the old man or father whose sexual potency has diminished, and who must be killed by the vigorous young sons so that they can take over the sexual role and enable life to continue. Another psychological interpretation springs from the role the dragon has in many legends as guardian of treasure. In this case the treasure is seen either as the son's sexual drives, to be guarded or restrained by the mother in the role of dragon, or as the daughter's virginity, to be preserved by her father in the dragon role.

Below: an Italian artist's version of the St. George legend in about 1502. The earliest stories about St. George made him a Christian martyr of the 4th century in North Africa. During the first crusades the nature of his character changed, and he became a warrior-saint in knight's armor. The first trace of his legendary battle with the dragon to save the life of the princess appeared early in the 13th century. In these accounts he was offered the princess and the kingdom as a reward, but nobly refused and rode off to do more good deeds. Some later accounts, however, have him marrying the princess Sabra and going to live happily in England.

In contrast to the West, the dragon in China is the embodiment of gentleness and goodwill. The Chinese dragon legends and interpretations therefore differ greatly. But whatever the symbolism, why should these strange hybrid creatures exert such power and fascination over our minds? There are land dragons, water dragons, flying dragons, fierce and timid dragons. There are dragons of many shapes in nearly every part of the world. Where do they spring from? Were they created to fulfill some deep need in humans, to personify the otherwise inexplicable forces of Nature, to provide some explanation for arbitrary fate? It seems that this might have been so. But while the West took the dragon to symbolize the evil, ungovernable, and destructive side of Nature, the East used it to portray the life-giving, benevolent, and restorative side. Both aspects were equally incomprehensible and mysterious, and lent themselves to interpretation by symbols

10

Left: *Perseus and Andromeda* by Italian Renaissance artist Piero di Cosimo. In the Greek myth on which this is based, Andromeda is left fastened to the rocks as a sacrifice to a sea dragon which has been ravaging her homeland of Ethiopia. Perseus rescues her with his magic weapons, and takes her as his wife. With this story the Greeks added a new element to the dragon legend: that the beast could be appeased by the sacrifice of a virgin, most often a royal princess. It was probably this story that later was shaped in Christian terms to become the legend of brave St. George and the dragon. Below: this is how one medieval miniature painter envisioned the rescue of Andromeda by Perseus.

that made them easier to understand for ordinary people.

Just as our early ancestors endowed many of the gods with a mixture of human and animal attributes to make them more powerful than either humans or animals, so they may have conceived of dragons as a mixture of different creatures in order to suggest their supernatural power. It seems that, just as different peoples interpreted the character of dragons to fulfill their own needs, so they concocted the appearance of the dragon from the beasts they found most significant. Thus in India we find an elephant dragon, in China a stag dragon, and in Western Europe —where the dragon myths stem from those of the serpent—we find a reptilian dragon. The Western dragon is so reminiscent of prehistoric reptiles that one is led to wonder whether the conception stems from folk memories of giant dinosaur fossils, or even a late freak survival of a prehistoric monster.

Since the serpent was in many civilizations the ancestor of the dragon, we find that in many myths the identity of the two creatures overlaps. The serpent sometimes becomes a dragon in later phases of the same legend. One of the first dragons to appear in myth is thought to be Zu. He arises in the legends of the Sumerians who settled in Mesopotamia possibly as early as 5000 B.C. The dragon Zu was said to have stolen tablets setting out the laws of the universe from the chief god of the Sumerians, Enlil. As a punishment Enlil ordered the sun god, Ninurta, to kill the dragon. This battle between the dragon and the sun god is repeated in the myths of many later civilizations, and seems to symbolize the struggle between light and darkness, between good and evil.

When in about 1800 B.C. the Babylonians gradually replaced the Sumerians as a leading power, they took over many of the Sumerian myths. Their story of creation is the story of the struggle between order and chaos, good and evil. The forces of chaos are personified by the sea goddess Tiamat, who adopted a dragon for her symbol. She led a fierce army that included serpents and dragons with crowns of flame, and attacked the gods, who stood for order. The dragon, representing Tiamat, was therefore associated with forces of destruction. Marduk, the

Below: a depiction of the battle in heaven between Archangel Michael and a dragon, described in the New Testament book of Revelation. The dragon, which was the Devil in this case, was overcome by the forces of good.

chief god of the Babylonians and god of the sun, was determined to fight Tiamat in single combat. He used the winds as his main weapon. When Tiamat opened her mouth to consume him, he drove the winds into her mouth and body. Her body became distended and she was unable to close her mouth. Marduk then shot an arrow down her throat, killed her, and severed her body in half. One half became the earth and the other the heavens. Thus the dragon is involved in the myth of creation.

Babylonian and Sumerian ideas spread to Egypt, and probably inspired the legend of the enormous serpent Apophis, the enemy of the Egyptian sun god. Later this serpent became identified with the ocean, which in Egyptian myth held the world together but constantly threatened to destroy it. Then the myth developed into the struggle between night and day, light and darkness. In some versions the serpent or dragon, representing night, swallowed the sun at sunset and disgorged it the next morning. In others the sun went down to the underworld each night to fight the dragon and, having each time succeeded in hacking him to pieces, came up to earth again in the morning. Throughout the West and Middle East dragons were generally regarded as carriers of evil and bad luck. They might vary greatly in appearance—some resembling serpents, others being formed from such

Below: this medieval tapestry shows the seven-headed dragon that, according to St. John's book of Revelation, menaced the earth after being cast out of heaven. It is sometimes called the Great Beast of the Apocalypse.

In the Far East the dragon is a benevolent creature associated with prosperity and good luck.

Right: this rich silk robe with an embroidered dragon was made for an 18th-century Chinese ruler. The dragon motif was a favorite one among the Chinese emperors.

Left: illuminated to glow across the water, this giant sea dragon was part of the festivities held in Singapore to mark the 1953 coronation of Queen Elizabeth II.

Below: the coronation dragon's head in close up shows its huge size and intricate construction.

unlikely combinations as a lion, a crocodile, and a hippopotamus—but they nearly all have a common characteristic: an endless hostility against human beings.

Some Western medieval scholars believed that the majority of dragons lived beneath the earth in an area honeycombed with caves. Dragons preferred to be underground, and the only ones seen above ground were those that had somehow gotten lost and strayed into the world of sky and sunshine. Unable to find their way back, they vented their frustration on any person nearby. In psychological terms, the dragons from the dark depths become the evil thoughts dwelling in all of us which, once they are allowed out into the open, bring trouble, pain, and sometimes death to our fellow beings.

It was an early dream expert, the 2nd-century Greek Artemidorus, who first mentioned dragons in connection with guarding treasure. He believed that dragons were to be found where treasure was hidden, and that therefore dreams about dragons signified riches and wealth. The link between dragons and treasure, and the caves where treasure was usually hidden, is found in many legends in different countries. It became a popular theme in the early Christian and the medieval periods, probably because it lent itself to many symbolic interpretations. In the Teutonic legend of Siegfried, for example, the dragon watches over a hoard of treasure that is the source of life. Siegfried acquires invulnerability by bathing in the dragon's blood after he has killed it. Also by drinking the dragon's blood he learns the language of the birds. In other words, he gains a new understanding of Nature. In many other legends the heroes gain new kinds of power from killing and eating parts of the dragon.

The English writer J. R. R. Tolkien gives a vivid picture of a dragon as treasure keeper in his modern fable of the struggle between good and evil, *The Hobbit*. He calls the beast Smaug and describes him this way: "There he lay, a vast red-golden dragon, fast asleep; a thrumming came from his jaws and nostrils, and wisps of smoke . . . Beneath him, under all his limbs and his huge coiled tail . . . lay countless piles of precious things . . ."

Britain has many dragon legends. One they owe to the Danish invaders of the mid-6th century, who brought with them their epic of King Beowulf. Although he beheads the murderous monster Grendel, Beowulf is killed by a dragon whose treasure has been stolen. An even earlier folk story concerns the legendary British monarch King Lludd, who lived happily in the city he had built in the southeast of the island—a city later called Londinium by the Romans and London by the Saxons. Suddenly peace was destroyed by an evil that "went through people's hearts, and so scared them, that the men lost their hue and strength, and the women their children, and the young men and the maidens lost their senses, and all the animals and trees and earth were left barren."

King Lludd sought the advice of his older brother, King Llevelys of France. "The plague in your kingdom is caused by a red dragon," King Llevelys said. "Another dragon of a foreign race is fighting with it, and striving to overcome it. And therefore does your dragon make a fearful outcry." King Llevelys gave King Lludd careful instructions about how to rid his land of the

15

Opposite: according to English legend, the Yorkshire knight Moore of Warncliffe killed the dreaded Dragon of Wantley. Then, in keeping with the romantic ideas of the age of chivalry, he demanded a fair young maiden as reward.

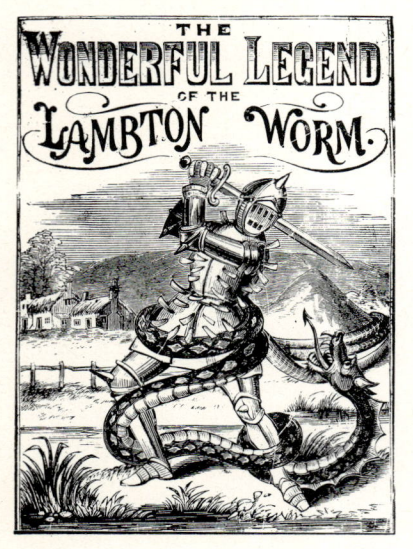

Above: the title page of an 1875 book on the Lambton Worm, one of the most popular and persistent English dragon stories. There is no beautiful damsel involved in this legend of a young lord who overcame the huge worm by following a witch's advice and wearing armor studded with blades to cut up the monster. This old tale also has the twist of a family curse brought about because the knight unwittingly breaks a vow.

Below: the red dragon of the Welsh flag. It is thought that dragons may have once been used on flags carried in battle as a kind of psychological warfare to give the enemy an added fright.

monsters. King Lludd returned home and, following his brother's directions, had a pit dug in the exact center of his domain. As Llevelys had predicted, the dragons grew tired of battling one night, and fell exhausted into the pit. They drank the mead that had been poured in and fell asleep. This made it easy to take them in two stone chests to the Welsh mountain of Snowdon for burial. The red dragon later became one of the war symbols of the ancient Britons and Welsh, and today is one of the symbols of Wales.

Among Britain's other dragon legends are those in which the monster takes the form of a giant worm. England is rich in stories of such creatures. Of these the most renowned is the Lambton Worm, which was discovered by John de Lambton in the fast-flowing Wear River near his ancestral home in northeast England. It was a Sunday, and Lambton, the heir to the estate, should have been attending church. Instead he defiantly went fishing. It was not much fun for him when he hooked a great worm with nine holes on either side of its mouth. Foot by foot he dragged the huge, grotesque monster onto dry land, cursing the thing's size and ugliness. He thought he had caught "the Devil himself," and to get rid of it he threw it into a deep well nearby. He then went back home hoping that he had seen and heard the last of the worm. He shortly resumed his "God-defying" habit of Sunday fishing.

Some weeks later the worm reappeared. It crawled out of the well, coiled itself round a rock in the middle of the river, and lay there all day long. At night, however, it snaked ashore and pillaged the district. It attacked cattle, mangled cows and drank their milk, swallowed lambs in a single bite, and terrorized the local women and children. On witnessing this, and on seeing how the beast froze its victims on the spot with its "great big goggly eyes," Lambton confessed his responsibility for the worm's presence. In an attempt to lessen the monster's fury by good works, he joined one of the crusades to the Holy Land and was away for seven years. On his return to England, he learned from his father that the beast had increased its plunder. It uprooted trees in the area, killed all who tried to destroy it, and paid a daily visit to Lambton Hall to drink a large amount of milk it demanded as tribute. The heir to the estate determined to kill the worm, and visited a local sage, the so-called Wise Woman of Brugeford, to get advice on how to win the battle. "You will succeed," she told him, "but remember this. You must vow to kill the first being or person you meet as you recross the threshold of Lambton Hall. If you fail to do so, then none of the Lambtons for the next three-by-three generations will die in his bed."

Lambton agreed to the condition, put on a special suit of armor studded with blades, and went out to face his enemy. A desperate battle ensued. After an hour or more of savage fighting, in which the worm wound itself tightly around the knight's body, Lambton slew the monster. He then waded ashore and walked wearily to the Hall. Before entering the great manor he blew three notes on his bugle—a prearranged signal for the release of his hound Boris so that it would be the first to greet him as he entered. However, the plan misfired, and it was old Lord Lambton who reached the warrior before the rest. As the father started to embrace his son,

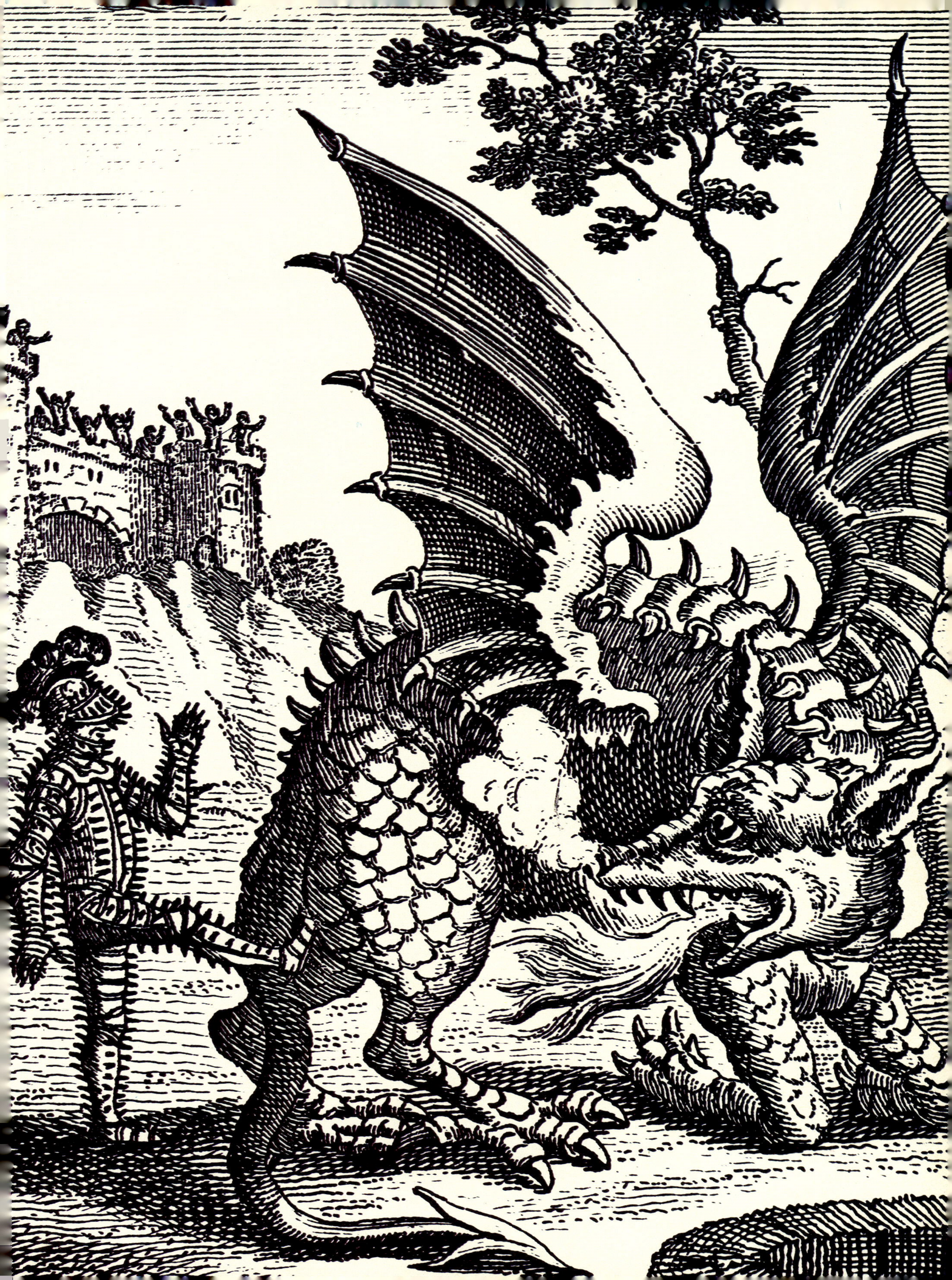

The Kiss That Conquered a Dragon

Once long ago a fiery dragon ate the two older sons of an emperor, whose youngest son went out to save them. This prince discovered that the dragon's great strength lay in a distant kingdom. There in a lake dwelled another dragon. Inside that dragon was a boar. Inside the boar was a hare. Inside the hare was a pigeon. Inside the pigeon was a sparrow. And inside the sparrow was the dragon's strength.

The brave young prince went to the faraway land and found the dragon. For two days they fought furiously, and each day the fight ended in a draw. During the fight the prince cried out: "If the princess would only kiss me on the forehead, I would throw you up to the sky!" This was reported to the emperor, who sent his daughter with the prince on the third day. The girl was deadly afraid, but she ran forward swiftly and kissed the prince on the forehead when he called for her. The prince then tossed the dragon high into the sky where it shattered into a hundred pieces. This freed the boar, the hare, the pigeon, and the sparrow in turn. The prince seized the first dragon's strength—but before he returned home to free his brothers, he married the beautiful princess.

the heir avoided him, called for Boris, and ran the hound through. But it was too late, for the vow had been broken. The Wise Woman's prediction came true, and the next nine generations of Lambton men died away from their beds. The first to die according to the prophecy was the monster-killer himself, who was slaughtered while on another crusade. The ninth Lambton to meet an unnatural death was Henry Lambton, Member of Parliament who represented the city of Durham. He was killed in June 1761 when his coach was in an accident on a bridge over the Wear River.

In China the dragons that stalked the land created no need for the country's heroes to kill them, eat their hearts, or drink their blood in order to become as strong, mighty, or keen-sighted. Dragons were regarded as benevolent rather than baleful. Far from gobbling up infants, violating virgins, and tangling with knights, they were gentle, charming creatures that brought hap-

Below left: in a German fairy tale a young couple decided to kill a dragon to gain his golden treasure for their marriage portion. They were both killed themselves—but, says the story, had the girl only known to tickle the dragon's chin, he would have purred contentedly while her lover safely took away the gold. Below: Fafnir, the fierce dragon of Norse and Germanic legend. He was once a man, but turned himself into a dragon in order to guard the treasure he had obtained by killing his father. The monster meets his death at the hands of a young hero with a magical sword.

piness and plenty. They could be found in rivers, lakes, and even —when they magically shrank themselves—in raindrops. Along with three other wholesome and well-intentioned creatures of legends—the tortoise, the phoenix, and the unicorn—they enjoyed lolling and basking in the sun. Occasionally they snacked on a swallow that flew into their jaws while pursuing flies. They were honored as the makers of humanitarian laws, and were held in particular esteem during the Ch'ing dynasty (1644–1912), when the emperors sat on dragon thrones, traveled by dragon boats, ate at dragon tables, and slept in dragon beds.

The Chinese affection for the beasts was made clear in this dictionary definition of around 1600, which stated: "The dragon is . . . the largest of scaled creatures. Its head is like a camel's, its horns like a deer's, its eyes like a hare's, its ears like a bull's, its neck like a snake's, its belly like a frog's, its scales like a carp's, its claws like an eagle's, and its paws like a tiger's. Its scales number

Right: a medieval manuscript illumination vividly illustrates the men of Alexander the Great battling terrible dragons. During his eastern campaign, Alexander reportedly encountered many monsters.

81, being nine by nine, the extreme odd and lucky number. Its voice is like the beating of a gong... When it breathes the breath forms clouds, sometimes changing into rain, at other times into fire... it is fond of beautiful gems and jade. It is extremely fond of swallow's flesh; it dreads iron, the *mong* plant, the centipede, the leaves of the Pride of India [the azedarac tree] and silk dyed in five different colors. When rain is wanted a swallow should be offered; when floods are to be restrained, then iron; to stir up the dragon the *mong* plant should be employed."

In spite of the help dragons gave, they were occasionally used for food and medicine. According to legend, a tasty soup was made of one particular dragon that fell into the palace grounds of the Emperor Hwo during a heavy shower around 100 B.C., and the hot liquid was served to the emperor's ministers. Dragons were also chopped into mincemeat and served at the tables of other emperors. In parts of China today pharmacies sell powdered and dried alligators, which are said to be descended from dragons, to cure anything from warts to lovesickness. However, even in the Far East the dragon was sometimes a malicious and predatory beast. Whenever upset or insulted, it could gather up all the neighborhood's water in containers and cause a drought. It could also turn on its old enemy the sun and cause an eclipse. The Japanese version of the monster often behaved more in keeping with the Western image. Some Japanese dragons demanded the sacrifice of a virgin once a year.

Legends from all over the world and, in particular, the legend of St. George and the dragon, once inspired a booming trade in fraudulent dragons and monsters throughout Europe. Imitation dragons were manufactured and sold as being straight from the caves and sandy banks of the Middle and Far East. The bogus monsters were displayed as early as the 16th century, when the renowned Italian physician and mathematician Hieronimus Cardanus saw some in Paris. "They were two-footed creatures with very small wings, which one could scarcely deem capable of flight, with a small head... like a serpent, of a bright color, and without any feather or hair," he recorded. The fake dragons were no larger than a kitten, so their sellers tried to pass them off as dragon babies. In fact, they were probably made by mutilating specimens of small flying lizards found in the Malay Peninsula and the East Indies. A scholar who examined one of the ugly specimens felt that all was not right. "Its head is serrated," he wrote, "and its crest comes to a peak... It has a flexible tail, two feet in length, and bristling with prickles. The skin is like that of a skate." Other false specimens were made by using parts of a giant ray fish, or by adding bat's wings to the dried-up body of a lizard.

Reports of dragons continued throughout the centuries, and many of them were included in various respected books. A 17th-century collection of fables, *Historie of Serpents*, told how dragons killed elephants by dropping on them from trees. In *The Subterranean World*, published in Amsterdam in 1678, the author Father Athanasius Kircher wrote that: "All the world's

Right: a fanciful illustration in an early book on the exploration of America shows an encounter with a dragon-like creature. It is possible that explorers met up with alligators which, in the retelling of them, became dragons. Below: an attempt at a scientific drawing of a crocodile in 1582. However, it has many of the usual attributes of the fabled dragon.

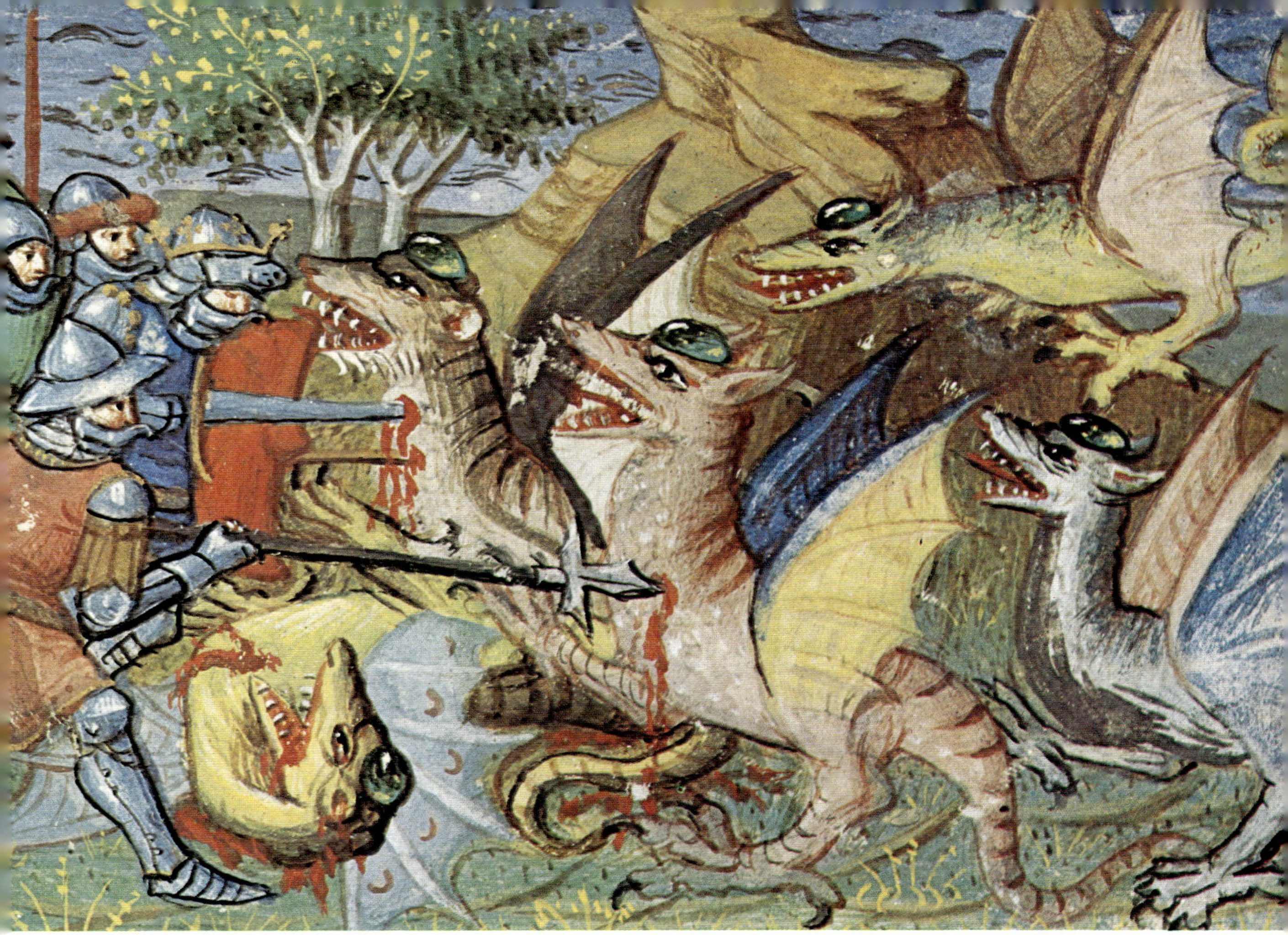
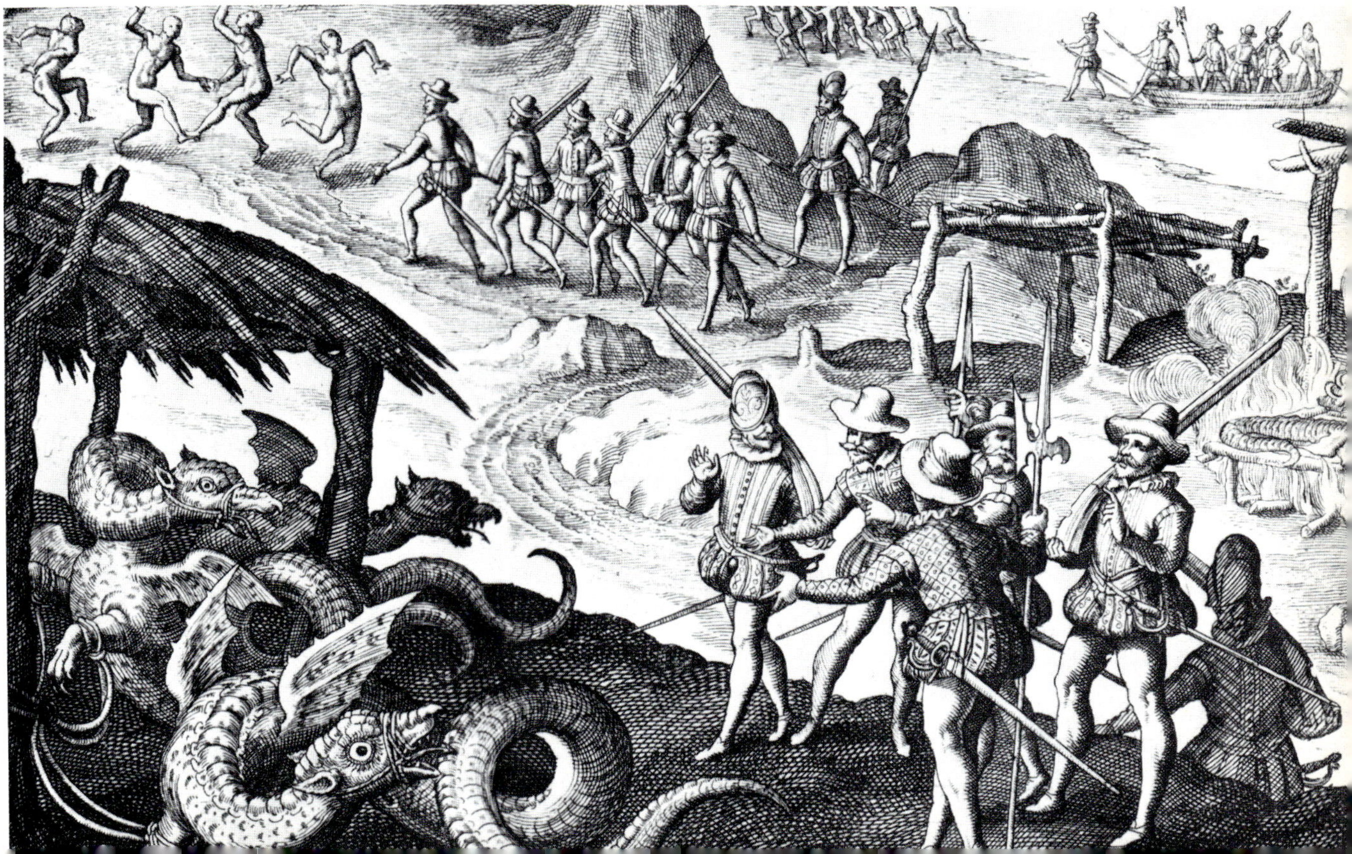

Reports of dragons in Europe were still current up to the 18th century. Left: a dragon was reportedly seen in a region of the Alps in 1660. Below: a sea dragon said to have been caught off the English coast in 1749 was four feet in length.

volcanoes are fed by one great main fire situated in the very bowels of the earth. Down in this area is a labyrinth of passageways, all running into each other, and most filled with lava, liquid fire, and water. Some of these caves and passageways, however, are empty, and it is here that you will find dragons, the kings of the underground beasts."

One of the most startling of dragon reports came from the small island of Komodo in the Malay Archipelago as recently as 1912. The pilot of a plane that crash-landed on Komodo afterward spoke of the "giant, lizard-like creatures" he had encountered. Although most people dismissed his story as "preposterous," the curator of the Botanical Gardens on Java decided to investigate the aviator's claims. He asked the Dutch Civil Administrator of the district to visit Komodo and see what he could find out. The administrator came back with the skin of a seven-foot-long creature, reporting that the local people swore there were similar beasts of up to 30 feet in length. On receipt of the skin and the information, the curator sent a Malay animal hunter to the island in search of a live monster. A local rajah provided special assistants and dogs. The hunt party captured four dragon-like animals, the biggest of them almost 10 feet long. They were later classified as belonging to a new species of giant monitor lizard, and are now known popularly as Komodo dragons.

In the summer of 1960 dragons again made the news. The place was New Guinea. The story was that local residents in an area of the island under Australian administration had been attacked by dragons some 20 feet long. Rumors flew that the monsters belched smoke and fire and sucked the blood from their victims' bodies. Some corpses also had wounds of more than a foot in length, said to have been made by the dragons' claws. There was so much panic that the government authorities moved people into police stockades, and posted a substantial reward for the capture of one of the beasts dead or alive. Perhaps not surprisingly, no one tried to collect the reward. Whether from boredom or overfeeding, the dragons themselves appeared no more.

The dragon is now considered by most people as a purely mythical beast. But its history and symbolism are so rich and diverse that the creature fascinates us more than many a real animal.

Below: a Komodo Dragon, a giant species of monitor lizard found on Komodo Island off the Malay peninsula. It is the closest thing to an actual dragon that has been scientifically reported. It first became known in 1912 when an airman made a forced landing on Komodo, and came back with tales of huge dragons that ate pigs and deer. Later investigation proved the existence of giant lizards on Komodo, of which at least one measured over nine feet.

2

Mermaids and Unicorns

On a warm summer day in the late 1890s William Munro, a teacher, was walking along the beach in the county of Caithness, Scotland. Suddenly he spotted a figure that resembled a naked woman seated on a rock jutting out to the sea. If he had not known that it was too dangerous to swim out to the rock, Munro would have assumed the figure to be human. But realizing that something was odd, he examined the figure closely. The lower part of the body was covered by water, but the creature was using her exposed arms to comb her long, light brown hair. After three or four minutes the figure dropped into the sea and vanished from view.

Unlike the fierce fire-breathing dragon, the seductive mermaid and the graceful unicorn breathe the eternal fragrance of a land of magical romance. Above: a unicorn drawn by the Swiss scientist Conrad Gesner in 1551. He speculated that the unicorn may have perished in the biblical great flood, and that bones found in Germany in his day might be unicorn horns washed there during the flood.

Right: the sheet music of an English variety show song popular in the 1860s. In this humorous ditty, at least one lonely sailor found a bride on the ocean floor.

25

"She lures unresisting sailors to their doom"

As the result of an argument 12 years later, Munro wrote to *The Times* of London. In the published letter he described his earlier experience in careful and unemotional language. "The head was covered with hair of the color above mentioned [brown] and shaded on the crown, the forehead round, the face plump, the cheeks ruddy, the eyes blue, the mouth and lips of natural form resembling those of a man; the teeth I could not discover, as the mouth was shut; the breasts and abdomen, the arms and fingers of the size of a full-grown body of the human species, the fingers, from the action in which the hands were employed, did not appear to be webbed, but as to this I am not positive."

Munro went on to say that, although other reliable people had reported seeing the figure, he had not believed them until he had seen it himself. Having seen it, he was convinced that the figure was a mermaid. He finished by saying that he hoped his letter might help to establish "the existence of a phenomenon hitherto almost incredible to naturalists, or to remove the skepticism of others, who are ready to dispute everything they cannot comprehend . . . ."

This clear account shows that a belief in mermaids was not held only by half-crazed sailors on lengthy ocean voyages. In fact, the mermaid—like the dragon—seems to be a nearly universal symbol. She is found in most countries of the world, and where there is no sea, she adapts her home to a lake or river. Like the dragon, she seems to answer some deeply felt need in man. She is the unobtainable enchantress, seemingly sexual and voluptuous but underneath cold and elusive. With her eternal youth and beauty, her magical voice and seductive power, she lures unresisting sailors to their doom. She seems, in modern

Below: a German illustration of 1895 takes the erotic view of a mermaid ensnaring a human lover.

psychological interpretation, to symbolize the mingling of sex and death, the desire by man to lose himself totally even when he knows it means his own destruction.

Behind the mermaid legend lies a long sequence of romantic yearning, the longing for an ideal if unattainable woman whose favors were like those of no mere mortal. The very spot on which Munro had his "arresting experience" was the scene of an earlier and even more eventful happening. According to local stories a mermaid had given a young man gold, silver, and diamonds that she had gathered from a wrecked ship. The youth took her gifts but gave some of the jewels to young women he desired. Worse than this, he failed to meet the mermaid a number of times as planned, so arousing her jealousy and wrath. One day she met him in a boat and rowed him to a nearby cave, saying it held all the treasures ever lost in the estuary. Once there, the youth fell asleep. He awoke to find himself tied to a rock by gold chains that allowed him to walk only as far as a mound of diamonds at the mouth of the cave. Although he had riches and a mate who satisfied his lust, he was but a prisoner. He was trapped, a victim of his own greed.

Mermaids were well-known for taking ruthless revenge if thwarted or slighted in any way, and there are many stories that illustrate this characteristic. This theme may stem from man's sexual fantasy of a wild untameable creature bent on

Above: an illustration of the hero Odysseus, or Ulysses, and the sirens who lured men to their death by eerily beautiful singing, from the Greek epic poem by Homer. Although the poet did not describe the sirens physically, the early Greek artists usually portrayed them as part-woman, part-bird. Later, as in this version, they acquired the mermaid's tail. Odysseus resisted the sirens' songs by having himself lashed to the mast, and prevented his men from hearing them by plugging up their ears with beeswax.

Right: mermen are very rare, but this drawing is supposed to be of one seen with his mate in the Nile in ancient times. It appeared in a book by the Italian naturalist Ulysses Aldrovandi in 1599. In an 18th-century account of the event, it was said that the creatures remained in full view of several people for at least two hours.

Right: a magnificent French 16th-century pendant of pearls and rubies in the shape of a merman. By logical development of the many factual and mythical tales of treasure ships sinking to the bottom of the sea, mermaids came frequently to be associated with fabulously rich hoards of jewels and great heaps of bright gold.

fulfilling her own desires. Even more sinister in terms of sexual symbolism is the idea of the mermaid as a fallen angel who could only eat living flesh. She captured sailors by her singing and sweet music. If this technique failed—which it rarely did—she relied on a unique body smell that no man could resist. Once she had snared her victim, and lulled him to sleep, she tore him to pieces with her spiky green teeth.

Slightly less savage as a fantasy was the myth that mermaids and mermen lived in a kingdom of great riches beneath the sea to which mermaids took their victims and kept them prisoner. From this tale grew the seaman's belief that it means bad luck to see a mermaid. It was supposed to foretell death at sea by drowning.

The roots of the mermaid legend go back to the powerful Babylonian fish deities associated with the sun and the moon. Oannes, who represented the sun, had a human form but wore a fish head as a cap and a fish skin as a cloak. He was gradually replaced by the fish god Ea who was half man and half fish, and can be seen as the ancestor of the merman. The moon goddess Atargartis, half woman and half fish, was the precursor of the mermaid. The Babylonians believed that when they had finished their respective journeys through the sky, the sun and moon sank into the sea. So it seemed appropriate that the gods of the sun and moon should have a form that allowed for life both above and below the water. The strange form of these gods, part human and part fish, and their power to vanish into the unfathomable oceans gives them a mysterious, elusive quality. This mystery and elusiveness was inherited by mermaids. The mirror the mermaid often holds is thought to represent the moon, which also seems to add to her power because of the way the moon influences the tides. Because the fish deities were accorded enormous power in pre-Christian times, their link to the mermaids helped strengthen the mermaid legends.

Other forerunners of the mermaids were the tritons of Greek mythology. Also half human and half fish, the tritons calmed the waves and ruled the storms. The sirens of Greek mythology, although half bird and half woman, like the mermaid lured men to destruction by their beautiful singing. When the Greek hero Ulysses was forced to sail past them, he plugged the ears of his sailors with wax, and had himself bound securely to the mast in order to be able to resist them.

The Apsaras of India were beautiful water nymphs, but despite their human shape, they had much in common with mermaids. Besides their beauty and "fragrance," they were skilled musicians, especially on the lute, and shared the mermaid's power of prophecy. However, though promiscuous and always eager for new conquests, they were friendly toward man, and intent on giving happiness.

With the establishment of Christianity, the mermaid legend took on a new aspect in which the mermaid longed to have a soul. According to Christian thought, the mermaid could only gain a soul by promising to live on land and giving up all hope of returning to the sea. This was impossible for the half-fish creature, so it doomed her to an unhappy struggle with herself.

Above: in ancient Hindu sculpture the important god Vishnu is seen as a semi-fish. In the story of how Vishnu saved humankind during his first incarnation, the god appeared "on the vast ocean in the form of a fish, blazing with gold."

29

240. Monstre semblable à une Sirenne pris à la côte de l'isle de Borné ou Boeren dans le Departement d'Amboine Il étoit long de 59. pouces gros à proportion comme une Anguille. Il a vecu à terre dans une Cuve pleine d'eau quatre jours et sept heures. Il poussoit de temps en temps des petits cris comme ceux d'une Souris. Il ne voulut point manger, quoy qu'on luy offrit des petits poissons, des coquillages, des Crabes, Ecrevisses, etc. On trouva dans sa Cuve apres qu'il fut mort quelques excremens semblables à des crottes de chat.

Above: the mermaid of Amboina, caught on the coast of Borneo, was reported to have lived for over four days after capture. This picture was said to have been "drawn from life," and was published in an elegant volume—lavishly illustrated—published by Louis Renard in Amsterdam in 1717. The drawings were made by Samuel Fallours from specimens in the collection of the governor-regent of the province of Amboina.

Thus the mermaid, who had been a simple figure representing the most elemental urges and desires, became far more complex, with her own internal conflicts. There is a sad and charming story of a mermaid in the 6th century A.D. who daily visited a monk in the holy community of Iona, a small island off Scotland. She begged to be given a soul, and the monk prayed with her to give her the strength to abandon the sea. But despite her desire for a soul, and despite the fact that she had fallen passionately in love with the monk, she was unable to give up the sea. In the end, weeping bitterly, she left the island forever. It is said that the tears she shed became pebbles, and to this day, the gray-green pebbles found on the shore of Iona are known as mermaid's tears.

The seal, with its sleek form and human characteristics, has long been linked with the mermaid. Many believe that reports of mythical mermaids are based on glimpses of real seals. In mermaid lore, however, the seal is known as the constant companion of the mermaid. There is a story that a fisherman once stunned and skinned a seal, and then threw it back live into the sea. A mermaid, taking pity on the animal, volunteered to search for its skin. However, she was captured by the fisherman's companions and died from exposure to the air. Ever since then, in gratitude for her bravery, the seal has been the special guardian of the mermaid.

The Scandinavians, Scots, and Irish had many stories about seal people who were forced to live as seals at sea, but who could at certain times assume their true human shape on land. Some thought seals were fallen angels, others that they were the souls of drowned people or humans under a spell. Certain Irish families claimed descent from seals, and an entire nation in Asia Minor traced their ancestry back to a seal maiden

Right: in the last century the Japanese made skillful mermaid fakes with torsos of monkeys and tails of fish—but they were far from the beauties of the myths. **Below:** another unattractive fake mermaid of the type exhibited by P. T. Barnum in the 1870s. He fooled the public with pictures of lovely mermaids outside the tent.

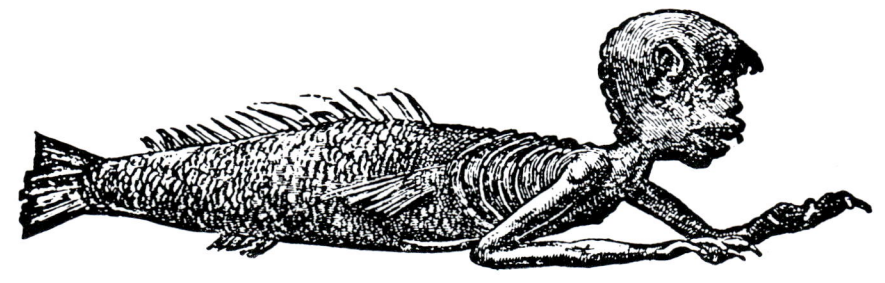

mentioned in Greek mythology. In the myth a water nymph transformed herself into a seal to evade the unwelcome attentions of the son of Zeus. However, her precautions were too late, for soon after her transformation she gave birth to a son. He was named Phocus, which means seal. The Phocian people commemorated their descendance from the seal maiden by showing a seal on their earliest coins.

Seal maidens had much in common with mermaids, and the two creatures became inextricably mixed in many legends. Mermaids and seal maidens both liked to dance and sing. They also both shared the gift of prophecy. There are stories of both seal maidens and mermaids marrying humans and remaining on land for many years. It was said that a mermaid had an enchanted cap without which she could not return to sea. If a man managed to steal her cap and hide it, he might marry her; but if she ever found it she would immediately vanish into the waves. In the same way a man could marry a seal maiden if he could steal and hide her sealskin. An old story from the Scottish highlands is one of many on this theme. A man fell in love with a beautiful seal maiden, stole her sealskin and hid it carefully, and married her. They had many children and were happy. But one day one of her sons discovered where the skin was hidden and told his mother. She eagerly put it on and, leaving her children forever, swam joyfully out to sea.

In 1403 a mermaid reportedly floated through a broken dyke near Edam in Holland, and was taken into captivity. Her fate was different from most other captured mermaids. She spent the next 15 years in Haarlem where she was taught to spin and to obey her mistress. On death she was given a Christian burial.

In some areas mermaid legend survived a long time. As recently as 1895 the inhabitants of the Welsh seaport of Milford Haven believed that mermaids or underwater fairies regularly shopped at the town's weekly market. They got to the town by means of a covered road on the sea bed, quietly made their purchases, such as tortoiseshell combs for their hair, and vanished till next market day.

Most sightings of mermaids, however, have been by sailors. For instance, during his first voyage, the previously skeptical Christopher Columbus recorded seeing three mermaids leaping high out of the sea off the coast of Guiana. Mermaids were regularly seen by sailors suffering from months of boredom and sexual frustration at sea. Could sexual fantasizing have made them see a beautiful half-woman in sea mammals such as graceful seals, or even ungainly dugongs or manatees? Who knows?

The famous English navigator Henry Hudson told his mermaid story matter of factly. On June 15, 1625, while sailing in search of the North West Passage, he wrote in his diary: "One of our company, looking overboard, saw a mermaid. From the navel upward, her back and breasts were like a woman's . . . her skin very white, and long hair hanging down behind, of color black. In her going down they saw her tail, which was like the tail of a porpoise, speckled like a mackerel." There are reports of sightings from Russia—where the mermaids were "tall, sad, and pale"—from Thailand, and from Scotland. In the last country in May 1658 mermaids were found at the mouth of the River Dee and the *Aberdeen Almanac* promised visitors that they "will undoubtedly see a pretty Company of Mermaids, creatures of admirable beauty."

Right: an 18th-century French engraving showing two views of a manatee seen in the Congo River. It was called a "woman fish."
Below: the manatee under water. It is hardly a tribute to women that men—even womenless men—saw this cumbrous animal as a mermaid.

Pesce-Dona ou poisson femme sur le dos

As the fame of mermaids spread, so the inevitable fakes and frauds began to appear. Usually false mermaids were carefully constructed from the top half of a monkey joined to the tail of a fish. One of these, probably made in the 17th century, was shown in an exhibition of fakes mounted by the British Museum in London in 1961. Most of these so-called mermaids were extremely ugly, but they seemed to have aroused great interest.

In a book published in 1717 there is a picture of a supposedly genuine mermaid. The description with the picture said: "A monster resembling a Siren caught on the coast of Borneo in the administrative district of Amboina. It was 59 inches long and in proportion like an eel. It lived on land for four days and seven hours in a barrel filled with water. From time to time it uttered little cries like those of a mouse. Although offered small fish, molluscs, crabs, crayfish, etc., it would not eat . . . ."

As the fame of this mermaid spread, Peter the Great, Czar of Russia, got interested and tried to get more information from François Valentijn, a Dutch colonial chaplain who had written on the subject. Valentijn didn't add much but reported on another Amboina mermaid. This time the creature was accompanied by her mate, and was seen by more than 50 witnesses. The writer was convinced that the mermaid story was true. "If any narrative in the world deserves credit," he wrote, "it is this . . . Should the stubborn world, however, hesitate to believe it, it matters nothing; for there are people who would even deny the existence of such cities as Rome, Constantinople, or Cairo, simply because they themselves have not happened to see them."

Despite the fact that mermaids were supposed to be wanton and cruel they were sought after by seamen as if they were virginal and kind. Such was the enthusiasm to find a mermaid— and then presumably keep her for private pleasure—that the ships' lookouts began to see the heroine of their erotic dreams everywhere. As one writer later put it, "These hauntingly beautiful goddesses of the sea, full of mystery and danger, were surely conjured from the chaos of the water in answer to some primal human need." But the great 18th-century German naturalist, G. W. Steller, seemed to have a rather different image of the origin of mermaids. Up to the time that he joined an expedition seeking a sea route from Siberia to Alaska, sightings of mermaids had been dismissed by some experts as being distorted glimpses of the dugong or manatee. Such water mammals suckled their young and, ran the explanation, a sight of mother mammal suckling her baby gave rise to tales about beautiful sea maidens with shapely naked breasts.

On the expedition's return voyage, Steller's ship was wrecked. He and others were washed up on Copper Island in the Commander Group near Bering Island. It was there at high tide that Steller saw some "hump-backed" objects in the water. At first they reminded him of capsized boats. On seeing them again, however, he realized that they were seal-like animals of a previously unknown class. He gave them the name of *Rhytina stelleri,* or Steller's sea-cow, and claimed that it was these somewhat unfortunately named creatures that had for so long been taken for mermaids. He was the first trained observer

Above: mermaids and wild men together in a 15th-century French coat-of-arms. Mermaids became a favorite heraldic emblem early, and the graceful maids from the sea rode into battle on countless banners.

Right: perhaps it was the dream of every fisherman to take as his catch the fabled creature with the body of a voluptuous woman.

to have seen this animal alive. He estimated that they were an average of 30 feet long and weighed some $3\frac{1}{2}$ tons each. They had small heads and large forked tails. Subsequent investigation proved that they mated like human beings—especially in the spring on evenings when the sea was calm.

"Before they come together," he wrote, "many amorous preludes take place. The female, constantly followed by the male, swims leisurely to and fro, eluding him with many gyrations and meanderings until, impatient of further delay, she turns on her back as if exhausted and coerced, whereupon the male, rushing violently upon her, pays her the tribute of his passion, and both give themselves over in mutual embrace."

Throughout the Middle Ages carvings and stone and wooden representations of mermaids adorned churches and cathedrals in almost every part of Europe. But by the middle of the more scientific 19th century, belief in them was ebbing. As steamships replaced sailing ships and the duration of voyages grew shorter, seamen less and less claimed to have been seduced, tempted, or taunted by the lethal sirens. In spite of this, the mermaid had not yet completely submerged. One was seen again in 1900 by Alexander Gunn, a landholder in the far north of Scotland. While he and his dog were out rescuing a sheep that had become stuck in a gully, he glanced up and locked eyes with a mermaid reclining on an adjacent ledge. With red-gold wavy hair, green eyes, and arched eyebrows she was extremely beautiful. She was also of human size. It was hard to tell who was the more startled—she, Gunn, or his dog. However, it was the dog which, with a terrified howl, gave vent to its feelings first. It fled with its tail between its legs, followed close behind by the landholder who had seen anger as well as fear in the mermaid's expression. "What I saw was real," he told a friend later. "I actually encountered a mermaid."

More than 50 years later, two girls sauntering along the same shore also chanced upon a mermaid stranded by the tide. Her description fitted that of Gunn's. Shortly after this, in a completely different part of the world, the adventurer Eric de Bisschop added to the relatively few 20th-century accounts of mermaids. His experiences occurred shortly after midnight on January 3, 1957, when he was sailing his reconstruction of an ancient Polynesian raft from Tahiti to Chile. In his book, *Tahiti-Nui*, published two years later, he told how one of the sailors on watch suddenly began to act like he had gone mad. The man claimed he had seen a strange creature leap out of the water and onto the deck. The being, with hair like extremely fine seaweed, stood upright on its tail. The sailor approached and touched the intruder, which immediately knocked him flat and then jumped into the sea. It was the shining fish scales on the seaman's arms that convinced de Bisschop the man was telling

The Little Mermaid and the Sea Witch

Hans Christian Andersen's little mermaid was the most beautiful of the Sea King's six daughters. She longed for a life on land and an immortal soul. When she saw the handsome young prince and learned that if she gained the love of a mortal she could have a soul that would live forever, she determined to do so — even though the Sea Witch warned her that the price of failure was instant death. The Sea Witch changed her fishtail into legs, but every step hurt her as if she were treading on a sharp-edged knife. In return for the charm, the Sea Witch demanded the mermaid's tongue, and she became mute.

The prince found the exquisite speechless girl and lovingly took care of her, but he did not think of taking her as his wife. At length he met a beautiful princess and married her. The mermaid's sisters appeared and told the little mermaid that if she plunged a knife in the prince's heart she could still be saved. The little mermaid refused, and for this act of mercy she was swept into the skies to become one of the Air Spirits, who after 300 years of good deeds are rewarded with a soul and go to heaven.

Right: one panel of the tapestry series *The Hunt of the Unicorn* woven in France around 1480. It is an example of popular Christian belief about the unicorn in the Middle Ages, which held that the fierce little animal could only be captured after being lulled to sleep by a virgin. Here the beast tries to escape.

Left: this 17th-century print of three different species of unicorn indicates that belief in them still persisted in a period of reasoned scientific inquiry.

the truth, and that he had been in contact with a mermaid. Four years later, in 1961, the Isle of Man Tourist Board introduced an angling week and offered a prize to anyone catching a live mermaid in the Irish Sea. This followed several reports of red-headed water nymphs sporting in the foam. However, the Gaelic mermaids proved as elusive as their sisters of centuries before, and none was caught.

Though there are probably only a few people today who would genuinely subscribe to a belief in real mermaids, it might be said that mermaids have attained a degree of reality. The legend is so powerful and universal that, like the dragon, the mermaid has become a symbol—part of man's unconscious imagination. The same can be said for the unicorn.

This mythical creature is based on a variety of animals, but is always distinguished from others by its long single horn. Like the dragon, its general appearance and characteristics varied according to place and legend. Sometimes it strongly resembled one animal such as a goat, a horse, or even a serpent, and sometimes it combined the features of different animals. In the West it tended to be fierce and untameable, a lover of solitude, but in China it was peaceful and gentle and heralded good fortune.

Like other mythical beasts the unicorn provides a rich field for symbolic interpretation, both of a specific and of a generalized kind. The single horn indicates both virility and kingly power, and is also, in some legends, a sign of purity. The unicorn combines both male and female elements with its masculine horn and female body. Its Chinese name, ki-lin means male-female. This reconciliation of the opposing forces of male and female in one creature meant, in symbolic terms, that the

37

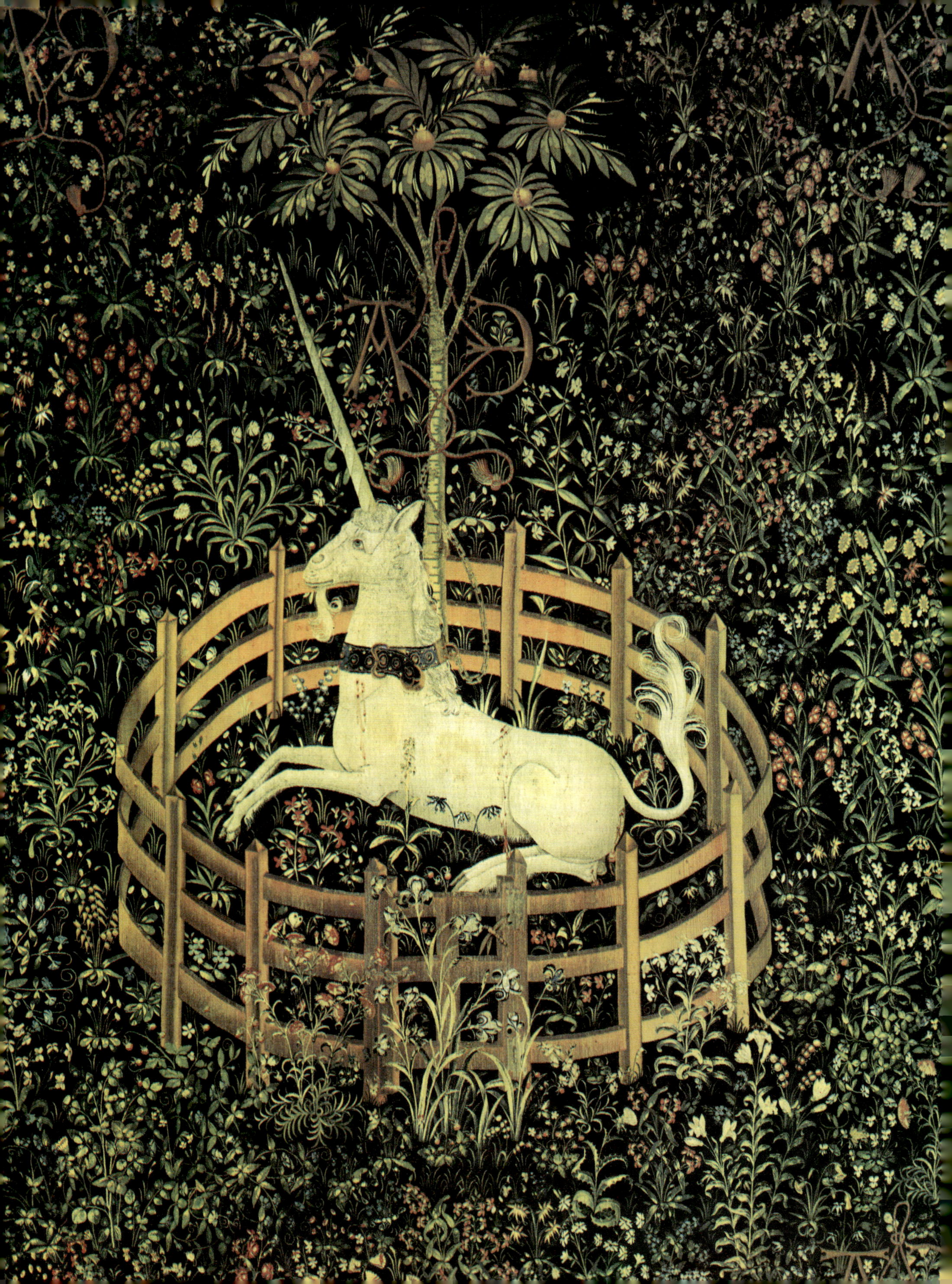

Left: the last panel of *The Hunt of the Unicorn* shows the mythical creature in captivity. The theme of the unicorn and the hunt was a favorite of artists throughout the Middle Ages. They were drawn by the grace of the animal and the richness of the complex symbolism surrounding the whole legend.

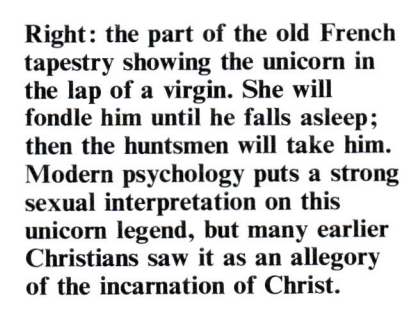

Right: the part of the old French tapestry showing the unicorn in the lap of a virgin. She will fondle him until he falls asleep; then the huntsmen will take him. Modern psychology puts a strong sexual interpretation on this unicorn legend, but many earlier Christians saw it as an allegory of the incarnation of Christ.

unicorn stood for the reconciliation of other opposites. The harmony of opposites was the greatest ideal of Western magicians and alchemists, and the unicorn therefore has an important place in the history of magic.

The first mention of the unicorn in the West was in a book on India written by the Greek historian Ctesias in about 398 B.C. Part of his description went: "There are in India certain wild asses which are as large as horses, and larger. Their bodies are white, their heads dark red, and their eyes dark blue. They have a horn on the forehead which is about a foot and a half in length." The description seems to be based on conjecture and travelers' tales. The unicorn appears to be a mixture of the rhinoceros, the Himalayan antelope, and the wild ass. Its horn was said to have come to a long sharp point, and to be white at the base, black in the center, and crimson at the tip. It is probable that Ctesias had seen drinking cups made of horn and decorated in these colors inasmuch as such drinking horns were often used by Indian princes. He reports that dust scraped from the horn was an antidote to poison, and that those who drank from the horn would be protected from convulsions and from poisoning. This belief persisted up to the Middle Ages, and the rich and powerful paid enormous prices for drinking vessels believed to be made from the horn of the unicorn.

Apothecaries often claimed to keep a unicorn's horn in their shop in order to cure ailments. Some even thought it had the

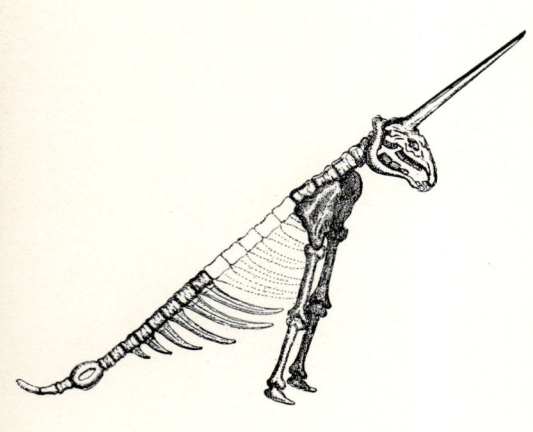

Above: a unicorn skeleton reconstructed from fossil bones in 1749. By that time, scientists were more skeptical about unicorns. Then, in the next century, a leading naturalist declared that a single-horned animal with a cloven hoof was genetically impossible. With that, the graceful unicorn finally withdrew into the mists of legend and myth.

Below: the British royal coat-of-arms. When James VI of Scotland became James I of England in 1603, he added the unicorn as a heraldic emblem. This mythical animal had long been one of the royal beasts of Scottish rulers.

power to raise the dead. Even in the 17th and 18th centuries alicorn, a powder allegedly made from unicorn horn, was featured on the drug lists issued by the English Royal Society of Physicians. It was extremely expensive, and gave rise to the saying "weight for weight alicorn for gold." The druggists explained the high costs by the fact that unicorns were mostly caught in India, and that the powder had to be shipped from there.

In 1641 a French marquis visiting London wrote that he had seen a unicorn's horn on display in the Tower of London. It had been the property of Queen Elizabeth I, and was said to have then been worth about £40,000. He wanted to test its authenticity by placing it on a piece of silk and putting both articles on a hot coal fire. If the horn was genuine, he said, the silk would not burn. However, perhaps fortunately, the presence of the guards prevented him from carrying out this test.

The purifying nature of the unicorn's horn is apparent in a famous medieval legend. In this story many animals gather at dusk by a pool to quench their thirst, but the water is poisoned and they are unable to drink. Soon they are joined by the unicorn who dips his horn into the water and cleanses it. In some Christian versions, the horn stands for the cross and the water for the sins of the world.

Another famous and symbolic medieval legend is the capture of the unicorn by a young virgin. The unicorn, a small goat-like creature, was too fierce and swift to be captured by hunters. It could only be tamed by a virgin seated alone in a forest under a tree. Attracted by her perfume of chastity, the unicorn would approach and lay its head in her lap. She would stroke its horn and lull it to sleep. Then she would cut off his horn and betray him to the hunters and dogs. The sexual symbolism of this story is fairly obvious, and it gave rise to many erotic elaborations. There was also an attempt to put a Christian interpretation on it. In this case the virgin is the Virgin Mary, the unicorn is Christ, and the horn signifies the unity of father and son. Christ, as embodied in the unicorn, is slain for the sake of a sinful world.

For centuries naturalists suggested that it should be possible to produce a unicorn by genetic engineering, and in March 1933 it was done. An American biologist, Dr. Franklin Dove, performed a simple operation on a day-old male Ayrshire calf at the University of Maine. By transplanting the animal's two horn buds and placing them together over the frontal bones, he forecast that a single unicorn-like horn would grow. His experiment was a total success and he was able to show the world a one-horned bull. It was nothing like the unicorn of the Middle Ages, which through courtly literature had gradually assumed the sleek lines of a horse. But it was not bullish in character. Could people centuries ago have performed the same experiment and produced a one-horned creature, with characteristics that differed from its two-horned brethren? And could these creatures have inspired the original legends of the unicorn? Or did the unicorn, a mysterious and magical creature, spring purely from man's mind, meeting some psychological and imaginative need?

Right: an advertisement for unicorn's horn—usually called alicorn—which throughout the Middle Ages was considered a powerful antidote against poison. It was also supposed to be a cure for the plague and other diseases. A unicorn's horn purified water, and a drinking cup made of this horn guaranteed that any poison placed in it would be rendered harmless—an obvious asset for insecure monarchs of the day. The powdered form was the easiest way to take alicorn internally, but avaricious pharmacists produced "unicorn water" merely by standing one end of the horn in water, as in this 17th-century illustration.

Below: the one-horned rhinoceros, almost certainly one of the main sources for the unicorn myth. Even at the height of belief in the unicorn, learned men were aware of the existence of the rhinoceros, and certain that it was definitely distinct from the unicorn—although this did not prevent them from confusing rhinoceros and unicorn attributes.

UNICORNS HORN

Now brought in Ufe for the Cure of Difeafes by an Experienced DOCTOR, the AUTHOR of this Antidote.

A Moſt Excellent Drink made with a true *Unicorns Horn*, which doth Effectually Cure theſe Difeaſes:

Further, If any pleaſe to be ſatisfied, they may come to the Doctor and view the *Horn*. *Viz*.

- Scurvy, Old Ulcers,
- Dropſie,
- Running Gout,
- Conſumptions, Diſtillations, Coughs
- Palpitation of the Heart,
- Fainting Fits, Convulſions,
- Kings Evil, Rickets in Children,
- Melancholly or Sadneſs,
- The Green Sickneſs, Obſtructions,

And all **Diſtempers** proceeding from a Cold Cauſe.

The Uſe of it is ſo profitable, that it prevents Diſeaſes and Infection by fortifying the Noble Parts, and powerfully expels what is an Enemy to Nature, preſerving the Vigour, Youth, and a good Complexion to Old Age: The Virtue is of ſuch force, as to reſiſt an Injury from an unſound Bedfellow; None can excel this, for it is joyned with the Virtue of a true *Unicorns Horn*, through which the Drink paſſeth, and being impregnated therewith, it doth wonderfully Corroborate and Cure, drinking it warm at any time of the Day, about a quarter of a Pint at a time, the oftner the better, the Price is 2 s. the Quart.

2. Alſo as a preparative for this excellent Drink, and good againſt the Diſeaſes above mentioned, and all Crudities in the Body, is ready prepared twelve Pils in a Box to be taken at three Doſes, according to Directions therewith given, the Price is 2 s. the Box.

3. Likewiſe he hath Admirable Medicines for the Cure of the **POX**, or Running of the Reins, with all Simptoms and Accidents thereto belonging, whether Newly taken or of long Continuance, and (by God's Bleſſing) ſecures the Patient from the danger of the Diſeaſe preſently, and perfects the Cure with the greateſt Speed and Secreſie imaginable, not hindering Occaſions, or going abroad: Whoſoever makes Uſe of theſe Admirable Medicines, may have further Advice from the Doctor without Charge.

The Doctor Liveth in Hounſditch, next Door to Gun-Yard, have-

3

Monsters of the Deep

In 1938 a strange fish was picked up in the nets of a South African trawler. It turned out to be a coelacanth, a fish that had been in existence about 300 million years ago, and was believed by scientists to have been extinct for about 70 million years. The coelacanth had no special protective features, so its survival all these millions of years was particularly remarkable. If the lowly coelacanth had such powers to survive, why not other ancient marine species? Might there be a few survivors somewhere in the depths of the ocean? The sea is vast and incredibly deep. Ships travel over only a small portion of the surface, and trawlers

The oceans, so full of unknown possibilities, have fascinated generations of sailors passing over their surface, and also land-dwellers staring out over the apparently empty expanses. In such vastness, surely anything might live? In such unimaginable depths, surely some terrible gigantic creature might find a cold, silent, but safe refuge? Right: a mermaid and a sea serpent leap out of their watery element on the cover of a German magazine published in 1897.

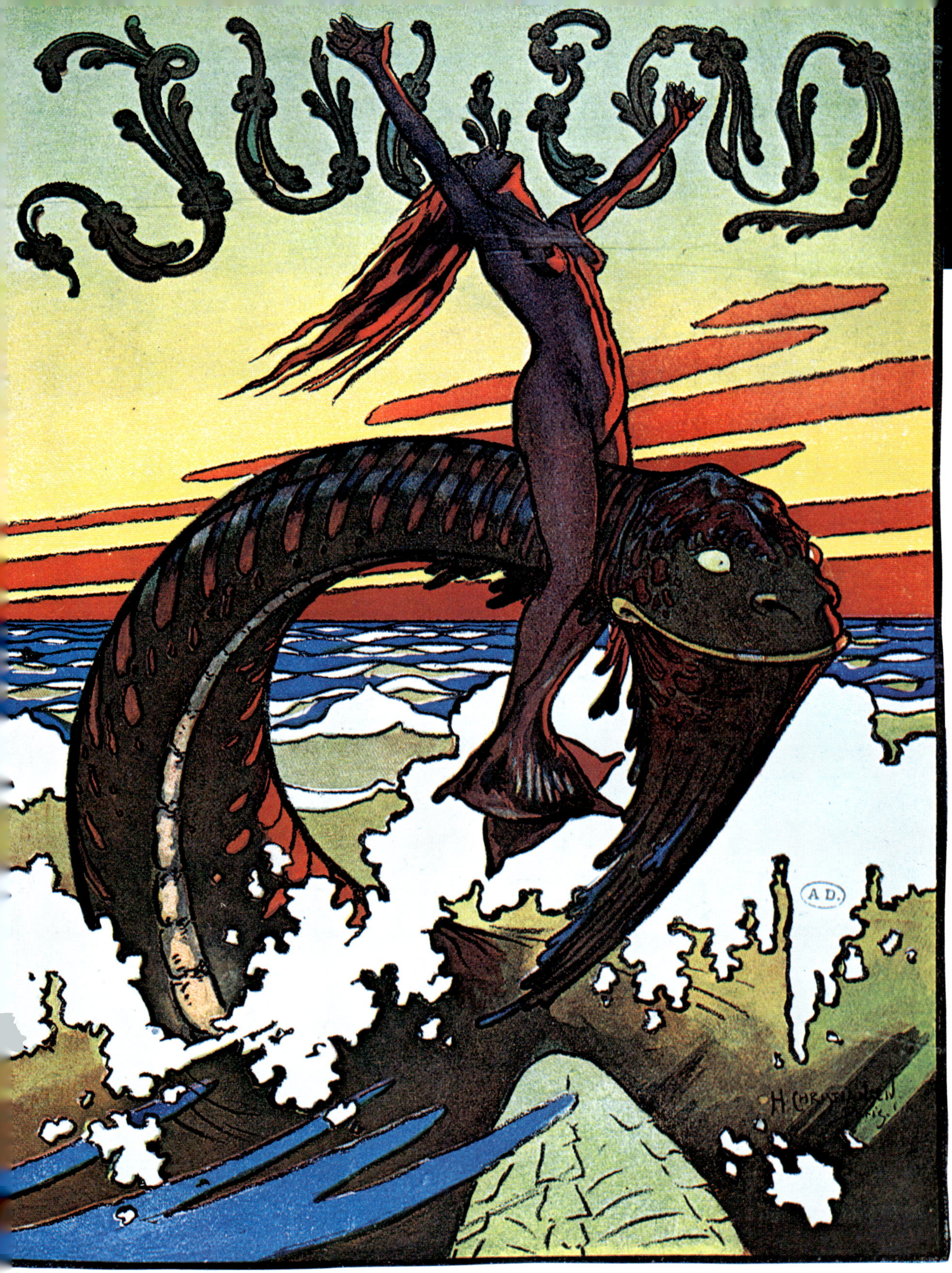
A D.

"Suddenly, a giant sea monster emerged"

Below: this illustration for a Jules Verne story shows a giant squid "brandishing the victim like a feather." Do the huge and terrifying sea monsters of fiction have real-life counterparts? That is still an unanswered question.

normally sink their nets to a depth of about 60 feet. Until recently scientists believed that fish could not survive at great depths, but a research vessel has now brought up a fish from a depth of over 26,000 feet. Although the ocean at that level is totally black, that fish still retained two small eyes—evidence that it had once lived far closer to the surface. We know that marine creatures are amazingly adaptable. Salmon leap rapids. A variety of lung fish can live out of water for four years. It is not impossible that certain prehistoric sea monsters have adapted to living in the ocean deeps.

At one time, perhaps as long as 200 million years ago, the sea was filled with giant monsters. There were massive sharks far larger than any we know today, enormous crabs, sea serpents of fantastic lengths, and huge lung fish, skates, and rays. Many of these creatures developed body armor and protective devices such as stings to insure their survival. In 1930 Dr. Anton Brun caught the six-foot-long larva of an eel at a depth of only 1000 feet. On the assumption that it would mature to 18 times its length—although some eels reach 30 times their larval size—this eel would grow to a mammoth 110 feet. Perhaps there are still larger species existing at still greater depths.

But whether they exist or not, sea monsters have long been a part of mariners' tales. Among the many stories is one that took place in the late 18th century when a Danish sailing ship had been becalmed off the coast of West Africa. Her captain, Jean-Magnus Dens, decided to put the time to good use and ordered the crew to scrape and clean the outside of the boat. To do this the men worked from planks on the ship's side. Suddenly, without warning, a giant sea monster emerged. Wrapping two of its enormous arms around two of the men, it dragged them into the sea. A third arm went around another sailor, but, as he clung desperately to the rigging, his shipmates freed him by hacking off the monster's arm. Despite repeated attempts to harpoon the monster, it sank out of sight into the water. The bodies of the first two victims were never recovered, and the third sailor died that same night. The captain later described the part of the arm that had been hacked off. He said it was very thick at one end and tapered to a sharp point at the other. It was about 25 feet long and covered with large suckers. Judging from the size of the cut-off portion, the captain estimated that the whole arm must have been between 35 to 40 feet in length.

This is a typical seaman's story of a monstrous sea creature—exaggerated, fantastical, but fascinating. Such stories were often believed in earlier times. However, even in the late 18th century, Captain Dens could find few to credit his. The big exception was the young French naturalist Pierre Denys de Montfort, who was determined to prove to the skeptical scientific world that octopuses of collosal size existed. Choosing to believe that Dens' monster was a huge octopus, he included Dens' account in his unfinished six-volume work *The Natural History of Molluscs*. These books were published in Paris between 1802 and 1805, and, unfortunately for Denys de Montfort's reputation, he included a mixture of science and imagination in which fact was hard to distinguish from fiction. The Frenchman's one

Above: a painting said to have been presented to a church by the grateful crew that escaped death at the hands of the monster shown. The original had been lost, but French naturalist Pierre Denys de Montfort had another painted from word-of-mouth description because he felt it was proof of the existence of monstrous sea creatures.

Left: the capture of a giant squid by the French gunboat *Alecton* on November 30, 1861. Attracted by a huge, mysterious floating mass off Tenerife, the commander, Lieutenant Bouyer, went over to investigate. He discovered an oversized squid between 15 and 18 feet long with arms of five to size feet. The men succeeded in harpooning it, but when they tried to haul it ashore the body broke, and they recovered only the end of the tail. Although the fragment looked and smelled like animal matter, French scientists concluded that it was probably a piece of seaweed.

Above: a 19th-century woodcut of a kraken—legendary Norwegian sea monster—attacking a sailing ship. It has been speculated that the silent sailing ships, gliding across the surface as they did, were far more likely to encounter sea creatures than noisy engine-driven craft, which create warning vibrations in the water for considerable distances. Below: an artist's impression of the gigantic squid caught off the coast of Newfoundland in 1878, shown with a man next to it to indicate scale. The body was 20 feet long, and one of the arms alone was 35 feet. It is the biggest specimen accepted by science as a genuine giant sea animal.

scientific supporter was the German naturalist Lorenz Oken, who, for all his renown, was slightly suspect because he also believed there were more and stranger things beneath the surface of the sea than had ever been seen above it. Despite great ridicule and criticism, Denys de Montfort continued to compile reports of "the sightings of monsters and serpents of the sea by mariners whose sincerity I do not and will not doubt."

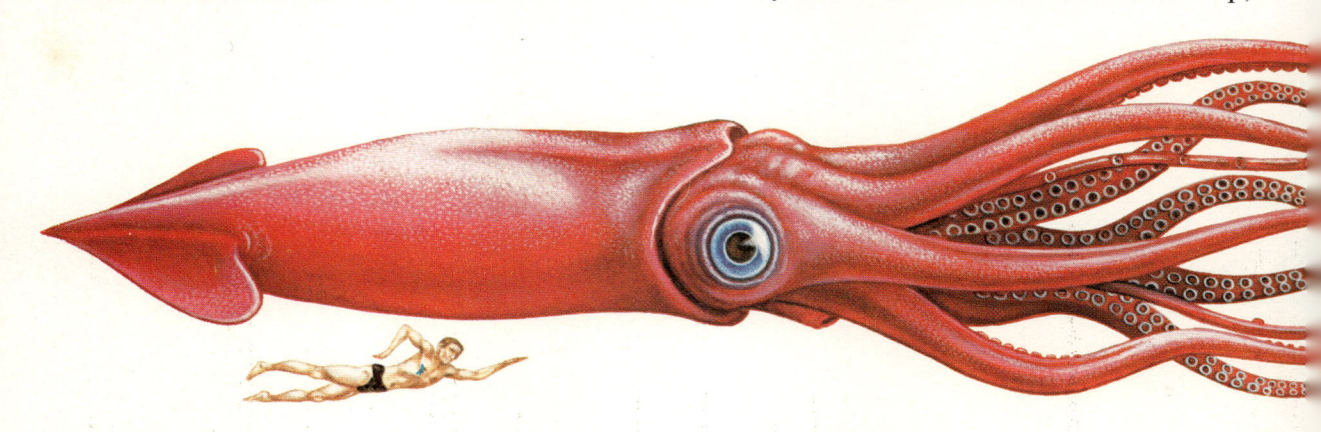

True to his word, he followed every lead to find his giant octopus. Sometime in the 1790s he journeyed to the northern port of Dunkirk, where a group of American whale fishers were living and working. He wanted to interview the seamen and hear at first hand of the experiences that few people apart from himself would credit. For example, here is a report he repeated: "One of these captains, named Ben Johnson, told me that he had harpooned a male whale, which, besides its very prominent penis placed under the belly, seemed to have another one coming out of its mouth. This surprised him greatly, and also the sailors, and when they had made the whale fast to the ship, he had them put a hook through this long round mass of flesh which they hauled in with several running nooses . . . They could hardly believe their eyes when they saw that this fleshy mass, cut off at both ends and as thick as a mast at the widest point, was the arm of an enormous octopus, the closed suckers of which were larger than a hat; the lower end seemed newly cut off, the upper one . . . was also cut off and scarred and surmounted by a sort of extension as thick and long as a man's arm. This huge octopus's limb, exactly measured with a fishing line, was found to be 35 feet long, and the suckers were arranged in two rows, as in the common octopus. What then must have been the length of arm which had been cut off at its upper extremity where it was no less than six inches in diameter?" It seemed to Denys de Montfort that at least 10 feet had been sliced off the upper end, and a further 10 to 25 feet off the lower—making a total length of some 80 feet.

During his stay in Dunkirk, he found that the whale fishers were eager to speak of their encounters with monsters. He gave an account of what was told by an American captain named Reynolds. "One day," Denys de Montfort recorded, "he and his men saw floating on the surface of the water a long fleshy body, red and slate colored, which they took to be a sea serpent, and which frightened the sailors who rowed the whaleboats." However one sailor noticed that the supposed snake had no head and was motionless, so they found the courage to haul it aboard. They then discovered from the suckers that it was an octopus or squid arm—one that measured 45 feet in length and 2½ feet in diameter.

The arm, which would have been a convincing piece of evidence, was nowhere to be found by the time Denys de Montfort heard about it. Although disappointed at not seeing it, the naturalist's hopes rose when he heard of an extraordinary painting of a sea monster on view further along the coast in St. Malo. He hurried to go to St. Thomas's chapel where the picture, given in thanksgiving for their survival by a ship's crew, was hanging. Before inspecting it, however, he quizzed several of the port's fishermen about its story. They related how a local sailing ship had run into trouble off the West African coast, and how her crew had been set upon by a "monster straight from Hell." As Denys de Montfort told it from the accounts he heard:

The Monster from the Sea

Late in the 18th century a sailing ship off the coast of West Africa found itself becalmed in a placid ocean. The wind had dropped, and Jean-Magnus Dens, the Danish captain, ordered his crew to lower planks off the side from which they could scrape and clean the ship. Three men climbed onto the planks and began their work. They were scraping energetically when suddenly, out of the quiet sea around them, rose an immense octopus or squid. It seized two of the men and pulled them under the water. The third man leaped desperately into the rigging, but a gigantic arm pursued him, getting caught up in the shrouds. The sailor fainted from shock, and his horrified shipmates frantically hacked at the great tentacle, finally chopping it off. Meanwhile, five harpoons were being driven into the body of the beast in the forlorn hope of saving the two who had disappeared. The frightful struggle went on until, one by one, four of the lines broke. The men had to give up the attempt at killing the monster, which sank out of view.

The unconscious sailor, hanging limply in the shrouds, was gently taken down and placed in his bunk. He revived a little, but died in raving madness that night.

47

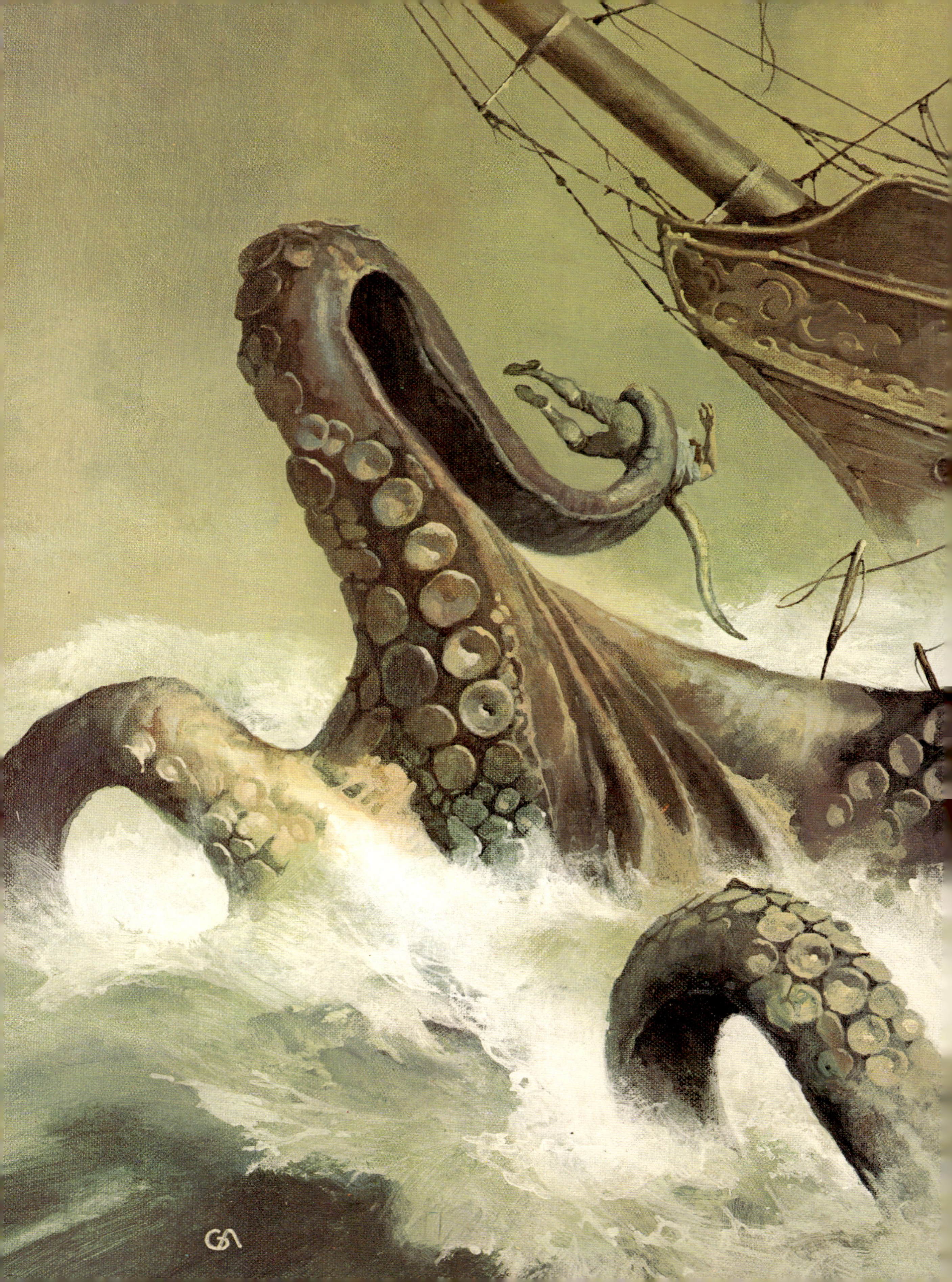

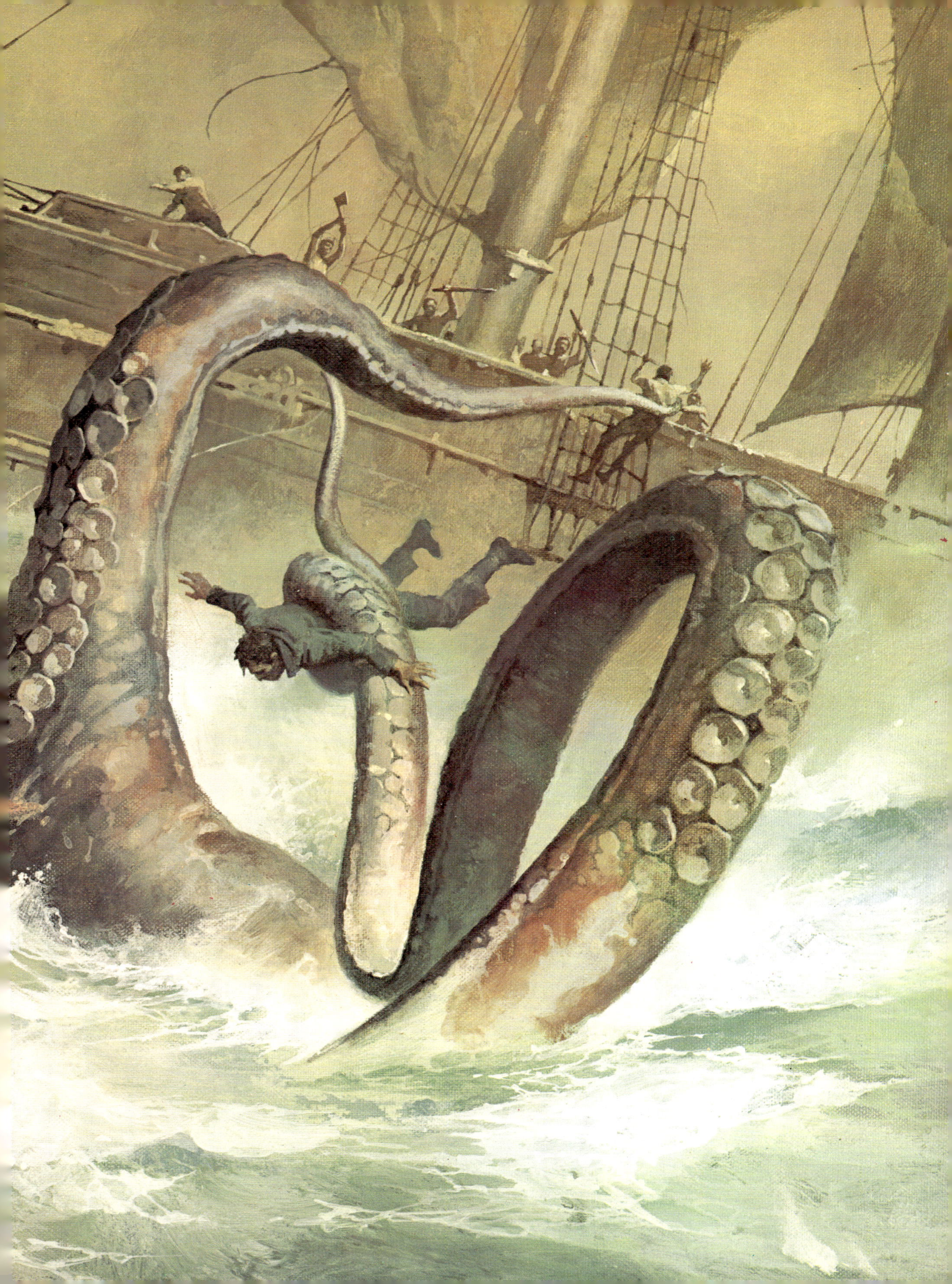

Right: a decorated Greek vase showing the struggle of the hero Heracles with the river-god Achelous to win Deianeira. The god is represented with a man's torso atop a sea serpent's body. The Greeks usually depicted river-gods with beards and horns, the latter being a symbol of power.

Above: a sea monster described by Olaus Magnus and illustrated in his book published in 1555. His sea monster is a long serpent-like creature with a head about the size of a man. Olaus Magnus felt that the appearance of a creature like this was a portent of change, probably for the worse.

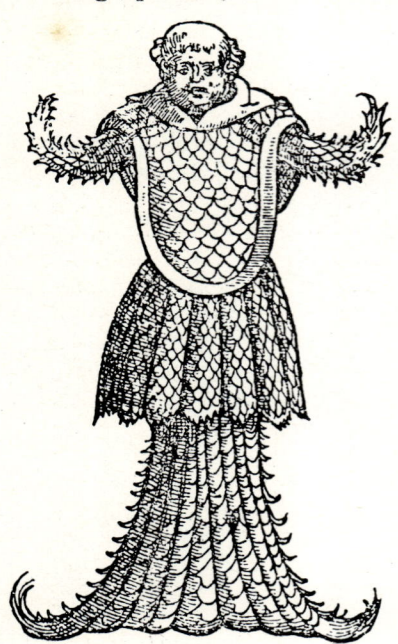

Above: the legendary sea monk of 16th-century Norway. It was said to have a head like a monk's cowl, a human face, and a fishtail.

"The ship had just taken in her cargo of slaves, ivory, and gold dust, and the men were heaving up anchor, when suddenly a monstrous cuttlefish appeared on top of the water and slung its arms about two of the masts. The tips of the arms reached to the mastheads, and the weight of the cuttle dragged the ship over, so that she lay on her beam-ends and was near to being capsized. The crew seized axes and knives, and cut away at the arms of the monster; but, despairing of escape, called upon their patron saint, St. Thomas, to help them. Their prayers seemed to give them renewed courage, for they persevered, and finally succeeded in cutting off the arms, when the animal sank and the vessel was righted. Now, when the ship returned to St. Malo the crew, grateful for their deliverance from so hideous a danger, marched in procession to the chapel of their patron saint, where they offered a solemn thanksgiving, and afterwards had a painting made representing the conflict with the cuttle, and which was hung in the chapel."

On hearing this story, Denys de Montfort rushed into the chapel as eagerly as the seamen themselves had done, and gazed up at the fantastic and fearsome scene that the painting depicted. The monster, whose arms were wound around the tops of the three masts, was as gigantic and hideous as the naturalist could have yearned for, and he was grateful for the boost it gave to his theories. He took the painting to be an exact description of a real event, which his obsessional belief in monstrous octopuses made entirely plausible to him. He had a copy of the painting made by an artist who had not seen the original, and who therefore made it seem even more fantastic. On publication of the copy, critics called it an even bigger fake than his books. He was branded "the most outrageous charlatan Paris has known," and no one accepted his challenge to travel the 200 miles to St. Malo to see the original for themselves. The picture was later taken from the chapel and either hidden or destroyed. Denys de Montfort sank into disrepute and obscurity. He wrote a phrase book and a book on bee-keeping, and, on their failure, became a pedlar of sea shells. Having fallen into deep poverty, he was found dead in a gutter in 1820 or 1821. His reputation as an eccentric overshadowed his fine early work on mollusc shells, and it was too soon forgotten that he had created 25 new genera still in use today.

For some decades after, no naturalists were prepared to risk their career by writing about marine monsters, whether or not they thought some of the tales might have a basis in fact. A more recent author views the whole subject in more perspective, however, and writes: "The sea serpent—or at any rate his cousin, the sea monster . . . is at least as ancient, and therefore as respectable, as the fairies, and a good deal older than the modern ghost." Tales of the Norwegian monkfish, for instance, go back to medieval times. The first one was caught off the coast after a great tempest. It "had a man's face, rude and ungraceful with a bald, shining head; on the shoulders something resembling a monk's cowl; and long winglets instead of arms. The extremity of the body ended in a tail." According to the historian who described it, the monkfish was given to the King of Poland who took pity on it and had it placed back in the sea.

In 1680 a frightful kraken, which is a legendary giant sea monster, swam too close to the shore of Norway, became jammed in a cleft of rock, and remained there until it died. The stench from the kraken polluted the entire neighborhood, and it was months before the local people could go within miles of the rotting carcass. More than 50 years later, in 1734, another kraken was observed by the celebrated Danish missionary Hans Egede—this time near Greenland. He recorded the experience in his diary stating: "The monster was of so huge a size that, coming out of the water, its head reached as high as a mainmast; its body was as bulky as the ship, and three or four times as long. It had a long pointed snout, and spouted like a whalefish; it had great broad paws; the body seemed covered with

Below: a drawing of a kraken in the form a huge sea serpent as reported in 1734 by the Norwegian missionary Hans Egede. His was an eye-witness account, and one of the first by a person whose integrity could hardly be doubted.

Below: a suggestion by the 19th-century naturalist Henry Lee of how Egede's kraken could be a partially hidden giant squid.

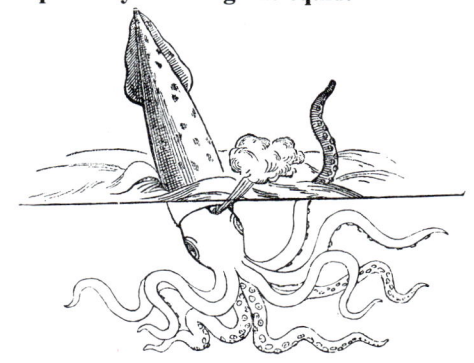

Above: a sketch of the head of the sea serpent sighted from the *Daedalus*. This drawing, like the top one, was based on sketches by M'Quhae, and executed under his personal supervision.

shellwork, and the skin was very ragged and uneven. The under part of its body was shaped like an enormous huge serpent, and when it dived again under the water, it plunged backward into the sea, and so raised its tail aloft, which seemed a whole ship's length distant from the bulkiest part of its body."

Another 18th-century writer on the kraken was the Norwegian Bishop of Bergen, Erik Pontoppidan. He wrote a book about the natrual history of Norway in 1752, and, although he did not see a sea monster himself, he believed the scores of fishermen who told him that they had. He described the kraken as it was described to him. "Its back or upper part, which seems to be about an English mile-and-a-half in circumference, looks at first like a number of small islands surrounded with something that floats and fluctuates like seaweed . . . at last several bright points or horns appear, which grow thicker and thicker the higher they rise above the water. . . . After the monster has been on the surface for a short time it begins slowly to sink again, and then the danger is as great as before, because the motion of his sinking causes such a swell in the sea and such an eddy or whirlpool, that it draws everything down with it . . ."

In 1765, the same year that Bishop Pontoppidan's book appeared in English translation, *The Gentleman's Magazine* in London stated that "the people of Stockholm report that a great dragon, named Necker, infests the neighboring lake, and seizes and devours such boys as go into the water to wash." This did not stop the Bishop of Avranches from swimming

Left: on August 6, 1848, the captain and six members of the crew of H.M.S. *Daedalus*, which was returning to England from the East Indies, sighted a sea serpent that traveled alongside the ship for 20 minutes, never out of sight of their glasses. Captain M'Quhae's report to the Admiralty, which demanded an explanation from him after a report appeared in *The Times*, is a clear and detailed account of the creature. He said that it was at least 60 feet long, and that the head was snakelike and 15 or 16 inches in diameter.

Below: an attempt by the English naturalist Lee to show that the *Daedalus* serpent, like Egede's kraken, was a giant squid seen from an angle. In his book *Sea Monsters Unmasked*, published in 1884, Lee tried to prove that all sea serpents sighted in the past had really been huge squids.

there on a sunny summer day, although the onlookers "were greatly surprised when they saw him return from imminent danger."

With some three-fifths of the earth's surface covered with water, it is hardly surprising that stories of sea monsters arose. Sightings were reported in many parts of the world, including North America after it was settled by Europeans. The coast of New England soon became a popular place for serpent encounters, and between 1815 and 1823, hardly a summer went by without someone meeting up with a sea monster. In June 1815 a strange animal was observed moving rapidly south through Gloucester Bay. Its body, about 100 feet long, seemed to have a string of 30 or 40 humps, each the size of a barrel. It had a head shaped like a horse, and was dark brown in color. Two years later it was again seen in the bay, and the *Gloucester Telegraph* reported: "On the 14th of August the sea serpent was approached by a boat within 30 feet, and on raising its head above water was greeted by a volley from the gun of an experienced sportsman. The creature turned directly toward the boat, as if meditating an attack, but sank down...."

The following year, the same or a similar creature was observed in Nahant. One of the clearest accounts was given by Samuel Cabot of Boston. Mr. Cabot was standing on the crowded Nahant beach when he noticed that a number of boats were speedily making for the shore. "My attention," he wrote, "was suddenly arrested by an object emerging from the water at the distance of about 100 or 150 yards, which gave to my mind at the first glance, the idea of a horse's head. It was elevated

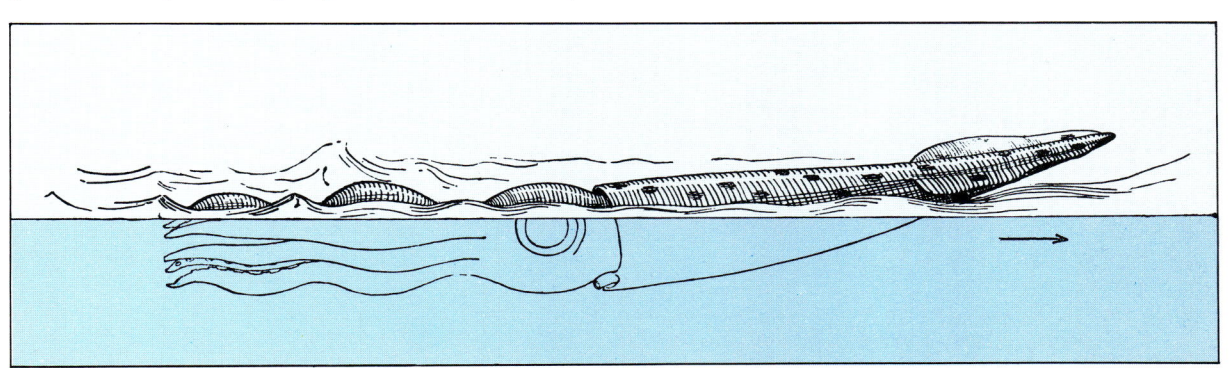

Right: the enormous skeleton of a sea serpent, 114 feet long, exhibited by Albert C. Koch in New York in 1845. Unfortunately for Koch, the skeleton was very closely examined by a Boston zoologist who exposed the fraud. Koch had assembled the creature from vertebrae of many *Zeuglodon*, an extinct distant relative of the modern whale. After the exposure, Koch packed up his bones and went to Germany, where he exhibited them again. Again, the fraud was discovered.

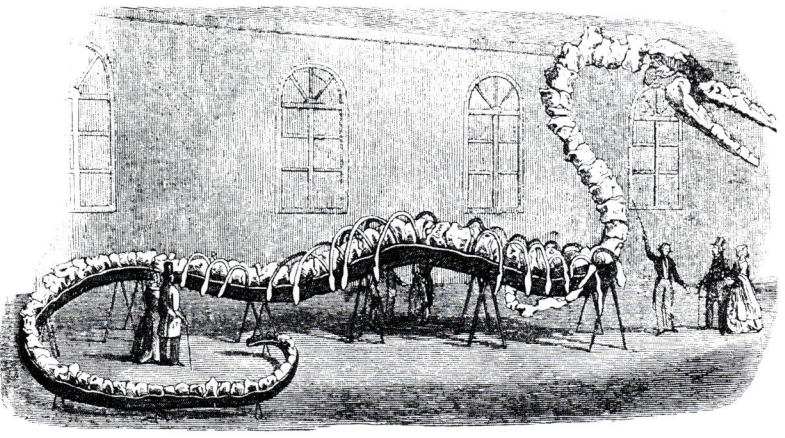

Right: sailors of old went in fear of an attack by a sea monster, as shown in this 18th-century print.

Below: illustration of a sponge diver swallowed whole by a sea monster said to be the size of a small boat. Fear of this monster was reported by the British vice-consul in 1875 as the reason for a sharp drop in the supply of sponges from Mount Lebanon—and a subsequent rise in their price.

Above: in 1891 a sea monster was reported to have appeared suddenly among the bathers at Pablo Beach, Florida, causing great consternation and panic.

Below: the great monster of Lake Utopia surprises two canoeists. Sightings of this huge creature in the Canadian lake have been reported for more than 100 years.

about two feet from the water, and he depressed it gradually to within six or eight inches as he moved along. His bunches appeared to me not altogether uniform in size. I felt persuaded by this examination that he could not be less than 80 feet long." The horse-like monster reappeared again the next summer, and it was watched by dozens of vacationers. "I had with me an excellent telescope," declared one knowledgeable witness, "and . . . saw appear, at a short distance from the shore, an animal whose body formed a series of blackish curves, of which I counted 13 . . . This at least I can affirm . . . that it was neither a whale, nor a cachalot [sperm whale], nor any strong souffleur [dolphin], nor any other enormous cetacean [water mammal]. None of these gigantic animals has such an undulating back."

Within a short while the creature had shown itself to the crew of the sloop *Concord*. The captain and the mate made a deposition of what they had seen before a local Justice of the Peace as soon as they reached shore. In his sworn statement the mate said in part: "His head was about as long as a horse's and was a proper snake's head—there was a degree of flatness, with a slight hollow on the top of his head—his eyes were prominent, and stood out considerably from the surface . . ." The same animal was later seen and identified by Reverend Cheever Finch, who said he spent a half-hour watching its "smooth rapid progress back and forth."

Many lakes are immensely deep, and could provide suitable habitats for large monsters. In fact, the next North American area to be infiltrated by sea serpents was British Columbia, where deep-water lakes are spaced between the Rockies and the Pacific. It was while taking a team of horses across Lake Okanagan in 1854 that an Indian halfbreed claimed to have been "seized by a giant hand which tried to pull me down into the water." He managed to struggle out of the grip, but the horses in his charge were not so lucky. The monster—which apparently had several long and powerful arms—got a hold on the animals and pulled them under the surface; all of them drowned. The sea serpent was known as Naitaka to the Indians and Ogopogo to the settlers. It was seen regularly from then on, and a pioneer named John McDougal later recounted an experience similar to the halfbreed's. Again the man escaped with his life, and again the horses were the victims. By the 1920s the "thing in the lake" was internationally famous, and a London music hall ditty immortalized it with the words: "His mother was an earwig / His father was a whale / A little bit of head / And hardly any tail / And Ogopogo was his name."

From Canada the story of the serpents moved south to the Mormon settlement of Salt Lake City. In July 1860 the newspaper there, *The Desert News*, offered new testimony about the monster of Bear Lake. Up to that time, the Shoshone Indians of Utah had been the principal witnesses of the "beast of the storm spirits," and they were seldom taken seriously. The newspaper story, however, recounted the experience of a respected local resident who had been going along the east shore of the lake. "About half-way," wrote a reporter, "he saw something in the lake which . . . he thought to be a drowned person . . . he rode to the beach and the waves were running pretty high. . . . In a few

The Captain, the Sailing Ship, and the Sea Serpent

From the 1860 report of Captain William Taylor, Master, *British Banner*: "On the 25th of April, in lat. 12 deg. 7 min. 8 sec., and long. 93 deg. 52 min. E., with the sun over the mainyard, felt a strong sensation as if the ship was trembling. Sent the second mate aloft to see what was up. The latter called out to me to go up the fore rigging and look over the bows. I did so, and saw an enormous serpent shaking the bowsprit with his mouth. It must have been at least about 300 feet long; was about the circumference of a very wide crinoline petticoat, with black back, shaggy mane, horn on the forehead, and large glaring eyes placed rather near the nose, and jaws about eight feet long. He did not observe me, and continued shaking the bowsprit and throwing the sea alongside into a foam until the former came clear away of the ship. The serpent was powerful enough, although the ship was carrying all sail, and going at about ten knots at the time he attacked us, to stop her way completely. When the bowsprit, with the jibboom, sails, and rigging, went by the board, the monster swallowed the foretopmast, staysail, jib, and flying-jib, with the greatest apparent ease. He shoved off a little after this, and returned apparently to scratch himself against the side of the ship, making a most extraordinary noise, resembling that on board a steamer when the boilers are blowing off. The serpent darted off like a flash of lightning, striking the vessel with its tail, and staving in all the starboard quarter gallery with its tail. Saw no more of it."

Left: the Gloucester sea monster, named after the New England port in which it was sighted. It was said to be a 65-foot-long snake-like creature with a head the size of a horse's skull. There were hundreds of eye-witness reports during the month of August, 1817. Right: whatever the 19th-century scientists said, seamen still reported seeing huge sea monsters—as depicted in paintings like this. Below: an engraving showing the attack of a sea serpent on the American schooner *Sally* in 1819, off the coast of Long Island. The crew resisted with musket fire.

minutes . . . some kind of an animal that he had never seen before . . . raised out of the water. He did not see the body, only the head and what he supposed to be part of the neck. It had ears or bunches on the side of its head nearly as big as a pint cup. The waves at times would dash over its head, when it would throw water from its mouth or nose. It did not drift landward, but appeared stationary, with the exception of turning its head." The next day, July 28, the creature was seen by a man and three women—but this time it was in motion and "swam much faster than a horse could run on land."

Reports of the Bear Lake serpent continued for several decades, but were temporarily eclipsed in 1941 with the advent of Slimey Slim, the serpent that inhabited Lake Payette in Idaho. During July and August that summer more than 30 people—most of them boaters on the lake's seven miles of water—saw the monster. For a while, they kept quiet about it. Then Thomas L. Rogers, City Auditor of Boise, Idaho, decided to speak up. He told a reporter: "The serpent was about 50 feet long and going five miles an hour with a sort of undulating movement. . . . His head, which resembles that of a snub-nosed crocodile, was eight inches above the water. I'd say he was about 35 feet long on consideration."

With the publication of this story the lake was inundated with camera-wielding tourists hoping for a glimpse of Slimey Slim. After an article about him appeared in *Time* magazine, the monster seemed to turn shy, and little more was heard or seen of him. With Slim's disappearance, attention returned to Ogopogo, who, having been seen by a captain in the Canadian Fishery Patrol, had been described as being like "a telegraph pole with a sheep's head." An American visitor to Canada was struck "dumb with horror" on catching sight of the monster. On July 2, 1949, Ogopogo was seen by the Watson family of Montreal together with a Mr. Kray. Newsmen reported of their experience: "What the party saw was a long sinuous body, 30 feet in length, consisting of about five undulations, apparently separated from each other by about a two-foot space . . . . The length of each of the undulations . . . would have been about five feet. There appeared to be a forked tail, of which only one-half came above the water."

Three summers later Ogopogo presented himself to a woman visitor from Vancouver, swimming within a few hundred feet of her. "I am a stranger here," she said shortly afterward. "I did not even know such things existed. But I saw it so plainly. A head like a cow or horse that reared right out of the water. It was a wonderful sight. The coils glistened like two huge wheels. . . . There were ragged edges (along its back) like a saw. It was so beautiful with the sun shining on it. It was all so clear, so extraordinary. It came up three times, then submerged and disappeared."

Reports of the sea serpent mounted until 1964, when Ogopogo apparently went into retirement. However, one of the most graphic accounts of the creature was featured in *The Vernon Advertiser* of July 20, 1959. The writer, R. H. Millar, was the newspaper's owner-publisher, and the sighting of "this fabulous sea serpent" was clearly the highlight of his journalistic life. "Returning from a cruise down Okanagan Lake, traveling at 10 miles an hour, I noticed, about 250 feet in our wake, what appeared to be the serpent," he recorded. "On picking up the field glasses, my thought was verified. It was Ogopogo, and it was traveling a great deal faster than we were. I would judge around 15 to 17 miles an hour. The head was about nine inches above the water. The head is definitely snakelike with a blunt nose. . . . Our excitement was short-lived. We watched for about three minutes, as Ogie did not appear to like the boat coming on him broadside; [he] very gracefully reduced the five humps which were so plainly visible, lowered his head, and gradually submerged. At no time was the tail visible. The family's version of the color is very dark greenish. . . . This sea serpent glides gracefully in a smooth motion . . . . This would lead one to believe that in between the humps it possibly has some type of fin which it works . . . to control direction."

The publicity given to Ogopogo brought eye-witness versions of serpents in other North American lakes, including Flathead Lake in Montana; Lake Walker, Nevada; Lake Folsom, California; and Lake Champlain, Vermont. From Monterey in Southern California came reports of the so-called "monster of San Clemente," who was also known as the Old Man of Monterey. Further north, on Vancouver Island, a serpent nicknamed "Caddy" made a rival bid for the headlines. The most sober and authentic sounding account of Caddy goes back to 1950, when he was seen by Judge James Thomas Brown, then one of Saskatchewan's leading members of the judiciary. He was spending a winter holiday on the island when he, his wife, and daughter spotted Caddy some 150 yards from shore.

"His head [was] like a snake's [and] came out of the water four or five feet straight up," stated the judge. "Six or seven feet from the head, one of his big coils showed clearly. The coil itself was six or seven feet long, fully a foot thick, perfectly round and dark in color. . . . It seemed to look at us for a moment and then dived. It must have been swimming very fast, for when it came up again it was about 300 yards away . . . I got three good looks at him. On one occasion he came up almost right in front of us. There was no question about the serpent—it was quite a sight. I'd think the creature was 35 to 40 feet long. It was like a monstrous snake. It certainly wasn't any of those sea animals we know, like a porpoise, sea-lion and so on. I've seen them and know what they look like."

Monsters of the lakes and seas continued to make appearances in the present century. Passengers and crews of the *Dunbar Castle* in 1930, and again of the *Santa Clara* in 1947, sighted such monsters in the Atlantic. It must have been an added thrill for the passengers as they spotted the serpents swimming nearby. In the summer of 1966, while rowing across the Atlantic in their boat *English Rose III*, Captain John Ridgway and Sergeant Chay Blyth were nearly rammed by one of the marine monsters. It was shortly before midnight on July 25, and Blyth was asleep. Captain Ridgway, who was rowing, was suddenly "shocked to full wakefulness" by a strange swishing noise to starboard.

"I looked out into the water," he recounts in their book *A Fighting Chance*, "and suddenly saw the writhing, twisting shape of a great creature. It was outlined by the phosphorescence in the sea as if a string of neon lights were hanging from

Above: the partially decomposed body of a big sea animal washed ashore on the Massachusetts coast in 1970. It was about 30 feet long and weighed 15–20 tons. Although it had a long neck, it was believed to be a species of whale. Finding dead sea creatures on the shore is fairly common, and big ones keep the monster story alive.

Left: a sea serpent supposedly captured off the coast of England in 1897. Its totally unreal quality and the way the captors are so carefully holding their hands over what could be segment joins make it appear to be a hoax—all in fun from the men's expressions.

Below: a joke photo of Ogopogo, the Canadian lake monster, surfacing for a coffee break in 1960.

it. It was an enormous size, some 35 or more feet long, and it came toward me quite fast. I must have watched it for some 10 seconds. It headed straight at me and disappeared right beneath me. I stopped rowing. I was frozen with terror . . . I forced myself to turn my head to look over the port side. I saw nothing, but after a brief pause I heard a most tremendous splash. I thought this might be the head of the monster crashing into the sea after coming up for a brief look at us. I did not see the surfacing—just heard it. I am not an imaginative man, and I searched for a rational explanation for this incredible occurrence in the night as I picked up the oars and started rowing again . . . I reluctantly had to believe that there was only one thing it could have been—a sea serpent."

As far back as 1820 the English naturalist Sir Joseph Banks, who had sailed around the world with Captain Cook, had given scientific credence and his "full faith" to "the existence of our Serpent of the Sea." He was followed in this a few years later by the botanist and director of Kew Gardens, Sir William J. Hooker, who said of the sea serpent that, "It can now no longer be considered in association with hydras and mermaids, for there has been nothing said with regard to it inconsistent with reason. It may at least be assumed as a sober fact in Natural History . . ."

Below: John Ridgway and Chay Blyth in the *English Rose III*, the small boat in which the two rowed across the Atlantic during the summer of 1966. Ridgway is certain that he saw a 35-foot-long monster which headed straight for the boat one night. It came fast, but disappeared right underneath him as he sat in frozen horror.

59

Since that time, much has been learned about life underneath the ocean and about the ocean bed itself. In 1865 a Frenchman descended to a depth of 245 feet. Within a hundred years that record was smashed by Dr. Jacques Piccard and Lieutenant D. Walsh of the U.S. Navy. On January 23, 1960, these two men took the bathyscaphe *Trieste* down to a depth of 35,802 feet at Marianas Trench in the Pacific. This is the world's deepest trench and, measured from top to bottom, is higher than Mount Everest. They described the bottom as a "waste of snuff-colored ooze." Being able to go so far into the ocean's depths has increased the chances of an encounter with a deep-sea monster that may date from prehistoric days.

Explorers such as Piccard and the world-famous Captain Jacques Cousteau have seen species of fish that were previously unknown to or unseen by man. Swimming through the deep troughs, trenches, and ridges that make the ocean bed a kind of underwater mountain area, are millions of hitherto unclassified creatures. "I was astounded by what I saw in the shingle at Le Mourillon," writes Cousteau of one of his expeditions, ". . . rocks covered with green, brown, and silver forests of algae, and fishes unknown to me, swimming in crystal clear water. . . . I was in a jungle never seen by those who floated on the opaque roof." In 1969 the world's largest research submarine—the electrically powered *Ben Franklin* designed by Jacques Piccard—drifted to a depth of 600 feet below the Gulf Stream. Its six-man crew surfaced with numerous reports of sightings made through one or another of the craft's 29 viewing ports, including the observation of the tiny purple colored Hatchet fish.

From these and other expeditions it is obvious that man is determined to explore and chart the world beneath the sea. Scientists state that before long some 98 percent of the ocean floor will have been explored, and that such exploration could mean the discovery of any monster or monsters which have been living in the ocean ridges. The U.S. Navy is developing a Deep Submergence Search Vehicle, which will be prepared if it encounters more dangerous inhabitants than the prawns, starfish, and copepods already found to be living in the low-level oozes. Underwater television, sonar sensing equipment, and electronic flash lamps and floodlights will compensate for the lack of light.

Men like Cousteau have pioneered in building underwater houses and villages—such as the U.S. Navy's *Sealab* machines—in which aquanauts can live beneath the oceans for periods of up to 30 days. In Switzerland today there is a special tourist submarine that takes visitors beneath the surface of a lake for a view of the wonders down below. From that it is just another large step to underwater cruise liners which are being planned to take tourists under the waters of the ocean.

In recent years giant sharks whose heads measure some four feet from eye to eye have been photographed on the sea bed. This suggests that even bigger fish—the traditional monsters—are waiting to be found. In their places of so-called eternal darkness, the oceans go down six miles or more—and it is there that the kraken survivors or descendants may lurk. Not long ago a giant pink squid was captured off the coast of Peru. Its 35-

Right: the secrets of the sea may not remain hidden for much longer. As science develops more and more sophisticated equipment to explore the greatest depths, the chances of solving the monster riddle become greater. Here A. B. Rechnitzer (left) and Jacques Piccard are shown on board the *Trieste*, which Piccard piloted to a depth of 18,150 feet. Below: this submersible can carry out maintenance work on undersea wellheads at 2000 feet.

Above: the grotesque hatchet fish, *Argyropelecus hemigymus*, one of the deep-ocean creatures. This monster is less than three inches long, but who knows if it has giant companions in the silent depths?

foot-long tentacles and its eyes of a foot in diameter caused a sensation. Scientists suggest that the pink squid is nothing compared to the creatures that have yet to be caught. To back up their argument, they point to certain pieces of squid that have been taken from the stomach of whales. Projecting the size of the whole squid from the pieces, they say it would be more than 100 feet in length.

It does not seem too fanciful to imagine that one day in the future a nuclear powered submarine, such as the U.S. Navy's *Nautilus*, could be drifting silently beneath the ice cap at the North Pole when it was suddenly attacked by an underwater monster in defense of its home or family. A similar fate could happen to one of the proposed deep-sea cruise liners. No one knows who would emerge the victor, or how many lives might be lost. But one thing is certain. It would make the most sensational sea monster news in centuries—and this time the accounts could not be put down to the imagination or exaggeration of sailors.

4

The Loch Ness Monster

Among lake monsters, Nessie of Loch Ness in Scotland holds a special place. She has been pursued by submarines, featured on front pages, and starred in the movies—but her "stand-in" was the model pictured here.

The African python, which is capable of swallowing a goat, has been seen swimming in the Indian Ocean, sometimes traveling from island to island in search of food. Attempts by large snakes such as this to board passing ships in search of a resting place have naturally given rise to tales of sea monsters. Bits of floating timber or shipwreck may account for other monster stories. But it is possible that some accounts of sea monsters are genuine. They are disbelieved mainly because the creatures seen have not yet been identified by scientists, or are thought to be long extinct.

About 80 to 90 million years ago giant

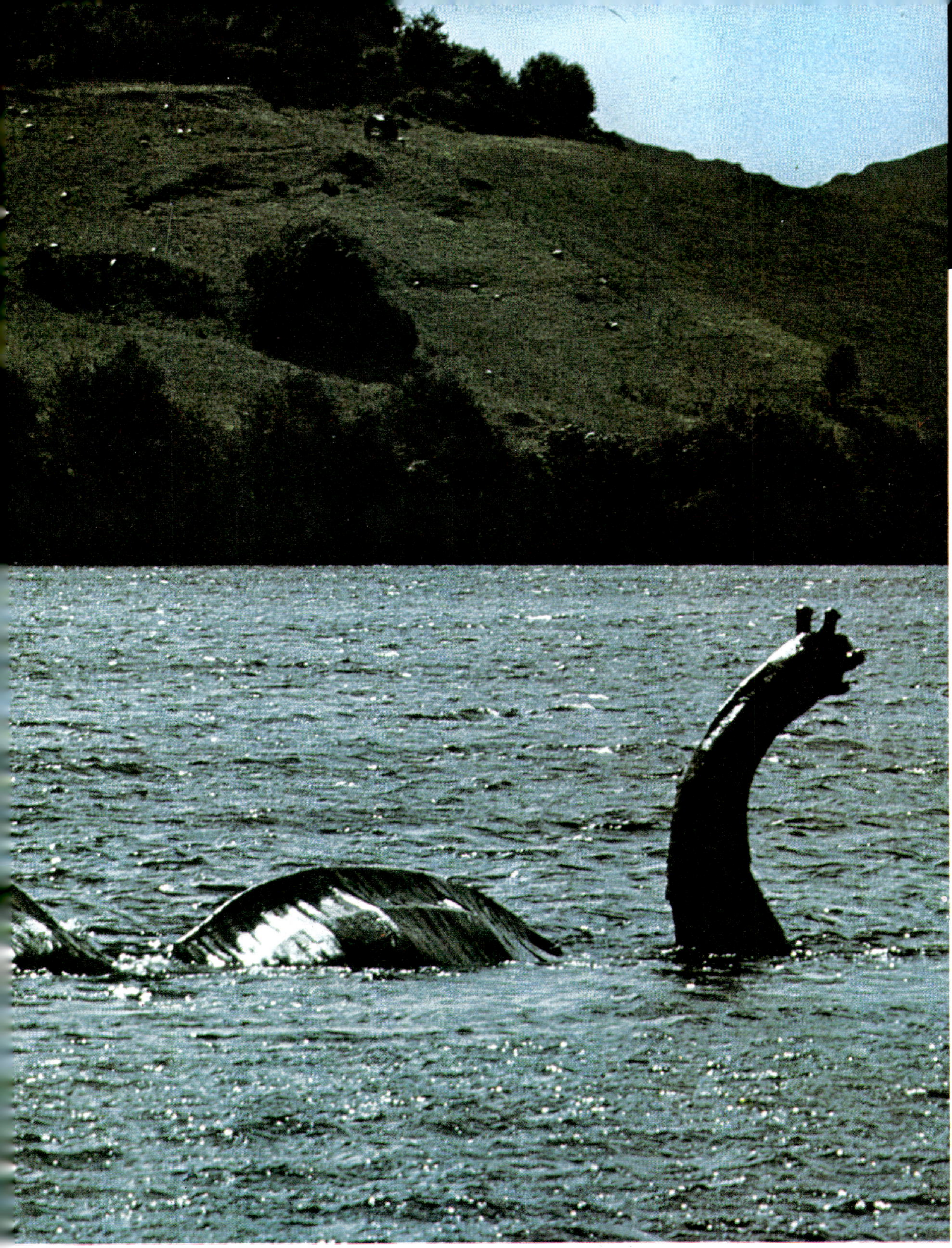

"A strange creature emerging from the bracken"

reptiles roamed the earth and scoured the oceans in search of food. For survival they depended on brute strength, adaptation to changing environments, and hiding from any danger they could not cope with. For many millions of years the seas were dominated by the fish-eating *plesiosaurus* with its barrel-shaped body and serpentine neck, and the sharklike *ichthyosaur*, or fish lizard. Gradually these animals were displaced by aggressive 40-foot-long sea lizards, the *mosasaurs*. We know that giant land animals began to disappear from the earth, but we do not know what happened to species of animals that were equally at home in the water. Could they have used their skills of adaptation and hiding to penetrate the depths of oceans and lakes and find a way to survive? It is not entirely impossible. After all, huge sea animals really did exist. They are not a figment of our imagination as some skeptics seem to imply. Let us explore the possibilities that may defy the skeptics.

Many of the Scottish lakes, or lochs as they are known in Scotland, are extremely deep. One of the deepest ones, Loch Ness, has become almost legendary because of its associations with repeated sightings of a monster. A dramatic and recent sighting took place in July 1933. Mr. and Mrs. George Spicer were driving home to London along the south bank of Loch Ness when they saw a strange creature emerging from the bracken. It appeared to have a long undulating neck little thicker than an elephant's

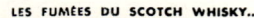

Above: a skeptical French cartoon makes the caustic suggestion that Scotch whisky provides the real source for the Loch Ness Monster.

Right: looking across the famous lake from the shoreline. Loch Ness is the largest body of fresh water in Great Britain, and its mean average depth is even twice that of the North Sea. Much of it is 700 feet deep, and it is 734 feet at the deepest recorded spot.

trunk, a tiny head, a thick ponderous body, and four feet or flappers. Carrying what seemed to be a young animal in its mouth, it lurched across the road, lumbered into the undergrowth, and disappeared with a splash into the lake. The whole startling incident lasted only a few seconds, but it left an indelible impression on the couple. Mr. Spicer later described the creature to a newspaper reporter as a "loathsome sight." He said it looked like "a huge snail with a long neck."

Despite the scorn heaped on Mr. Spicer by the leading scientists and zoologists of the day, there were many who believed his story of the 25-to-30-foot-long monster. Indeed, Spicer was not the only nor the first person to have seen—or claimed to have seen—the beast from the deep. Ever since the early 1880s there had been regular sightings of "Nessie," as the Scottish lake monster affectionately became known. Unaccountably, Nessie was popularly regarded as being female. At various times she was seen by a stonemason, a group of schoolchildren, and a forester working for the Duke of Portland. Further appearances were noted in 1912, 1927, and 1930, and descriptions of her personality and activities appeared in newspapers from Glasgow to Atlanta. However, it was not until the summer of 1933—the same summer that the Spicers reported their experience—that Nessie became an international pet. In that year, a new road was built on the north shore of the beast's lake home between Fort William and Inver-

The Creature from the Lake

It was four o'clock in the afternoon on July 22, 1933, and Mr. and Mrs. George Spicer were driving home to London after a tour of the highlands of Scotland. They were halfway between the villages of Dores and Foyer on the south bank of Loch Ness when Mrs. Spicer suddenly noticed something moving out from the bracken on the hillside.

She gave a shriek, and as they watched in horror, a long undulating neck, followed by a ponderous body, lumbered out of the bracken and across the road. It was dark elephant gray. Mr. Spicer said it looked like a huge snail with a long neck. It had a tiny head for its enormous size—about 25 to 30 feet long—and it was carrying what looked like a lamb in its mouth. It seemed to lurch along on flippers as the unbelieving Spicers stared at it. It paid no attention to them, although Mr. Spicer had braked the car hastily and leaped out onto the road. It plunged down a bank toward the lake, and disappeared with a splash into the otherwise still and placid waters. There was no trace left on the road of the incredible creature—just an ordinary man and woman staring at each other stunned, speechless, and very frightened.

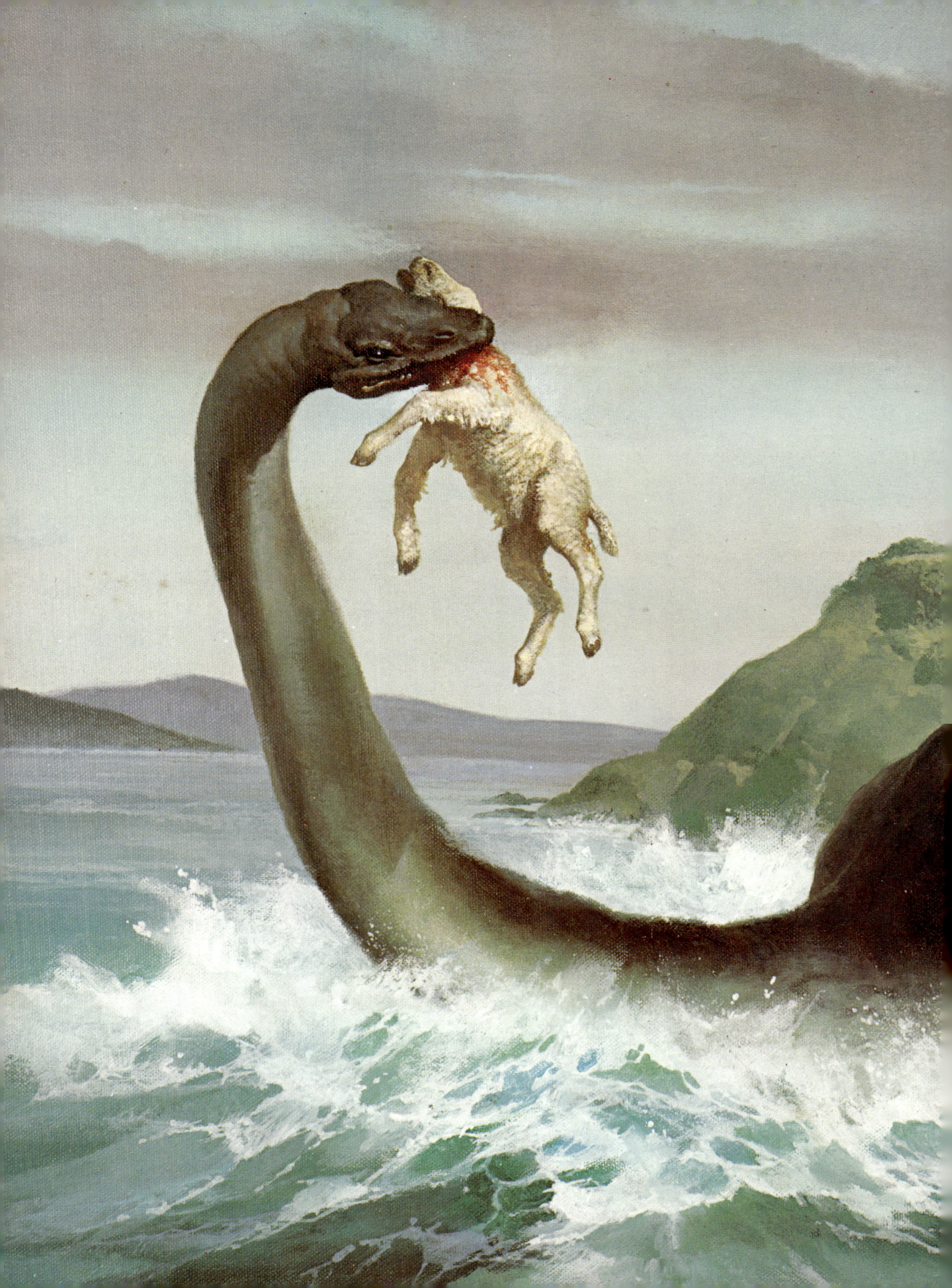

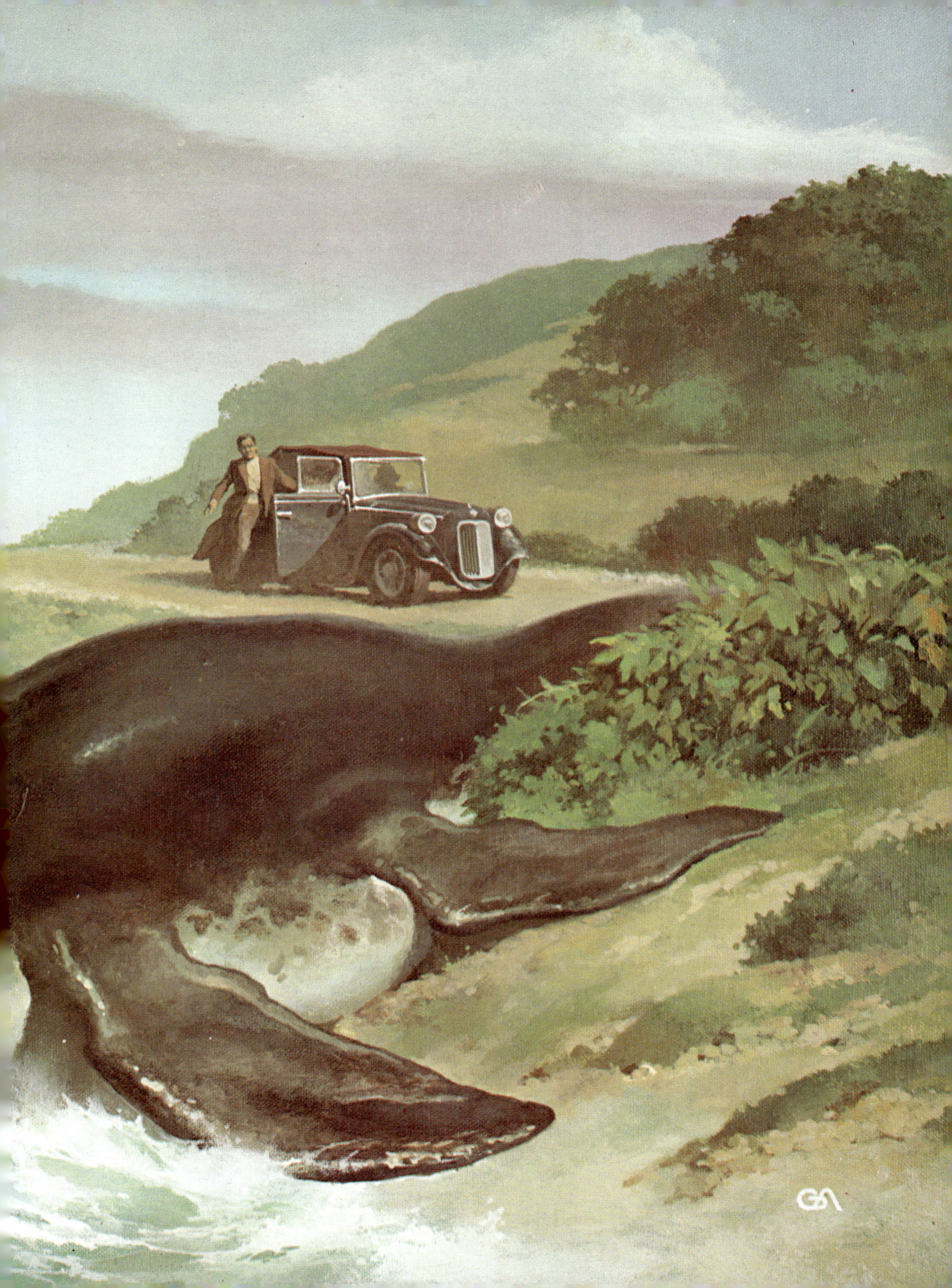

ness. According to local inhabitants, Nessie was roused from her sleep hundreds of feet beneath the surface of the lake by the noise of the drilling, the vibrations from the explosions, and the boulders that every now and then crashed down the banks. Annoyed at having her slumber disturbed, she broke water, clambered ashore, and proceeded to roam through the surrounding bracken feasting on any young animals she could get her teeth into.

It was around this period that an Automobile Association patrolman also spotted the sea serpent. He too described it as "a thing with a number of humps above the water line. . . . It had a small head and very long slender neck." Shortly after this a third person—local resident Hugh Gray—actually took a photograph of Nessie, and it was reproduced in newspapers and magazines throughout the world. This photograph, like many that were subsequently taken, was not well-defined. Doubters dismissed the object in the picture as a floating tree trunk or log. For those who accepted this theory, the explanations for the Loch Ness phenomenon was clear: some careless road construction workers had thrown a large piece of wood into the loch. Other disbelievers in the monster's existence preferred to think that someone was trying to pull the public's leg.

In order to seek the truth, journalists from all parts of the globe descended on the area—feature writers and photographers from New York, Rio de Janeiro, and Tokyo among them. They were joined in their watch for the monster by a troop of Boy Scouts. When an old lady disappeared from her home nearby, some said that she had become Nessie's latest victim, and declared that the beast was an agent of the devil. Others asserted that she wouldn't attack a human, and was timid and unaggressive by nature. However, both camps agreed that the monster could change shape at will, that she could rise and sink in the loch vertically, and that her body was iridescent, which made her color vary with the light.

Right: in 1934, the enthusiasm for the Loch Ness monster reached such proportions that the Illustrated London News devoted much of an issue to a discussion of the creature. The cover picture was a drawing made from a sketch by an eyewitness, B. A. Russell. Below: the best-known photograph of Nessie records the long neck and small head reported by many Nessie spotters. It was taken by Kenneth Wilson, a London doctor, on vacation in 1934, and was published in a newspaper. Since then it, and one other successful shot, have been inspected from every angle, analyzed, and argued about.

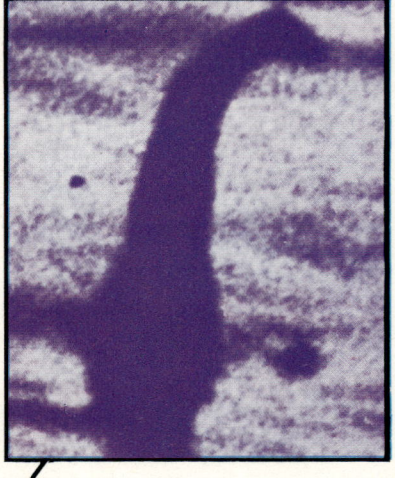

THE ILLUSTRATED LONDON NEWS

The Copyright of all the Editorial Matter, both Engravings and Letterpress, is Strictly Reserved in Great Britain, the Colonies, Europe, and the United States of America.

SATURDAY, JANUARY 13, 1934.

THE "MONSTER" SKETCHED BY MR. B. A. RUSSELL, OF FORT AUGUSTUS.

OUR SPECIAL ARTIST INVESTIGATES THE LOCH NESS MONSTER: THE APPEARANCE OF THE MYSTERIOUS CREATURE AS VOUCHED FOR BY MR. B. A. RUSSELL, M.A., OF FORT AUGUSTUS.

In view of the very great interest that is being taken in the so-called Monster of Loch Ness—even in the august pages of our contemporary, "The Times "—we sent our Special Artist, Mr. G. H. Davis, to the Loch, in order that he might record there the evidence of a number of reliable persons who are convinced that they have seen a strange apparition in the waters of the Loch—with the results shown on this page and on two succeeding pages. Our artist's method was to draw the "monster" from a sketch made by the witness concerned; and his drawings were passed as correct by the witnesses. The "monster" depicted above is that vouched for by Mr. B. A. Russell, M.A., of the School House, Fort Augustus. Mr. Russell, a very calm, level-headed man, states that he saw the mysterious head, as here drawn by himself and by Mr. Davis, on Sunday, October 1, 1933, between 10 and 10.30 in the morning, and that it was visible for twelve minutes. His observation-point was near Captain Meiklem's house, near Fort Augustus, at a height of over 100 feet. The sun, he told our artist, was shining and the Loch was absolutely calm. He watched the head and neck moving with a "horizontal undulation" about five feet above the surface, and noted that the creature covered half a mile during the twelve minutes he had it under view. It was some 700 yards from him and was silhouetted against the pale-grey water, so that it was very evident.

DRAWN BY G. H. DAVIS, OUR SPECIAL ARTIST AT LOCH NESS, FROM A SKETCH BY MR. B. A. RUSSELL, WHO PASSED THE DRAWING AS CORRECT. (SEE ALSO PAGES 40-41 AND 42.)

Below: part of the 1934 issue of the Illustrated London News, presenting a compilation of several eyewitness reports of the popular if elusive monster.

To support their view that Nessie was alive, well, and dwelling in the lake, her fans produced statistical and historical evidence.

First of all they pointed out that Loch Ness—the largest mass of fresh water in Great Britain—was 22½ miles long and 734 feet deep in the middle. This meant it could easily be the watery home of any huge monster, serpent, or "thing from the deep." They then delved back to the year 565 when a sighting of Niseag—to give Nessie her Gaelic name—was noted by the Irish Saint Columba. For two years previously, Saint Columba had been working to convert the heathen Picts, Scots, and Northumbrians

OUR SPECIAL ARTIST INVESTIGATES THE LOCH NESS MONSTER:

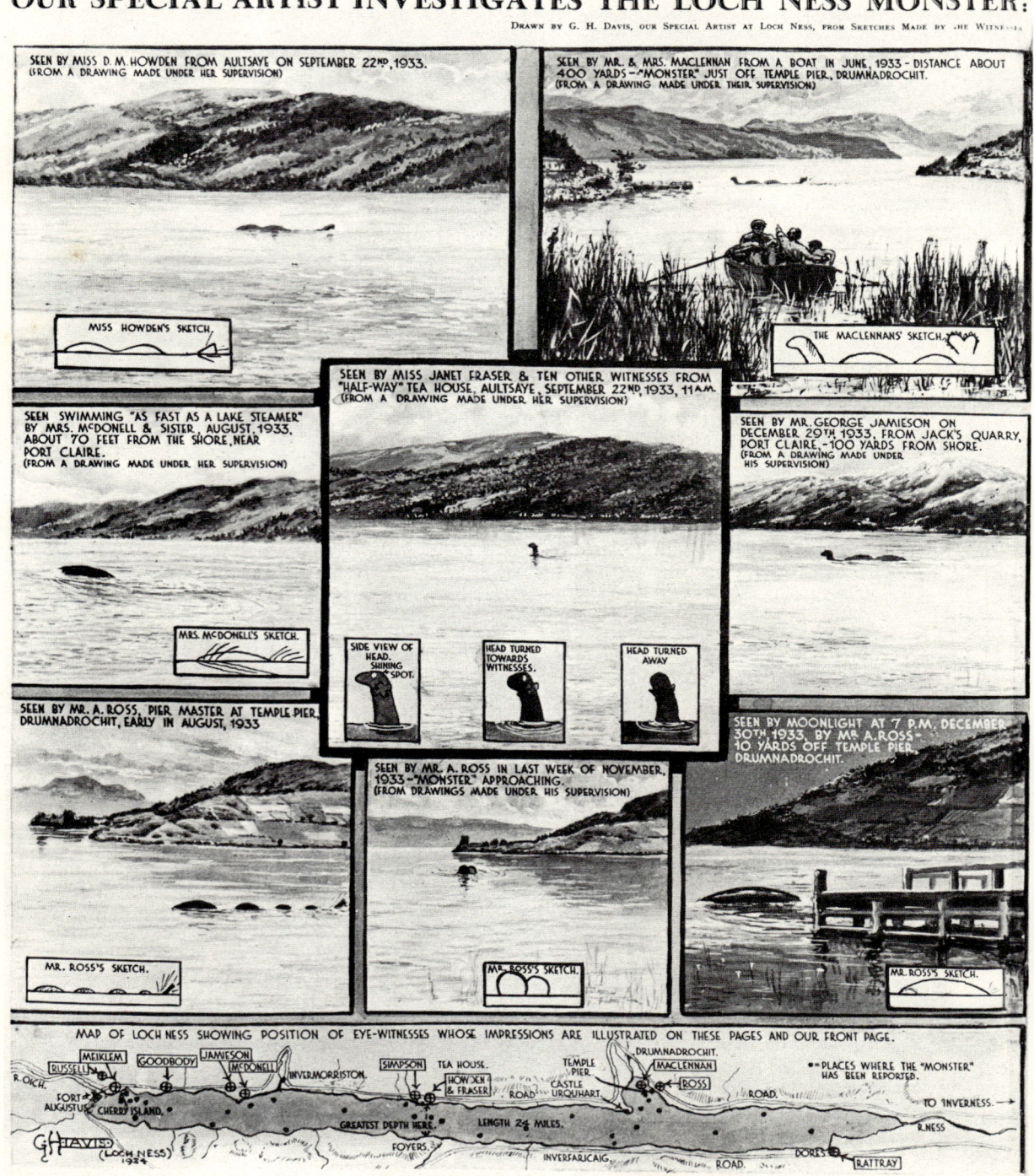

DRAWN BY G. H. DAVIS, OUR SPECIAL ARTIST AT LOCH NESS, FROM SKETCHES MADE BY THE WITNESSES

ACCORDING TO RELIABLE PERSONS WHO ARE CERTAIN THAT THEY HAVE SEEN A MYSTERIOUS

to Christianity from his new monastery on the island of Iona, off the west coast of Scotland. His mission took him throughout the north of the country. When he came to Loch Ness he found some of the local people burying a neighbor who had been badly mauled by the lake monster while out swimming, and who afterward died of his wounds. The corpse had been brought to land by boatmen armed with grappling hooks, but this did not deter one of the missionary's followers from swimming across the narrows at the head of the loch in order to bring over a small boat moored on the other side. Clad only in his loin cloth, the man was making

THE STRANGE CREATURE AS VOUCHED FOR BY EYE-WITNESSES

CREATURE IN LOCH NESS: THE "MONSTER" SKETCHED BY WITNESSES INTERVIEWED

good headway when he was suddenly confronted by a "very odd looking beastie, something like a huge frog, only it was not a frog."

After surfacing and gulping in some air, the monster proceeded to make an open-mouthed attack on the swimmer. She bore down on the defenseless man, and would undoubtedly have swallowed him alive had it not been for the intervention of Columba. Used to dealing with the "irreligious savages," he thought nothing of addressing a monster equally in need of God. With head raised and arms outstretched he commanded: "Go thou no further nor touch the man. Go back at once!" Then, according to an 8th-century biography of the saint, "on hearing this word... the monster was terrified and fled away again more

Below: John Cobb, the speedboat racer, shown in the cockpit of his jet-propelled *Crusader* on Loch Ness in 1952. He was trying to set a world water speed record.

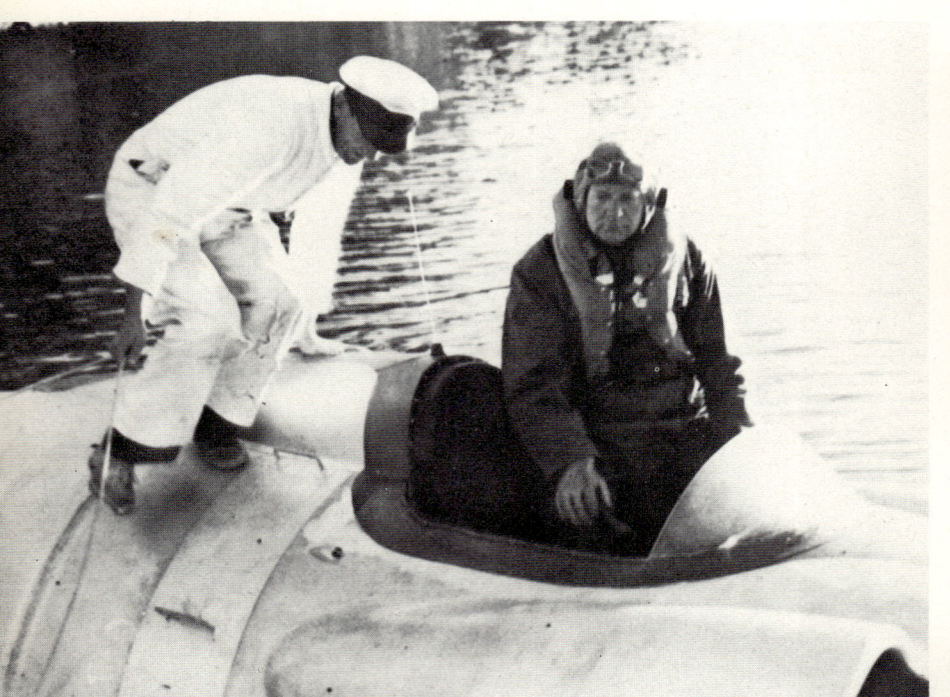

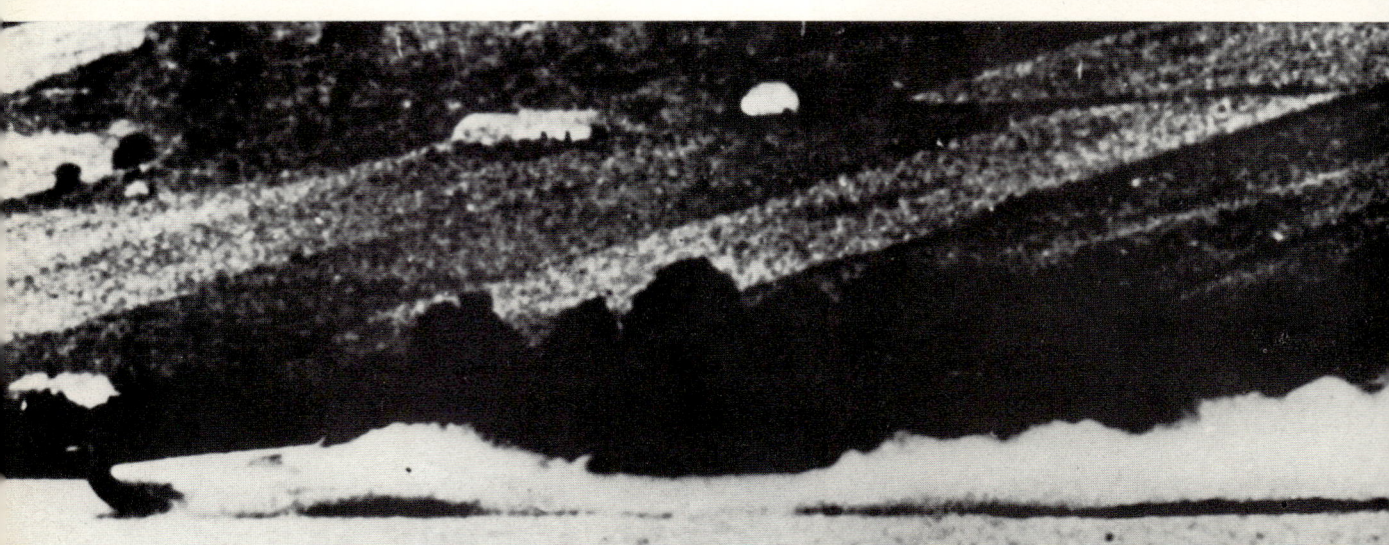

Below: 10 days after failing to break the world record, Cobb set out on Loch Ness to try again. **Bottom:** seconds after Cobb had succeeded in setting a record on September 29, 1952, he slowed down—and the pressure on his boat at such high speed caused it to break up. Cobb was flung to his death. Eyewitnesses claimed that they saw Nessie's wake at the spot where Cobb slowed, and believed that the creature had ruffled the water when disturbed.

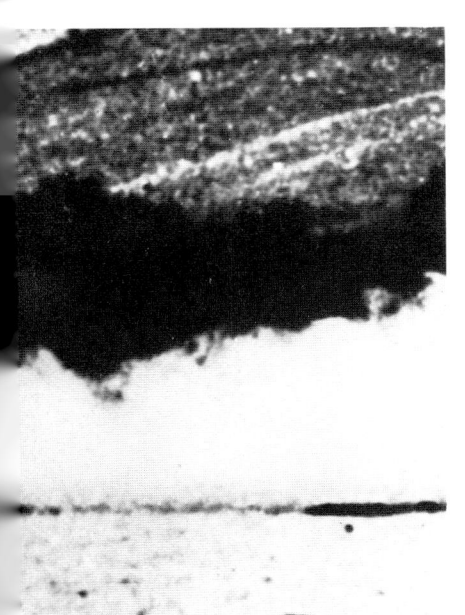

quickly than if it had been dragged on by ropes, though it approached Lugne [the swimmer] as he swam so closely that between man and monster there was no more than the length of one punt pole." This feat was hailed by the potential converts as a manifestation of holy power, and the saint—who was noted everywhere for his "cheerfulness and virtue"—recruited scores of new believers.

From then on the Loch Ness monster became as much a part of Scottish lore as the teachings of Columba himself. At the beginning of the 19th-century, children were warned against playing on the banks of the lake because it was rumored that Nessie was once again restless and about to pounce. Even such a level-headed, no-nonsense person as the novelist Sir Walter Scott perpetuated monster stories. On November 23, 1827, he wrote in his journal: "Clanronald told us . . . that a set of his kinsmen—believing that the fabulous 'water-cow' inhabited a small lake near his house—resolved to drag the monster into day. With this in view, they bivouacked by the side of the lake in which they placed, by way of nightbait, two small anchors such as belong to boats, each baited with the carcass of a dog, slain for the purpose. They expected the water-cow would gorge on the bait and were prepared to drag her ashore the next morning when, to their confusion, the baits were found untouched."

Perhaps the lake monster cleverly avoided the trap. In any case she seems to show herself only when she wants to, often unexpectedly. A few decades later, in 1880, a diver named Duncan McDonald came across the beast while attempting to salvage a boat wrecked on Loch Ness. "I was underwater about my work," he said, "when all of a sudden the monster swam by me as cool and calm as you please. She paid no heed to me, but I got a glance at one of her eyes as she went by. It was small, gray and baleful. I would not have liked to have displeased or angered her in any way!" By then the major feeling about Nessie was that although ugly of face and bad-tempered when aroused, she did not go out of her way to trouble or frighten people.

Another 19th-century account of the Loch Ness monster gives an entirely different view of the lake inhabitant. It said: "A noted demon once inhabited Loch Ness and was a source of terror to the neighborhood. Like other kelpies [water-spirits in the shape of a horse] he was in the habit of browsing along the roadside, all bridled and saddled, as if waiting for someone to mount him. When any unwary traveler did so, the kelpie took to his heels, and presently plunged into deep water with his victim on his back." The teller of this tale mustered up few believers, perhaps because of the great disparity between his description and the more generally accepted ones.

Coming up to the 1930s period when Nessie was at the peak of her popularity, hotelier John Mackay sighted the lake serpent on May 22, 1933. He said that he saw the lake animal make the water "froth and foam" as she reared her ludicrously small head in the air. Although Mackay beat the Spicers by two months in his encounter with Nessie, it was George Spicer's story that was most listened to and believed in nonprofessional quarters.

Before the year 1933 was out Loch Ness and its celebrated inhabitant had become one of the principal tourist attractions of

Left: Nessie's appearances at best are irregular and widely spaced. Conducting a systematic search for the monster requires patience, a certain disregard for cold damp mists, and special equipment. Here a 36-inch telescopic lens adapted to a 35mm camera is poised across the loch in the chill early morning.

Below: Tim Dinsdale, a former aeronautical engineer who now devotes himself to a study of the monster, with a model he made in 1960 based on film he himself succeeded in getting of Nessie. Since then he has refined his model from further information of sightings.

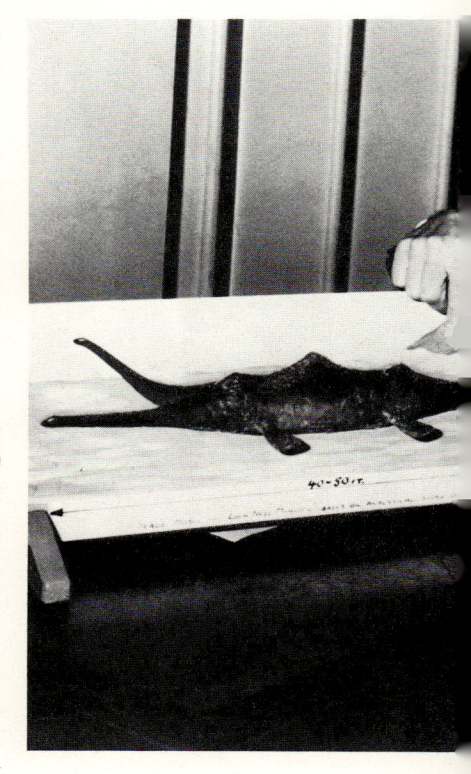

Great Britain. Holiday makers by the thousands got into their cars and headed north to park along the shores of the lake and gaze out over the water. Between 1933 and 1974, some 3000 people attested to having spotted Nessie as she surfaced, dived, or swam tranquilly along. Claims were also made that the monster made a sound—a cry of "anger and anguish" when nearly run down by a car. Waiting for Nessie rivaled watching flagpole squatters and marathon dancers, which were big vogues of the mid-30s. Hundreds of sun-dazzled or fog-smeared photographs—with an indistinct blur in them—were offered as Nessie at play. The eager Nessie-hunters were given short shrift by E. G. Boulenger, Director of the Aquarium in the London Zoo. He wrote in October 1933 that:

"The case of the Loch Ness monster is worthy of our consideration if only because it presents a striking example of mass hallucination ... For countless centuries a wealth of weird and eerie legend has centered around this great inland waterway ... Any person with the slightest knowledge of human nature should therefore find no difficulty in understanding how an animal, once said to have been seen by a few persons, should shortly after have revealed itself to many more."

Another reason for so many sightings was suggested by the more cynical, who pointed to the rewards being offered for the capture of Nessie alive. The money prizes included one for $500 from the New York Zoo, £20,000 ($50,000 at today's exchange rate) from the Bertram Mills circus, and a mammoth £1 million ($2½ million) from the makers of Black and White Whisky. The whisky firm stipulated that the monster, if taken, had to be declared genuine by officials of the British Museum. Debate on Nessie even reached the British House of Commons, and, on November 12, 1933, a member of Parliament called for an official investigation to settle the "monster matter" for once and all. The Government spokesman who replied stated that such an

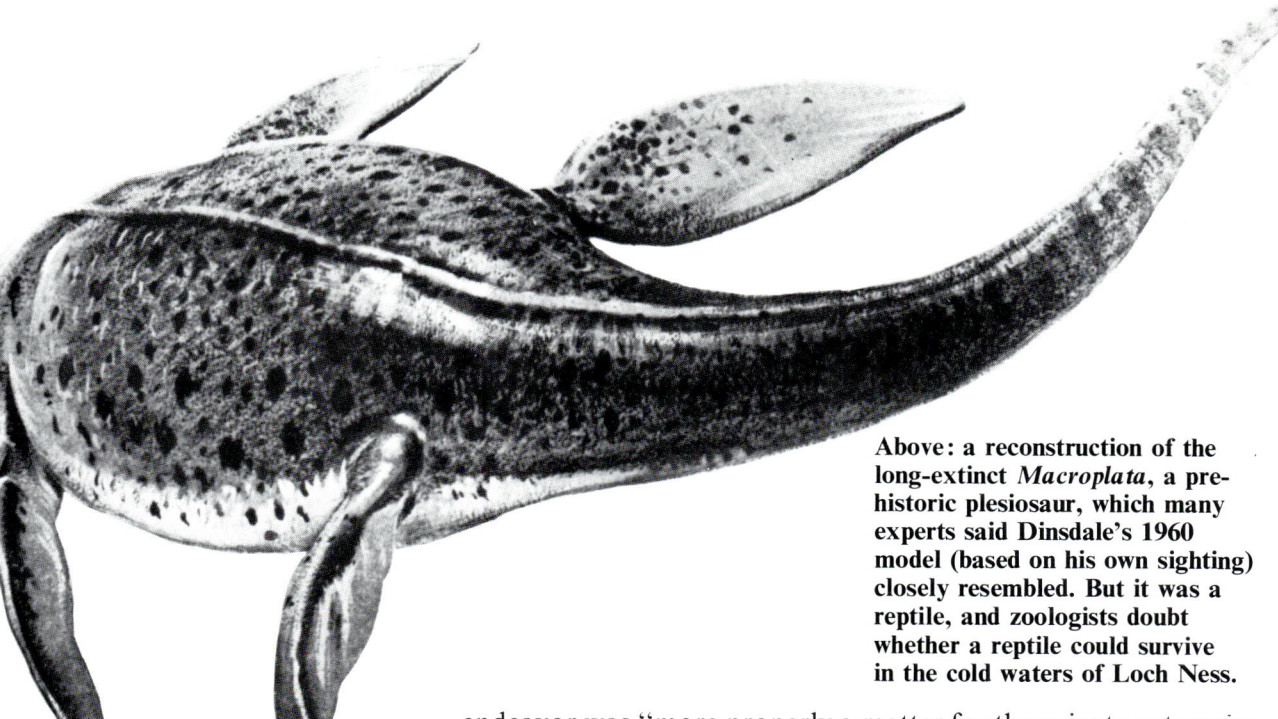

Above: a reconstruction of the long-extinct *Macroplata*, a prehistoric plesiosaur, which many experts said Dinsdale's 1960 model (based on his own sighting) closely resembled. But it was a reptile, and zoologists doubt whether a reptile could survive in the cold waters of Loch Ness.

endeavor was "more properly a matter for the private enterprise of scientists aided by the zeal of the press and photographers."

It was on the same day of the government debate that Mr. Hugh Gray took the famous picture mentioned before. It was published first of all in the Scottish *Daily Record*, and then reproduced throughout the world. That was all the confirmation Nessie's admirers needed. According to Gray, he was walking along the loch shore near Foyers, camera in hand, when, from his vantage point on a 30-foot-high cliff, he saw the quiet water beneath him "explode into commotion." A huge form reared in front of him and a long neck stretched out. During the few seconds that the monster was on the surface, Mr. Gray took five hasty shots of her. Due to the spray that was thrown up, the "object of considerable dimensions" was not clearly discerned. Later, four of the five negatives proved to be blank. The good negative was shown to technical experts of the Kodak camera company, who testified that it had not been tampered with in any way—and once again only the professional zoologists remained dissatisfied. Mr. J. R. Norman of the British Museum stated that "the possibilities leveled down to the object being a bottlenose whale, one of the larger species of shark, or just mere wreckage." Professor Graham Kerr of Glasgow University considered the photograph to be "unconvincing as a representation of a living creature."

A local bailiff, Alexander Campbell, held stage center in June 1934 when he told his Nessie tale. According to him, he had been out fishing in a row boat with two friends when a "dark gray, rocklike hump" rose from the water, stayed there for a moment, and then submerged without causing more than a few ripples. (Campbell was persistent if not consistent. In 1958 he said that Nessie had again appeared before him, but this time she created a "small tidal wave" that sent him toppling into the lake.)

In 1934, too, came the first of the numerous books about the celebrated Loch Ness monster. It listed 47 sightings complete with drawings and photographs. In January a newsreel film said to be of Nessie was shown in London to a private audience. The camera caught her about 100 yards away as she swam past. Of this event *The Times* on January 4 said: "The most clearly evident movements are those of the tail or flukes. This appendage is naturally darker than the body. The photographers describe the general color of the creature as gray, that of the tail as black. Indeterminate movements of the water beside the monster as it swims suggests the action of something in the nature of fins or paddles." Unfortunately, this film disappeared before any study of its authenticity was made.

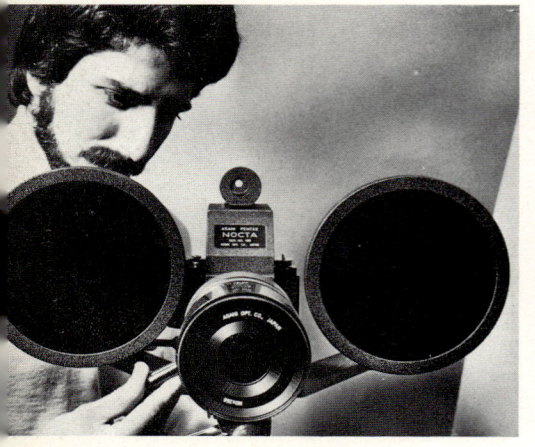

Three months later Nessie reached the attention of royalty when the Duke of York—who became King George VI—addressed the London Inverness Association, and told members:

"Its [Nessie's] fame has reached every part of the earth. It has entered the nurseries of this country. The other day, I was in the nursery, and my younger daughter, Margaret Rose [now Princess Margaret], aged three, was looking at a fairy-story picture book. She came across a picture of a dragon, and described it to her mother: 'Oh, look Mummy, what a darling little Loch Ness monster!'"

The Abbot of the Monastery in Fort Augustus, at the foot of the loch, added his opinion to the controversy with his announcement that, "the monster is a true amphibian, capable of living either on land or in water, with four rudimentary legs or paddles, an extraordinarily flexible neck, broad shoulders and a strong, broad, flat tail, capable of violently churning the waters around it." Then, in April 1934, came the famous "surgeon's picture" taken by a London surgeon named Kenneth Wilson. He had a telephoto lens on his camera for his hobby of photographing trains. While driving south from a vacation in northern Scotland, he stopped the car at 7:30 a.m. and got out to stretch his legs. He was on a slope 200 feet above the surface of Loch Ness when he suddenly saw the water begin to swirl, and spotted "the head of some strange animal rising." He ran back to the car, returned with the three-quarter plate camera, and rapidly took four pictures. Two of them turned out to be duds, but one showed the monster's long, arched neck, and the last plate revealed its out-of-proportion small head about to submerge. The picture of the head and neck appeared in the London *Daily Mail*. As so often in the past, the public showed interest, but the authorities remained skeptical.

How can a creature of Nessie's size hide out so well in a lake, even one as large as Loch Ness? Part of the answer is that this lake is the receptacle of peat particles from 45 mountain streams and five rivers. Little is visible below a depth of six feet, and underwater exploration by lung divers is stymied by the dense, impenetrable murk. For the most part, Nessie has been seen as a series of humps when she came up from the depths for air. This proved the case with the investigation backed by the insurance tycoon Sir Edward Mountain, who kept an intense five-week watch on the loch in the summer of 1934. Of the 17 monster sightings reported, 11 of them were of humps. This was also true when a Glendoe sawmill worker saw Nessie at 9 a.m. that same summer. He reported a series of 12 humps "each a foot out of water." He said in an article in the *Scotsman* of July 6, 1934: "The

Above: the endless watch on Loch Ness. Experts estimate that there is one sighting for every 350 hours spent watching the lake.

Below: even at night Nessie is pursued. An expedition in 1970 used this infra-red camera for seeing 100 yards in total dark.

day was so clear that I could distinguish drops of water as they fell when the monster shook itself. It reached Glendoe Pier and stretched its neck out of the water where a stream enters the loch. It did not actually come ashore, but seemed to be hunting about the edge, and I cannot see how it could move as it did without using flippers or feet."

The start of World War II in 1939 put an end to speculation about lake serpents for a time, and it wasn't until the early 1950s that Nessie made news again. Then came the usual spate of sightings and photographs. An account of one of the sightings appeared in *Harper's Magazine* in 1957. The witness, Mr. David Slorach, told how he had been driving to Inverness for a business appointment on the morning of February 4, 1954. On looking to his right to admire the view of Loch Ness, he saw something unusual in the water. Its shape reminded him of a "comic ornament popular at one time—a china cat with a long neck. The thing ahead of me looked exactly like the neck and head part. One black floppy 'ear' fell over where the eye might be, and four black streaks ran down the 'neck' ... The object [was] traveling through the water at great speed, throwing up a huge wave behind. I slowed to around 35 miles per hour, but the object raced ahead and was soon out of sight behind a clump of trees."

Inspired by the renewed interest in Nessie, the BBC sent a television team equipped with a sonic depth-finder to the loch in an attempt to prove or disprove the legend. Obligingly, a "mysterious object" came into range, was recorded some 12 feet below the surface, and was followed to a depth of 60 feet before it lost the depth finder. Experts of the British Museum and the Zoological Society of London were asked their opinions, but they scoffed at the idea of an unfamiliar beast. Instead they spoke of sturgeons, fin whales, sperm whales, and that old standby, the tree trunk. One man was not convinced by the scoffing professionals, however. This was the author and journalist F. W. Holiday. As he put it, his "consuming interest in the problem of the Loch Ness Orm or monster began in 1933 when I was 12 years old." One morning 29 years later, in August 1962, he settled himself on a hillside near Foyers, and, with his binoculars, waited for the monster to make an appearance. He described what happened in his book *The Great Orm of Loch Ness*:

"A dozen or so yards into the loch, opposite the leat [a water channel] an object made a sudden appearance. It was black and glistening and rounded, and it projected about three feet above the surface. Instantly it plunged under again, violently, and produced an enormous upsurge of water. A huge circular wave raced toward me as if from a diving hippopotamus ... Just below the surface, I then made out a shape. It was thick in the middle and tapered toward the extremities. It was a sort of blackish-gray in color ... When a chance puff of wind touched the surface, it disappeared in a maze of ripples; but when the water stilled, it was always there. Its size—judging from the width of the leat—was between 40 and 45 feet long."

Holiday also recorded that a film taken at the loch in 1960 was later shown to specialists at the Ministry of Defense's Joint Air Reconnaissance Intelligence Center. After carefully studying and analyzing the images—which showed the customary humped

Above: a Japanese skin diver is poised in readiness to snap a picture of Nessie in her home. A Japanese team went to Loch Ness to hunt the monster in 1973.

Below: in spite of the murkiness of the peat-laden waters of the loch, there have been underwater sightings. Here a strobe camera caught a flipper of a 30-foot-long creature in August 1972.

Above: an American skipper, Dan Taylor, and a British crew on his home-made mini-submarine in which they plumbed the depths of Loch Ness to find Nessie in 1969. Taylor's expedition was sponsored by an American encyclopedia firm.

object moving through the water—the experts decided that something, if not Nessie, existed in the deep. They came to the conclusion that the subject of the film "probably is an animate object." However, Nessie came the nearest to getting a certificate of authenticity in 1963 when on the evening of February 2 Grampian and Border Television, an independent British station, transmitted a program about her. The program was presented as a panel discussion, and one of the participants was David James, a Highland laird and a Member of Parliament at the time. He had a few months before kept a two-week, round-the-clock watch on the shores of the loch. Mr. James, founder of "The Loch Ness Phenomena Investigation Bureau," told viewers that his watch had been successful. He said:

"On October 19 [1962], in the middle of the afternoon, we had seven people at Temple Pier, and suddenly everyone was alerted by widespread activity among the salmon. After a few minutes the salmon started panicking—porpoising out in the middle of the loch—and immediately we were aware that there was an object following the salmon which was seen by practically everyone there for three or four minutes." On hearing that—and after sifting through years of recorded evidence—the panel announced that: "We find that there is some unidentified animate object in Loch Ness which, if it be mammal, reptile, fish, or mollusc of any known order, is of such a size as to be worthy of careful scientific examination and identification. If it is not of a known order, it represents a challenge which is only capable of being answered by controlled investigation on carefully scientific principles."

Six years after this television program, in August 1968, a team from the Department of Electronic Engineering of Birmingham University mounted a sonar system on one of the piers on the loch. The scan was directed at the southeast corner, and, according to author Holiday, the scientists achieved "dramatic success." The cathode display screen was photographed every 10 seconds by a movie camera, but for some days, nothing of interest was seen. Then, at 4:30 on the afternoon of August 28, there occurred a remarkable 13-minute sequence. "A large object rose rapidly from the floor of the loch at a range of .8 kilometer, its speed of ascent being about 100 feet a minute," Holiday wrote. "It was rising obliquely away from the sonar source at a velocity of about 6.5 knots, and was soon 1 kilometer away. Its upward movement had now slowed to about 60 feet a minute. This object then changed direction to move toward the pier at about 9 knots, keeping constant depth. Finally, it plunged to the bottom at about 100 feet a minute before rising again at .6 kilometer range, when it apparently moved out of the sonar beam and was lost to record. Meanwhile, a second large object had been detected at .5 kilometer from the pier which finally dived at the astonishing velocity of 450 feet a minute. Both objects remained many feet below the surface."

One of the leaders of the team, Dr. H. Braithwaite, later wrote a magazine article on the sonar experiment in which he stated that, "the high rate of ascent and descent makes it seem very unlikely [that the objects were shoals of fish], and fishery biologists we have consulted cannot suggest what fish they might

Left: the mini-submarine *Pisces* in 1969 in another underwater search for Nessie and the final answer to it all. *Pisces*, which was sponsored by an English newspaper, could stay under the surface for more than 12 hours, and was equipped with a sonar system. Skin divers were among the crew. Below: Elliott Sinclair, one of the *Pisces* team, inside the sub. He is surrounded by the electronic equipment designed to detect any sign of Nessie—who didn't show.

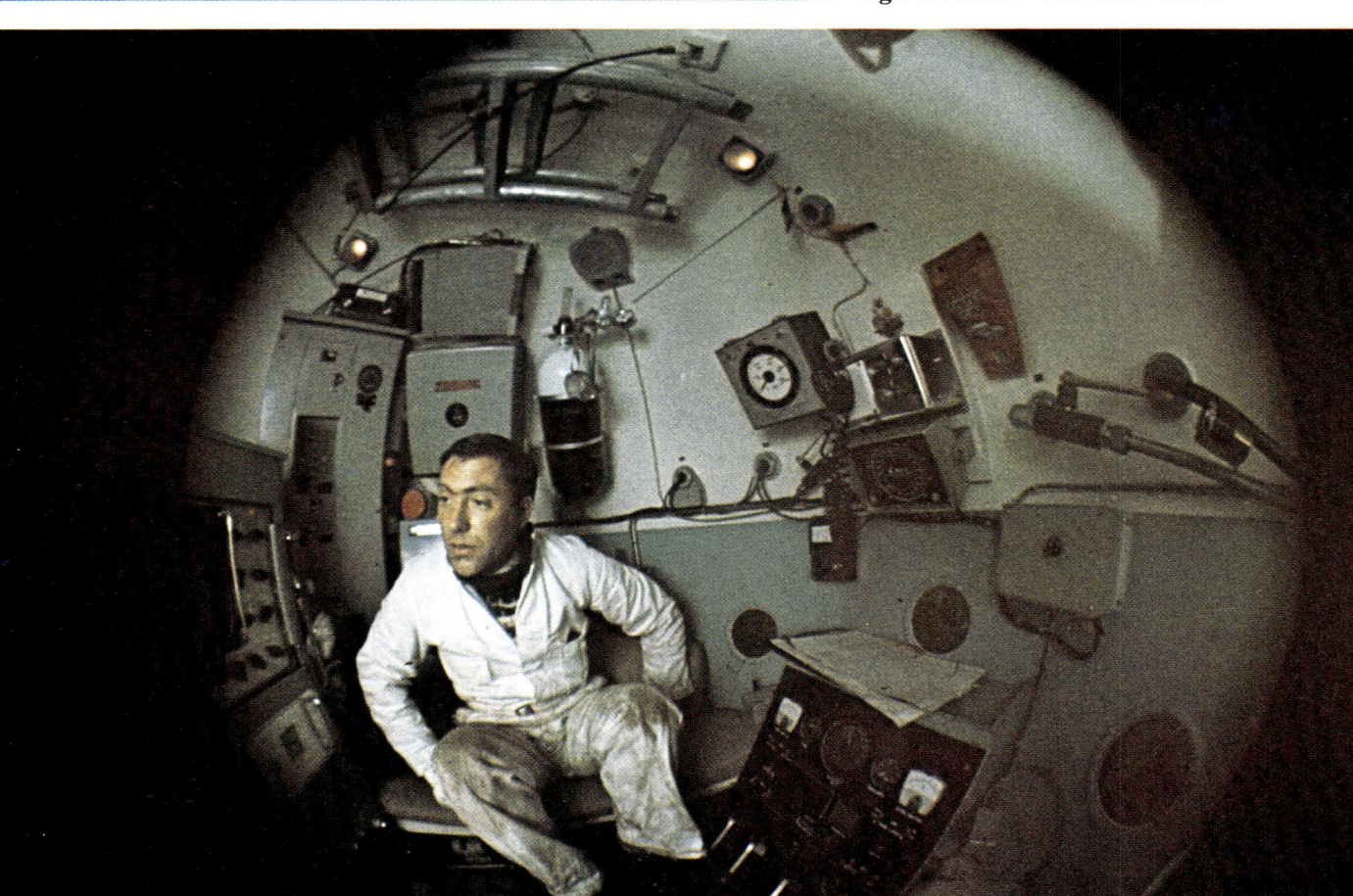

be. It is a temptation to suppose they must be the fabulous Loch Ness monsters, now observed for the first time in their underwater activities."

There the matter rested and there—admired or maligned, sought-after or ignored—lies Nessie. Among the latest to try to explain her away is Dr. Roy Mackal of the Biochemistry Department of the University of Chicago. On visiting Loch Ness in 1966, he suggested that the monster was most likely some kind of "giant sea slug." Four years later another American, Dr. Robert Rines of the Massachusetts Academy of Applied Science, took a Klein side-scan sonar to the banks of the loch. In the deeper water he detected several large moving objects, and said afterward in a radio interview: "We wouldn't have been here if we didn't have the suspicion that there is something very large in this loch. My own view now, after having personal interviews with, I think, highly reliable people, is that there is an amazing scientific discovery awaiting the world here in Loch Ness."

However, Loch Ness is far from being the only fresh-water lake with a quota of monsters. Loch Morar, some 30 miles to the west and completely separated from Loch Ness, has its own Great Worm. At the beginning of 1970 a scientific team headed by the British biologist Dr. Neill Bass began a survey of the site. The team's efforts were rewarded on the afternoon of July 14 when Dr. Bass and two colleagues went for a walk on the north shore of the loch. It started to rain and, while his companions sheltered under some nearby trees, Bass gazed out over the rain-flecked water. Then, just as the weather improved and a breeze came up, the surface was broken by a "black, smooth-looking hump-shaped object." It was some 300 yards away, and by the time his fellow scientists had joined him, the creature had submerged vertically. Thirty seconds later, however, there was another disturbance in the water. It was followed by what the survey's final report called "a spreading circular wake or ripple which radiated across the waves to about 50 yards diameter." For a while Bass thought the object might have been a giant eel, but then realized that the movement was uncharacteristic of such a fish. In the end the report declared it to be "an animate object of a species with which he [Bass] was not familiar in this type of habitat."

The following month a zoology student, Alan Butterworth, also spotted the monster through binoculars while keeping watch on Loch Morar. The water was calm, and visibility was good. The watcher observed a "dark-colored hump," dome-shaped and similar to a rocky islet. The object was about $1\frac{1}{2}$ miles away. Butterworth left to get his camera, and when he returned with it the Great Worm had disappeared. So the most important goal—to obtain authentic film of the monster—was not fulfilled.

Not to be outdone by Scotland, countries from France to Australia to Argentina have claimed that their inland lakes contain their own mysterious and outsized monsters. Ireland, whose legends of lake monsters go back to ancient times, easily heads the list.

Another region with a long tradition of lake monster stories is Scandinavia. It was while visiting Scandinavia and Iceland in 1860 that the English clergyman and author Reverend Sabine Baring-Gould heard of the Skrimsl, a "half-fabulous" monster said to inhabit some of the Icelandic lakes. Although he didn't see any of the beasts himself, he spoke to educated and respectable lawyers and farmers who told of one particular Skrimsl. It was almost 50 feet long and apparently looked much like the more famous Nessie. "I should have been inclined to set the whole story down as a myth," wrote Baring-Gould, "were it not for the fact that the accounts of all the witnesses tallied with remarkable minuteness, and the monster is said to have been seen not in one portion of the lake (the Lagarflot) only, but at different points."

The clergyman also learned of a similar creature in Norway—a

Right: Frank Searle, one of Nessie's most determined hunters. He first saw the monster in 1965, gave up his job four years later, and moved to Loch Ness to camp by the lakeside in hopes of getting absolute proof of her existence. He claimed 18 sightings by 1972. Searle spent up to 19 hours a day waiting by the side of the loch, camera poised and at the ready. **Left:** one of the photographs taken of Nessie at home in 1972 by the persistent Frank Searle.

Left: another Searle photograph of the dim humps of the monster.

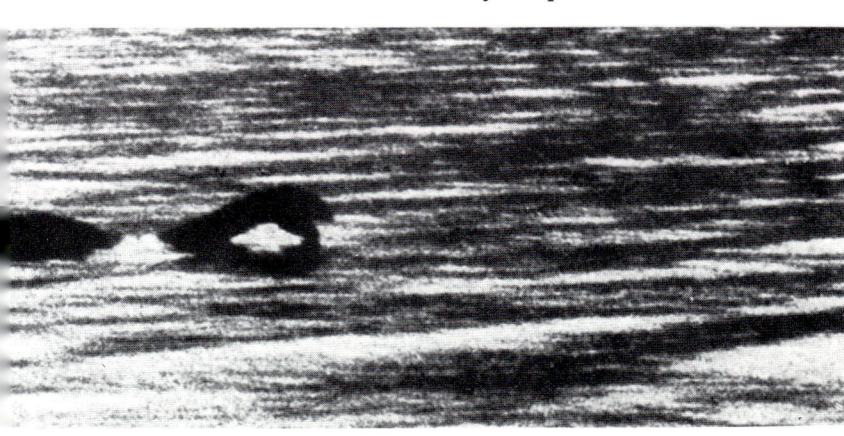

Below: even in the depths of winter, Searle keeps vigil. This photo was taken January 8, 1974.

Top: one of the special effects crew working on the enormous mechanical Loch Ness Monster created for a 1969 movie, *The Private Life of Sherlock Holmes*, filmed in Scotland. During the shooting the mechanical Nessie disappeared into the depths of the lake, presumably to provide a bizarre companion for the real Nessie lurking somewhere in the dark, mysterious loch herself. Above: a still from the film as the mechanical monster encounters Dr. Watson, Holmes, and Gabrielle in a small boat.

slimy, gray-brown animal that terrified the people living around Lake Suldal. Its head was said to be as big as a row boat. The story was told of a man who, crossing the lake in a small craft, was set upon by the monster and seized by the arm. The attacker let go only when the victim recited the Lord's Prayer. But the man's arm was mangled and useless thereafter.

In Sweden itself Lake Storsjö has long been associated with monsters, and a turn-of-the-century zoologist, Dr. Peter Olsson, spent several years analyzing and sifting through 22 reports containing numerous sightings. The Lake Storsjö monster, or leviathan, was said to be white-maned and reddish in color, more like an enormous seahorse than anything else. It was first spotted in 1839 by some farmers, and reports of it continued well into the 20th-century. The creature differed from its fellows by virtue of its speed, which was estimated at a rapid 45 m.p.h. Olsson regarded it as "the fastest and most fascinating of all lake dwellers," a view which was shared by the *New York Times* in 1946. Under the heading, "Normalcy?," an article in the paper stated that, after the insanity of World War II, things were getting back into their old familiar and comforting routine because monsters were being seen again.

Shortly afterward a Stockholm newspaper reported that a group of three people had seen the Lake Storsjö monster when the lake's "calm shining surface was broken by a giant snakelike object with three prickly dark humps. It swam at a good parallel to the shore, on which the waves caused by the object were breaking." More sightings were reported in 1965. This inspired the local tourist board to use a color picture of the monster in its brochures, and to boast that the beast was Sweden's answer to the Loch Ness monster.

Ireland is Scotland's nearest rival in the "creature in the lake" stakes, however. There are innumerable reports, accounts, and twice-told tales about such beings. In recent times the stories have proved as vivid and interesting as ever. For example, there is the one of three Dublin priests. On the evening of May 18, 1960, Fathers Daniel Murray, Matthew Burke, and Richard Quigly went trout fishing off Lake Ree—called Lough Ree in Ireland—on the River Shannon. They were exceedingly pleased with the warmth, the calmness of the water, and the way the fish were biting. All at once the tranquility was shattered by the approach of a large flat-headed animal they couldn't identify. It was about 100 yards from where they sat. When it swam up the lake toward them, the startled priests jumped to their feet. "Do you see what I see," one of them cried out, and the other two nodded their heads in amazement. "It went down under the water," stated one of the priests later, "and came up again in the form of a loop. The length from the end of the coil to the head was six feet. There was about 18 inches of head and neck over the water. The head and neck were narrow in comparison to the thickness of a good-sized salmon. It was getting its propulsion from underneath the water, and we did not see all of it."

Lough Ree, where this sighting took place, is one of many small lakes in Ireland, whose west coast is dotted with them. Each lake it seems has its own particular inhabitant. It was this fact which in the 1960s inspired Captain Lionel Leslie, an explorer and cousin of Sir Winston Churchill, to mount his own investigation of the monsters. In October 1965 he went to Lough Fadda in Galway, and exploded a small charge of gelignite against a rock. He hoped that this would bring a *Peiste*, or lake monster, to the surface. Sure enough, a few seconds later a large black object appeared some 50 yards from the shore. Dismissing the possibility of it being a piece of wood or debris, Captain Leslie later told a reporter from *The Irish Independent*, "I am satisfied beyond any doubt that there is a monster in Lough Fadda." A subsequent netting operation failed to capture the creature. Captain Leslie tried again in 1969. In the company of author F. W. Holiday, he plumbed the depths of Loughs Shanakeever, Auna, and Nahooin, but came up with nothing. Television cameras were on hand to record the hoped-for event, but all they were able to film was Captain Leslie, his disheartened band of monster hunters, and the constant rain.

Such experiences—even though they make ready fodder for newspapers and TV—tend to lessen scientific belief in the existence of lake creatures. John Wilson, warden of the bird sanctuary operated by the Royal Society for the Protection of Birds in Lancashire, England, is another skeptic. Writing in the Society's journal in the summer of 1974, he says that Nessie, and presumably those like her, could well be a group of otters at play. "Four or five otters swimming in line with heads, bodies, and tails continually appearing and disappearing combine to look like a prehistoric monster," he states.

For the steady line of Nessie-spotters since George Spicer hit the headlines in 1933, the Loch Ness monster is very much a reality. For the disbelievers, explanations like Dr. Mackal's sea slug or Mr. Wilson's otters are perfectly logical and satisfactory. What is the real truth? No one knows yet!

Below: a photograph of Nessie that is clearer than most. It was taken by a resident of Inverness, Scotland, on a sightseeing trip to Loch Ness with visitors in 1969.

5

Did the Dinosaurs Survive?

Because most of the world has been mapped out, we tend to forget that much still remains to be explored. Geographers may take bearings from distant mountain ranges, follow a river along its banks, or photograph regions from the air. However, they will not usually penetrate huge areas of swamp or forest, climb inaccessible peaks, or plumb the depths of lakes. Even discounting the vast wastes of Antarctica, nearly a tenth of the earth's land surface remains almost totally unexplored. Who can guess what lies in the unknown?

In the last 150 years, many new large animals have been discovered. Some, like

Every schoolchild knows that huge and fierce dinosaurs once roamed the face of the earth. The question now is whether there are still some stray survivors of that monstrous species living in the caves and jungles of little-known and unexplored areas—ready to attack. Right: an Asian dinosaur of giant size and frightening strength. It had powerful jaws and big pointed teeth that could tear its victims to pieces. This monster, which reached the overwhelming size of 20 feet high and 45 feet long, moved firmly on strong hindlegs.

85

"Harrowing adventure in the heart of West Africa"

Below: Ivan T. Sanderson, the naturalist and writer who spent most of his life in exotic and inaccessible parts of the world, photographed with one of his less frightening animal friends during a program for children.

the king cheetah, have been found in areas close to habitation and well-traveled by zoologists and big-game hunters. They had, for some reason, escaped notice. Others, such as the okapi, had taken refuge in remote and difficult country. Because they were believed to be extinct, descriptions of them by local residents had at first been discounted. It is always exciting to find a new species; but to discover that an animal, thought to have been long vanished, still survives is even more thrilling. It is as if, in a reassuring way, it had somehow managed to overcome both the forces of nature and our technological world.

If there is any likelihood of finding other living animals that we thought would never be seen again, it is in unexplored and difficult territory where they may have fled from the competition of newer and more successful species. We know that huge dinosaurs and giant reptiles became extinct about 60 million years ago, probably due to climatic changes that affected their food supply. But what happened to their smaller relatives needing less food? Were they able to find a better area and slowly adapt to changes? Perhaps so. For, although most of the world has undergone violent geological changes in the last 60 million years, Central Africa—hot and swampy—has remained geologically stable. It is essentially the same land mass it was when the giants roamed the earth, much of it almost impenetrable and unexplored. If any creature has survived from the age of dinosaurs it is here that it would be found. It is certainly here that tales of dinosaurs and other massive monsters abound and persist. Those who tell the tales are often respected scientists.

The well-known naturalist and writer Ivan T. Sanderson, for example, recounts a harrowing adventure on the Mainyu River in the heart of West Africa. The river ran "straight as a man-made canal," and Sanderson's canoe glided along with the paddles hardly being used. Ahead of him, in the lead canoe, was his fellow explorer and animal collector Gerald Russell. A hundred feet of water separated the two boats as they approached a deep shadowy gorge hemmed in by sheer high walls and huge black caves. The two explorers had only recently ventured that far inland, and their two African aides—Ben and Bassi—were equally strange to the area. The adventurers were near the middle of the winding mile-and-a-half-long gorge when their smooth progress was abruptly disturbed. "The most terrible noise I have heard short of an oncoming earthquake or the explosion of an aerial torpedo at close range, suddenly burst from one of the big caves on my right," declared Sanderson in his book More "Things." "Ben, who was sitting up front in our little canoe . . . immediately dropped backward into the canoe. Bassi in the lead canoe did likewise, but Gerald tried to about-face in the strong swirling current, putting himself broadside to the current. I started to paddle like mad, but was swept close to the entrance of the cave from which the noise had come."

A few moments later, when both canoes were opposite the mouth of the cave, an ear-splitting roar came out of it. In Sanderson's own words: "Something enormous rose out of the water, turning it to sherry-colored foam, and then, again roaring, plunged below. This 'thing' was shiny black and was the *head* of something, shaped like a seal but flattened from above to below. It was about the size of a full-grown hippopotamus—this head, I mean. We exited from the gorge at a speed that would have done credit to the Harvard Eight, and it was not until we entered the pool (from which the Mainyu stretched north) that Bassi and Ben came to."

Sanderson and Russell asked the two Africans about the monster, but, not being river people, they could provide no answer. Finally, however, they both yelled "M'koo-m'bemboo," grabbed their paddles, and sped across the pool. The group soon rejoined the rest of its 20-strong party. The other Africans were all local men, and showed great concern over their leaders' frightening experience. The river people among them confirmed Bassi and Ben's opinion that the dreadful creature was one of the M'koo. Said Sanderson: "These animals lived there all the time, they told us, and that is why there were no crocodiles or hippos in the Mainyu. (There were hundreds of both in the pool, the other river, and the Cross River.) But, they went on, M'koo does not eat flesh, but only the big liana fruits and the juicy herbage by the river."

Ivan Sanderson's fantastic encounter with a monster occurred in 1932, and he never did find out the exact nature of the gigantic thing that had so dramatically displayed itself. It is difficult to dismiss his experience as the product of an overstimulated imagination, for Sanderson's story has been accepted by a number of experts in the monster field. Among them is the reputable zoologist and author Dr. Bernard Heuvelmans, who refers to the incident in his wide-ranging and definitive book *On the Track of Unknown Animals*. In this book Heuvelmans stresses that the sighting of the M'koo and other monster evidence came from "a first-rate naturalist whose works are authorities all over the world." Indeed, as a well-traveled and well-informed expert in such matters, Sanderson knew that there had been a "very curious going-on in Africa for more than a century." What he had seen and heard led him to ask: could there still be dinosaurs living in some remoter corners of the African continent, and in other isolated parts of the earth?

To Sanderson, this idea was not too startling—even though dinosaurs are one of a group of huge reptiles that lived during Mesozoic times some 70 to 220 million years ago. After all, he and others had seen what could have been a monster left over from prehistoric times, and he felt that Africa was still a relatively unexplored continent. "Its vast jungle and swamplands have been by-passed in all the modern hubbub," he stated in *More "Things"* in 1969, "and thousands of locations that were fairly well known 50 years ago have now been virtually lost. The mere size of the place is quite beyond comprehension to those who have not visited it, so it is quite useless to suggest that there is not room in it for all manner of things as yet unknown." For proof of this, Sanderson and his fellow explorers did not need to go back further than 1913 when the German government sent a special expedition to its colony in the mountainous Cameroons. The expedition was led by Captain Freiherr von Stein, and its purpose was to make a general survey, map the area, and pinpoint the whereabouts of its vegetable and mineral fields.

Because of the outbreak of World War I the report was never

Was It Really a Dinosaur?

As recently as 1932 a Swedish rubber plantation overseer came across a huge monster in Central Africa. Out hunting in the swampy Kasai valley, J. C. Johanson and his African bearer suddenly saw a creature about 16 yards long with a lizard's head and tail. The men started for home without waiting to see more, but in crossing a swamp on the way they again stumbled on the giant. It was tearing lumps of flesh from a rhinoceros it had killed.

"It was simply terrifying," Johanson later wrote ". . . At first I was careful not to stir, then I thought of my camera. I could plainly hear the crunching of rhino bones in the lizard's mouth. Just as I clicked, it jumped into deep water. The experience was too much for my nervous system. Completely exhausted, I sank down behind the bush that had given me shelter. Blackness reigned before my eyes. . . . I must have looked like one demented when at last I regained camp . . . waving the camera about in a silly way and emitting unintelligible sounds . . . For eight days I lay in a fever, unconscious nearly all the time."

The photographs Johanson had snapped came out, but were not very clear. Might they really have been of a dinosaur that had survived extinction?

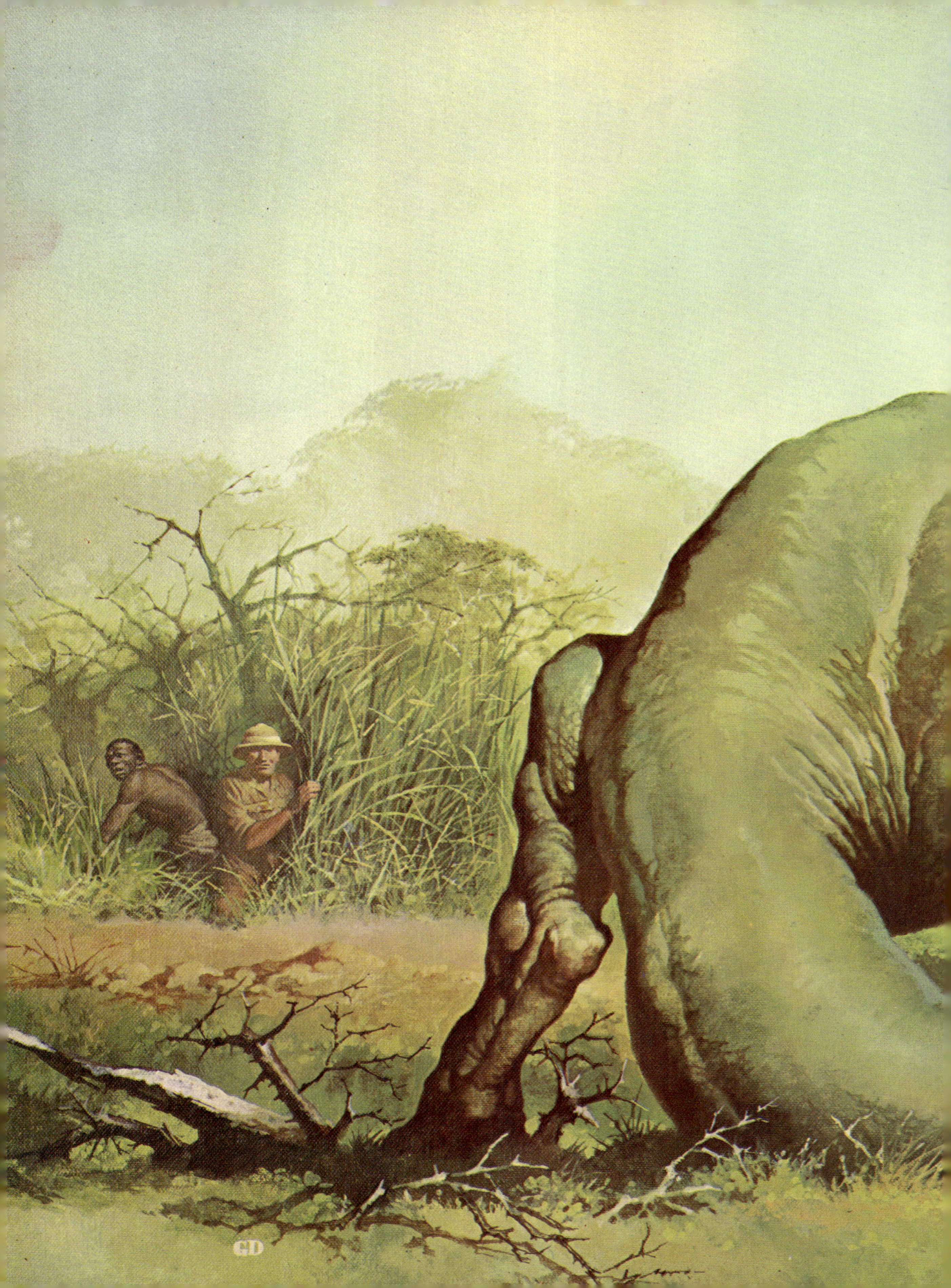

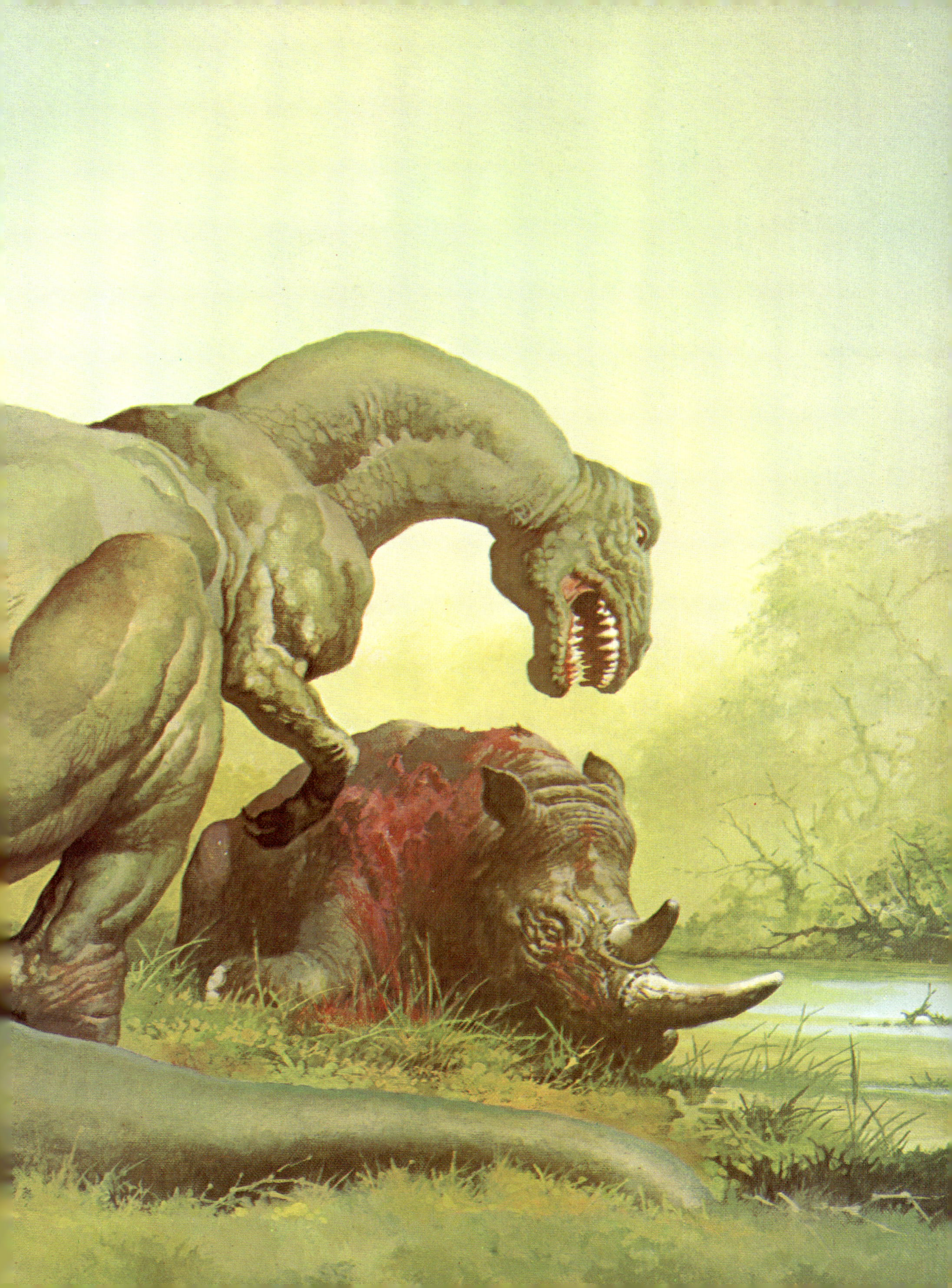

published, but the contents of the manuscript were later made available to those in search of sensational monster material. Captain von Stein, a disciplined and hard-headed soldier, wrote in the report that the people who lived by the rivers told him of a "very mysterious thing" that dwelt in the water. In his book *Exotic Zoology*, scientist Willy Ley quotes from the von Stein report. He points out that the captain recorded the experiences of respected guides who, without knowing each other, gave the same details and "characteristic features" about the water beast.

The creature—which at the time of the expedition was spotted in a section of the Sanga River previously said to be non-navigable—was described as of a "brownish-gray color with a smooth skin, its size approximately that of an elephant . . . It is said to have a long and very flexible neck and only one tooth, but a very long one; some say it is a horn. A few spoke about a long muscular tail like that of an alligator. Canoes coming near it are said to be doomed; the animal is said to attack the vessels at once and to kill the crews, but without eating the bodies. The creature is said to live in the caves that have been washed out by the river . . . It is said to climb the shore even at daytime in search of food; its diet is said to be entirely vegetable."

The fact that the monster was a vegetarian convinced von Stein that it was more likely to be a factual beast than a mythical one. The outsized animals of mythology showed no such reluctance to tear human flesh, drink blood, and crunch bones. His belief was strengthened when he was shown the creature's favorite food, "a kind of liana with large white blossoms, with a milky sap and apple-like fruits." He was also taken to a spot by another river where the monster had apparently trampled a fresh path in order to reach the food it liked best. Twenty-five years later, in 1938, the captain's findings were confirmed by another German, Dr. Leo von Boxberger. He was a magistrate who had spent many years working in the Cameroons. "The belief in a gigantic water-animal," he wrote, "described as a reptile with a long thin neck, exists among the natives throughout the Southern Cameroons wherever they form part of the Congo basin, and also to the west of this area . . . wherever the great rivers are broad and deep and are flanked by virgin forest."

However, neither man was the first European to have experiences of monsters on the so-called Dark Continent. This distinction probably lies with two others of their countrymen, Carl Hagenbeck and Hans Schomburgk. Their adventure took place in 1909.

Hagenbeck and Schomburgk were two renowned wild animal dealers. For years they had heard identical stories from locals and travelers about the existence of what Hagenbeck in his book *Beasts and Man* called "an immense and wholly unknown animal." Known as the King of the Zoos because of his work in supplying wild animals, Hagenbeck was fascinated by the creature reported to be half dragon and half elephant. It was said to have a single horn like the rhinoceros, but as Dr. Heuvelmans later points out, "an animal may look like a rhinoceros without being one." Hagenbeck believed the beast to be a dinosaur, one that was "seemingly akin to the brontosaurus." At "great expense" he later sent out an expedition to

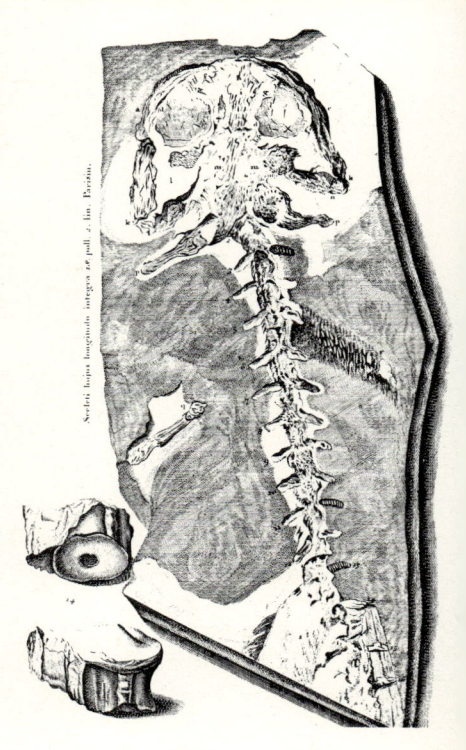

Above: how the earth must have trembled in those far-off times when monstrously huge dinosaurs battled each other! Here is what the scene might have looked like in an attack by *Tyrannosaurus rex*, largest biped dinosaur that ever lived, on the immense but weaker duck-billed *Trachodon*. Left: our knowledge of dinosaurs is comparatively new. For many centuries men took no particular note of fossil bones uncovered, or decided that they belonged to human giants. These bones of an *ichthyosaurus* were explained learnedly in 1726 as the bones of one of the vast numbers of people drowned in the biblical flood. Right: a 19th-century expedition collects dinosaur bones for the American professor Othniel Charles Marsh, one of the first scientists to study dinosaurs by using uncovered fossil material.

Above: drawing of a *Triceratops*, a three-horned dinosaur. When a Belgian named Lepage, reported being chased by a horned monster in Africa in 1919, the well-known naturalist Bernard Heuvelmans said that the animal described most resembled the *Triceratops*.

Below: the German wild game dealer Carl Hagenbeck. From his experiences in Africa at the turn of this century, he was convinced that a dinosaur-like reptile still existed in the jungle swamplands.

find the beast. Unfortunately, the party was forced to return without having discovered any evidence for or against the monster's presence.

It was not until ten years later—and after Captain von Stein had written his report—that the monsters of central Africa again made news. In the London *Times* of November 17, 1919, a story stated that an "extraordinary monster" had been encountered in what was then the Belgian Congo. In October it had charged a Monsieur Lepage, who was in charge of railway construction in the area. Lepage fired on the beast, and then fled with the creature in full pursuit. Only when the animal tired and gave up the chase was he able to examine it through his binoculars. The animal, he told *The Times* correspondent in Port Elizabeth, was some "24 feet in length with a long pointed snout adorned with tusks like horns and a short horn above the nostrils. The front feet were like those of a horse, and the hind hoofs were cloven. There was a scaly lump on the monster's shoulder."

Soon afterward the animal—by then said to be a dinosaur—rampaged through a nearby village, killing some of the inhabitants. Despite this, the Belgian government prohibited anyone from hurting or molesting the beast. Officials told a hunt that was organized that the animal was "probably a relic of antiquity," and therefore must not be harmed. "There is," added *The Times*, "a wild trackless region in the neighborhood which contains many swamps and marshes, where, says the head of the [local] museum, it is possible that a few primeval monsters may survive."

The Times account made a particular impression on Captain Leicester Stevens, who was even more excited when on December

Above: a sketch by big game hunter Walter Winans of the *brontosaurus* he claimed had been described to him by Carl Hagenbeck. Dr. Heuvelmans said that it was completely unlike a true *brontosaurus*, calling it the "mongrel offspring of a lion and a medieval dragon."

Below: a true *brontosaurus*, which was a herbivorous dinosaur up to 60 feet long. Bones have been found in the western United States.

4 he read a report from Africa that the monster had been seen in another part of the Congo. This time the beast, said to be a brontosaurus, had been trailed by a Belgian big game hunter. He had followed the "strange spoor" for some 12 miles, and had then come across an animal "certainly of the rhinoceros order with large scales reaching far down its body." He fired at the monster, which then threw its head up and lumbered off into a swamp. "The American Smithsonian expedition," the report ended, "was in search of the monster . . . when it met with a serious railway accident in which several persons were killed."

After the fatal accident, the Smithsonian Institution offered a $3 million reward for the monster, dead or alive. On learning this, Captain Stevens decided that he would hunt the dinosaur down. With his mongrel dog Laddie, which was part wolf, he set out by train from London's Waterloo Station on the first stage of his journey to central Africa. Laddie, a "barrage dog" which had been used as a front line message carrier in France in 1914–18, was prepared, according to Stevens, to take on anything from a tank to a dinosaur. "I am leaving for Cape Town on Christmas Eve," the captain told a newspaper reporter on the train. "From Cape Town I shall go 1700 miles north to Kafue, where my expedition will be organized."

Armed with a Mannlicher rifle, Captain Stevens claimed that he knew the location of a "vital spot" on the monster, which was

Above: *Steneosaurus bollensis*, one of the first true crocodiles. It appeared on earth in the early Jurassic period over 150 million years ago. It was one of the commonest, and grew to between 13 and 20 feet. Dr. A. Monard, who investigated the African stories of the *lipata*, a gigantic amphibian, concluded that it was a species of crocodile and not a prehistoric animal of any kind.

especially vulnerable to bullets. "Where that spot is," he said mysteriously, "is one of my secrets." His venture fired the imagination of both the general public and expert animal hunters. One of the latter, the American Walter Winans, supplied the London *Daily Mail* with a picture he claimed to have taken of a brontosaurus in the central African swamps. This was followed by a letter to the paper from another experienced big game hunter, R. G. Burton, in which he advised Captain Stevens to take a "more effective battery of guns" with him.

"If the animal is anything like the monster conjured up by Mr. Walter Winans," he wrote, "the hunter had better take a tank instead of his 'barrage dog.' To receive the charge of 80 feet of primeval monster, armor-plated and exuding poison from fangs and skin . . . Mannlicher and repeating Winchester rifles are quite inadequate. I would be sorry to face even a charging tiger with such weapons, while the shotgun, unless it is for the purpose of scattering salt on the tail of the creature, will prove worse than useless. He should take nothing less than a field gun—say an 18 pounder. Armed with a tank, with heavy artillery and with a supply of poison gas, the modern St. George might make 'merry music' against this 'dragon of the prime,' and have a fair chance of taking the £1 million offered by the Smithsonian Institution when he comes galumphing back with the skin."

It would appear that Burton's warning was a sound one. A single report came out that Captain Stevens had encountered his monster "crashing through the reeds of a swamp, and that it was the brontosaurus—a huge marsh animal, ten times as big as the biggest elephant." Nothing more was publicly heard of the hunter. The Smithsonian's reward went unclaimed, and in February 1920, a member of the Institution's expedition dismissed the monster stories as a practical joke. Whether or not this was true, there was no denying the fact that, from then on, the search for and sighting of dinosaurs was to be a regular feature of the central African scene.

One of the most dramatic dinosaur sightings took place 12 years later in February 1932. J. C. Johanson, a Swedish rubber plantation overseer, was out on a shooting trip in the Kasai valley when he and his African servant suddenly saw an incredible sight—a 16-yard-long monster with the head and tail of a lizard. The beast disappeared almost at once, but reappeared again in a large swamp that the two men had to cross to get home. Just 25 yards separated the hunters and the creature. The African fled. Johanson fainted, but just before he passed out, he managed to put his camera to use. The experience left the overseer ill for eight days.

The photographs taken by Johanson were later printed in Germany in the *Cologne Gazette*, and this was reported in the *Rhodesia Herald*. "The photos," the newspaper story went, ". . . were anything but clear, yet they revealed a discovery of great importance. Johanson stumbled on a unique specimen of a dinosaur family that must have lived milleniums ago." It was similar to an outsized lizard seen a few months later in the summer of 1932 by a young South African hunter. Even so, accusations of fake were once again made. Support for the possibility of such sightings came from the Swiss zoologist Dr. A.

Monard who, also in 1932, accompanied a dinosaur expedition to Angola.

"The existence of a large saurian descended from the reptiles of the Mesozoic era [the third major geological era] is by no means theoretically impossible," he wrote in a Swiss scientific journal. "Though every continent has been crossed and recrossed, most travelers follow much the same track, and there are still holes in the net to be explored. There have been several reports that some kind of 'brontosaurus' survives, and several expeditions have even gone to look for it; the fact that they failed may merely prove that this prehistoric beast is very rare or that it lives in country as inaccessible as the great swamps are. There are some reasons, based on the history of the continents and of the great reptiles, for thinking that they could survive . . . While it is not scientific to be too credulous, it is no better to be incredulous; and there is no reason for saying that the survival of some types of Mesozoic saurians is impossible."

Dr. Monard's optimism, however, was not borne out when he and his companions reached Angola later that year. They were hoping to find a *lipata*, an enormous and "very voracious" amphibian. It was much larger and fiercer than a crocodile, and was only seen at the end of the rainy season from July to September. In spite of paddling for days through the marshes in the sun and rain to follow up every lead, the animal was not found.

Seven years afterward Mrs. Ilse von Nolde, who had lived in eastern Angola for 10 years, had better luck. She actually heard the "water-lion" roaring at night, and knew that the local hippopotami fled the district whenever they heard the fearsome sounds. "All the people dwelling along the tributaries of the

Above: a *Stegosaurus*. This prehistoric animal most nearly fits the description of the fearsome *row* which the explorer Charles Miller claimed to have seen and photographed while in New Guinea. Below: jacket of Miller's book published in 1950. The photograph of the row was not in it.

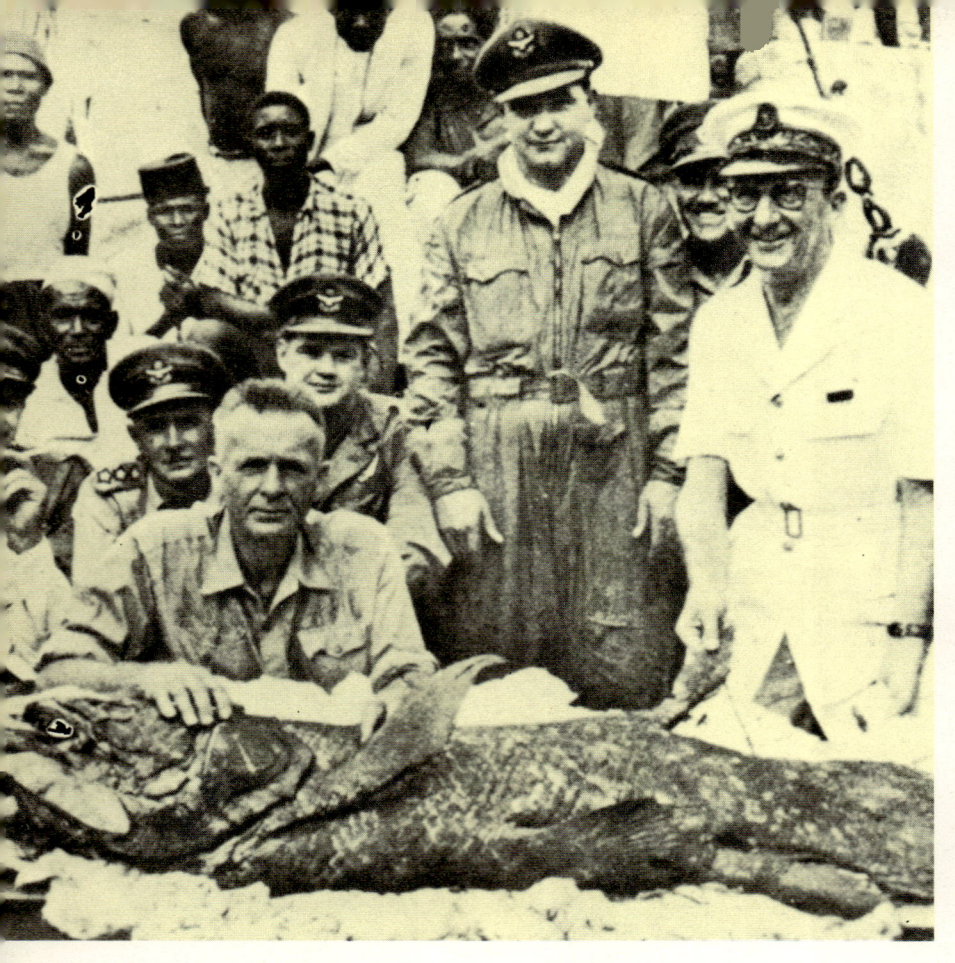

Left: Professor J. C. B. Smith, South Africa's best-known expert on fish, with the second coelacanth discovered in 1952. In 1938 Smith had seen the first one ever found only after it had decayed badly. He then put out a leaflet offering a reward for the fish, but had to wait 14 years until the next one was brought to him.

Below: scientists examining a coelacanth in a cold store. Since 1952 close to 100 more have been caught, but none has lived in captivity longer than a few hours.

Above: a coelacanth, living link with the unknown and far distant past. When the first of these big prehistoric fishes was caught, startled fishermen could not get near it because of its vicious snapping. It died in three hours.

Kuango know about the 'water-lion,'" she wrote in an article published in a German colonial gazette. "They had heard it roar during the night, but none of them has ever seen one—at least none of those I talked to—and they say it will come ashore during the night only, and hide in the water during the day."

After this partial anticlimax in 1939, the next decade was mostly taken up with stories and articles about World War II and its aftermath. It wasn't until the publication in London in 1950 of explorer Charles Miller's book *Cannibal Caravan* that the monsters of the unknown made news again. The material for the book had been gathered when Miller and his society bride had spent their honeymoon among the head-hunting cannibals of New Guinea. There they heard of a 40-foot-long lizard known among local people as *row*, because of the noise it made. The beast lived on the top of a high grassy plateau, and the couple decided to make their way up and take pictures of the animal. They reached the summit and looked over the edge of a cliff, where they saw a large triangular-shaped marsh. As they gazed, the reeds below them began to stir, and a long yellowy-brown neck swayed up toward the sky. Miller froze on the spot and his wife, who came over to join him, fell to the grass and lay there too scared to lift her head. Then Miller pointed his camera at the creature.

"As if in obedience to my wishes," he wrote, "the colossal remnant of the age of dinosaurs stalked across the swamp. Once its tail lashed out of the grass so far behind its head I thought it must be another beast. For one brief second I saw the horny point.

I heard it hiss—roooow, roooow, roooow . . . It was a full quarter mile away, it couldn't possibly hear the camera, but I found myself cowering back as if that snapping turtle-shaped beak would lash out and nab me. I gasped with relief when the creature settled back . . . Twice more the row reared up, giving me a good view of the bony flange around its head and the projecting plates along its backbone. Then with a click my camera ran out just as the row slithered behind a growth of dwarf eucalyptus."

Miller's book had numerous illustrations, but there was none of the row that had so frightened him and his wife. He offered his dinosaur film to several producers, but it was never commercially shown. However, as Dr. Heuvelmans stresses in his retelling of Miller's adventure, "it would be rash to assert that such an animal is impossible—zoology and paleontology [the study of fossils] are full of surprises . . ."

Despite this further disappointment, professional and amateur monster lovers refuse to believe that such creatures do not exist except in controversial books. Ivan Sanderson, who had first-hand experience of a monster in Africa, asserts that much of our present-day world is unknown, and he attacks the popular notion that there is little left to be fully explored and mapped. "There was never a greater misconception," he writes. "The percentage of the land surface of the earth that is actually inhabited—that is to say, lived upon, enclosed, farmed, or regularly traversed—is quite limited. Even if the territory that is penetrated only for hunting or the gathering of food crops be added, vast areas still remain completely unused. There are such areas in every continent, areas that for years are never even entered by man. Nor are these only the hot deserts of the torrid regions or the cold deserts of the poles . . . There might easily be creatures as big as elephants living in some profusion in, say, the back of the Guyanas, which are now only a few hours' flight in a commercial plane from Miami. Such animals might have been well-known to several thousand people for hundreds of years, but their presence would still be unsuspected by us, for few of the Amerindians—who from aerial surveys are known to exist in that area—have ever come out, or even been seen by anyone from outside."

That creatures we call monsters exist somewhere today is not totally impossible. This was demonstrated in 1938 with the discovery off the coast of South Africa of a live coelacanth—a huge fish dating from millions of years ago, and naturally assumed to be extinct long since. The fossils of other coelacanths showed the species to be some 70 million years old. Scientists were further amazed and delighted when, in 1952, a second live coelacanth was caught off Madagascar. Since then close to 100 more of these hardy survivors from the past have been discovered and studied, although most live for only a few hours in captivity. Their home is in the Indian Ocean near the Comore Islands. These discoveries now make it logical to ask: "If prehistoric coelacanths are still living today, why not dinosaurs?"

It is possible that dinosaurs exist in spite of all the doubters, and, like the coelacanth, are a link in the long chain of living beings. But, unlike the fish, they are savage, huge, lumbering monstrosities not so easily captured.

Mammoths in the Siberian Forest

A Russian hunter in 1918 was exploring the taiga—the vast forest that covers nearly three million square miles of Siberia—when he encountered huge tracks in thick layers of mud by a lake in a clearing. They were about 2 feet across and about 18 inches long, and appeared to be oval. The creature was obviously four-footed, and had wandered into the woods. The hunter followed the tracks curiously, from time to time finding huge heaps of dung apparently composed of vegetable matter. The tree branches were broken off about 10 feet up, as if the animal's enormous head had forced its way through. For days he followed the tracks. Then he saw traces of a second animal, and a trampling of the tracks, as if the two creatures had been excited by the meeting. Then the two went on together.

The hunter followed. Suddenly, one afternoon, he saw them. They were enormous hairy elephants with great white tusks curved upward. The hair was a dark chestnut color, very heavy on the hindquarters, but lighter toward the front. The beasts moved very slowly.

The last of the mammoths are believed to have died more than 12,000 years ago, and the hunter knew nothing about them. But did he see one?

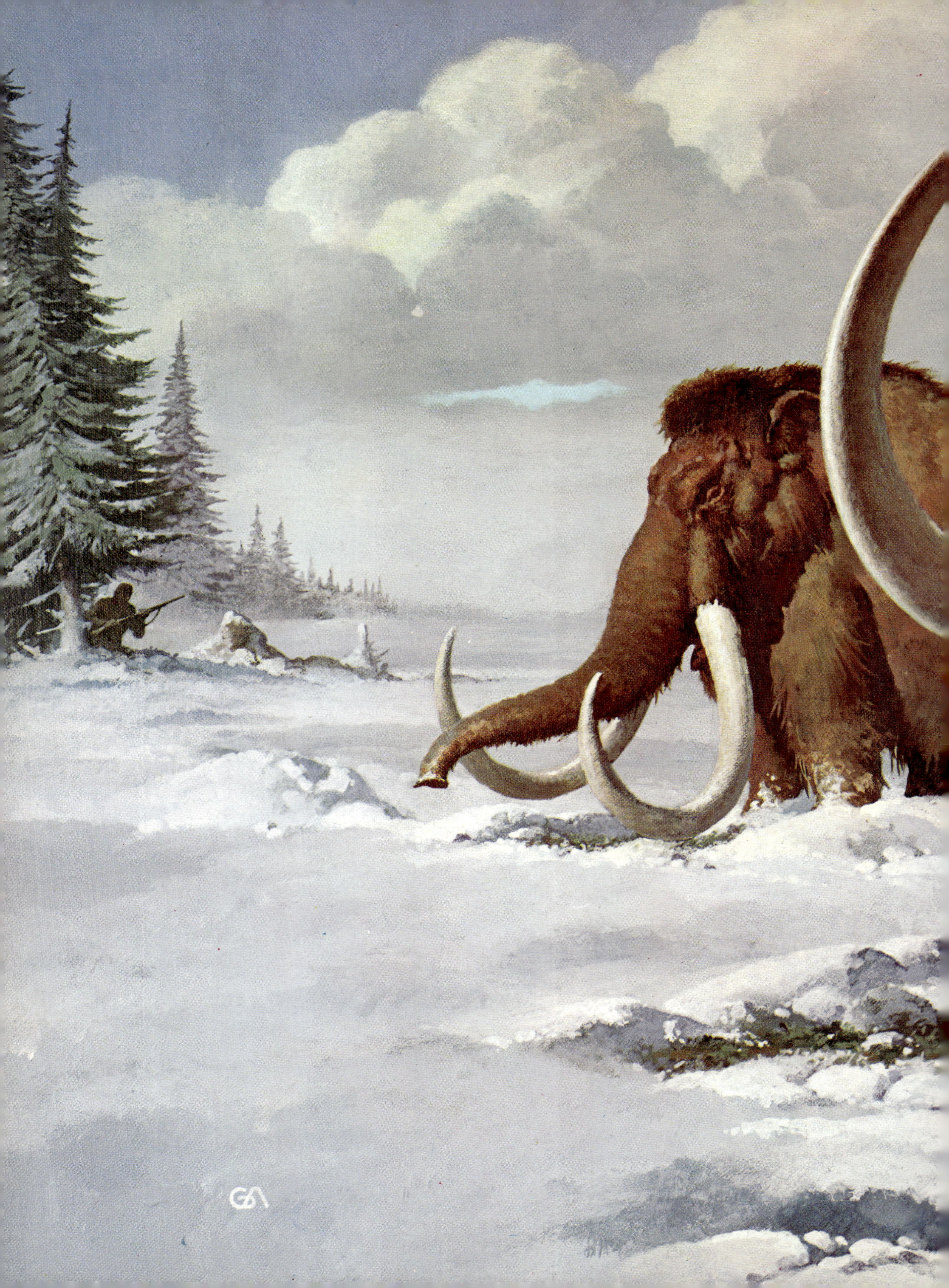

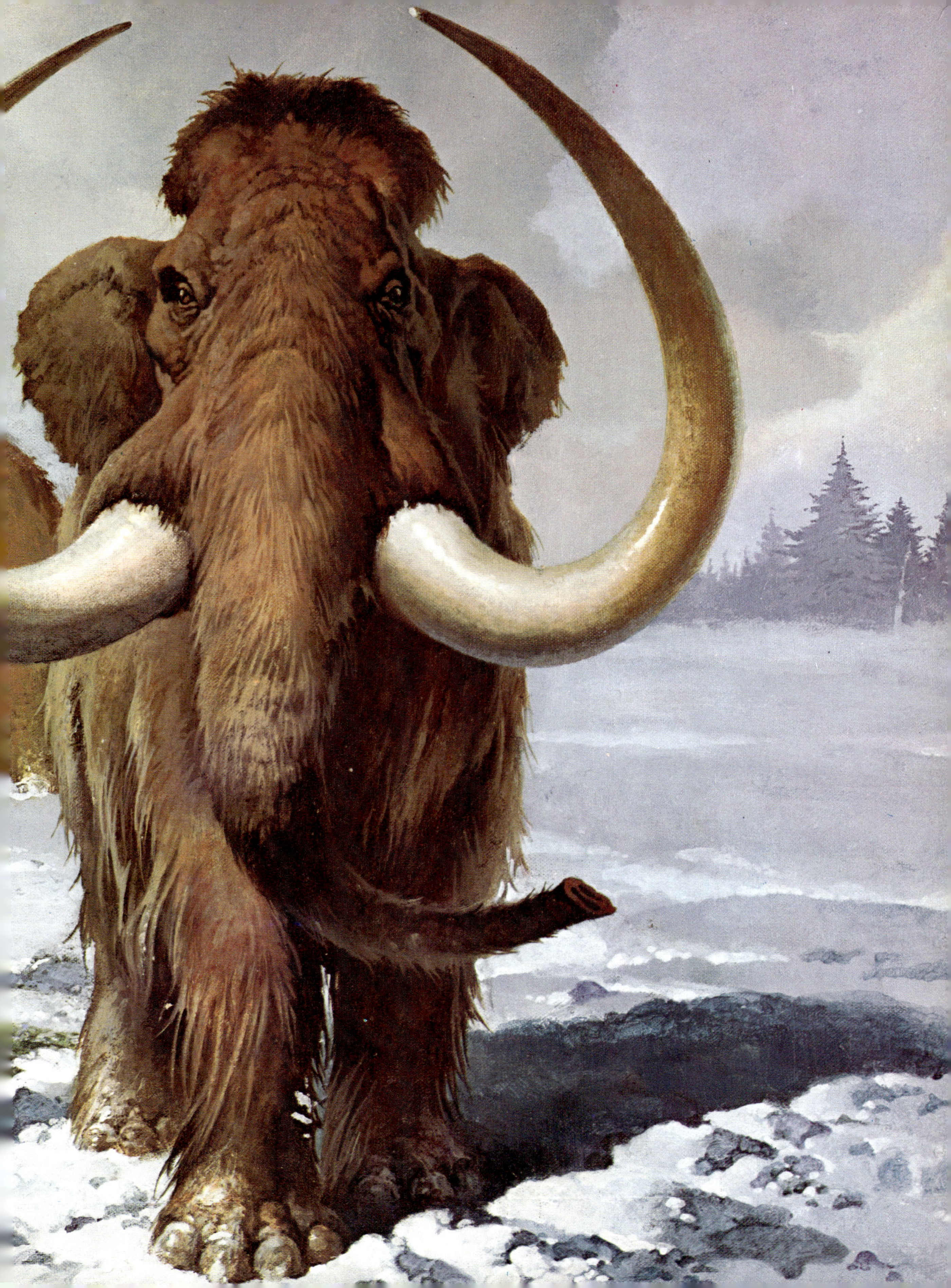

6

The Abominable Snowman

It was around teatime on a cold November afternoon in 1951. British mountaineers Eric Shipton and Michael Ward, returning from the Everest Reconnaissance Expedition, were making their way over the Menlung Glacier some 20,000 feet above sea level between Tibet and Nepal. Suddenly they came across a giant footprint in the snow. It measured 13 by 18 inches! As they saw it, the two men stopped and stared at each other. They knew the imprint had been recently made because it had not had time to melt. This meant that it was closer to actual size than a melted print, which appears larger. Therefore its size was the more

In the icy silent mountains of the Himalayas, it seems curious enough to find any animal life at all. But to find traces of giant two-legged creatures apparently making their home in eternal snow! Mountaineers came down from the heights with tales of the Yeti, and the public imagination was swiftly captured.

Above: a magazine illustration for a fictional surprise encounter of an armed man with the Snowman, a musk ox lurking behind him.

Right: mysterious tracks seen and photographed by climber Don Whillans in 1970 during an assault on the south face of Annapurna. That night he saw an apelike creature in bright moonlight bounding along the ridge above. He didn't see it again after that.

101

"Several sets of inexplicable tracks"

amazing. Had the footmark been made by a giant human or a huge snow monster? As they speculated, and before they could recover from their initial surprise, they noticed a set of fresh looking tracks in the deep snow lining the lip of the glacier. Almost too excited to speak, they followed the trail for nearly a mile before the snow became thinner and the tracks disappeared. The two seasoned mountain climbers realized that they could be on the verge of a major anthropological discovery, and quickly set about taking photographs of their find.

Using Ward's ice axe and snowboots to show scale, Shipton took two photographs in which the footprints were well defined and perfectly in focus. These photographs were to cause controversy, doubt, and sometimes downright disbelief in every country in which they were later reproduced. Despite those who called the photographs everything short of fake, there was no disputing the fact that the prints had not been made by monkeys, bears, leopards, or ordinary human beings. In that case, then, what kind of creature had preceded the explorers across that remote section of the Himalayas? Whatever it was, it had five distinct toes with the inner two toes larger than the rest, the smaller toes pressed together, and the heel flat and exceptionally broad. If Eric Shipton was in any doubt at the time he photographed the footmarks in 1951, he had certainly made his mind up 10 years later. In a foreword to Odette Tchernine's book *The Snowman and Company* he wrote:

"Before 1951, though like other travelers I had seen several sets of inexplicable tracks in the snows of the Himalayas and Karakoram, and had listened to innumerable stories of the 'Yeti' told by my Sherpa friends, I was inclined to dismiss the creature as fantasy. But the tracks which Michael Ward . . . and I found in the Menlung Basin after the Everest Reconnaissance Expedition, were so fresh and showed so clearly the outline and contours of the naked feet that I could no longer remain a skeptic. There could be no doubt whatever that a large creature had passed that way a very short time before, and that whatever it was it was not a human being, not a bear, not any species of monkey known to exist in Asia."

The newspapers of the day—and indeed those since then—seized upon the story as eagerly as they had earlier publicized the newsworthy Loch Ness Monster. Playing down the Tibetan name Yeti—meaning "magical creature"—they popularized the name "Abominable Snowman"—which got across the idea of horror associated with the being that was said to exist in the valleys, gaps, and glaciers of the Himalayas. The London Zoological Society and the Natural History department of the British Museum examined the photographs and came to the conclusion that the prints had been caused by a langur monkey or a red bear. The creature's stride alone—a length of some $2\frac{1}{2}$ feet—made nonsense of the monkey theory. But these austere authorities remained unconvinced, and it was left to the highly regarded British medical journal *The Lancet* to give credence to Shipton's Abominable Snowman claims. In an article published in June 1960, and headed "Giants with Cold Feet," it stated:

"Even in the 20th century there are many thinly populated and almost unexplored regions of the world, and in several of these

Above: Eric Shipton, the British mountain climber who is a veteran of expeditions on Mt. Everest. He and Michael Ward encountered peculiar and unfamiliar giant footprints during the Everest Reconnaissance Expedition of 1951, and photographed them. This fed the controversy about the Yeti.

Below: the giant footprints that Shipton, Ward, and their guide Sen Tensing discovered near the Menlung Glacier. Ward's ice axe is laid by the footprint to show the scale. Ward said that they followed the track for about half a mile. Where the animal had crossed a small crevasse it was possible to see how its toes had dug in to get a firm hold. It even appeared that there might be an imprint of the nails, but it wasn't possible to be sure.

there have arisen rumors of the existence of large animals still awaiting scientific discovery and classification. The publicity accorded to the 'Abominable Snowman' of the Himalayas is no doubt a tribute to the aura of mystery and endeavor surrounding the highest mountain on earth. It may also be due in part to the beguiling name bestowed upon the creature, almost certainly as a result of a losing battle with the local dialect."

Although the Yeti was big news in the 1950s and early 1960s, it was already old news, with sightings dating back to 1832. According to the well-known anatomist and anthropologist Dr. John Napier, the source of the Abominable Snowman stories were the "military and Civil Service pioneers in the last century, and the high mountaineers in this." Because of them, Napier says,

Above: how myths are made. These cloven-hoofed prints were long accepted as a Yeti trail simply because they were photographed on the same day and in the same area as the Shipton-Ward ones, and so filed together in the Mt. Everest Expedition archives. They are clearly goat footprints.

103

"the eastern Himalayas are better known than most of the other mountain ranges where monster myths are prevalent."

It was in 1832 that B. H. Hodgson, the British Resident in Nepal, published an article about a strange mountain creature in a scientific journal. He wrote that some Nepalese porters of his had "fled in terror" from an erect, tailless being with shaggy black hair that had ambled up to them. They called the creature a *rakshas*, the Sanskrit word for "demon," and informed him that references to such wild men went back to the 4th century B.C. In those early times, rakshas appeared in the Indian national epic *Rama and Sita*. Hodgson derided his servants' talk of a demon creature, and explained the intruder away as a stray orang-utan. Fifty-seven years later, however, in 1889, Major L. A. Waddell of the Indian Army Medical Corps became the first European to see footprints presumably made by one of the mountain monsters. He discovered the tracks 17,000 feet up in northeast Sikkim, but was reluctant to ascribe them to the then unnamed Snowman. In his book *Among the Himalayas*, he stated:

"The belief in these creatures is universal among Tibetans. None, however, of the Tibetans I have interrogated on the subject could ever give me an authentic case. On the most superficial investigation it always resolved into something that somebody had heard tell of." In his conclusion, Waddell insisted that the "so-called hairy wild men" were simply vicious, meat-eating yellow snow bears that frequently preyed upon yaks.

The next recorded sighting of tracks by a European came in 1914 when J. R. P. Gent, a British forestry officer stationed in Sikkim, wrote of discovering footprints of what must have been a huge and amazing creature. "The peculiar feature," he said, "is that its tracks are about 18–24 inches long, and the toes point in the opposite direction to that in which the animal is moving... I take it that he walks on his knees and shins instead of on the sole of his foot."

It was only a matter of time before the inevitable encounter between a European and a mysterious Yeti. It came in 1921 when Lieutenant-Colonel C. K. Howard-Bury led the first Everest Reconnaissance Expedition. He and his team were clambering over a ridge some 21,000 feet up. Suddenly one of his Sherpa guides gripped his arm excitedly and pointed to a dark upright figure moving rapidly through the snow. The Sherpas immediately jumped to the conclusion that this must be "the wild man of the snows." On his return to his own country, Howard-Bury read up on the ways and customs of the Himalaya wild man. He learned that naughty little Tibetan children are threatened into good behavior by warnings about him. "To escape from him they must run down the hill, as then his long hair falls over his eyes and he is unable to see them," Howard-Bury said.

There is also a female of the species, and the Sherpas say that Yeti women are hampered by the size of their breasts. One investigator of the creatures was told by a Sherpa, "We followed the track of two Yeti, they were both females—their breasts were so large they have to throw them over their shoulders before they bend down."

In the spring of 1925 a sighting was made by the British photographer N. A. Tombazi. He observed one of the elusive

Above: the vast trackless wastes of the high Himalayan mountains. This view is from the Western Cwm on the shoulder of Mt. Everest, looking at the giant peak of Pumori, 23,442 feet high.

Left: the chief lama of Khumjung with the scalp thought to be that of a Snowman. It is kept as a relic in the monastery.

Right: lamas perform a ceremonial dance to invoke certain deities. The religious and mythological content of Tibetan Buddhism is filled with demons, spirits, and other strange beings. Therefore it is natural for the people of the high mountains to believe in the Yeti as a supernatural creature.

Left: the only tangible evidence of the existence of the Yeti is the scalps treasured by various monasteries. This one comes from Pangboche on the trial to Mount Everest, so has been frequently reported by outsiders. There have been stories of Yeti skins, but so far there are no photographs. Sherpa porters have often said that tracks encountered by an expedition were Yeti tracks, but one authority reminds us that the Sherpas consider it highly ill-mannered to disappoint anyone.

Above: the Khumjung Yeti scalp, which is hundreds of years old. When it was brought to the West, Dr. Heuvelmans was one of the scientists who studied it. Without denying the existence of the Yeti, he said the scalp was a fake made from a mountain goat's. He explained that it was probably made long ago as a dance mask.

beings 15,000 feet up the Zemu Glacier and, as a Fellow of the Royal Geographical Society, his testimony was not to be laughed aside. Again it was a Sherpa who drew attention to the Snowman's presence, but to begin with the bright glare of the snow prevented the photographer from seeing the newcomer. Then, as his eyes grew accustomed to the dazzle, he spotted the creature some 200 or 300 yards away in a valley to the east of the camp. In his book *Bigfoot* John Napier quotes the photographer as follows:

"Unquestionably the figure in outline was exactly like a human being, walking upright and stopping occasionally to uproot or pull at some dwarf rhododendron bushes. It showed up dark against the snow and, as far as I could make out, wore no clothes. Within the next minute or so it had moved into some thick scrub and was lost to view. Such a fleeting glimpse, unfortunately, did not allow me to set the telephoto-camera, or even to fix the object carefully with the binoculars; but a couple of hours later, during the descent, I purposely made a detour so as to pass the place where the 'man' or 'beast' had been seen. I examined the footprints which were clearly visible on the surface of the snow. They were similar in shape to those of a man . . . The prints were undoubtedly biped, the order of the spoor having no characteristics whatever of any imaginable quadruped. From enquiries I made a few days later at Yokson, on my return journey, I gathered that no man had gone in [that] direction since the beginning of the year."

By now belief in the Yeti was growing from country to

country, and reports of the creature's habits and behavior were coming from men of prominence and responsibility. The English mountaineer Maurice Wilson, who died in 1934 while attempting to climb Everest alone, was convinced that the Snowmen existed, and that they were mystical hermits rather than wild beasts. This theory was shared by the German missionary-doctor, Father Franz Eichinger. He told the London *News Chronicle* that the Yeti were solitary monks who had withdrawn from the pressures of civilization, and who lived in cold but contemplative peace in their mountain caves. In 1938 the Yeti emerged as creatures of kindness and sympathy according to the story of Captain d'Auvergne, the curator of the Victoria Memorial near Chowringhee in Calcutta. Injured while traveling on his own in the Himalayas, and threatened with snowblindness and exposure, he was saved from death by a 9-foot-tall Yeti. The giant picked him up, carried him several miles to a cave, and fed and nursed him until he was able to make his way back home. Captain d'Auvergne concluded that his savior was a survivor from some prehistoric human tribe or sect. Like Father Eichinger, he believed that the Snowman and his fellows belonged to an ancient people called the A–o–re who had fled to the mountains to avoid persecution, and who then developed into beastlike giants.

All this was sensational enough, but an even more vivid, explicit, and dramatic encounter was to take place. It occurred in February 1942, but was not made public until the following decade when Slavomir Rawicz's best-selling book *The Long Walk* appeared. In it Rawicz, a Pole, tells how he and six friends escaped from a Siberian prisoner of war camp, and crossed the Himalayas to freedom in India. The book came under widespread attack as being more fiction than fact, many critics citing the physical unlikelihood of weakened escapees being able to make such a journey—which included a 12-day hike across the Gobi desert with little food and no water. There was also extreme skepticism about Rawicz's story of meeting two 8-foot tall creatures somewhere between Bhutan and Sikkim. For two hours, according to the author, he and his companions watched the outsize animals or men from a distance of 100 yards. He gauged the monster's height by using his military training for artillery observations.

In 1953 the Yeti again made international news when New Zealander Edmund Hillary and Sherpa Tenzing Norgay spotted giant prints during their conquest of Mt. Everest. In some quarters their feat was practically eclipsed by their discovery of the Yeti footmarks. Such prints were a familiar sight to Tenzing, who had grown up in a village on the Khumbu Glacier, and who told Hillary that his father—"who was no teller of lies"—had once almost been killed by one of the Snowmen. The older Tenzing had come across the creature while it was eating, and had been chased by it down a steep slope. He escaped by running downhill "for his life."

It was such anecdotes that led the London *Daily Mail* to organize its own Abominable Snowman Expedition in 1954. Two years before, Yeti tracks had also been seen by Dr. Eduard Wyse-Dunant, the leader of a Swiss Everest Expedition.

They Saw the Abominable Snowman

In the decade after World War II Slavomir Rawicz, a Polish refugee living in England, wrote about his experiences in *The Long Walk*. In this book he claimed that he and six others escaped from a Siberian prison camp and walked 2000 miles to freedom. During their grueling journey to India they crossed the Himalayas. It was there, one day in May 1942, that he said they saw two massive Yeti.

"They were nearly eight feet tall and standing erect," Rawicz wrote. "The heads were squarish and... the shoulders sloped sharply down to a powerful chest and long arms, the wrists of which reached the knees." One was slightly larger than the other, and Rawicz and his companions concluded they were a male and female. The unknown creatures looked at the humans, but appeared completely indifferent. Unfortunately, they were in the middle of the most obvious route for the refugees to continue their descent, and the men were disinclined to approach much closer in spite of the apparent lack of interest.

The refugee party finally moved off by another route. Behind them the Yeti watched their retreat with obvious unconcern, and then turned away to look out over the magnificent scenery.

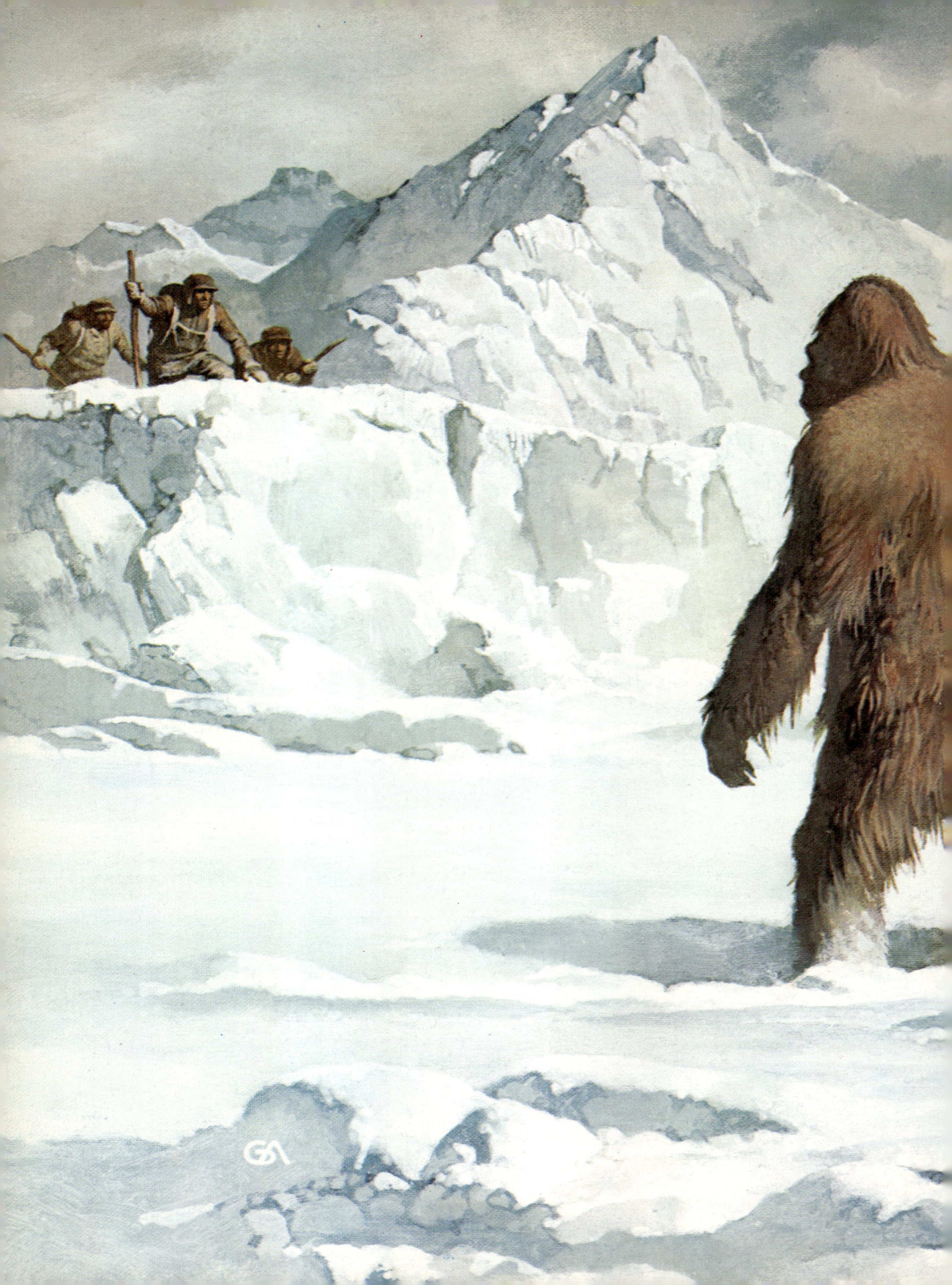

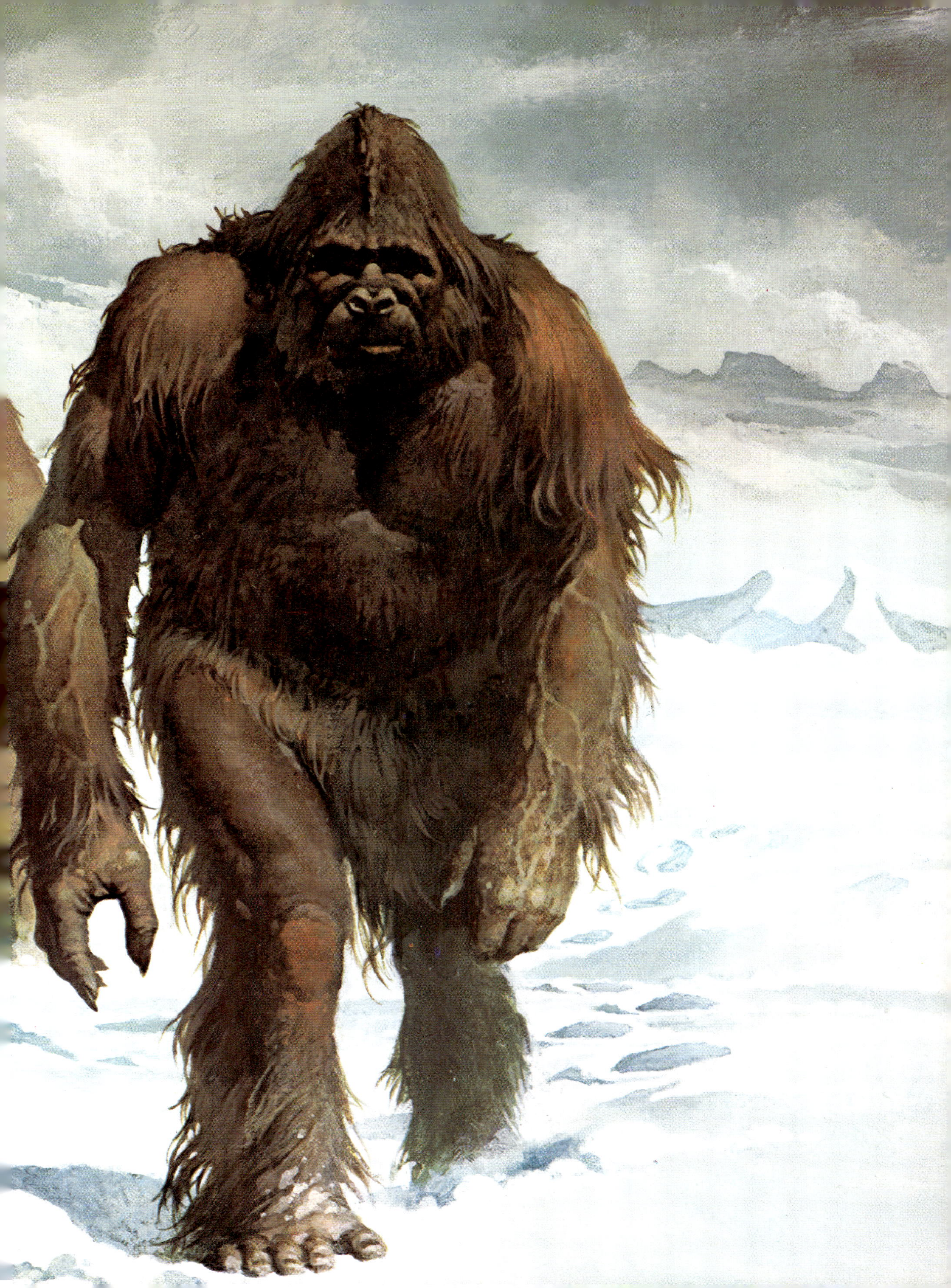

Above: Tenzing Norgay on the summit of Mount Everest, photographed by Edmund Hillary. It was on this climb to the top that the pair saw footprints which Tensing identified as those of a Yeti. Hillary was intrigued enough to mount an expedition later to investigate the existence of the Yeti, although the expedition also intended to find out about the adaptation of the human body to the effects of high altitudes.

Because he found "no trace of meals, nor yet of excrement," Dr. Wyse-Dunant believed that the "animal is only passing through and does not frequent these heights." His view was confirmed by the experience of the *Daily Mail* team, which came up with nothing more positive than a few hairs from a 300-year-old alleged Yeti scalp kept in a Buddhist temple. This scalp, conical in shape, was about 8 inches high and had a base circumference of 26 inches. It was photographed by *Mail* journalist Ralph Izzard, who later had the hairs analyzed. He was told they belonged to "no known animal."

In his book about the expedition, *The Abominable Snowman Adventure,* Izzard asserted that their effort, though a stunt to boost circulation, had not been worthless. "I am personally convinced," he wrote, "that sooner or later the Yeti will be found, and that it will be sooner rather than later because of our efforts. One must, however, add a word of warning to future expeditions. I think it is the opinion of all of us when we review our own experiences that the Yeti is more likely to be met in a chance encounter round say, a rock, than by an organized search . . . In such country there is no question of stalking an animal in the accepted sense of the term. For miles at a time there may be only one safe path used by men and animals alike, for to deviate from it would mean taking unacceptable risks from crevasses, avalanches, and other hazards. Often such a path . . . may cross the dead center of a snowfield where a party is as conspicuous as a line of black beetles on a white tablecloth and where, from the surrounding cliffs, a lurking animal can hold one under observation for hours at a time with freedom of choice to lie low or steal away across the next horizon . . . That we failed to see a Yeti signified nothing, either for or against its existence . . . There are, I know, many who rejoice that we failed in our main objective—that a last great mystery remains in this much picked-over world to challenge adventurous spirits."

Just as Izzard had observed, the "great mystery" inspired three American safaris in 1957, 1958 and 1959. They were financed and headed by the tycoons Tom Slick and F. Kirk Johnson. The expeditions carried hypodermic rifles and bullets, which the Yeti wisely stayed miles away from, and the nearest the well-equipped parties came to success was when the two millionaires took some excellent plaster casts of Yeti prints. Other well-substantiated reports of sightings continued to appear in books and interviews. Mountaineer John Hunt, in his account of the 1953 scaling of Everest, told about a story he heard from the dignified Abbot of Thyangboche Monastery. It seems that a few winters previously, the religious leader had seen a Yeti. Hunt reports the Abbot's story as follows:

"This beast, loping along sometimes on his hind legs and sometimes on all fours, stood about five feet high and was covered with gray hair . . . The Yeti had stopped to scratch . . . had picked up snow, played with it, and made a few grunts . . . instructions were given to drive off the unwelcome visitor. Conch shells were blown, and the long traditional horns sounded. The Yeti had ambled away into the bush."

During the 1950s several Soviet scientists took the Yeti seriously. Dr. A. G. Pronin, a hydrologist at Leningrad University, for instance, sighted one of the creatures in 1958 in the Pamir Mountains in Central Asia, and was duly impressed. Odette Tchernine gives an account of Pronin's encounter in her book *The Yeti*. "At first glance," he wrote, "I took it to be a bear, but then I saw it more clearly, and realized that it was a manlike creature. It was walking on two feet, upright, but in a stooping fashion. It was quite naked, and its thickset body was covered with reddish hair. The arms were overlong, and swung slightly with each movement. I watched it for about ten minutes before it disappeared, very swiftly, among the scrub and boulders."

Despite being attacked in some newspapers, the doctor's story was listened to in official circles. As a result, a professor of Historical Science, Dr. Boris Porshnev, was appointed head of a Commission for Studying the Question of the Abominable Snowman. His on-the-spot investigations convinced him that the Yeti was not just another traveler's tale, but actually existed. "In the 15th century such wild people lived in the mountain fastnesses near the Gobi desert," he stated. "They had no permanent homes. Their bodies, except for hands and faces, were covered with hair. Like animals they fed on leaves, grass, and anything they could find." A third Soviet authority who refused to discount the Snowman was Professor Stanyukovich. Around 1960, he went to the Pamirs with a Yeti expedition that included some of his country's most expert zoologists, archeologists, botanists, and climbers. After nine months of patient endeavor, during which cameras with telescopic lenses were at the ready in concealed observation posts, the creatures had still not been seen—either in person or by way of footprints. The Yeti had prudently ignored the 20 goats and rams put out as bait, and avoided the dozens of snares, nets, and the team of snow-

Above: Edmund Hillary before the 1960–61 Yeti expedition. He shows newsmen a drawing of the Abominable Snowman based on the reports of several witnesses who claimed to have seen the elusive mountain monster. Ward, who had seen the footprints with Shipton, was an expedition member. Below: Hillary with the Khumjung Yeti scalp that he brought back, and Khumbo Chumbi, the Sherpa assigned as caretaker of the scalp.

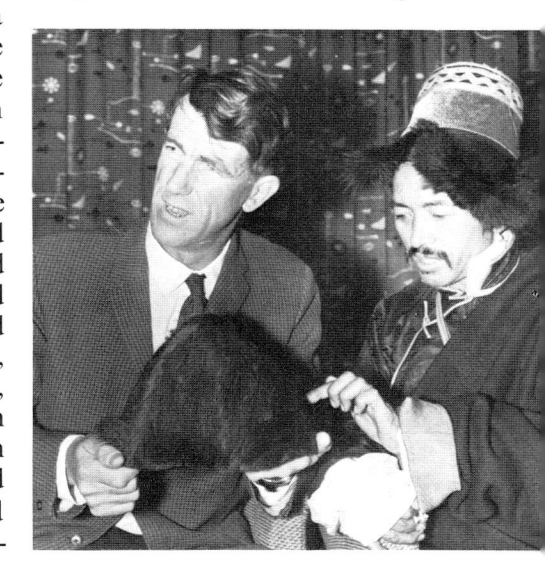

leopard hunters who spent more than three months lying in cunningly hidden dugouts.

The professor took it philosophically, however. "Farewell, you fascinating riddle," he wrote. "Farewell, inscrutable Snowman, ruler of the heights and snows. A pity, a thousand pities that you are not to be found. What, not at all? Not anywhere? Perhaps you are yet to be found in the remotest mountains of Nepal. Perhaps!"

Edmund Hillary led his own commercially backed Yeti expedition in 1960–61. Although he returned with a Snowman scalp lent to him by the Khumjung monastery, the Yeti remained as evasive as ever. Zoologists classified the scalp as that of a serow, or goat antelope, which is a native of eastern Asia—and only some unfamiliar parasites found among the hair were new to them. At this time, information about the Abominable Snowman had been systematized, and it had become clear that there are three distinct types: the *Rimi*, which can be up to 8 feet tall and dwells at the comparatively low level of 8000 feet; the *Nyalmot*, an improbable 15 feet in height and a meat eater that feeds on mountain goats and yak; and the *Rakshi-Bompo*, a mere 5 feet in stature and a vegetarian that lives on grain and millet. A shy and retiring being, the Yeti of all three types prefers to come out at night, and is rarely seen in more than twos. It also appreciates it if bowls of water and food are left where it can find them. The Nepalese and Tibetans will not kill or harm the beast in the belief that to do so will result in bad luck and general misfortune. The creature is usually described as having long reddish hair and feet that, according to the Sherpas, are placed back to front. They get this idea from its prints, which appear to be going in a contrary direction.

The Yeti is reputed to have a body odor that makes a skunk smell good, and to possess such strength that it can throw boulders around as if they were marbles and uproot trees as if they were flowers. Descriptions of the Yeti's voice range from shrill whistles to high-pitched yelps to lion-throated roars. It is also said to be fond of any kind of alcohol.

As more evidence about the Yeti piled up, the Nepal government took a definite stand in 1961. The Yeti, it claimed, positively existed, and was to be found in an S-shaped area incorporating Siberia and Southeastern USSR, India, Alaska, Canada, and the USA. Therefore, the Nepalese granted licenses at a cost of $10,000 to hunters dedicated and rich enough to stalk the beast through the Himalayas. Special triangular stamps were issued by the enterprising Bhutanese Post Office, which depicted the Snowman as a being peculiar to the mountains of Bhutan.

Some experts believe not only that the Yeti exists, but also that it will sooner or later be caught and brought down to civilization —and, presumably, to a caged life in one of the world's leading zoos. The latest theory about the Snowman's origins comes from a team of three zoologists who, toward the end of 1972, set out to hunt the fabled beast. They believe that the Yeti may be a descendant of the giant ape *Gigantopithecus*, which 500,000 years ago retreated to the mountains of southern Asia. At that time the Himalayas were rising by as much as 2400 to 3000 meters. Because of this increase in the height of the mountains, the

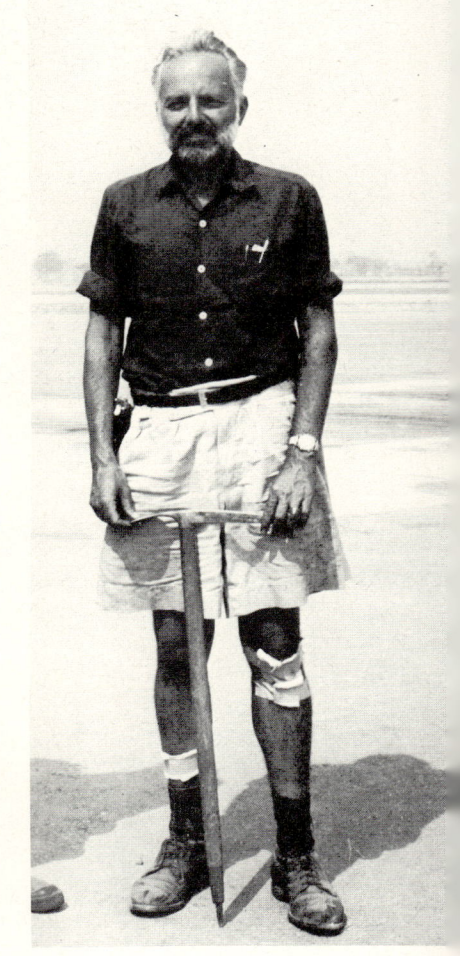

Above: Texas oilman Tom Slick, bandaged from a truck accident on the approach to the mountains. He had financed three attempts to find the Snowman. Slick said he was almost convinced of the Snowman's existence when he photographed Yeti tracks and collected a few wisps of hair that he brought back for analysis.

Above: the London *Daily Mail* Yeti team of the 1954 Himalayan Expedition, photographed at base camp with the expedition Sherpas. Above right: Sherpa Ang Tschering pointing to a line of Yeti tracks that ran alongside the tracks made by the expedition. This was as close to a Yeti as the expedition managed to get. Right: the Russian historian Boris Porshnev, a scholar of wide learning who holds doctorates in historical and philosophical sciences. He is convinced that the Yeti exists and that it will so be proved one day. He believes that the best approach would be not to capture the Snowman, but to make contact with it and attempt to get it semi-domesticated. Then a Yeti Reserve should be set up to protect the creature and allow full scientific research to proceed. Below right: Don Whillans, who made the most recent sighting of the mysterious Snowman on the Annapurna expedition in March 1970.

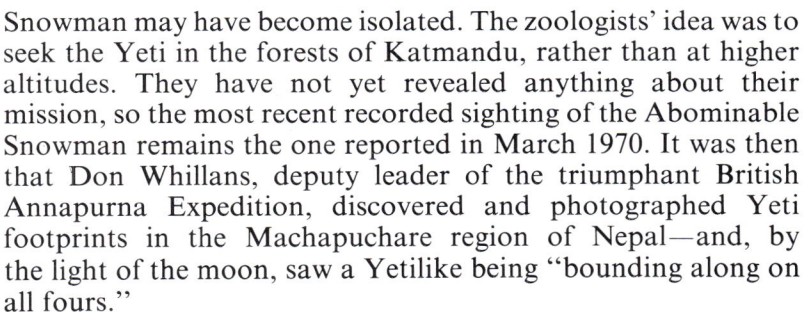

Snowman may have become isolated. The zoologists' idea was to seek the Yeti in the forests of Katmandu, rather than at higher altitudes. They have not yet revealed anything about their mission, so the most recent recorded sighting of the Abominable Snowman remains the one reported in March 1970. It was then that Don Whillans, deputy leader of the triumphant British Annapurna Expedition, discovered and photographed Yeti footprints in the Machapuchare region of Nepal—and, by the light of the moon, saw a Yetilike being "bounding along on all fours."

In his best-selling book *Annapurna South Face*, team leader Chris Bonnington quotes Whillans as saying: "The following morning I went up to make a full reconnaissance to the permanent Base Camp site, and I took the two Sherpas along. I thought I'd see their reaction at the point where I'd photographed the tracks the day before. The tracks were so obvious that it was impossible not to make any comment, but they walked straight past and didn't indicate that they had seen them. I had already mentioned that I had seen the Yeti, not knowing exactly what it was, but they pretended they didn't understand and ignored what I said. I am convinced that they believe the Yeti does exist, that it is some kind of sacred animal which is best left alone; that if you don't bother it, it won't bother you."

Whillans also had the British Medical Association magazine *The Lancet* on his side, for in a 1960 article the journal concluded: "Now that the Himalayas are more frequented by mountaineers than formerly, information is likely to accumulate more rapidly,

Below: whether it exists or not, the Yeti goes to work to provide funds for its homeland. In 1966 Bhutan, claiming the Snowman as its "national animal," issued a set of commemorative stamps with various versions of the beast.

and this most popular of mysteries may become a mystery no more."

Why has our imagination been so captured by the Yeti? It cannot just have been the kind of news coverage it got. Publicity could have been responsible for a Seven Days' Wonder, but not for the fact that in the 25 years since the publication of Eric Shipton's photographs, the yeti has become firmly established in people's minds—almost part of folk history. It may be that we have a desire to discover lost peoples or creatures akin to humans. But, although the discovery of unknown tribes of about 100,000 people in New Guinea in 1954 created interest, it did not capture public imagination in the same way as the Yeti. The people of New Guinea are now a fact. The Yeti is still a mystery. We do

Left and below: three creatures, each of which has been proposed by experts as the real Abominable Snowman. At the far left is a composite drawing of a Yeti, as witnesses report it to appear; in the center is a red bear which Charles Stonor, formerly with the London Zoo, suggested might fit at least some of the Yeti descriptions; and below, a langur monkey, which the British Museum in 1937 felt was the only rational explanation for the footprints.

not know whether it exists or not. The only evidence we have is footprints and occasional sightings—not enough to form a scientific theory, but enough to stimulate our curiosity.

Perhaps this is the function that the Yeti serves for most of us. We need creatures to inhabit that strange borderland between fact and fantasy, and our interest lies not so much in whether they really exist, but in the possibility that they may exist. It is as if the very uncertainty, the remoteness, and the scanty evidence on which our ideas are based, increases the hold on us, and gives life an extra dimension it would lose if final proof came. These large creatures hovering between man and ape, grappling with nature to survive, satisfy a psychological need for many of us—just as dragons and mermaids did for our ancestors.

7

North American Monsters

North America has its own equivalent of the Yeti, which is known as the Bigfoot in the United States and the Sasquatch in Canada. Like the Yeti, these creatures are said to be hairy, to walk on two feet, and to resemble humans in appearance. For centuries the American Indians had passed on stories of the Bigfoot, whose footprints were said to measure anything from 16 to 22 inches, and whose height when fully grown was thought to be from 7 to 12 feet. The creature also featured in the folklore of South and Central America. This fact is emphasized by Dr. John Napier, curator of the primate collection of the Smithsonian Institution, who

Out of the dense California forest looms the giant figure of a man—but is it real? This one is not. It is an eight-foot redwood statue of a Bigfoot, North America's own equivalent to Asia's Abominable Snowman. Stories of the Bigfoot—called Sasquatch in Canada—are old and many, and as difficult of proof as the reports of the Yeti. This wooden figure was done by Jim McClarin, and is an attraction of the town of Willow Creek.

117

"Wild men of the woods..."

Above: an artist's conception of a Sasquatch, whose name comes from an Indian word that means "hairy giant." The Sasquatch is said to be up to 12 feet tall. Below: the "S-map" suggested by Snowman enthusiast Odette Tchernine as a theory of the distribution of the Snowman and its apparently closely related North American friends, the equally mysterious and elusive Bigfoot and Sasquatch monsters.

writes in his book *Bigfoot*, published in 1973: "Although in the last 20 years there has been a tremendous revival of public interest since these creatures have come to the attention of the 'white settlers,' it is a reasonable assumption, from what we know of early written records that, like Peyton Place, the story of Sasquatch has been continuing for a great many years."

The first recorded sighting of a Sasquatch track by a non-Indian occurred in what is now Jasper, Alberta, in 1811. While crossing the Rockies in an attempt to reach the Columbia River, the explorer and trader David Thompson came across a set of strange footprints measuring 14 inches long by 8 inches wide. Four toe marks were shown in the deep snow. This was unlike the five-toe print of a bear, and convinced those who heard of the track that it did not belong to a grizzly. About 70 years after this, on July 4, 1884, an account of the capture of a supposed Sasquatch appeared in the *Daily Colonist*, the leading paper of British Columbia. The creature—subsequently nicknamed Jacko—had been spotted by the crew of a train traveling along the Fraser River between the towns of Lytton and Yale. The railmen had stopped the train, given chase to the gorilla-like being with coarse, black hair, and, on catching it, had placed it safely in the guard's van. After being on show for the citizens of Yale and the surrounding country for a time, Jacko was sold to Barnum and Bailey's Circus.

As time went on and more and more giant "wild men of the woods" were seen and written about, it became clear to experts that these creatures were more violent and dangerous than their kin the Yeti. This was confirmed in 1910 when two prospectors, brothers named MacLeod, were found in the Nahanni Valley in the Northwest Territories of Canada with their heads cut off. The Sasquatches who had been seen in the area were blamed for the double murder, and from then on the area became known as Headless Valley. Eight years later the fearful

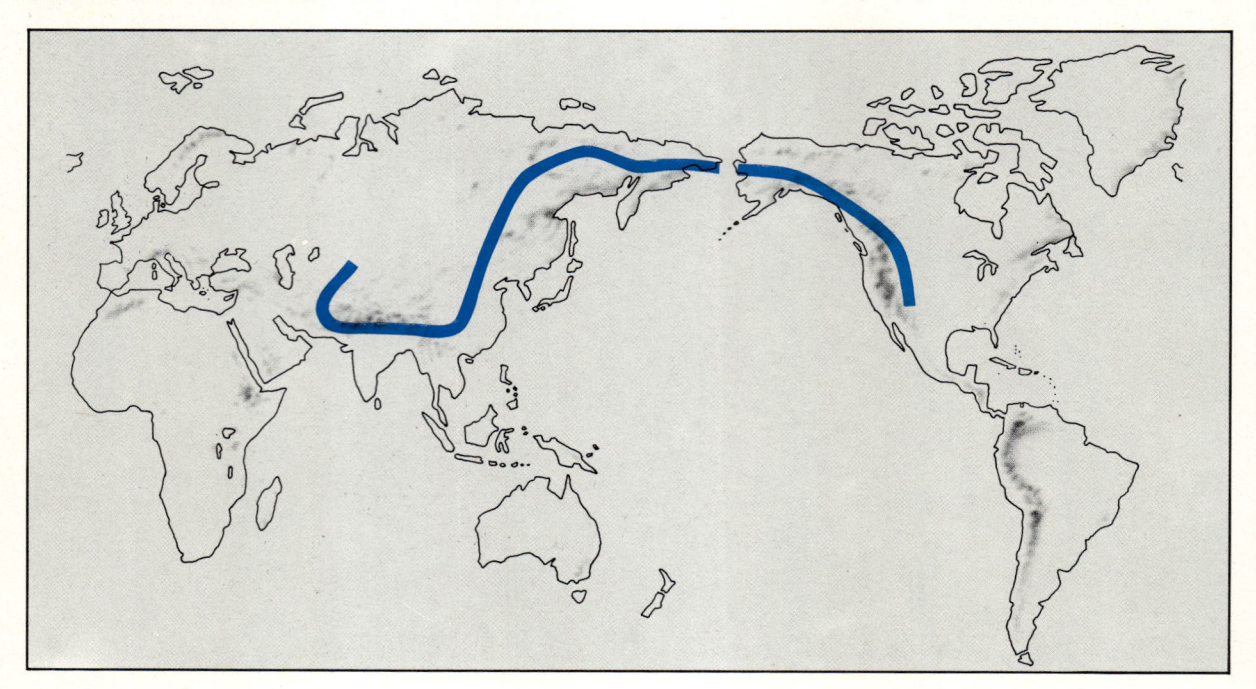

Bigfoot struck again with an attack on a prospector's shack in Mount St. Lawrence, Washington. According to the *Seattle Times*, which reported the incident, the assailants were about eight feet tall, were "half-human, half-monster," and were able to hypnotize people, to use ventriloquism, and to make themselves invisible at will.

Throughout the next few decades the Sasquatch and Bigfoot made frequent and much-publicized appearances in British Columbia, Northern California, and the state of Washington. One of the most fully documented accounts took place in 1924 in British Columbia.

At first, the few people who heard it refused to believe lumberjack Albert Ostman's story of being kidnapped in the mountainous hinterland of British Columbia, of being kept prisoner in a remote "cliff-enclosed" valley for more than a week, and of escaping from his "relentless captors" and making his way thankfully back to civilization. What caused his friends and family to doubt his tale was the fact that his kidnappers, so he said, were no ordinary hoodlums or gangsters. They were a family—father, mother, teenage son, and young daughter—but a family of "near-human hairy beasts." According to Ostman, he fell into their clutches in the summer of 1924 while on vacation. Having decided to mix business with pleasure, he had traveled to the head of Toba Inlet, near Vancouver Island, to look for traces of the gold that had formerly been mined there. Equipped with a rifle, cooking utensils, and cans of food, he spent some six or seven days roaming through the district. He got farther and farther off the beaten track. Finally he came across a secluded glade surrounded by cypress trees and containing a tempting freshwater spring in its center. Tired but contented, he resolved to spend some time there, and pitched his sleeping bag beneath the stars. On the second night in the glade, however, he woke up to find himself being carried "inside my bag like a sack of potatoes, the only thing in sight being a huge hand clutching the partly closed neck of the bag."

Ostman's kidnapper walked rapidly, and the journey was rough and painful for the bagged lumberjack. He was glad when the bag was suddenly dropped on the ground and he was able to crawl out of it. Dazed and bruised he looked around him, and met the curious stares of a weird family—all huge, hairy, and beastlike. Ostman feared for his life, but his giant captors did not bother him. In fact, they even allowed him to prepare his own meals from his supply of canned provisions. They turned out to be vegetarians who ate sweet grass, roots, and spruce tips from the evergreen forests. They also gave him a certain amount of freedom to explore his new valley home. Ostman noticed that it was the mother and son who did the family chores, wandering off into the trees and returning with tubers and hemlock tips. The father and daughter kept a careful watch over him.

Ostman feared he might be meant for the daughter later. It was this consideration, plus the obvious fact that he did not want to spend the rest of his life as the family's pet, that made Ostman resolve to escape. He got away one day when his kidnappers had become so used to him that they seemed to

Kidnapped by the Hairy Monsters

Albert Ostman, a Canadian lumberjack, in 1924 combined a vacation with a bit of gold prospecting. He camped near the head of the Toba Inlet opposite Vancouver Island, spent a week exploring, and decided to stop in a lovely glade under some cypress trees. The second night there he awoke to find himself being carried away in his sleeping bag like a sack of potatoes. He saw a huge hand around the partly open neck of the bag.

When Ostman was later dumped out on the ground, he was in the middle of a family of four big-footed monsters—the Sasquatch or Bigfeet. They were all enormous and hairy: father, who had kidnapped him, mother, a nearly adult son, and a younger daughter. The father was eight feet tall, the mother about seven. For six days Ostman was held prisoner, though no harm was done him. He observed that they were vegetarians, eating the grass, roots, and spruce tips gathered mainly by the mother and son. The daughter and father kept an eye on Ostman, but grew increasingly trustful of him. Finally he got the chance to escape.

Fearing to be locked away as a madman, Ostman said nothing publicly about his adventure for many years.

119

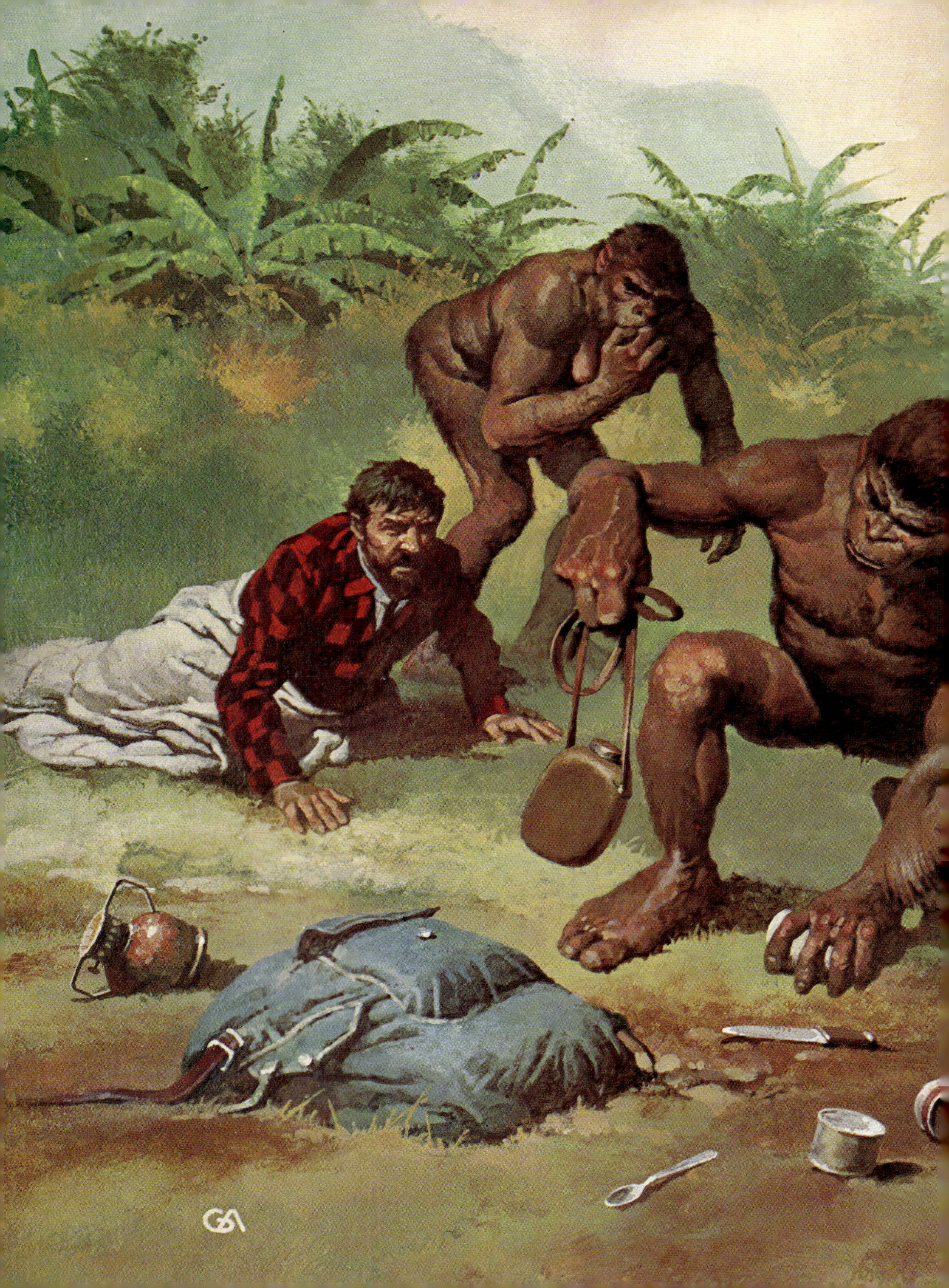

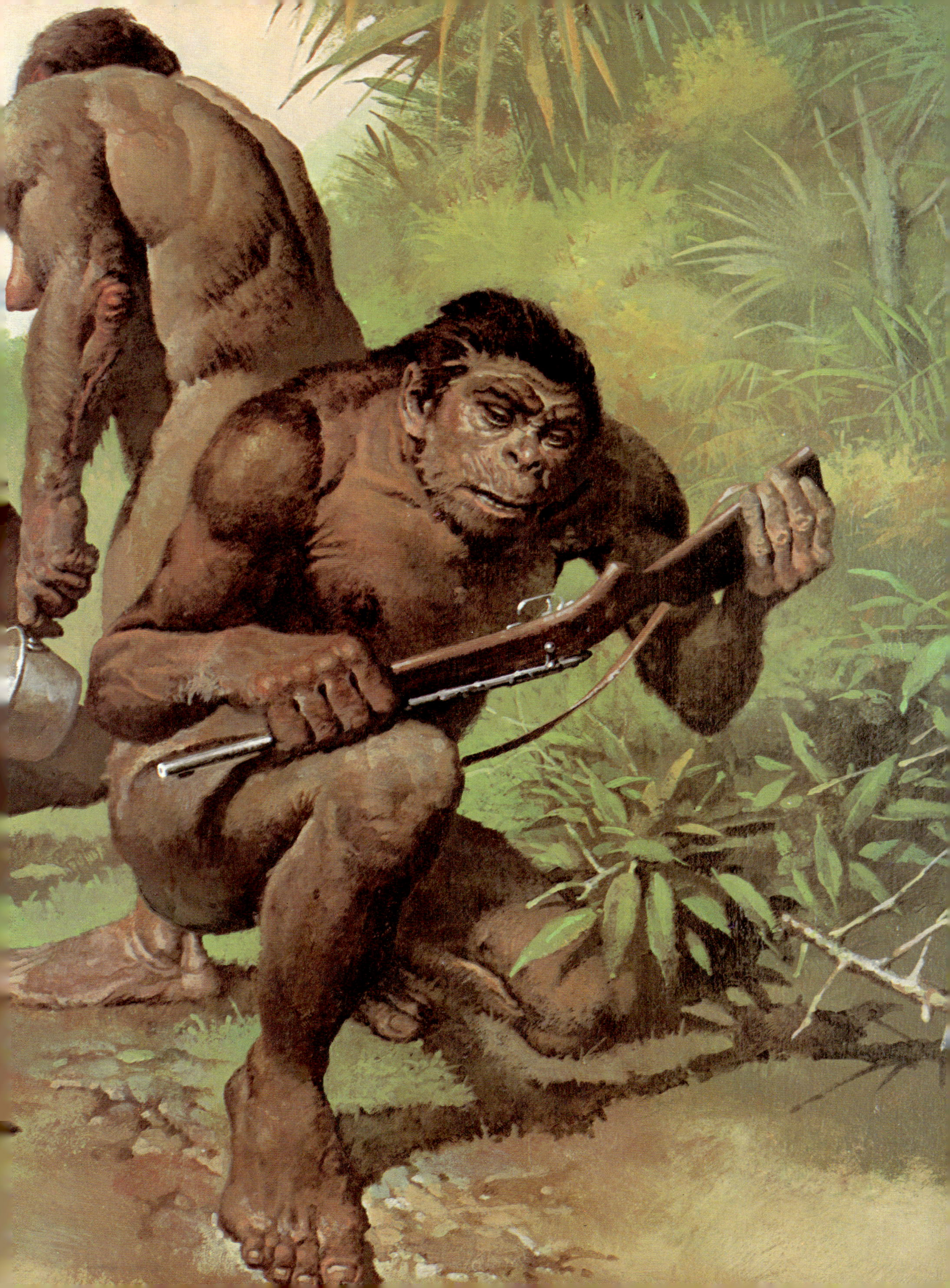

Above: John Green, author and intrepid investigator of Bigfoot stories. Here he is studying a set of 15-inch footprints found on Blue Creek Mountain in northern California in 1967.

think he was as happy in the wilds as they were, and so let their vigilance slip temporarily. On his return home Ostman was at first reluctant to tell of his unique and unsettling experience. Those whom he did mention it to regarded him as a crank—or worse. So he said no more about it until 33 years later in 1957. Only then did he come forward and tell newspapermen and anthropologists of his enforced stay with the monstrous family. Asked why he hadn't made a public statement earlier, he understandably replied that he had thought no one would take him seriously—or even that they might question his state of mind. In a belated attempt to gain credence, he swore the truth of his story before a Justice of the Peace at Fort Langley, British Columbia, on August 20, 1957, and later agreed to be interviewed by experts.

Ostman's account appeared honest in most respects, but his report of the creatures' eating habits did cause doubt. Considering that the Sasquatch family in all must have weighed more than 2000 pounds—as much as five male gorillas or fourteen adult humans, for example, it seemed unlikely that such outsize beings could have kept alive and active on the kind of low-calorie diet Ostman described. The province's Minister for Recreation and Conservation received a report from Frank L. Beebe of the British Columbia Provincial Museum in 1967. In it the expert stated that the type of vegetation used by Ostman's giants "produces the very poorest quality of low-energy food and the least quantity of high-energy food of any forest type on the planet."

A look back at the year that Ostman actually claimed to have met up with the Sasquatches revealed that 1924 had also provided another version of the monsters' activities. This time the incident took place in Ape Canyon, Washington. It was there that a group of coal miners were attacked by a "horde of Bigfeet" after one of the workers, Fred Beck, had met a Bigfoot at the edge of a canyon, and, terrified, had shot it three times in the back. A running battle then ensued between the dead monster's companions and the miners. It ended with the Bigfeet driving the panic stricken men from the area forever. Beck's version, as told to two well-known Bigfoot investigators, was given by Dr. John Napier in his book *Bigfoot*:

"At night the apes counterattacked, opening the assault by knocking a heavy strip of wood out from between two logs of the miners' cabin. After that there were assorted poundings on the walls, door, and roof, but the building was designed to withstand heavy mountain snows and the apes failed to break in . . . There was . . . the sound of rocks hitting the roof and rolling off, and [the miners] did brace the heavy door from the inside. They heard creatures thumping around on top of the cabin as well as battering the walls, and they fired shots through the walls and roof without driving them away. The noise went on from shortly after dark until nearly dawn . . . The cabin had no windows and of course no one opened the door, so in fact the men inside did not see what was causing the commotion outside. Nor could Mr. Beck say for sure . . . that there were more than two creatures outside. There were that many because there had been one on the roof and one pounding the wall

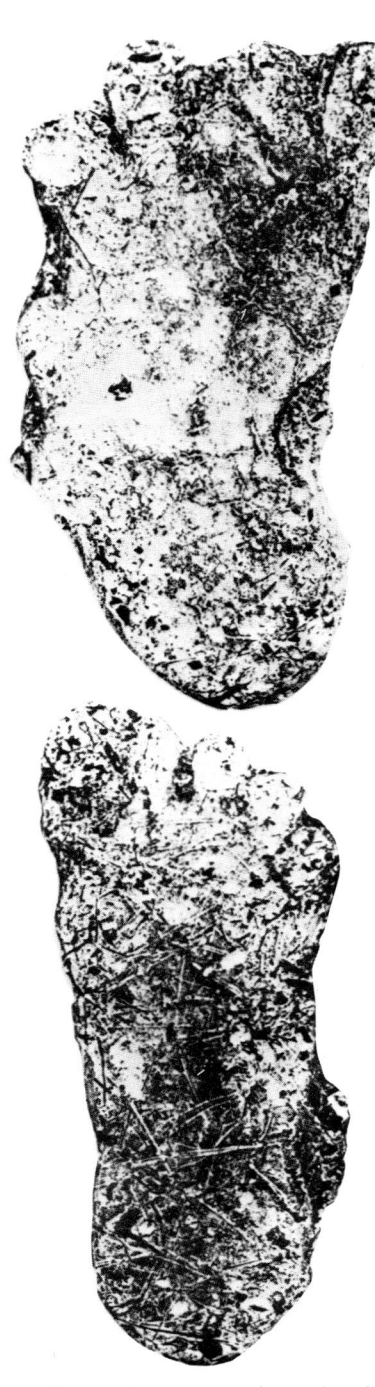

Above: two casts of a pair of human-type footprints of great size even for a Bigfoot—they measure $17\frac{1}{2}$ inches long. The left foot (top) is deformed: the unfortunate Bigfoot appears to have a clubfoot, probably from an injury during its youth.

Right: Green with a footprint cast he presented to a local museum. Officials declared it to be a fake.

simultaneously. However many there were, it was enough for the miners, who packed up and abandoned their mine the next day."

In 1940 a Bigfoot male that was eight-foot tall raided a farmstead in Nevada. The farmer's wife had to grab her children and flee. When she came back later, she found the house encircled by huge footprints. A large barrel of salted fish had also been knocked over and its contents spilled. In 1958 a truck driver named Jerry Crew found some impressively big tracks in the California mud. He followed them up hill and down into low ground before sensibly taking a plaster cast of one of them. He had himself photographed holding the cast up, and the picture caused a sensation in the newspapers and periodicals in which it appeared. Five years later Texas oil millionaire Tom Slick died in a crash in his private plane while trying to get at the truth about the Bigfoot. The findings of the various expeditions he financed have never been made public. However, the stories about his Bigfoot searches kept the interest in the monster alive. Between June 1964 and December 1970, 25 Bigfoot sightings were reported, bringing the grand total of eye-witness reports of footprints and monsters to more than 300. In 1969 in Canada alone there were no less than 60 different accounts of Sasquatches and their doings.

Toward the end of the 1960s came a publicity stunt involving the Bigfoot. It was known that the monsters were usually seen in midsummer or fall. Operating on this knowledge, a one-time rodeo worker, Roger Patterson, announced in October 1967 that he and a half-Indian friend had encountered a female Bigfoot near Bluff Creek, California, and had taken 20 feet of film of her as she ambled along the outskirts of a dense forest. Patterson said he operated the camera while on the run, and that explained why the opening frames of his 16mm color movie jumped about so much. The film was of a creature some seven feet high and weighing between 350 and 450 pounds. It was shown to Dr. Napier, who duly noted its heavy build, reddish-brown hair, and prominent furry breasts and buttocks.

Dr. Napier viewed the movie six times at a private screening in Washington, D.C. on December 2, 1967, before forming an opinion about it. He was dissatisfied with the alleged Bigfoot's "self-conscious walk," which seemed to him to be that of a human male. He felt that the cone-shaped top of the skull was "definitely nonhuman," but was suspicious of the being's center of gravity—as he said, "precisely as it is in modern man"—and could only accept the buttocks as a "human hallmark."

"The upper half of the body," he went on, "bears some resemblance to an ape, and the lower half is typically human. It is almost impossible to conceive that such structural hybrids could exist in nature. One half of the animal must be artificial. In view of the walk, it can only be the upper half. Subsequently, I have seen and studied the film, frame by frame, a dozen times or more . . . I was [also] puzzled by the extraordinary exaggeration of the walk: it seemed to me to be an overstatement of the normal pattern, a bad actor's interpretation of a classical human walking gait . . . There is little doubt that the scientific evidence taken collectively points to a hoax of some kind. The creature

Below: Rene Dahinden (on left) the Swiss-Canadian investigator into the Sasquatch, with Roger Patterson, who claimed to have taken approximately 100 feet of color movie film of a female Bigfoot wandering through a California forest in 1967. They are holding plaster casts of footprints of manlike animals that they identify as Bigfeet.

Above and right: a frame from the movie Patterson shot, with an enlargement of the creature herself. She has a cone-shaped skull, which is a characteristic of large adult male gorillas and orang-utans, and she also seems to have furry but otherwise human buttocks and breasts. Her walk was described by experts as that of a self-conscious human.

shown in the film does not stand up well to functional analysis. There are too many inconsistencies . . . Perhaps it was a man dressed up in a monkey-skin; if so it was a brilliantly executed hoax and the unknown perpetrator will take his place with the great hoaxers of the world." By the time Dr. Napier had reached this last conclusion, the film had been shown commercially to audiences both in Canada and the United States.

A couple of years after the Patterson film, a sensational headline in the *National Bulletin* screamed, "I Was Raped by the Abominable Snowman." The rape victim, a young woman by the name of Helen Westring, claimed that she had met her assailant some three years earlier while on a solo hunting trip in the woods near Bemidji, Minnesota. Hypnotizing her with its pink eyes, she said, the monster with huge hairy hands and long arms had ripped her clothes off "like one would peel a banana." It then stared at her intently, particularly at "the area between my legs," threw her to the ground, and went about its "beastly purpose." Fortunately for the victim she fainted; on coming to she took her rifle and shot the rapist through the right eye.

As the story unfolded it was clear that Helen Westring was not talking about a Bigfoot, and that the newspaper was capitalizing on the wide interest in the Himalayan Abominable Snowman by using such a headline. The gory rape-murder story referred instead to the Minnesota Iceman, who was famous in

125

126

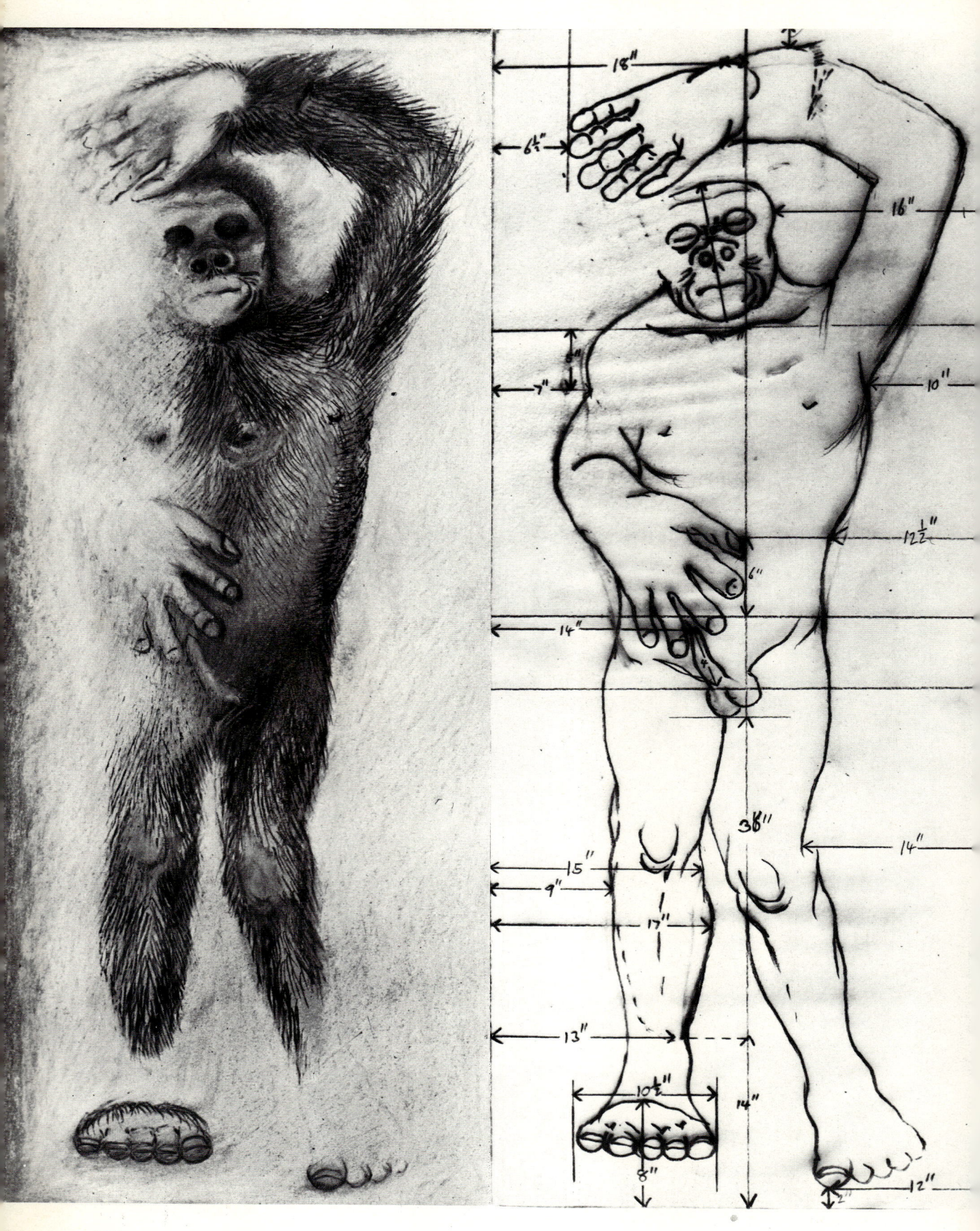

Left: scale drawings by Ivan T. Sanderson of the Minnesota Iceman. To do them Sanderson had to lie on the plate glass lid of the chilly coffin, nose-to-nose with the monster. Sanderson and Bernard Heuvelmans, both greatly interested in the existence of unknown animals, happened to be staying together when word reached them of the Iceman, and they investigated it together.

Below: Bernard Heuvelmans. He was trained as a zoologist, and holds a doctorate. He has written several books exploring the idea of whether there is any scientific foundation for a belief in the existence of unknown animals.

his own right as a monster—and, possibly, as the biggest hoax of the century.

In the late 1960s, the Minnesota Iceman was taken around the carnivals and fairgrounds of the United States, and shown to vast audiences for 25 cents admission. The "mysterious hairy body" was in the possession of Frank Hansen who, in May 1967, first exhibited the so-called "man left over from the ice age" to the American public. Hansen claimed that the body on display had been found preserved in a 6000-pound block of ice in the Bering Straits.

For more than 18 months the monster was taken from area to area. News of its existence spread until it was heard by the well-known Belgian scientist and writer Dr. Bernard Heuvelmans and his associate Ivan Sanderson. The two men journeyed to inspect the Iceman at Hansen's farm near Winona, Minnesota out of their interest in monsters, for by then the creature's identification as a prehistoric man had seemed to evaporate. They found him encased in a block of ice and enclosed in a refrigerated coffin. The monster's right eye had been penetrated by a bullet and the back of his skull shattered. Hansen said he had been murdered. Their examination began on December 17, 1968, and, although it lasted for two days, they had only restricted access to the creature. The coffin was kept in a small poorly lit trailer, and in order to sketch the Iceman, Sanderson had to lie on top of the plate glass lid of the coffin, his nose almost touching that of the monster's. Photographs were also taken. Heuvelmans later wrote a paper for the Royal Institute of Natural Sciences in Belgium, which he called "Preliminary Note on a Specimen preserved in ice; an unknown living hominid." From this it seemed that the two scientists had accepted the Iceman as fact, and Hansen's explantion as to the bullet wound on the monster as truth. Heuvelmans statement was given by Odette Tchernine in her book *The Yeti* as:

"The speciman at first sight is representative of man . . . of fairly normal proportions, but excessively hairy . . . His skin is of the waxlike color characteristic of corpses of men of white race when not tanned by the sun . . . The damage to the occiput [back of the head], and the fact that the eyeballs had been ejected from their sockets, one having completely disappeared, suggests that the creature had been shot in the face by several large-caliber bullets. One bullet must have penetrated the cubitus [forearm] when he tried to protect himself. A second bullet pierced the right eye, destroying it, and causing the other to start out of its cavity. This caused the much larger cavity at the back of the cranium, producing immediate death."

With the Iceman's acceptance both in popular and academic circles, Hansen then announced that the creature, nicknamed "Bozo" by Sanderson, was not his at all: he was merely its keeper. Its real owner was a mysterious "Mr X," a millionaire Hollywood film maker who had bought the Iceman from an emporium in Hong Kong, and had had it flown to the United States. If Hansen was to be believed, Bozo had been shuttled around the Far East from Soviet sealers, to Japanese whalers, to Chinese dealers, all the while causing consternation of Customs and other officials. The Hollywood tycoon was said to be interested only in allowing ordinary people to view their "Neanderthal ancestor," and so in 1969 the Iceman returned to the carnival circuits. This time he was billed as a "Creature frozen and preserved forever in a coffin of ice" in a return to the prehistoric man idea. It was apparent to those who saw it that the second exhibit was no fossil.

As it happened, Sanderson had approached Dr. John Napier just before the carnival tour to see if he might be interested in having the monster fully and scientifically investigated. At first Napier was enthusiastic to undertake a study. But then a number of things happened to squash his enthusiasm. First, the Secretary of the Smithsonian, S. Dillon Ripley, learned from Hansen that the creature about to go on exhibition was a latex model, which, Hansen was careful to say, resembled the original Iceman. Second, after the murder theory was put forward, Ripley immediately wrote to the FBI to see if the Bureau would cooperate in tracing the original exhibit. As no federal law had been broken, the Bureau would not intervene—but this did not stop Hansen from preparing a new display sign for his monster, calling it "The near-Man . . . Investigated by the FBI."

The Smithsonian then withdrew its interest in the Iceman, which only seemed to spur Hanson on. He held a press conference at his ranch, timing it prior to taking the Iceman to St. Paul. He admitted to reporter Gorden Yeager of the *Rochester Post-Bulletin* that the monster was "man-made, an illusion." From St. Paul the exhibit moved to Grand Rapids where it was filmed by a team from *Time-Life*. This film showed distinct differences between the model then on display and the Iceman as drawn and photographed by Heuvelmans and Sanderson. The original creature had only one yellowish tooth, while this one boasted at least four.

After the Helen Westring story of the murder of the Minnesota Iceman, Hansen came up with a final version of how the monster had met his death. In *Saga* magazine in 1970 he declared that it was he, not Helen Westring, who had shot the monster in the woods. He had done so while in the US Air Force on a hunting trip with some fellow officers in the north of the state. The creature had fallen mortally wounded in the snow, and had stayed there for two months until Hansen removed the body to the deep-freeze at his camp quarters. "Let's not tell a single person about this," he warned his wife. "We'll just leave it there until Spring." After seven years, Hansen took the corpse to his nearby farm. Later, and for reasons never explained, he had a latex replica made of it by special technicians in Hollywood. From then on he simply switched the exhibits when necessary, and talked as fast as he could in order to fool the press, the public, and the experts.

One person who didn't believe Hansen's "transparently dubious" confession is Dr. Napier, who is as close to the story as anyone. But however skeptical he is about the Iceman, he feels that the "North American Bigfoot or Sasquatch has a lot going for it . . . Too many people claim to have seen it, or at least to have seen footprints, to dismiss its reality out of hand. To suggest that hundreds of people at worst are lying or, at best, deluding themselves is neither proper nor realistic."

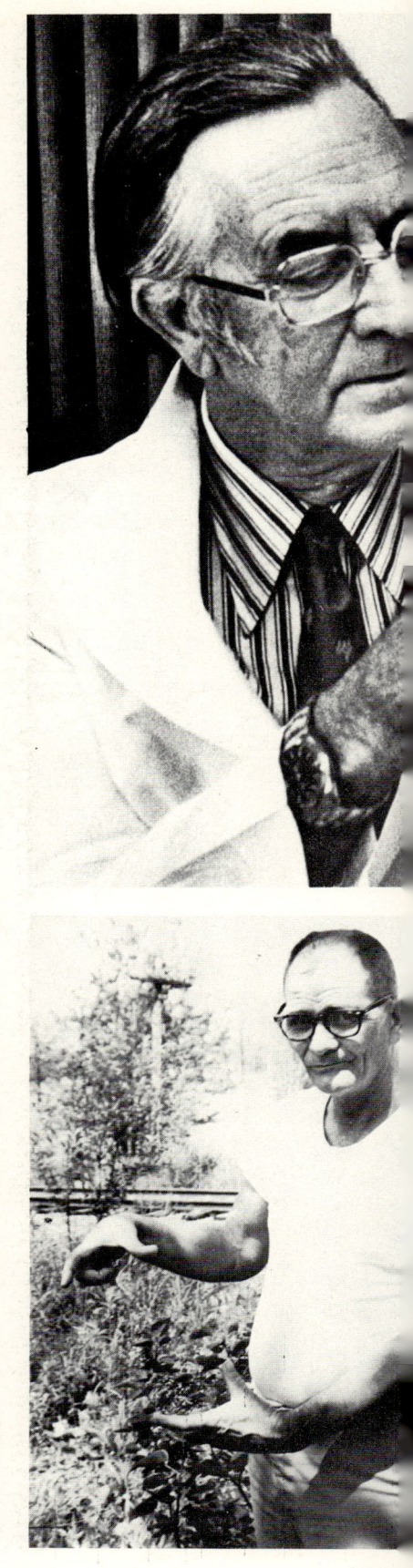

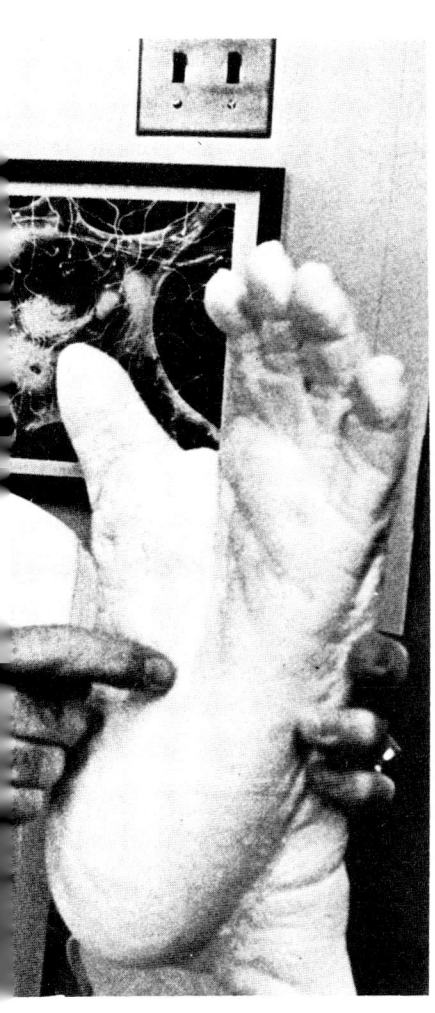

Above: Dr. Joeffrey H. Bourne of the Yerkes Regional Primate Center in Georgia, holding a print of a gorilla's foot. Like many scientists, he believes the existence of giant humanoids such as the Yeti and the Bigfoot is possible, but decidedly unproved.

Left: Henry McDaniel, a disabled war veteran of Illinois, showing the size of footprints he said were made by a gray, hairy, three-legged monster with pink eyes bulging from a huge head. He claims he saw the thing twice.

Right: another alleged Bigfoot photo, taken somewhere northeast of Spokane, Washington. Skeptics remark on the odd similarity of the Bigfoot's method of descent with that of a cowardly human.

8

The Monster Business

We have always been of two minds about our monsters. Although in a sense we have tried to conquer them, we have also in a sense yielded to them. Monsters of old usually inhabited some difficult and inaccessible place. For many people today the scientific laboratory is difficult and inaccessible—as frightening as the dragon's cave was to our ancestors. Monsters, usually developed under extraordinary circumstances, have extraordinary features and can only be destroyed by special skills and equipment. Perseus needed winged sandals, a helmet of invisibility, and a mirror to kill the Gorgon. If he had looked at the horrible creature he would have turned to

Are there real monsters hidden in the distant and inaccessible parts of the world? We play with the question, and while waiting for the answer, keep ourselves happily frightened with fictional creations guaranteed to make us shiver with dread, and settle into our movie seats with anticipation. Right: Boris Karloff, best-known of the actors who have portrayed Frankenstein's man-made monster, in the *Bride of Frankenstein*. It was filmed in Hollywood in 1935.

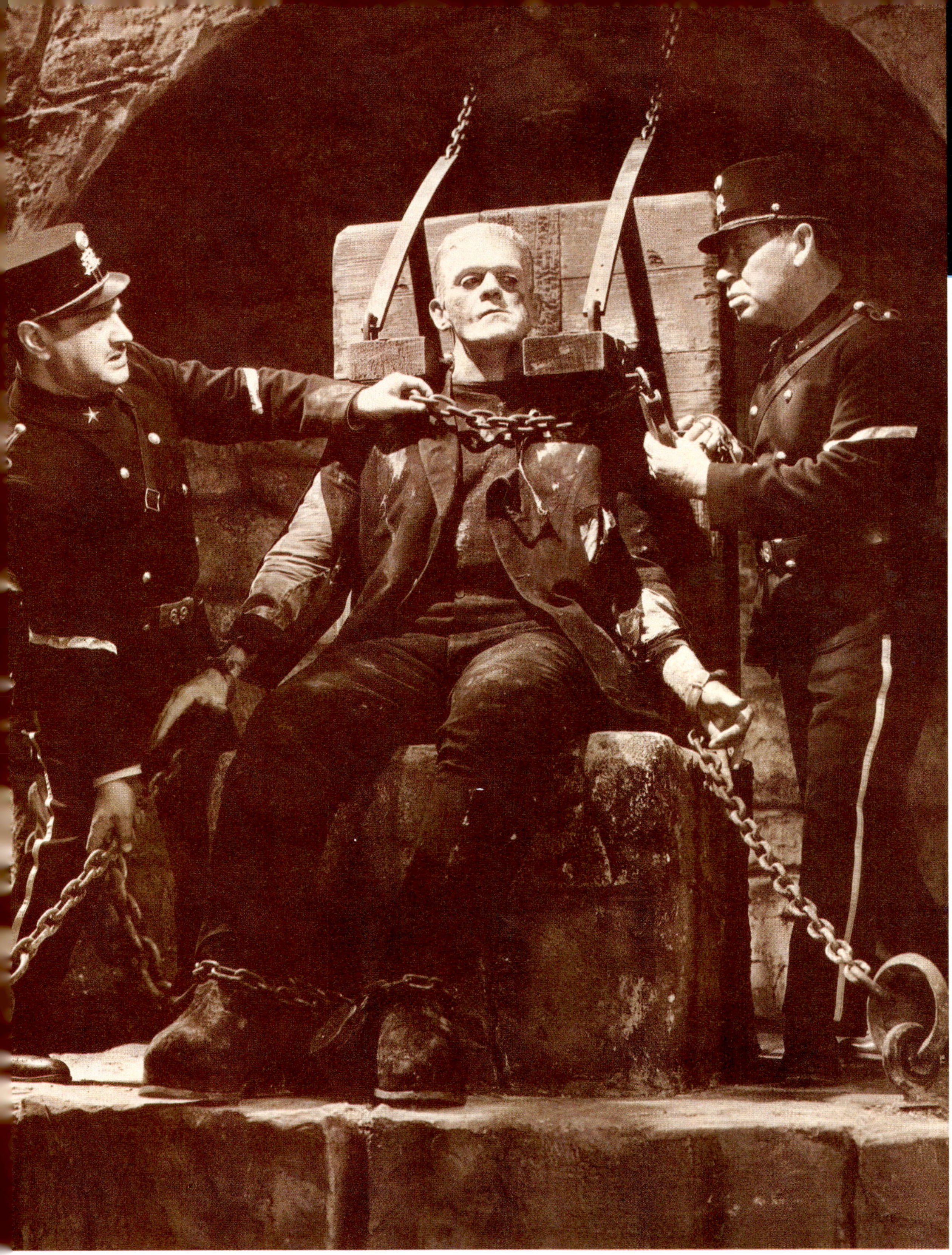

"I saw the hideous phantasm of a man stretched out..."

stone. St. George needed Christian faith and courage to master the dragon. In our time, a scientific formula is usually more appropriate.

As our understanding of our own emotional responses increased, some people became aware of the possibility of creating fictional monsters for commercial ends. Just the right mixture of terror and sex could provide safe and pleasureable titillation for the public—and profit for the creators.

The monster business might be said to have started more than 150 years ago when a young English girl went to Switzerland for vacation. The girl, 21-year-old Mary Wollstonecraft Shelley, had run away to the continent four years earlier with poet Percy Bysshe Shelley. They had lived together without marriage until the death of his wife allowed their marriage to take place in 1816. Two years later, in the wet and miserable Swiss summer of 1818, they were staying with their friend, the poet Lord Byron, on the shores of Lake Geneva. For entertainment at night Byron, the Shelleys, and a doctor friend sat around a blazing log fire reading volumes of German ghost stories. After enduring several days of cold and constant rain, Byron suggested that each of the four of them should write a "truly horrific" story for amusement. The winner of the literary contest would be the person who succeeded in scaring the others most.

By the term ghost story, Byron said he meant anything that depicted the "monstrous, the horrendous, the unusual." Mary Shelley, who had never written anything before, naturally experienced the greatest creative difficulty. "I busied myself to think of a story—a story to rival those which had excited us to this task," she stated. "One which would speak to the mysterious fears of our nature and awaken thrilling horror—one to make the reader dread to look around, to curdle the blood, and quicken the beatings of the heart. If I did not accomplish these things, my ghost story would be unworthy of its name."

Morning after morning she confessed to her competitors that inspiration had not come in the night. Evening after evening she listened to the long and macabre conversations between the two major poets. Their talk centered mostly around the experiments being made at the time by an English doctor who, it was said, could make a "piece of vermicelli in a glass case" move "by some extraordinary means . . . with voluntary motion." This led them to such statements as: "Perhaps a corpse could be reanimated; perhaps the component parts of a creature might be manufactured, brought together, and [given] vital warmth." It was after midnight when this particular discussion ended, and Mary Shelley and her husband went wearily to bed. However, tired as she was, she had difficulty sleeping. Later she wrote of the extraordinary vision that came to her in a kind of waking dream.

"I saw—with shut eyes, but acute mental vision—I saw the pale student of unhallowed arts kneeling beside the thing he had put together. I saw the hideous phantasm of a man stretched out, and then, on the working of some powerful engine, show signs of life and stir with an uneasy, half-vital motion. Frightful it must be, for supremely frightful would be the effect of any human endeavor to mock the stupendous mechanism of the Creator of the world."

Above: Mary Wollstonecraft Shelley, the wife of the poet and the sweet-faced creator of the classic horror tale *Frankenstein*.

Above: the title page of Mary Shelley's *Frankenstein*, which was published in London in 1831. Below: the popularity of the novel naturally led to a stage version. This engraving of 1850 shows a scene from the production entitled *Frankenstein, or, The Model Man*, as it was presented at the Adelphi Theater in London.

Below: an engraving from the 1831 edition of *Frankenstein*. The gloomy scene with the monster stirring captures the frightful moment when "by the glimmer of the half-extinguished light I saw the dull, yellow eye of the creature open; it breathed hard and a convulsive motion agitated its limbs . . . I rushed out of the room."

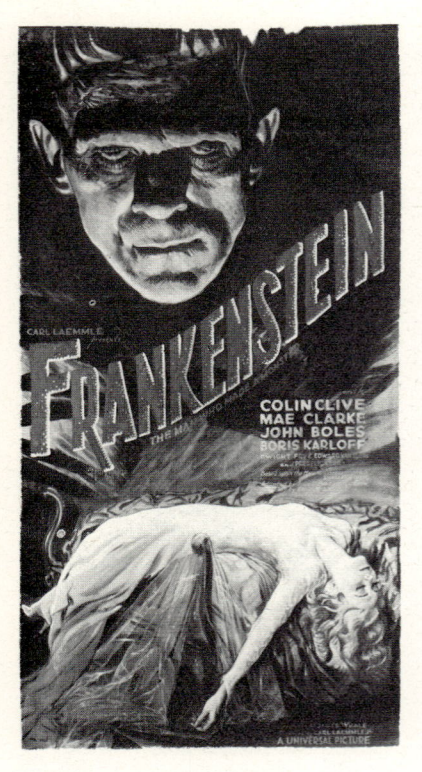

Above: publicity for the movie *Frankenstein*—here, a poster for display outside the theater—made the sexual aspect explicit.

Below: this scene of the monster and a little girl was too strong for 1931, and was cut. In it, the monster encounters a small girl floating flowers in the river, and happily joins in. When they run out of flowers, he unthinkingly throws her in. She doesn't float.

"He [the student] would hope that, left to itself, the slight spark of life which he had communicated would fade, that this thing which had received such imperfect animation would subside into dead matter, and he might sleep in the belief that the silence of the grave would quench forever the transient existence of the hideous corpse which he had looked upon as the cradle of life. He sleeps; but he is awakened; he opens his eyes; behold, the horrid thing stands at his bedside, opening his curtains and looking on him with yellow, watery, but speculative eyes. I opened mine in terror."

That night, Baron Victor Frankenstein and the monster he made in his laboratory were born. From then on the inhabitants —especially the young girls—of the fictitious village of Ingoldstad, Transylvania, would sleep uneasily in their beds. A monster was in their midst, and there was no more peace. Little realizing that she had created a classic theme of sexual potency and fear, Mary Shelley gleefully reported the next morning that she had thought of "a few pages, of a short tale." Shelley was so intrigued by her idea that he urged her to develop it at greater length. So she wrote more, produced the novel called *Frankenstein, Or, The Modern Prometheus*, and bid her "hideous progeny" to "go forth and prosper." The book did exactly that, making her reputation and starting her on a writing career.

Over the years the book went into edition after edition, but in 1931 it reached an even wider audience when Hollywood filmed it as *Frankenstein* with the then unknown Boris Karloff as the man-made monster. By then the novel's sexual implications were seen and better understood: the monster, though only half a human, had the drives of a man and wanted a mate like other men. Of course, Hollywood was wary of making the sexual content too explicit, and the director compromised by limiting the monster's attempts to take a mate to one time. He approaches a child whom he discovers floating petals in a lake, and although his advances are innocuous enough, he ends up by killing the youngster and throwing her into the water. This scene was considered too brutal for the sensibilities of the time, and it was cut before the film was released. But in the sequel, *Bride of Frankenstein*, made four years later, the monster's sex life was openly admitted. It was handled by the creation of a wife, played by Elsa Lanchester. "With Karloff," writes film historian Carlos Clarens in his book *Horror Movies*, "she manages to communicate . . . a delicate suggestion of the both the wedding bed and the grave."

By the early 20th century it had become obvious that most monster stories—and the films inspired by them—were little more than sex sagas in disguise. In the 20th century it was no longer enough to fob readers and audiences off with what the Scottish prayer calls ". . . ghoulies and ghosties and long-leggety beasties/And things that go bump in the night. . . ." There had to be spicier nocturnal goings on, activities that appealed to the beast in people and to primitive instincts. "Rather than sheer perversity," Clarens asserts, "horror films require of the audience a certain sophistication, a recognition of their mythical core, a fascination of the psyche."

This angle had been appreciated before Hollywood brought sex into its monster pictures. It was one of the most exploited factors in early German films. The basic theme was that of the fairy tale's Beauty and the Beast, of the beautiful and virginal princess forced to live with a monster that both repels and fascinates her. In the fairy story the princess' love frees the beast from an evil spell, and turns him into a handsome prince who marries her. However, things did not always work out as happily in celluloid life. In *The Golem*, made in Berlin in 1914, a giant clay statue is bought by an antiquarian and brought to life by magic. The Golem becomes the antiquarian's servant, but falls in love with his master's young and desirable daughter. Sickened by the monster's attentions and appearance, she spurns him. The Golem goes berserk. After creating havoc, he falls to his death from a tower, an obvious phallic symbol, and the girl's purity is preserved.

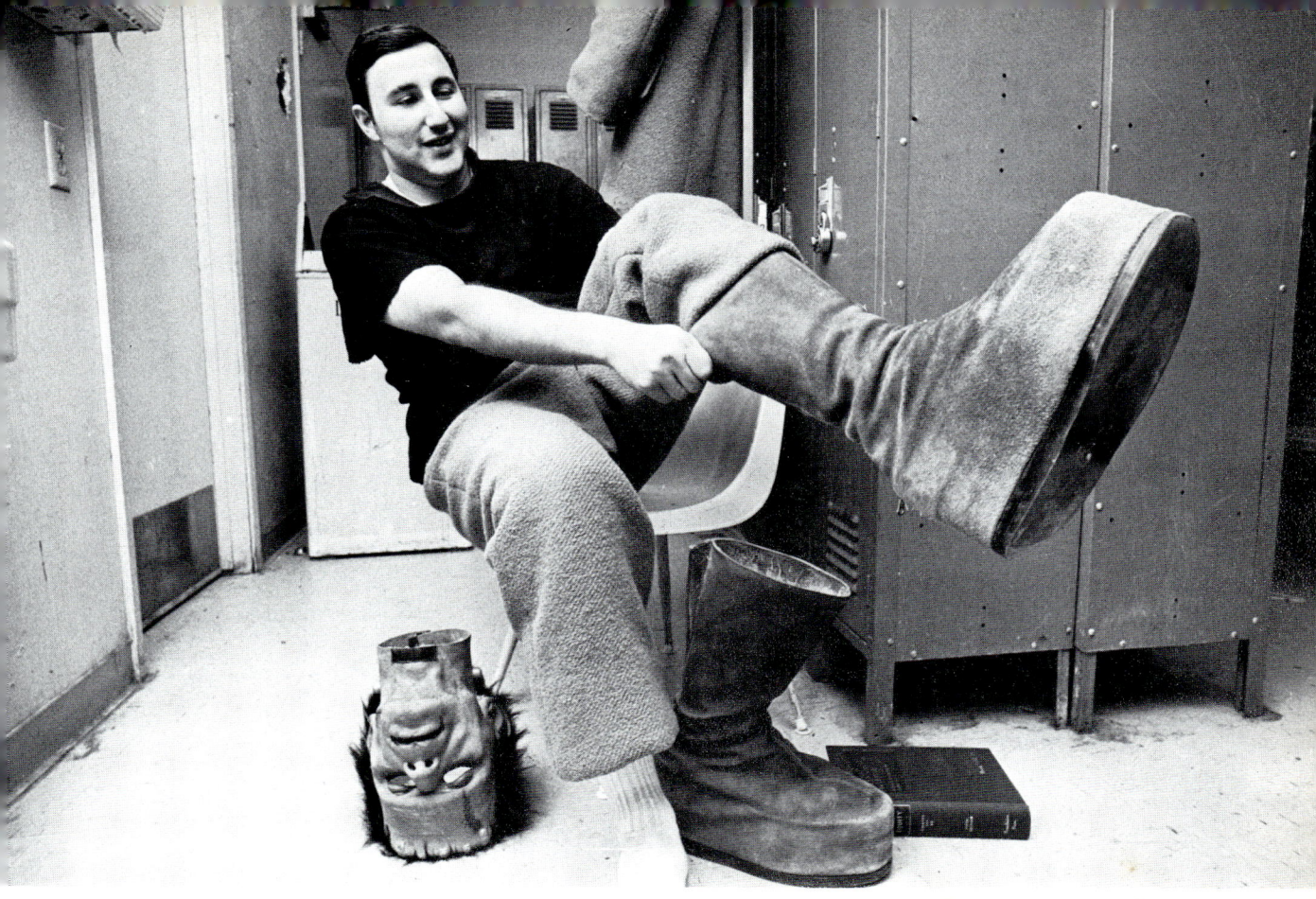

Monsters became bolder as time went on. They were no longer content to gaze down upon their adored one as she slept. They picked her up bodily and carried her away over marshes, across swamps, into jungles, and up alleyways. The heroines were always in danger of being ravished by the beasts, but the implication was that they might have dreamed about or secretly and subconsciously yearned for this fate. The idea of sleep—the unreal events within it and the realities without—was expanded in the 1919 classic *The Cabinet of Dr. Caligari*. This film, which deals with a man who seduces and kills women while he is hypnotized, was based on a real-life sex murder in which a human monster raped and murdered a girl at a fair in Hamburg. The film monster is a staring sleep walker who snatches a nubile

Above: the Frankenstein monster became part of the entertainment on Universal Studio tours. Here a guide gets into monster gear. Below: in his gruesome costume, which the tourists seem to love, the guide greets excited visitors at the starting point of their trip around the famous studio.

135

Left: an erotic scene from *The Golem*, a movie made in Germany in 1920 by the same director who had made the first version of this Hebrew legend in 1914. In it he developed the successful formula of many horror films: monster is created, monster tries to win heroine, monster meets violent end. The Golem, which is a clay statue brought to life by magic, is killed when a child accidentally drops the magic emblem that gives it life.

Above: Lon Chaney, the man of a thousand disguises (most of them usually repellent), became *The Phantom of the Opera*, made in 1925. This scene is of the ghastly moment when the girl, played by Mary Philbin, snatches off the phantom's ever-present mask and sees his visage in all its horror.

brunette from her bed and flees with her over rooftops and fields. He is pursued by the townsfolk, and dies of exhaustion. Once again the maiden survives, and we know she will find a lover who is well-intentioned and acceptable.

The females in *The Head of Janus*, made in 1920, were less fortunate. For the first time on the screen monsters influenced the behavior of the mildest and most respectable of men. The upstanding hero, played by Conrad Veidt, has an obsession for the two-faced Roman god Janus, representing the good and the evil in man. Influenced by the evil side, Veidt becomes a vicious sex criminal. First he assaults his fiancée and forces her to work in a brothel, and then he attacks and kills a small girl in the street. In the end he dies by swallowing poison. Audiences have learned to their horror that wickedness and lust are contagious, and it is not enough merely to defy monsters. Each of us must also beware that we do not start to behave like a monster, assaulting and degrading those nearest and dearest to us.

It was not until 1925 that the concept of beauty and the beast was presented both with realism and chilling fantasy. The film was *The Phantom of the Opera* in the first of three versions made by Hollywood. The star was Lon Chaney. The scene is Paris where a hideously disfigured creature lurks in the catacomb of cellars beneath the Opera House. Despite his handicaps he is madly in love with a young soprano, and does all he can to aid her career. Her success pleases him, but he is not satisfied until he has lured her down to his dank and watery living quarters. There he keeps her captive in a weird and gruesome bridal suite. Reaching a dramatic climax in the movie, the heroine tears the mask from her captor's face, and recoils in horror and disgust at the sight of his disfigurement. The film ends with a mob invading the phantom's subterranean chambers and killing him. Some commentators have seen the film as deeper and more symbolic than just another shocker. The mask the phantom wears, they say, is that of every man who devotedly and courteously woos the girl of his choice. Behind this mask of conventionality, however, is the real person: a leering, unscrupulous

Above: a chilling scene of murder from *The Mummy's Ghost*, made in 1944. In this gruesome fancy, Lon Chaney plays the mummy that returns to life after being buried for thousands of years. He tries to kidnap the beatiful young girl who is the reincarnation of his ancient love—and goes on a murderous spree in the process.

Above: the huge gorilla in *The Murders in the Rue Morgue* bearing yet another luscious lady off to his psychopathic master, a doctor who is carrying out secret grotesque experiments. Bela Lugosi, who was best known as Dracula, played the doctor in this 1931 Hollywood movie.

sex fiend who thinks of nothing of subjecting his chosen one to imprisonment, bondage, and rape.

With the phantom setting box office records—and making people realize that there was probably a Frankenstein's monster hidden somewhere in all of us—American film makers turned from human to animal monsters. The increasing number of reports that giant creatures existed in remote parts of the world sent producers to stories such as Edgar Allan Poe's *Murders in the Rue Morgue*. Again Paris is the setting, again a lustful monster is on the loose. In the movie version, which differs from the original work, the monster is a huge gorilla employed by a mad doctor to kidnap women for his "unholy experiments." The gorilla carries out his task with relish. There are gruesome scenes of a prostitute bleeding to death on a torture rack, and of a dead woman shoved into a chimney upside down. Once more the monster carries the scantily dressed heroine over rooftops in the dark of night, and once more the women in the audience shivered—as much with pleasurable anticipation as with fear, some analysts would say.

As aware as any psychiatrist of the underlying sexual content in such plots—and of the second-hand thrills that they provided—the movie moguls looked for the ultimate in monster-and-sex stories. One producer felt he had found it in *King Kong*, which had been partly written by the English thriller writer Edgar Wallace.

Above: Hollywood hadn't invented horror. Back in the 1870s the Illustrated Police News thrilled London readers with real-life sensational blood and gore. (If real-life proved a bit too tepid, it was embellished as necessary.) Here two women are overcome as the magazine headline screams "Murderous Attack by a Gorilla." **Below:** the gorilla charges on in *Gorilla at Large*, made in 1954.

It was released in 1933, and the producer was right: *King Kong* was a smash hit. In it the giant ape called King Kong snatched up the fair-haired heroine in one huge hand and made off with her into the wilderness. Puzzled by her strange, human, female smell, he at one point tears off her dress and sniffs the scent of her on his fingers. This was suggestiveness run riot, and Hollywood compensated for such blatancy by showing that the nice guy got the girl in the final reel—and that the beast in us was always rendered impotent. King Kong, like the Golem of 1914, dies in a tumble from what is clearly a phallic symbol—the Empire State Building, then the tallest in the world. The hero has the last word in the film, and it is a comment with sexual undertones. He says: "'Twas Beauty killed the Beast!" If the movie beast couldn't be transformed into an eligible prince charming then he had to die in order to observe the prevailing morality code. *King Kong*, which was a year in the making and had a huge budget for the period, was and still is the most famous of all monster movies.

There is at least one monster movie that was successful without the sex element. It was made in 1925 and was based on Sir Arthur Conan Doyle's novel *The Lost World*, published 13 years earlier. Conan Doyle had read a book on extinct animals by the zoology professor Ray Lankester, and was inspired by it. He was especially impressed by its illustrations of "nightmare-shapes of sabre-teeth and witless eyes," and thought it was not too fantastic that such creatures still existed. "Suppose," he said, "one misty evening, a stegosaurus came looming over the misty downs? Better still: suppose in some remote corner of the earth—a high plateau in the jungle, say, untouched and untouchable in primitive life—such creatures were yet alive? What game for a sportsman! What wonders for a zoologist!"

The repercussions to his book, which was a mixture of imaginitive fiction and solid fact, were immediate. Professor Lankester, author of the scientific work that had inspired Conan Doyle, wrote to him saying: "You are perfectly splendid in your story of the 'lost world' mountaintop. I feel proud to have had a certain small share in its inception . . . I notice that you rightly withold any intelligence from the big dinosaurs, and also acute smell from the apemen." About a year after Conan Doyle's book appeared, a group of American explorers set out from Philadelphia in the yacht *Delaware* for the broad waters of the Amazon. According to a newspaper account of April 1, 1913: "The yacht is the property of the University of Pennsylvania, and is bound for Brazil with a daring party of explorers, who propose penetrating to the far reaches of the Amazon, and to the headwaters of many of its tributaries in the interest of science and humanity. They seek Conan Doyle's 'lost world,' or some scientific evidence of it." They were unsuccessful, but their very attempt demonstrated mankind's willingness—need, almost—to accept monsters as real.

It was not until the 1950s that there was a serious revival of the horror film, and it was then that such curiosities as the Yeti and the Loch Ness Monster came into their own. Movies ranging from *The Abominable Snowman of the Himalayas* to *The Monster That Challenged the World* were made about the Yeti or their kin. The trend continued into the 1960s, and today it is as strong if

Above: King Kong, carrying the hapless heroine in one huge hand, looms ominously over the tall skyscrapers of New York City.

not stronger than ever. We are living in what film director Alfred Hitchcock calls the Age of Monsters. "Monsters are all around us," he writes. "They abound on the motion picture screens, coming from the depths of the sea, from under the Arctic ice, from outer space, or other such unexplored regions." Recognizing that the desire to be shocked and shaken starts early, publishers are now putting out Make-Your-Own-Monster books which show children how to construct such long-lasting favorites as the bearded dragon, the dinosaur, the Golem, the lake monster, and the sea serpent. However, as Hitchcock points out, "... a monster does not have to be a beast so large he wipes out a suburb every time he lashes his tail. Nor does he have to be a roughly human-shaped creature with his head bolted to his neck."

There are also monsters of the soul, the mind, and the subconscious. It is apparent that men and women respond to monsters and mythic creatures, whether mermaids, unicorns, dragons or underwater snakes, in a way that is ambiguous and erotic. Monsters both stimulate and repel, excite and nauseate. On

King Kong created a perfect blend of monster-and-sex. The story was hardly a model of subtlety, but within it were opportunities to exploit every shiver of dread and gasp of astonished shock, and the movie used them skillfully. Audiences flocked in, and King Kong as the giant ape became a permanent addition to American folk imagination. Above: King Kong, straddling the Empire State Building, waves a plane around just before his fall.

Right: the giant ape torments some pursuers on his own home ground. He was hard to capture.

Right: the drawing of a monster that was used by Sir Arthur Conan Doyle to start the action in his popular 1912 novel *The Lost World*. In the book, this drawing is supposed to have been found in the sketchbook of a dead artist who had traveled in the Amazon. It was in hopes of proving the existence of such monsters that the fictional party of explorers sets off into the deep, unknown Amazonian jungle.

Below: the fictional Professor George E. Challenger, hero of *The Lost World*. This picture was used as the frontispiece in the 1912 edition of the novel.

Opposite: beyond the torrid and tangled Guyana jungle lie the sheer and unfriendly cliffs of the Roraima plateau—the real Lost World. This photograph was taken by an expedition in 1973. It took the team 17 days of inching along some of the world's most difficult terrain to reach the peak—and they could not stay to explore it. Couldn't Roraima—and places like it—be the home of monsters surviving from the past? What else could live there?

another and equally important level, our interest in monsters and mythic beasts seems to have much to do with an awe of hugeness, and an admiration of courage and fortitude in the face of forces of the unknown.

"On the one hand," anthropologist Dr. John Napier writes, "we are delighted when bigness is overthrown, be it the small and good overcoming the big and bad (David and Goliath) . . . or simply man putting a monster in its place (St. George and the dragon). It gives us great satisfaction to see financial barons topple, commercial empires dissolve, bosses dismissed, boxing champions knocked out, and the World Cup winners soundly beaten. On the other hand, man seems to admire the big instinctively: the tall man is often esteemed without regard to his capabilities, the tall building attracts our admiration, and the large animals . . . our benevolence. We both love and hate large size, depending on whether or not it constitutes a threat to our survival . . . I believe our attitude toward legendary monsters is equally ambivalent. We laugh at them and we fear them, we love them and we hate them, but overall in a curious way, we respect them simply for being monstrously big."

From primitive times to the present day human beings have needed monsters. Frightening though they may be, monsters nevertheless reduce to a comprehensible form our inner fears and dread of external forces beyond our control. Perhaps for the early Greek sailors a six-headed brute such as Scylla, who was said to suck men to their deaths under the sea, was a way of coming to terms with the arbitrary nature of the elements and the ever-present danger of drowning. In times when life for most people in many parts of the world was little more than a daily struggle for survival, dragons and other mythic beasts may have channeled people's anxieties away from disease, starvation, and invasion. More important, perhaps, fabulous creatures may have added an element of mystery and excitement to otherwise drab lives. With the progress of science and technology, we have unleashed a new set of fears to replace those we have conquered. Monsters are still with us. Today they spring from outer space or from the experimental laboratory.

Picture Credits

Key to picture positions: (T) top (C) center (B) bottom; and in combinations, e.g. (TR) top right (BL) bottom left

2	Kunstmuseum, Basel/Colorphoto Hans Hinz	50(R)	Michael Holford Library photo	100	Culver Pictures
4	Vatican Museum	51-3	Aldus Archives	101	Photo Don Whillans (Annapurna South Face Expedition, 1970)
6	Aldus Archives	54(T)	Roger-Viollet	102	Aldus Archives
7	National Gallery of Art Washington; Ailsa Mellon Bruce Fund	54(CL)	Aldus Archives	103	Royal Geographical Society
		54(CR)	The Bettmann Archive	104(B)	London *Daily Mail*
		54(B)	Courtesy of the New Brunswick Museum	105(T)	Chris Bonington/Bruce Coleman Ltd.
8(L)	Alte Pinakothek, München/Photo Scala, Florence	56(T)	Reproduced with the permission of the Naval Historical Foundation from a print owned by Rear Admiral Henry Williams	105(B)	Romi Khosla
9, 10	Giraudon			106(T)	London *Daily Mail*
11(R)	Reproduced by permission of the British Library Board			106(B)	Syndication International Ltd., London
12(L)	Condé, Chantilly/Giraudon	57(T)	The Bettmann Archive	108-9	Gino d'Achille © Aldus Books
13	Giraudon	57(B), 58(T)	Snark International	110	Royal Geographical Society
14	Ivan Polunin/Susan Griggs Agency	58(B)	Compix, New York	111	Popperfoto
		59(C)	Photo *Penticton Herald*	112(B)	Compix, New York
15(T)	Gulbenkian Museum of Oriental Art, University of Durham/Photo Jeff Teasdale	59(B)	Central Press Photos	113(T)	Ralph Izzard, *The Abominable Snowman Adventure*, Hodder & Stoughton Ltd., London
		61(TL)	Barnaby's Picture Library		
		61(TR)	Popperfoto		
		61(BL)	Stern Archiv		
16(T)	Durham County Library	63	Keystone	113(CR)	Novosti Press Agency
16(B)	Aldus Archives	64(L)	*Radio Times* Hulton Picture Library	113(B)	Chris Bonington/Bruce Coleman Ltd.
17	Mary Evans Picture Library				
18(T)	Aldus Archives	65(B)	Photo Dmitri Kasterine © Aldus Books	114(L)	Stamps kindly loaned by Mr. R. A. Topley. Reproduced by permission of the National Postal Museum
18(B)	J.-L. Charmet, Paris				
19	Mary Evans Picture Library	66-7	Gino d'Achille © Aldus Books		
20(B)	Snark International	68	*London Daily Mail*		
21(T)	Reproduced by permission of the British Library Board	69-71	*Illustrated London News*	114(R)	John Francis/Linden Artists © Aldus Books
		72(TL)	Press Association Ltd.		
21(B), 22(TL)	Aldus Archives	72(TR)	Popperfoto	115(L)	John Francis/Linden Artists © Aldus Books after Spectrum
22(TR)	Mary Evans Picture Library	72(B)	Keystone		
23	Bruce Coleman Ltd.	74(T)	Photo Tim Dinsdale	115(R)	John Francis/Linden Artists © Aldus Books after Ardea
24	Snark International	75(T)	Aldus Archives		
25	Photo © J. G. Ferguson taken from The Raymond Mander and Joe Mitchenson Theatre Collection	75(B)	Compix, New York	117	Eastman's Studio
		76(T)	The Associated Press Ltd.	118(T)	Compix, New York
		76(B)	Popperfoto	118(B)	© Aldus Books
		77	Compix, New York	120-1	Gino d'Achille © Aldus Books
26, 27	J.-L. Charmet, Paris	78-81	Syndication International Ltd., London	122, 123(L)	John Napier, *Bigfoot*, © 1972 by John Napier. First published in the U.S.A. by E. P. Dutton & Co., Inc., and reprinted with their permission
28(T)	Aldus Archives				
28(B)	Museo degli Argenti, Firenze/Photo Scala	82	The Associated Press Ltd.		
		83	*London Express*		
29	Michael Holford Library photo	85	Zdenek Burian, *Life Before Man*, by permission of the publishers, Artia, Prague		
30-2(T)	Aldus Archives			123(R)	Compix, New York
32(B)	R. Kinne/Photo Researchers, Inc.			124	John Napier, *Bigfoot*, © 1972 by John Napier. First published in the U.S.A. by E. P. Dutton & Co., Inc., and reprinted with their permission
34(T)	Giraudon	86	Culver Pictures		
35(T)	Aldus Archives	88-9	Gino d'Achille © Aldus Books		
35(B)	Fotogram	90(B)	Aldus Archives		
36(L)	Snark International	91(T)	Zdenek Burian, *Life Before Man*, by permission of the publishers, Artia, Prague		
37-8	The Metropolitan Museum of Art, The Cloisters Collection, Gift of John D. Rockefeller, Jr., 1937			125(R)	Compix, New York
				126	Courtesy Sabina W. Sanderson and The Society for the Investigation of the Unexplained
		91(B)	Peabody Museum of Natural History, Yale University		
39	Giraudon	92(T)	Trustees of the British Museum (Natural History)	127	Raymond Vanker
40(T)	Aldus Archives			128-9	Compix, New York
40(B)	Photo Mike Busselle © Aldus Books	92(B)	Bilderdienst Süddeutscher Verlag	131	Kobal Collection
		93(T)	London *Daily Mail*	132	National Portrait Gallery, London
41(T)	Bodleian Library, Oxford	93(B)	Trustees of the British Museum (Natural History)		
41(B)	Aldus Archives			133	Mary Evans Picture Library
43	J.-L. Charmet, Paris	94	Zdenek Burian, *Life Before Man*, by permission of the publishers, Artia, Prague	134	Kobal Collection
44	Mary Evans Picture Library			135	Rex Features
45(L)	Aldus Archives			136-8	Kobal Collection
45(R)	Culver Pictures	95(T)	Trustees of the British Museum Natural History)	139(T)	Aldus Archives
46(T)	Mary Evans Picture Library			139(B)	*Movie Star News*
46(B)	Richard Orr/Linden Artists © Aldus Books	95(B)	Courtesy Pitman Publishing, London	140-1	National Film Archive
				142	Aldus Archives
48-9	Gino d'Achille © Aldus Books	96	Aldus Archives	143	*Observer*/Transworld
50(L)	Aldus Archives	98-9	Gino d'Achille © Aldus Books		